# The History of English Spelling

# THE LANGUAGE LIBRARY
Series editor: David Crystal

*The Language Library* was created in 1952 by Eric Partridge, the great etymologist and lexicographer, who from 1966 to 1976 was assisted by his co-editor Simeon Potter. Together they commissioned volumes on the traditional themes of language study, with particular emphasis on the history of the English language and on the individual linguistic styles of major English authors. In 1977 David Crystal took over as editor, and *The Language Library* now includes titles in many areas of linguistic enquiry.

The most recently published titles in the series include:

| | |
|---|---|
| Christopher Upward and George Davidson | *The History of English Spelling* |
| Geoffrey Hughes | *Political Correctness: A History of Semantics and Culture* |
| Nicholas Evans | *Dying Words: Endangered Languages and What They Have to Tell Us* |
| Amalia E. Gnanadesikan | *The Writing Revolution: Cuneiform to the Internet* |
| David Crystal | *A Dictionary of Linguistics and Phonetics, Sixth Edition* |
| Viv Edwards | *Multilingualism in the English-speaking World* |
| Ronald Wardhaugh | *Proper English: Myths and Misunderstandings about Language* |
| Gunnel Tottie | *An Introduction to American English* |
| Geoffrey Hughes | *A History of English Words* |
| Walter Nash | *Jargon* |
| Roger Shuy | *Language Crimes* |
| J. A. Cuddon | *A Dictionary of Literary Terms and Literary Theory, Fourth Edition* |
| Florian Coulmas | *The Writing Systems of the World* |
| Ronald Carter and Walter Nash | *Seeing Through Language* |

# The History of English Spelling

Christopher Upward
and
George Davidson

A John Wiley & Sons, Ltd., Publication

This edition first published 2011
© Christopher Upward and George Davidson 2011

Blackwell Publishing was acquired by John Wiley & Sons in February 2007.
Blackwell's publishing program has been merged with Wiley's global Scientific,
Technical, and Medical business to form Wiley-Blackwell.

*Registered Office*
John Wiley & Sons Ltd, The Atrium, Southern Gate, Chichester,
West Sussex, PO19 8SQ, UK

*Editorial Offices*
350 Main Street, Malden, MA 02148-5020, USA
9600 Garsington Road, Oxford, OX4 2DQ, UK
The Atrium, Southern Gate, Chichester, West Sussex, PO19 8SQ, UK

For details of our global editorial offices, for customer services, and for information
about how to apply for permission to reuse the copyright material in this book please
see our website at www.wiley.com/wiley-blackwell.

The right of Christopher Upward and George Davidson to be identified as the
authors of this work has been asserted in accordance with the UK Copyright,
Designs and Patents Act 1988.

*Library of Congress Cataloging-in-Publication Data*
Upward, Christopher.
 The history of English spelling / Christopher Upward and George Davidson.
   p.  cm.
 Includes bibliographical references and index.
 ISBN 978-1-4051-9024-4 (alk. paper) – ISBN 978-1-4051-9023-7 (pbk. : alk.
paper)  1. English language – Orthography and spelling – History.  2. English
language – Etymology.  I. Davidson, George.  II. Title.
 PE1141.U69 2011
 421'.5209 – dc22
                                                              2011008794

A catalogue record for this book is available from the British Library.

This book is published in the following electronic formats:
ePDFs [ISBN 9781444342963]; Wiley Online Library [ISBN 9781444342994];
ePub [ISBN 9781444342970]; Mobi [ISBN 9781444342987]

Set in 10/12.5pt Plantin by Graphicraft Limited, Hong Kong
Printed in Malaysia by Ho Printing (M) Sdn Bhd

1  2011

In Memoriam
Christopher Upward
1938–2002

# Contents

# Figures and Tables

# Preface

In his novel *Three Men on the Bummel*, the writer Jerome K. Jerome says of English spelling that it 'would seem to have been designed chiefly as a disguise for pronunciation'. Certainly, no one who reads any passage of modern English can fail to notice the frequent mismatch between the sounds of English and the letters used to record them, as, for example, in the well-known set of -OUGH words *cough, rough, though, through, thorough, plough*, or in the case of -OW as in *now, know, knowledge*. Given that in many languages there is a clear and predictable relationship between speech-sounds and the written characters that represent them, one might well ask why this is not the case with English.

The answer lies in the history of the English language, and the purpose of this book is to trace that history in so far as it pertains to the development of modern English spelling and its relationship to modern English pronunciation. We begin with the Old English base and trace the development through the centuries, describing in turn, and in detail, the contributions made to English spelling by Old Norse (the language of the Vikings), French (both Norman and Parisian), Latin, Greek and the many other languages from which English has borrowed vocabulary. These chapters form the bulk of the book, and are its main contribution to the study of English spelling. We also note the internal developments in the language, such as the Great Vowel Shift, the contribution of the early Civil Service (the Court of Chancery) and the printers, and the work of lexicographers and spelling reformers.

The original idea for this major study of English spelling was Christopher Upward's, and the greater part of the material contained in this book was written by him before his untimely death in 2002. Some time after her husband's death, Mrs Janet Upward commissioned the present writer to edit and complete her husband's work and to see it through to publication. It then remained for us to find a publisher, and we are very grateful to Professor David Crystal, the general editor of the *Language Library* series, and to Danielle Descoteaux of Wiley-Blackwell for their willingness to include this book in that series.

Of course, in a book of this length much must remain unrecorded and undiscussed. By the time of his death, Christopher Upward had written a great deal more material than could be included here, much of it based on his own exhaustive study of the Old English, Franco-Latin and Greek elements in present-day English. (For example, the Franco-Latin chapter alone as originally written by Christopher amounted to over 150,000 words – considerably longer than the whole of this book as it now stands.) A general introductory chapter on writing and spelling and another on the origin and development of the alphabet were also felt, with regret, to be outside the scope of the present book. In order to make the results of Christopher's immense work of scholarship available to all those who have an interest in English spelling, all the material that could not be included here is now available on a website (www.historyofenglishspelling.info) hosted by Aston University in Birmingham, UK, and we are very grateful to them for being willing to offer us this facility.

Bibliographical references to books and articles are omitted from the text, but for the benefit of readers who might wish to follow up particular points they are provided in the chapter end-notes.

I would like to thank Julia Kirk of Wiley-Blackwell for her advice and support throughout this project, and Fiona Sewell and the two anonymous readers of the typescript who provided many helpful suggestions and necessary corrections. Any remaining errors are, of course, my responsibility.

Finally, my thanks are due once again to David Crystal and Danielle Descoteaux, and also to Janet Upward and her family, and not least to my wife Nancy, for bearing with me while I made my best efforts to produce a book worthy of the work Christopher Upward had put into it, a task which took rather longer than originally expected.

George Davidson
Edinburgh

# Abbreviations and Symbols

## Abbreviations

| | | | |
|---|---|---|---|
| AmE | American English | OE | Old English |
| ANorm | Anglo-Norman | OFr | Old French |
| BrE | British English | ON | Old Norse |
| EModE | Early Modern English | VLat | Vulgar Latin |
| Eng | English | WSax | West Saxon |
| Fr | French | | |
| Gr | Greek | BCE | before the Christian era |
| Ital | Italian | CE | of the Christian era |
| Lat | Latin | d. | died |
| LGr | Late Greek | GVS | Great Vowel Shift |
| LLat | Late Latin | poss. | possibly |
| ME | Middle English | prob. | probably |
| MFr | Middle French | s.v. | at that word |
| ModE | Modern English | ult. | ultimately |
| ModFr | Modern French | usu. | usually |
| ModGr | Modern Greek | vs. | versus |

## Symbols

- \>   'becomes'
- \<   'is derived from'
- \*   indicates a hypothetical reconstructed form
- ~   indicates an alternative or variant

Letters, letter-groups and word-elements under discussion are generally printed as small capital letters (e.g. GH, -OUGH, -ITY). However, where necessary for clarity in particular contexts, letters and letter-groups may be printed between angle brackets (e.g. <g> rather than G).

## Phonetic symbols

### Consonants

p as in *paw*

b as in *bow*

t as in *to*

d as in *do*

k as in *cow*

g as in *go*

tʃ as in *chew*

dʒ as in *jaw*

f as in *foe*

ɸ an F-like sound made with the lips close together

v as in *vow*

θ as in *thin*

ð as in *the*

s as in *so*

z as in *zoo*

ʃ as in *show*

ʒ as in *regime*

m as in *my*

n as in *now*

ŋ as in *song*

ɲ as in French *signe*, Spanish *señor*

l as in *low*

ɬ an L-like sound with audible friction, as in Welsh *llan*

r as in *row*

h as in *how*

w as in *woe*

j as in *you*

ɟ a G-like sound formed at the hard palate

x as in *loch*

ɣ voiced equivalent of x

ç as in German *ich*

### Vowels

iː as in *sea*

ɪ as in *him*

ɛ as in *get*

e as in Fr *été*

æ as in *cat*

a as in French *patte*

ɑː as in *car*

ʌ as in *sun*

ɒ as in *cot*

ɔː as in *cord*

o as in French *côte*

ʊ as in *put*

uː as in *do*

ɜː as in *bird*

ə as in **about,** fath**er**

y as in French *tu*

eɪ as in *hay*

aɪ as in *high*

ɔɪ as in *boy*

əʊ as in *so*

aʊ as in *how*

ɪə as in *here*

ɛə as in *air*

aɪə as in *fire*

aʊə as in *our*

ʊə as in *poor*

Where vowel symbols with ː are not specifically listed above, the vowels are to be considered longer equivalents of vowels without ː. Similarly, where vowel symbols without ː are not listed above, they are to be considered shorter equivalents of vowels with ː.

/. . ./  indicates a phonemic transcription (i.e. a transcription of contrasting speech-sounds)

[. . .]  indicates a phonetic transcription (i.e. actual sounds as pronounced)

ˈ  precedes the syllable which carries the main stress in a word, e.g. /ˈdɪstrɪkt/ *district*, /dɪˈstrækt/ *distract*

# Language Periods Referred to in the Text

(Dates given are, of course, approximations; see comments *passim* in the text.)

Old English (5th century–c.1150)
Middle English (c.1150–c.1476)
Early Modern English (c.1476–c.1660)
Modern English (c.1476–present)
Old Norse (8th century–1350)
Old French (8th century–1400)
Middle French (14th and 15th centuries)
Modern French (16th century–present)
Late Latin (200–600)
Vulgar Latin (the spoken Latin of the classical period)
Late Greek (200–700)

# 1

# Introduction and Overview

English has frequently been criticized for the complexity of its spelling rules and for a lack of system and consistency in the relationship between the sounds of the spoken language and the symbols of the written language. In the Preface we have already noted Jerome K. Jerome's thoughts on English spelling as a 'disguise for pronunciation'. Others have made similar criticisms.[1] The Danish linguist Otto Jespersen, for example, refers to English spelling as a 'pseudo-historical and anti-educational abomination'; an American linguist, Mario Pei, has described it as 'the world's most awesome mess' and 'the soul and essence of anarchy'; Mont Follick, a former professor of English who as a British Member of Parliament twice, in 1949 and again in 1952, introduced bills into Parliament advocating the simplification of English spelling, said of our present-day spelling that it is 'a chaotic concoction of oddities without order or cohesion'; and more recently the Austrian linguist Mario Wandruszka pronounced it to be 'an insult to human intelligence'. Only slightly gentler in its reproach is Professor Ernest Weekley's opinion that the spelling of English is, in its relationship to the spoken language, 'quite crazy'. One could quote many other similar remarks.

A now classic lament on the state of English spelling, written from the viewpoint of a foreign learner, is the poem *The Chaos* by a Dutchman, Gerard Nolst Trenité, an amusing 274-line (in its final version) catalogue of about 800 English sound–spelling inconsistencies such as *verse* and *worse*; *oven* and *woven*; *Susy, busy, dizzy*; *how, low, toe*; *nature, stature,*

*The History of English Spelling*, First Edition. Christopher Upward and George Davidson.

*mature*; and *font, front, wont, want*.[2] Nolst Trenité's complaint is much the same as Jerome's: it is not so much the spelling as such that is lamented as the mismatch between spelling and pronunciation, with the consequence that learners of English cannot predict the pronunciation of many words they encounter in writing.

Such opinions are not new. As early as the late 1500s, scholars such as Sir Thomas Smith, John Hart and William Bullokar put forward proposals for reforming English spelling,[3] recognizing that, as Hart put it, 'in the moderne and present maner of writing . . . there is such confusion and disorder, as it may be accounted rather a kind of ciphring' that one can learn to decipher only after 'a long and tedious labour, for that it is unfit and wrong shapen for the proportion of the voice' (i.e. spelling does not accurately reflect the sounds of speech). A century and a half later, the actor and lexicographer Thomas Sheridan wrote in his *General Dictionary of the English Language* that:

> Such indeed is the state of our written language, that the darkest heiogliphics [*sic*], or most difficult cyphers [*sic*] which the art of man has hitherto invented, were not better calculated to conceal the sentiments of those who used them from all who had not the key, than the state of our spelling is to conceal the true pronunciation of our words, from all except a few well educated natives.[4]

But do the above remarks constitute a fair assessment of English spelling? Is it really nothing more than a 'chaotic concoction of oddities'? There are some linguists who have expressed rather more positive judgements on present-day English orthography.[5] Geoffrey Sampson, for example, has suggested that 'our orthography is possibly not the least valuable of the institutions our ancestors have bequeathed to us'. The eminent lexicographer Sir William Craigie, in the preface to his *English Spelling, Its Rules and Reasons*, pointed out that the impression that 'English spelling is a hopeless chaos' is quite false, and Joseph Wright, one-time professor of comparative philology at Oxford University, was of the opinion that 'English orthography . . . far from being devoid of law and order . . . is considerably more systematic than would appear at first sight' and that one would be quite wrong to think of it as 'existing by pure convention without rhyme or reason for its being, or method in its madness'. The linguists Noam Chomsky and Morris Halle are famously of the opinion that, in fact, 'English orthography turns out to be rather close to an optimal system for spelling English'. And in his discussion of the systematization of English orthography in the 17th century,

2

Brengelman affirms that the spelling system that developed during that period 'is not a collection of random choices from the ungoverned mass of alternatives that were available at the beginning of the century but rather a highly ordered system taking into account phonology, morphology, and etymology and providing rules for spelling the new words that were flooding the English lexicon'.

So how irregular, in fact, is English spelling? While it is very easy to home in on examples such as *streak* and *steak*, *now* and *know*, *blood* and *stood*, *here* and *there*, and of course the infamous -OUGH words mentioned in the Preface, the question must also be asked: how typical are such irregularities of English spelling as a whole? Analyses of English vocabulary suggest not nearly as much as the above critics, and others, seem to believe. English spelling is often perfectly phonetic, representing with absolute clarity and consistency the actual sound of many words by appropriate strings of letters. One study in the United States found that in a computer analysis of 17,000 words, 84 per cent were spelled according to a regular pattern and only 3 per cent were so irregular and unpredictable in their spellings that they would have to be individually learned,[6] a state of affairs very far from a supposed 'chaotic concoction of oddities'. One figure that is often quoted is that English spelling is about 75 per cent regular. (The statistics gained from such studies depend, of course, on what is or is not included in the analysis and how it is carried out. Are personal names and place-names to be included in or excluded from the study? And if, for example, a word such as *plough* is deemed irregular, are *plough* and *ploughs* to be counted as one irregular word or two? There is also the question of what should or should not be considered an English word for the purposes of a study of English spelling, a matter to which we will give some consideration below.) What makes English spelling *appear* to be very irregular is simply that the majority of the 400 or so most irregular words are also among the most frequently used words. It is their frequency, not their number, that creates the impression of great irregularity in English spelling.

We will say no more here about the pros and cons of English spelling, though we will return to the subject again briefly in the final chapter of this book. The main purpose of this *History of English Spelling* is neither to criticize nor to extol the current state of English spelling, but rather to describe its origins and development, to outline the factors, both linguistic and non-linguistic, that have led to its having the form it has today, and to analyse the complexities of its sound–spelling correspondences. For as Jespersen says,[7] referring in this instance to the pronunciation of

3

-OUGH in *though, through, plough, cough, enough*: 'However chaotic this may seem, it is possible to a great extent to explain the rise of all these discrepancies between sound and spelling, and thus to give, if not rational, at any rate historical reasons for them.' What holds true for these five words is equally true for many others in which the Modern English sound–spelling relationships are unsystematic and unpredictable, and in some cases seem to be almost beyond comprehension. To provide historical descriptive explanations for the facts of present-day English spelling is the chief purpose of this book.

# The Development of English Spelling: A Brief Introductory Overview

The symbols used in spelling modern English are the 26 letters of the Roman or Latin alphabet as it is currently established for English. (When speaking about English, we can refer to this particular set of letters as the English alphabet, in order to distinguish it from the different sets of Roman letters used in writing other languages, such as the German alphabet or the Spanish alphabet.) As we will see, however, the English alphabet did not always consist of 26 letters.

The alphabet evolved very gradually,[8] being applied in various forms in ancient times to languages as different as Greek, Etruscan and Latin. Originally, each letter of the Roman alphabet stood for one (or in the case of x, two) of the speech-sounds of spoken Latin, and when it came to be applied to Old English, the broad sound–spelling relationships of the Roman alphabet were retained as they had applied in Latin; but since Old English contained sounds for which the Roman alphabet provided no letters, a few new letters were introduced from a Germanic alphabet known as the futhark or futhorc. Although there were still more phonemes[9] (that is, contrasting speech-sounds such as, for English, /p/ and /b/, /m/ and /n/, /s/ and /ʃ/) in the Old English sound system than there were individual letters to write them with, over some four centuries preceding the Norman Conquest, the Anglo-Saxons evolved quite a successful system for writing their language down, using a generally regular and predictable system of sound–symbol correspondences.

The sound-to-symbol/symbol-to-sound simplicity of that original system, however, was undermined by subsequent events, such as the Norman Conquest itself, after which French-speaking scribes applied some of their own spelling rules to English (replacing, for example, cw, as in Old English

4

*cwen*, by QU, as in Modern English *queen*), the introduction of printing from continental Europe (with Flemish printers introducing Flemish spellings for English speech-sounds, such as GH for /g/; compare Old English *gast*, Flemish *gheest*, Modern English *ghost*), and by the desire of many scholars in the 16th century to add into English words letters reflecting the Latin and Greek words from which the English words were derived (hence Modern English *doubt*, with a silent B reflecting the B of Latin *dubitum*, although *dubitum* had developed into *doute* with neither the sound /b/ nor letter B in Old French, whence Middle English *doute*).[10] Unfortunately, some of the spelling changes made at this time are based on false etymologies. A classic case is Modern English *island*, from Old English *iȝland* (ȝ is a form of G) written correctly without s in Middle English *iland* but now with an s reflecting a supposed but non-existent connection with *isle* (< French *isle* < Latin *insula*, the source of Modern French *île*). Moreover, while there is a universal tendency for the pronunciation of a language to change over time, the changes needed to maintain a match between sound and symbol are not usually carried out once a writing system has become established, and even less so after the introduction of printing. It is this that has led to much of the irregularity and unpredictability that characterizes the spelling system of present-day English.

The formative stage of modern English spelling began in the early 15th century when Henry V was on the throne. Between 1417 and his death in 1422, Henry wrote almost all his letters in English. From Henry's Signet Office (by whose clerks the king's personal letters were written), the use of English in an increasingly standardized orthography passed to the Chancery Office, and thence in legal documents throughout England. Not surprisingly, this 'official' English spelling was then copied by professional scribes across the whole country. The introduction of printing in 1476 also tended towards an increasingly standardized non-regional spelling. English spelling has never, however, been subject to any overall centralized plan, since England never established or authorized a body, such as the Académie Française (established in 1634) for French, by which such developments could be guided. Modern English spelling has, therefore, emerged by a slow process of increasing consensus among printers and lexicographers, reinforced by teachers, authors of literacy primers and published writers. (These matters will be discussed in more detail in Chapter 9.) Prior to this, spelling was, despite the above-mentioned standardizing tendencies, much more fluid, and words could be spelt almost according to a writer's whim, though the variety and inconsistency in spelling was not without limits: spelling varied more between writers than within the writing of any one individual, and also varied according to the writer's education and temperament (consistency in spelling generally being the mark of someone of a scholarly frame of mind).[11] It is also the case that spelling was more consistent in published works than in private correspondence and diaries.[12]

In the second half of the 18th century Samuel Johnson's *Dictionary of the English Language* (1755) became widely used as a source of reference by the literate section of the population and hence contributed to the general acceptance of a standard, and by the late 19th century there was a fair degree of unanimity among printers, dictionaries and private writers as to how most English words should be spelt. The consensus was, however, never totally formalized or formally applied to all words. When one begins to explore some of the less familiar corners – as well as a few familiar areas – of English vocabulary, one discovers that a surprising number of words still have accepted alternative forms (the figure has been put as high as 25 per cent; it depends, of course, on the size of the dictionary one consults – generally speaking, the smaller the dictionary the fewer the variants listed), and are thus testimony to a continuing element of fluidity in English spelling. Amongst the best known in Britain are *gaol/jail, despatch/dispatch, enquire/inquire, adviser/advisor*, and the endings -ISE/-IZE in verbs such as *organise/organize*. Many of the words in this category are borrowings from 'exotic' foreign languages (which will be the subject of detailed analysis in Chapter 8): the lack of an accepted, standard system of sound–symbol correspondences in English shows up particularly when it comes to transliterating or transcribing loanwords from languages that do not use the Roman alphabet, for which the 'correct' or 'best' spelling to use may not be at all obvious. Hence we find alternative spellings for foodstuffs such as *lichi/litchi/lichee/lychee* (from Chinese), *borsht/borscht/borsch/borshch* (from Russian), *poppadum/popadum/popadom/poppodom/poppadam* (from Tamil) and *yogurt/yoghurt/yoghourt* (from Turkish). And from Russian *tsar[j]* we have the alternative forms *czar/tsar/tzar*.

## Geographical and Historical Variation

The above examples show us that English spelling is not one single, clear-cut system with every word only ever being spelt in one way. But in addition to the type of spelling variation illustrated above, English spelling is subject to variations of two other kinds, geographical and historical:

6

- Geographical variation is seen in the spelling differences found in the different orthographic usages of Britain and the United States of America, such as *colour/color* and *plough/plow*. (These differences will be described in detail in Chapter 9.) Elsewhere in the English-speaking and English-learning world, either British or American norms are adopted, or occasionally (as in Canada) a mixture of the two. Within the British Isles, too, there can be some minor spelling differences: for example, Scottish lakes are *lochs* /lɒxs/, while in Ireland the spelling is *loughs* (with the same pronunciation).[13]

- The above geographical variations are also a manifestation of historical change, in that they have arisen in particular historical circumstances. Other, less dramatic, changes slowly accumulate over time, mostly without the average reader being particularly aware of them. Two changes that became general in the 20th century in Britain were the discontinuation of the form *shew* in favour of *show*, and reversion to the older form *fantasy*, replacing *phantasy*, which had been in common use for several centuries. These are isolated cases, however, and have not entailed corresponding changes to such parallel spellings as *sew* and *phantasmagoria*.

- Another form of historical change is the recognition as correct, or at least as acceptable in some contexts, of spellings that have previously been considered incorrect. One example is *miniscule* for *minuscule* (doubtless from the influence of words beginning in MINI-), still condemned as a 'common error' in *The New Oxford Dictionary of English* in 1998, for example, but earlier gaining a shade of respectability as an 'alternative, less acceptable spelling' in *Chambers English Dictionary* in 1988. Another example is *alright*, once rejected as an error but now increasingly accepted as an alternative to *all right*. The Internet is now a major disseminator of misspellings, at least some of which may through frequency of occurrence achieve a degree of acceptability in the future which they do not enjoy at present.

# The Word–Stocks of English and their Contributions to Modern English Spelling

An examination of present-day English vocabulary shows that English consists for the most part of four main word-stocks: a Germanic base (mostly Anglo-Saxon but with some Scandinavian elements), overlaid with French and with some elements from Latin and Greek. Each of these word-stocks has its own spelling system. A key feature of English spelling, therefore, is that it is *polysystemic*, a mixture composed of or based on the differing spelling systems of several languages: Anglo-Saxon, Scandinavian, French (of at least two dialects – Norman and Parisian), Latin and (through a fairly standardized system of transliteration) Greek. The detailed analysis of the contributions that these languages and their spelling systems have made to modern English spelling forms the main part of this book (see Chapters 3, 5 and 7), the Latin and French elements being considered together in one chapter, with some overlap also between Latin and Greek.

The vocabulary of English is, however, not a closed set. The Roman alphabet is not peculiar to the English language and ever since it was first applied to English it has been the vehicle for an unceasing flow of vocabulary items between English and other languages, in both directions. Every language (whether or not written with the letters of the Roman alphabet) that has contributed one or more words to modern English vocabulary may thereby also have contributed to English orthography elements of its own particular sound system or sound–spelling system – directly, if the language is written with the Roman alphabet, as for example the GH of *spaghetti* or the GN of *bolognese*; via a system of transliteration from a non-Roman alphabet, as is the case with the BH of *bhaji* and *bhangra*, the KH of *khaki* or the Q of *qadi*; or from the phonetic transcription of words written in a non-alphabetic writing system, as in Chinese *taijiquan*, or of words from languages with (at least originally) no writing system at all, such as native languages of North and South America or Australia. The polysystemic structure of English spelling, to which it owes much of its apparently chaotic and unsystematic nature, derives therefore not only from the four major spelling systems (Old English, French, Latin, Greek) that underlie it, but also from a large number of minor ones (Spanish, Italian, Russian, Turkish, Malay, Chinese, etc.) that have each contributed some elements to English vocabulary and thereby to English spelling – 'major' and 'minor' to be understood only in the sense of the relative size of the contributions made.[14] The contribution made to English spelling by these minor languages will be analysed in Chapter 8.

# English Spelling and English Words

If English spelling is, by definition, the spelling of English words, by what criteria can one decide what to include in the data for a study such as this and what to exclude? Is every word that is or has been used by at least some English-speakers, even if only rarely or only in particular contexts or only in certain parts of the English-speaking world, to be included in the data for a history of English spelling, or are there words and phrases which, although found in otherwise undoubtedly English sentences, one may nevertheless exclude from a study of English spelling on the grounds that they are not actually English but foreignisms, i.e. foreign words or expressions which do not truly belong to the word-stock of English?

The question is not new. As Sir James Murray wrote in his introduction to the first edition of the *Oxford English* Dictionary:[15]

> English vocabulary contains a nucleus or central mass of many thousand words whose 'Anglicity' [i.e. 'Englishness'] is unquestioned . . . But they are linked on every side with other words which . . . pertain ever more and more distinctly to the domain of local dialect . . . and . . . the actual language of other lands and peoples. And there is absolutely no defining line in any direction: the circle of the English language has a well-defined centre but no discernible circumference.

Murray expects, therefore, that 'opinions will differ as to the claims of some [words] that are included and some that are excluded [in the dictionary]'.[16] In a similar vein, Serjeantson, in her study of foreign words that have entered English, admits that 'Probably no two people would agree entirely as to what words should be admitted to such a volume as this, especially when the words in question come from the more remote languages such as Chinese, Maori, and so on.'[17]

What applies to English lexicography and lexicology is no less applicable to the study of English spelling, and the issue remains as problematic today as it did in the last century. Of course, there are some guidelines and rules of thumb that can be applied. For example, if a word has been respelt as it has entered or developed in English, it is without question an English word: thus *shamrock* < Irish Gaelic *seamróg*. But if *taoiseach*,[18] also of Irish origin, appears in English sentences only in that form (rather than, for example, as *\*teeshock*), is it or is it not an English word? Should one, or should one not, include AOI = /iː/ in a list of English sound–spelling correspondences? By what criteria does one decide? Similarly, if a loanword has been given an English pronunciation even if the spelling is still 'foreign', it has fairly clearly become an English word: thus *eisteddfod*, usually pronounced /aɪˈstɛdfəd/ in English as opposed to the Welsh /əɪˈsdɛðvod/.[19] This rule of thumb would make *cynghanedd*,[20] pronounced /kəŋˈhænɛð/, a less certain case although the word appears in several English dictionaries, its pronunciation not having been much anglicized from the Welsh, and in particular with a sound–spelling correspondence DD = /ð/ that is not normal in English. At the other end of the scale, words and phrases that are considered foreignisms are generally printed in italic type in English: thus

'Stamp collecting is my hobby, it isn't my *raison d'être*.'

This practice is also found in some dictionaries.[21]

In the cline from clearly accepted loanwords to clearly non-absorbed foreignisms, there is no place where a definite dividing line between English words and non-English words can be drawn. This is an issue particularly in Chapter 8. It is our intention in this book neither to over-simplify the description of English spelling by excluding 'exotic' loan-words nor to over-complicate it by including obvious foreignisms. We have tried to strike a balance, even if it is necessarily subjective and open to criticism.[22] While we have concentrated as far as possible on words that have, regardless of their form or pronunciation, without doubt become fully naturalized in English, nevertheless some words whose 'Anglicity' might be questioned have also been included in order to illustrate a particular spelling, word-structure or sound–spelling correspondence.

## Word-Origin Irrelevant after Integration

Once a word has been absorbed into the language, it joins the common stock of English words and regardless of its origin generally undergoes the same sound and spelling changes as other words with the same sound and spelling structure. (This process can, of course, therefore only be seen in older borrowings into the language, not in the more recent addition to our word-stock.) For example, the word *bishop*, which came into Old English in the form *biscop/bisceop* via Latin *episcopus* from Greek ʼεπίσκοπος (*episkopos*), shows the same development of Old English SC > SH = /ʃ/ as do words of Germanic origin such as *ship* and *fish* (Old English *scip, fisc*). Similarly, both words of Old English origin such as *hus* 'house' and *hlud* 'loud' and words of French origin such as *flour* and *doute* 'doubt' underwent the same shift of vowel sound from /uː/ to /aʊ/ during the Great Vowel Shift of the 15th and 16th centuries. (Compare, on the other hand, the Modern English pronunciation of *group* (< French *groupe*), a word which first entered English in the late 17th century, i.e. some time after the Great Vowel Shift was over, and in which the vowel therefore did not shift to /aʊ/. Other factors, of course, may influence the outcome in particular cases, such as the 16th-century etymology-based spellings of words such as *doubt* and *debt*, discussed in Chapter 6 (see p. 191).

## Aim and Limitations of the Study

The focus of this book is very much on current English spelling, how it came to be as it is and, to a lesser extent, how efficient it is as a means of symbolizing English pronunciation. A book of this size cannot hope or pretend to provide a complete history of English spelling, and its relationship to English pronunciation, in all its facets from the earliest times to the present century. As we have noted in the Preface, much must remain unrecorded and undiscussed. The following points in particular should be noted:

- The provision of examples of Old French, Anglo-Norman, and Middle and Early Modern English spelling has inevitably required a great deal of selectivity. A full range of spellings, or anything approaching such, would have been quite beyond the bounds of this study. (The *Oxford English Dictionary* records, for example, three forms for the Anglo-Norman root of the verb 'maintain', and no fewer than 122 variant English spellings of the word recorded between Middle English and the 19th century.) It must be stressed, therefore, that for a complete spelling history of any particular word, one must have recourse to the *Oxford English Dictionary* to supplement such limited information as can be provided in this book or even on the website (www. historyofenglishspelling.info).
- The focus in this book is on the spelling of general vocabulary, with little attention being paid to personal names and place-names. These do, however, receive more coverage in the material on the website.

## Notes

1   References for the following remarks are: Jespersen (1905: 246; also 1956: 231); Pei (1953: 310, 311); Follick (1965: 1); Wandruszka (1990: 104); Weekley quoted in Vallins (1965: 11).

2   *The Chaos* is quoted in full and commented on in Upward (1994).
3   Smith (1568); Hart (1569) quoted in Vallins (1965: 94); Bullokar (1580). For further remarks on these and other proposals for spelling reform, see Chapter 9.
4   Sheridan (1780: 13).
5   Sampson (1985: 213); Craigie and Wright quoted in Robertson (1936: 299–300); Chomsky and Halle (1968: 184, footnote); Brengelman (1980: 334). The opinion of Chomsky and Halle is frequently quoted in this incomplete form, e.g. Carney (1994: xvii), Vachek (1973: 67), and without reference to the context in which it was made. The full quotation reads: '*In this case*, as in many other cases, English orthography turns out to be rather close to an optimal system of spelling English' because 'it turns out to be close to the true phonological representation' (emphasis added). The specific case referred to is the spelling of *divine/divinity, serene/serenity, profane/profanity*. Since acceptance of Chomsky and Halle's opinion requires acceptance of the theoretical framework underlying their analysis and of their view on what constitutes the 'true phonological representation' of these and other words, one could readily echo the comment of Vachek (1973: 68) that 'as a piece of apology for present-day English spelling, the argumentation adduced by Chomsky and Halle is hardly convincing, and if it is mentioned here this is only done for the sake of completeness'.
6   Hanna et al. (1971).
7   Jespersen (1933: 61).
8   A detailed account of the origins of the Roman alphabet can be found in the material on the website accompanying this book, www. historyofenglishspelling.info.
9   Technical terms are fully explained in the Glossary of Technical Terms, pp. 315–19. An explanatory list of the phonetic symbols used in this book can be found on p. xii.
10  For the dates of language periods referred to in this book, see p. xiv.
11  Baugh and Cable (1993: 203).
12  Sönmez (2000: 407). Sönmez also questions the hitherto generally accepted belief that women's spelling was worse than men's, noting that comparisons have generally been made between examples of men's published writing and women's private writing.
13  *Loch* is from Scottish Gaelic *loch*; *lough* is from Middle English, from Old English *luh*, of Celtic origin, but with the pronunciation of Irish Gaelic *loch*.
14  In the figures for the second edition of the *Oxford English Dictionary* quoted by Hughes (2000: 370), English has 50,725 borrowings from Latin, 37,032 from French and 18,675 from Greek. Among what we are calling the minor languages, some are, not surprisingly, more minor than others: English has, at one end of the scale, 12,322 words of German origin, 7,893 from Italian, 6,286 from Dutch and 5,795 from Spanish, and, at the other end, twelve

from Korean, nine from Thai and Xhosa (a language of southern Africa), seven from Tahitian and Iroquois, six from Vietnamese and Tongan, and four from Hopi.

15  Murray et al. (1884–1928: xvii).
16  Murray et al. (1884–1928: xxvi).
17  Serjeantson (1944: viii).
18  The taoiseach is the prime minster of the Republic of Ireland.
19  Wells (1990: s.v.).
20  An eisteddfod is a Welsh festival of music and poetry. Cynghanedd is a complex system of rhyme and alliteration used in Welsh poetry.
21  Thus, for example, in *Collins English Dictionary* (6th edn., 2003: x, §2.4): 'Foreign words or phrases are printed in boldface italic type and are given foreign-language pronunciations only unless they are regarded as having become accepted in English.' The criteria by which such acceptance or non-acceptance is judged are not stated.
22  Carney (1994: 105) states that 'unassimilated' words of foreign origin were excluded from his study of English spelling, admitting that the choice he made was 'inevitably idiosyncratic'.

# 2

# England and English from the Romans to the Vikings

## Latin and Celtic in Roman Britain

At the time of the Roman invasion in the 1st century CE, most of Britain was inhabited by Celtic-speaking tribes referred to collectively as Britons. The British language, the ancestor of Welsh, Cornish and Breton, was spoken over the whole of the country as far north as central Scotland. During the period of Roman rule, from 43 CE until the early 5th century, Celtic continued to be spoken, but Latin was the medium of written communication for the administration of Britain and was used by educated Britons as well as by their Roman rulers. Latin continued to be the official language in Britain in the first half of the 5th century, even after Roman administration came to an end in or around 410, and was still used into the 6th century by the British upper class in the west and north of the country,[1] but, unlike on the Continent, it did not replace Celtic.

That, then, was the linguistic situation in Britain when and after the Germanic tribes began to settle in the country.

## Anglo-Saxon Kingdoms and Old English Dialects

By the early centuries CE, there were Germanic-speaking tribes in territories along the North Sea coast of Europe, and it is these tribes,

*The History of English Spelling*, First Edition. Christopher Upward and George Davidson.
© 2011 Christopher Upward and George Davidson. Published 2011 by Blackwell Publishing Ltd.

whom we will refer to as Anglo-Saxons,[2] who brought English to Britain, beginning in or about 449. For more than a hundred years bands of these Anglo-Saxons crossed over from the Continent and settled in the south and east of Britain, gradually extending the area under their control northwards and westwards until it reached as far north as south-east Scotland and included everything to the south of that apart from Wales and Cornwall. The initial multitude of small territories so created gradually coalesced into seven kingdoms known as the Anglo-Saxon Heptarchy: Kent, Sussex and Wessex along the south coast, Essex and East Anglia in the east, Mercia covering the vast area of the midlands from the Thames to the Humber, and Northumbria northwards from the Humber to the Firth of Forth.

At the same time, dialect boundaries formed within the Old English speech area, creating four major dialects: Kentish, West Saxon, Mercian and Northumbrian (see Figure 1).

Mercian and Northumbrian are together referred to as Anglian. As one might expect, there was a broad, though not absolute, correlation between the dialect boundaries and the political boundaries of the Heptarchy: with some simplification of detail, we can say that Kentish was spoken in Kent; West Saxon was spoken in Sussex and Wessex; Mercian in Mercia, Essex and East Anglia (though Saxon settlers north of the Thames had some specific dialect features of their own); and Northumbrian in Northumbria.

## Anglo-Saxon Literacy and the Runic Alphabet

Although the Anglo-Saxons are generally described as illiterate, they did nevertheless possess a writing system which they brought with them to England. That system was the runic alphabet. Since, as will be seen, runes play a small part in the history of English spelling, we will include a brief consideration of them here.[3]

Runes may have been first devised around the 1st century CE by an Alpine Germanic people as an adaptation from a North Italic alphabet similar to the Etruscan or Roman alphabets. From its place of origin, runic writing was disseminated northwards and eastwards, and by the 3rd century it was being used in the regions of the North Sea coast and Scandinavia. Runes first came to England with the Anglo-Saxon settlers.

The Germanic runic character set is known as the *futhark*, after its first six letters F, U, TH, A, R, K, but the particular set which developed in

15

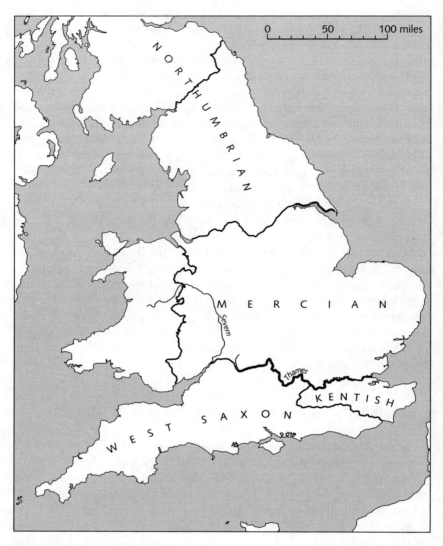

**Figure 1**  Map of Old English dialects.

Britain is generally known as the *futhorc* (reflecting Germanic-to-English sound changes affecting the fourth and sixth letters). The original Germanic character set contained 24 runes, but as brought to Britain it had acquired an additional two characters. In subsequent centuries further runes were added, especially in northern Britain, producing an eventual total of 31 signs.[4] Some of the later runes seem to have been added by analogy with already established Roman-alphabet spellings in Old English, several of them reflecting vowel sounds that evolved in Old English but were not present in earlier Germanic. Other, later, runes reflect awareness of the inadequacies of the Roman alphabet, being created to distinguish different values of alphabetic c (as /k/ and /tʃ/) and G (as /g/ and /j/).

English runes are found in three areas of England: Northumbria, Mercia and Kent; there are no runic inscriptions from Wessex. Most of the surviving runic inscriptions which have been found date from the 7th century or later, and were therefore written after the Anglo-Saxon conversion to Christianity and the concomitant adoption of the Roman alphabet (see below). In fact, the most important runic inscriptions include text in the Roman alphabet as well as in runes, while other shorter inscriptions mix Roman letters and runes in the spelling of individual words. Conversely, individual runes were sometimes used as abbreviations for full words in text which was otherwise written in the Roman alphabet; for example, the M-rune as an abbreviation for *man*, the D-rune for *day*.[5]

Runes are relevant to the history of English spelling for the following reasons:

- Firstly, by bringing runes with them to Britain, the Anglo-Saxons showed that they had among them people ('rune-masters') who had already analysed the sound system of their language sufficiently to apply the alphabetic principle (i.e. the representing of each speech-sound of the language by one symbol) to its representation, and, at least in the north of England, were capable of recognizing that sound-changes necessitated the introduction of new characters.
- Secondly, though limited in size, number and quality, and mostly rather late in composition, the runic inscriptions found in Britain give an alternative insight into the Anglo-Saxons' ideas about sound–symbol correspondences in the writing of their language.
- Thirdly, as will be described below (pp. 22–3), some runes were added to the Roman alphabet for the purpose of writing Old English.

17

## Old English and the Roman Alphabet

Whether the Britons were exterminated, driven out or assimilated by the Anglo-Saxons, there was a significant cultural decline in the territory the incomers entered, and the knowledge and use of the Roman alphabet decreased or possibly even totally ceased in these areas. Although there was continued use of the Roman alphabet in the British kingdoms, the evidence for the adoption of the Roman alphabet by the Anglo-Saxons does not suggest any significant influence from British sources. Literacy in the Roman alphabet returned to England through the work of Irish and continental Christian missionaries.

The Roman alphabet was introduced into Kent with Augustine's mission in 597. It was apparently applied to English in Kent during the following century at least for the purpose of drawing up law-codes, among them one for King Ethelbert before his death in 616. Yet although the Roman alphabet appears to have been first applied to English in Kent, and although Kent was eventually to assert itself as the dominant force in religious matters throughout Britain through the see of Canterbury (the Kentish capital), it is not from Kent that the main development of writing in Old English is to be traced. The earliest surviving Old English texts show that the decisive development occurred in the north, and emanated from Ireland.

Irish Christianity had produced a strong tradition of monastic literacy. Around 563, the Irish prince and monk Columba established a monastery on the island of Iona off the west coast of Scotland. The Iona monastery became a centre of learning where various offspring of Northumbrian ruling families later enjoyed sanctuary in exile, and it is from there that the Christianization of the northern English kingdom of Northumbria was to proceed, along with the introduction of the Roman alphabet. The initial conversion to Christianity of Northumbria under King Edwin took place in 627 under the auspices of the Augustinian mission (i.e. representatives of Roman Christianity), but Edwin's subsequent defeat and death in 632 led to a brief relapse into paganism. His successor, Oswald, on the other hand, had been baptized into the Celtic church on Iona, and around the year 635 he invited missionaries from Iona to his kingdom. Under the leadership of Aidan, this Irish mission set about the conversion of Northumbria to Christianity, founding monasteries which became famous centres for Latin book-learning and writing. For writing in English, these monasteries used the Irish script, a different style of letter-shapes from those of the Roman script. The

Irish style of lettering eventually became the standard for Old English throughout Britain, though continental styles were often preferred for writing in Latin.

# A First Look at Old English Spelling

The amount of written material surviving from the Old English period (not counting variant copies) has been estimated as equivalent to only about 30 medium-sized modern novels.[6] One of the oldest surviving examples of English is the nine-line poem attributed to Cædmon, a 7th-century lay brother of Whitby Abbey, but not much material survives from before the 9th century, and the bulk of the Old English texts we have today originated in or after the 10th century.

Old English spelling does not lend itself to a simple description, for a number of reasons:

- Firstly, the spelling changed in the course of time. The earliest texts show a greater dependence on the inventory of letters provided by the Latin alphabet than do later texts,[7] as successive generations of Old English writers evidently built up the experience and confidence to innovate and expand the received alphabet to meet the different needs of their own language.
- In addition, the language itself changed over the more than five centuries during which Old English was written. To take one example, the earlier distinct vowels of unstressed final syllables tended to merge towards the weak vowel /ə/, and were increasingly all written as E.
- There are also differences of dialect. In so far as the writing system was designed to represent speech-sounds, those dialect differences inevitably meant some differences in spelling too, especially of vowels. Thus, for example, what in West Saxon was written *eald* 'old' was elsewhere written *ald*, and *myrʒe* 'merry' (<ʒ> = G) elsewhere as *merʒe*. See pp. 33–4 for more on this.
- Again, there was no single official standard of spelling (although in later years something close to one did evolve in West Saxon), and there were no works of reference such as dictionaries against which a 'correct' standard spelling for words could be checked.
- Lastly, there was the element of individualism in the production of written text. With each copy of an Old English text being the work of an individual scribe, it is not surprising that no two copies would

be absolutely identical. Even if a number of scribes wrote simultaneously to dictation in a monastery scriptorium (i.e. the room where the copying of manuscripts was carried out), what they wrote depended ultimately on the degree of concentration and hand–eye co-ordination of each individual. Furthermore, the Old English alphabet provided more than one possible spelling for certain sounds, and individual scribes vacillated between them even in successive occurrences of the same word.

There was, therefore, a good deal of fluidity in Old English spelling. But we may nevertheless speak of spelling standards of a rough and ready kind. The craft of writing was confined to a relatively small number of people, chiefly clerics, who were typically trained to the orthographic standards of a particular monastic scriptorium. The monasteries were, in part, local institutions, and to that extent the spelling they cultivated reflected the regional dialect; but since first Northumbria and later Wessex tended to dominate literary output with their respective dialects at different times (Northumbrian in the 8th century, West Saxon from the 10th century), many surviving texts from a particular time-period reflect the spelling of the then dominant dialect. Political developments from the time of King Alfred (king of Wessex from 871, and by the time of his death also of Kent and western Mercia) onwards gave particular force to this tendency in the later Old English period. His campaign to restore education and literacy after the ravages of the Vikings involved a highly organized training programme for scribes and the distribution of a copy of each book produced to every bishopric. The West Saxon dialect of Alfred's kingdom came to form the basis for a spelling standard for Old English for some two hundred years, although some changes did occur during this period. Some features of the West Saxon dialect, however, set it rather apart from the dialects of the rest of Britain[8] and the spellings used for this standard appear to represent something of a compromise between dialects, being intended for readers and writers not only from Wessex but across England.[9]

To illustrate some of the spelling differences between Northumbrian and West Saxon, below are two versions of Cædmon's hymn,[10] composed in the late 7th century. The first, known as the Moore version, is found on the last page of a manuscript (the Moore Manuscript) of Bede's *Ecclesiastical History*, written about 737 (Bede gives a Latin translation of the poem in the body of this text); see the top lines of Figure 2. The second version is a West Saxon version made some 200 years later:

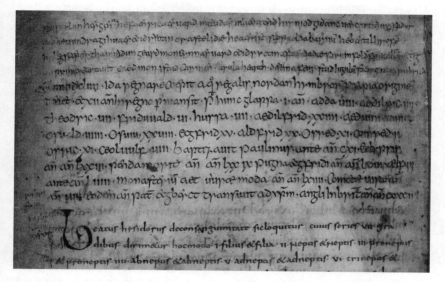

**Figure 2** Cædmon's *Hymn*. Reproduced by kind permission of the Syndics of Cambridge University Library.

### Northumbrian, c.700

*Nu scylun herȝan   hefaenrıcaes Uard*
*Metudæs maectı   end his modȝıdanc*
*uerc Uuldurfadur   sue he uundra ȝıhuaes*
*ecı Dryctın   or astelıdæ*
*he aerıst scop   aelda barnum*
*heben tıl hrofe   haleȝ Scepen*
*tha mıddunȝeard   moncynnæs Uard*
*ecı Dryctın   æfter tıadæ*
*fırum foldu   Frea allmectıȝ.*

### West Saxon, c.900

*Nu þe sculan herıan   heofonrıces peard*
*Metodes mıhte   and hıs modȝeþonc*
*peorc puldorfæder   spa he pundra ȝehpaes*
*ece Dryhten   ord onstealde*
*He ærest gesceop   eorðan bearnum*
*heofon to hrofe   halıȝ Scyppend*
*ða mıddanȝeard   moncynnes peard*
*ece Dryhten   æfter teode*
*fırum foldan   Frea ælmıhtıȝ.*

21

A fairly literal translation of this might be as follows (words which have survived into Modern English are given in italics in square brackets; words in round brackets appear only in the West Saxon version):

> Now (we) must [*shall*] praise   heaven-kingdom's guardian [*ward*]
> Creator's powers [*might*]   and his mind-thought [*mood, think*]
> Work of glory-father   as he of wonders each
> Eternal lord   the beginning established
> He first [*ere-est*] shaped   of men (earth) for children [*bairns*]
> Heaven as roof   holy Creator [*shape*]
> Then earth [*middle-yard*]   mankind's Guardian [*ward*]
> Eternal Lord   afterwards [*after*] created
> For men a world [*fold*]   Lord almighty.

Comparing these two versions, we find that over a quarter of the letters in the Northumbrian version do not occur in the West Saxon, and that of 42 words in the Northumbrian only six occur with the same spelling in the West Saxon (though these figures are slightly exaggerated by the occasional use of different words and word-forms in the two versions). The chief differences occur in the inventory of letters used and in the spelling of vowels, as for example when Northumbrian spells the Old English form of Modern English *heaven* as *hefaen* where West Saxon has *heofon*.

Some letters and letter-forms are not found in the Modern English alphabet:

- The letter <i> is written without a dot in both manuscripts.
- The 'open' G, <ȝ>,[11] is found in both texts. <ȝ> was a letter variant preferred by the Irish/English script to the 'closed' continental form <g> used for Latin texts in England and generally on the Continent. (In Middle English the open letter-form came to be known as 'yogh'.) The distinction between <ȝ> and <g> later became significant for a time in that they represented contrasting speech-sounds, especially after the Norman Conquest, but did not survive the introduction of printing.
- These variant letter-forms apart, the Northumbrian version of Cædmon's hymn confines itself to inherited Roman letters. Northumbrian used D to represent both /d/ (e.g. the first D in *modȝidanc*) and /ð/ (e.g. the second D of *modȝidanc*). The West Saxon version of the hymn, however, introduces three new letters: Þ/þ (called *thorn*); Ð/ð (for which the name *eth* was coined in the 19th century); and

22

Ƿ/ƿ (called *wyn*). The first two of these replace the Northumbrian TH and the D which = /ð/. The *thorn* is (with its name) taken from the runic *futhorc*, in which it was the third symbol, while the letter-form of *eth* is an adaptation of the D of the Irish/English insular script mentioned above. But whereas these two new letters, *thorn* and *eth*, avoided the ambiguity of D found in early Northumbrian, they were not used to distinguish the voiced and voiceless values of TH ([ð] and [θ]). Instead, Old English scribes used them more or less inter-changeably to represent both values (though with some preference regarding position rather than pronunciation, Þ/þ tending to pre-dominate word-initially and Ð/ð word-finally); thus in *Beowulf* we find the word for 'since' spelt with four different variations of these letters in the space of a few hundred lines: *syþþan, syððan, sypðan, syðþan*. Since in Old English a consonant standing between voiced sounds was itself always voiced (as TH is in Modern English *then*) while in other contexts or when doubled it was voiceless (as TH is in Modern English *thin*), it was of less importance to show the voiced/voiceless distinction with this pair of letters in Old English than arguably it is in Modern English (see also pp. 56–7 under 'TH').

• The letter *wyn*, ƿ, is another one that occurs in the West Saxon but not in the Northumbrian version of Cædmon's hymn. The latter makes use instead of a rather unsatisfactory device of Latin spelling, U being used to represent both the vowel /u/ and the consonant /w/ which is today spelt W (compare Modern English, where U = /w/ in *suede* but /uː/ in *sued*). Outside Northumbria, the originally runic letter *wyn*, ƿ, regularly came to be written for /w/. Hence we see that where Northumbrian has *uundra* for 'wonders', the West Saxon has *ƿundra*.[12]

There were two other innovations in Old English writing which arose from the development of the Old English vowel system. Old English had many more vowel sounds than Latin, and the letters A, E, I, O, U, Y were insufficient to distinguish them all. Latin spelling, especially in its transliterations from Greek (see p. 197), had used AE and OE, which by Anglo-Saxon times had in Latin merged in pronunciation as /e/. Old English adopted these symbols, but gave them other sound values: AE, early written separately but by 800 normally ligatured as Æ/æ (both ligatured and non-ligatured forms are seen in the two versions of the Cædmon hymn above), was used to represent /æ/. The ligatured Æ was called *ash*, and a symbol for it was developed for the later runic futhorc as well. The vowel of Old English *bæc* ('back') was thereby distinguished from the vowel in Old English *batt* (/bat/, 'bat, cudgel'). *Ash* occurred very widely in Old English writing, but in the Middle English period it fell into disuse, as the two *a*-vowels merged into a single sound. Less commonly used in Old English was Œ, typically a dialect variant of o or E; thus *dœhter* is more commonly written *dehter* (both forms being the dative singular form of *dohtor* 'daughter'). In pronunciation Œ is a front rounded vowel, corresponding perhaps to German ö, e.g. in Old English *œle* 'oil'.

None of these alphabetic innovations survived into Modern English. In the case of Æ and Œ, the sounds they were devised to represent had dropped out of the speech-sound system by Middle English (though /æ/ re-entered the sound system of English in the Early Modern English period), and so no longer needed to be written. (Both letters were re-introduced in more recent times, chiefly in words of Graeco-Latin derivation such as *Cæsar* and *cœnobite*, with the sound value /iː/.) Of the letters Þ (*thorn*), Ð (*eth*) and Ƿ (*wyn*), *thorn* was increasingly preferred to *eth* in the Middle English period, while w increasingly displaced *wyn*. However, it was the arrival of printing in Britain in the 15th century, with its imported continental typefaces, which put a stop to the remaining uses of such non-standard Roman letters. Vestiges of Þ are seen deformed in the Early Modern English abbreviations *y^e*, *y^t* for *the*, *that*, the former still occurring in pseudo-archaic signs such as *Ye Olde Englishe Tea Shoppe*.

## Long Vowels and Double Consonants

Two further features of Old English spelling may be commented on:

- Each vowel spelling in Old English (whether a single vowel represented by a single letter or a ligature such as Æ, or a diphthong represented by a digraph such as EA) could be pronounced either short or long, the long values being essentially just lengthened versions of the short values, but Old English spelling had no systematic way of showing the difference in quantity. However, because there was a danger especially of some monosyllables otherwise being misunderstood,[13] early manuscripts sometimes doubled the vowel letter, as in *ʒood, tiid*, to show the long O or I of the standard spelling *ʒod* 'good' or *tid* 'tide'; other manuscripts freely (if not consistently) used an acute accent over long vowels (e.g. *jód, tíd*), though this could also indicate a stressed vowel. Modern editions of Old English texts commonly mark long vowel values with a macron to aid readers not only as to pronunciation, but also sometimes to distinguish meaning, e.g. Old English *jod* 'god', but *jōd* 'good', *hara* 'hare', but *hāra* 'hoary'. It should be noted that in order to give a truer picture of Old English spelling as it was originally used, the long and short values of vowels will not be graphically distinguished in the examples in this book.

- Double consonants in Old English were pronounced 'geminated', that is, pronounced with double the length of the corresponding single consonants. Thus the N and NN in a pair of Old English words such as *sunu/sunne* 'son/sun' were pronounced differently, much as the NN in Modern English *inner* and *thinness* respectively. Gemination could vary in different forms of the same word: for instance *ic fremme* 'I do', *he fremeð* 'he does'; *steppan* 'to step' with a past tense *stopon* 'stepped'. Consonant doubling also appears in Modern English (e.g. *ride/ridden, omit/omitted, fez/fezzes, afraid/affray*) but usually does not imply a lengthened pronunciation as it does in Old English (but compare the pronunciation of the NN in *unnatural* or the BB in *subbasement*). Geminated consonants in Old English tended to cause shortening in preceding vowels which were originally long (as in, for example, *hlædder* 'ladder', *foddor* 'fodder', *cyððo* 'kith'), so establishing a pattern of long vowels or diphthongs before single consonants and short vowels before double consonants that is common in Modern English too (as in *write/written, hoped/hopped, caned/canned*). This pattern is also seen in the phonetic spelling devised by the Augustinian canon Orm in his poem the *Ormulum*, written in the second half of the 12th century (see p. 74). Nevertheless, consonant doubling is sometimes inconsistent in Old English, as in the alternative spellings *æppel/æpl* 'apple'; this occurs especially in final consonants of monosyllables, giving rise to alternatives such as *sac/sacc* 'sack', *bed/bedd, eall/eal* 'all', *man/mann*.

## Early Celtic and Graeco-Latin Elements in Old English: Their Zero Effect on English Spelling

It has been estimated that Old English absorbed over 500 foreign words at different periods, nearly all of them from Latin.[14] When adopting loanwords from other languages, there is the choice of either preserving their spelling in the source language or adapting them to the spelling patterns of the borrowing language. While English today usually keeps the foreign spelling of fresh loanwords (such as *pâté de foie gras, spaghetti, apartheid, machismo*) with consequent unpredictable sound–spelling correspondences, Old English tended to represent loanwords as they were pronounced in English, and so the sound–spelling correspondences in these words are no different from those of the original Anglo-Saxon word-stock, and their subsequent development into Modern English word-forms is therefore the same in both cases. Thus, in very few cases is the origin of these loanwords apparent from their Old English spelling, let alone their Modern English spelling: for example, as already noted (p. 10), Old English *biscop* (< Greek *episkopos* via Latin *episcopus*) develops into Modern English *bishop* in exactly the same way as Old English *fisc* (from a Germanic root) becomes Modern English *fish*. Similarly, *stræt* (< Latin *strata*) > *street* is an example of an Old English contribution to Modern English spelling, not a Latin contribution. Recording the Graeco-Latin contribution to Modern English spelling, it must be stressed, is not the same as recording the Graeco-Latin element in Modern English vocabulary. Such loanwords therefore constitute part of the Old English legacy to Modern English spelling[15] rather than belonging to the later Latin or Greek legacy which will be discussed in later chapters. (Of course, some Modern English words have forms similar or identical to their Old English equivalents. For example, Modern English *disc* is first seen in the 18th century, deriving directly from Latin *discus* and reinforced by French *disque*. Old English had also borrowed *disc* over 1,000 years earlier from the same Latin source, with the meaning of 'dish'. Thus Old English *disc* is the ancestor of Modern English *dish*, but not of Modern English *disc*.)

## The Vikings in England

The Vikings began ravaging Britain at the end of the 8th century: Wessex was raided in 787, and in the north the monastery of Lindisfarne was burnt in 793, and that of Jarrow the following year. But as with the Anglo-Saxons centuries earlier, so with the Vikings: raiders became settlers, and small bands were followed by larger numbers. Most of the settlers were Danes, but there were Norwegian settlements in the north and north-west of England. In 878 England was divided into two parts, with the eastern part under Danish rule and henceforth known as the

Danelaw.[16] By the middle of the 10th century, a large part of eastern England, though still strongly Danish in population and custom, was under English rule again. But after further Danish victories, the Danish king Svein seized the English throne in 1014; his son Cnut (Canute) and his successors ruled England till 1042.

The early relations between the Viking invaders/settlers and the English would doubtless at first be hostile, but there was eventually peaceful co-existence and intermarriage. Although in some places the Viking settlers seem to have soon adopted English, there were also communities in which for some time Danish or Norwegian remained the everyday language. There would doubtless also have been considerable bilingualism. These factors all created conditions favourable to extensive Scandinavian influence on English.

## Scandinavian Elements in English Vocabulary and Spelling

The Vikings did not have a developed literacy culture as the Anglo-Saxons did by the 8th century. Early Scandinavian inscriptions are written in runes, not the Roman alphabet, and early English records of the language of the Vikings in the Roman alphabet come chiefly from the relatively few examples of isolated Scandinavian words in Old English texts. The similarity between Old English and the language of the Scandinavian settlers can make it difficult to decide whether a word in Modern English is of Old English origin or borrowed from Scandinavian. Some Scandinavian words were indistinguishable from Old English (e.g. *folk, hus* 'house') or acquired an Old English spelling so close to the Scandinavian that the Modern English form appears to relate to both equally (e.g. *fellow* from Old English *feolaʒa* or Old Norse *felage*). Other words differed slightly more: Modern English *silver, sister* have a closer affinity to the Scandinavian form than to the Old English (compare Old English *seolfor*, Old Norse *silfr*, Middle English *selver/silver*; Old English *speostor*, Old Norse *systir*, Middle English *soster/sister*). There are about 900 words of definite Scandinavian origin in English, and an equal number for which a Scandinavian origin is probable or in which there has at least been some Scandinavian influence on the form of the word.[17] Although this borrowing must have been taking place in the 10th and 11th centuries, words of Scandinavian origin are mostly not attested in writing until the 13th century or later.

The written forms of Scandinavian-derived words generally apply standard English sound–symbol correspondences. Viewed from the perspective of Modern English, the Scandinavian word-stock has integrated almost indistinguishably into the spelling patterns of English as a whole: compare, for example, *window* (< Old Norse *vindauga* 'wind-eye') and *widow* (< Old English *widewe*); similarly, Scandinavian-derived *cast* beside Old English *last*, *take* beside *make*, *(boat)swain* beside *rain*.

- Most Scandinavian-derived words in Modern English are simple monosyllables with unremarkable spellings representing their pronunciation in a predictable way: *bait, bark* (of a tree), *bask, bloom, boon, brink, call, clip, crawl, crook, cut, die, dirt, down* 'feathers', *droop, flat, flit, fog, gait, gap, gasp, gust, hit, ill, lift, link, loan, loose, muck, odd, rid, sly, snub, sprint, stab, stack, swirl, till, trust, want, wing*.
- Two-syllable words are few, but include *anger, blather, filly, freckle, glitter, rotten, rugged*, though some of these include suffixes.
- Other Modern English disyllabic words derive from Scandinavian compounds made up of monosyllabic elements: *awk+ward, happ+y, har+bour, hus+band, hus+ting, marr+am, mid+den, ran+sack, rein+deer, wass+ail*.

## Scandinavian-derived consonants in Modern English

Scandinavian-derived words are found in Modern English with various digraphs (i.e. two-letter groups, often representing a single sound, or sometimes in Modern English no sound at all) which are otherwise typical of words descended from Anglo-Saxon English:

- GH in *slaughter, slight, tight*;
- TH in *their, they, thrift, thrust, tether, both, birth, sleuth*;
- WH in *wheeze, whin, whirl*;
- WR in *wreck, wrong*.

The digraphs CH and SH are not common in words of Norse origin. As was the case in the Middle English period with a few words of Old English origin (e.g. *mys* respelt *mice*), a Scandinavian final s may later be replaced by the French-derived spelling -CE, as in Scandinavian *fors* (= 'waterfall') aligned with French-derived *force* and *ras* (= 'speed race') aligned with French-derived *race* (= 'ethnic race').

One recurring spelling feature in words of Scandinavian origin that sets them apart from Anglo-Saxon-derived words is the retention of /g/

before a front vowel, as in *get, give, begin* (if these words had derived from Anglo-Saxon English, it should have resulted in Modern English forms such as *\*yet, \*yive, \*beyin*). The G in Scandinavian-derived *anger*, pronounced /g/, likewise contrasts with G pronounced /dʒ/ in French-derived *danger*. Further examples are:

- The G of *gill* 'liquid measure', deriving from French, is pronounced /dʒ/ in Modern English whereas *gill* 'stream', deriving from Scandinavian, has /g/ (as do the *gills* of a fish, though a Scandinavian origin for that word has not been conclusively demonstrated).
- Two further examples of Scandinavian /g/ before a front vowel are *girth* (< Old Norse *gjorð*) and (with an optional U) *gild/guild* (< Old English *ʒield*, influenced by Old Norse *gildi*).
- In the verb *geld* (< Old Norse *gelda*), the /g/ was alternatively written GU in the 16th and 17th centuries, giving the form *gueld*, a spelling device that has continued to be used in Modern English in Scandinavian-derived *guest* (Old Norse *gestr*).

Elsewhere in Scandinavian-derived words there is a similar tendency for the sounds /k/ and /g/ to be retained in certain positions where they contrast with /ʃ/, /tʃ/, /dʒ/ or with an orthographic W in words derived from Anglo-Saxon English:

- Words such as *kid, kilt, kindle* derive from Scandinavian.
- For the contrast between *dyke, wreck*, of ultimate Scandinavian origin, and *ditch, wretch*, which are Anglo-Saxon-derived cognates, see p. 38, with other examples not necessarily of Scandinavian origin (e.g. *church/kirk*).
- There are parallel contrasts in voiced consonants, e.g. between standard (southern English) *bridge* and northern dialect *brig*.
- A number of Scandinavian-derived words end in /g/: *dreg(s), egg, keg, leg, lug, rag*. In some words, there is a contrast with Anglo-Saxon English equivalents whose original G has changed to Modern English W: *drag/draw, nag/gnaw* (and the pair *flag(-stone)/flaw* show a similar development). However, although of Scandinavian origin, *awe* and *law* have undergone the change to W.
- A straightforward spelling pattern which commonly shows Scandinavian derivation arises from word-initial /sk/, usually spelt SC before what were back vowels in Old English (whether or not they are back vowels in present-day English) e.g. *scab, scale*, and SK before

what were front vowels in Old English (whether or not they are front vowels in present-day English) e.g. *skin, sky*. (SC before a front vowel such as E or I in Old English was pronounced /ʃ/, as for example in *scip* 'ship'. See 'SC', p. 55, for the relation of this pattern to SH in words descended from Old English.) Examples of such Scandinavian-descended spellings are *scab, scale, scanty, scar* (= 'rock-face'), *scare, scathe* (e.g. as in *unscathed*), *scorch, score, scout, scowl, skate* (= 'type of fish'), *skill, skin, skip, skirt, sky*; not surprisingly, spellings varied in the past, with forms such as *scate* for Modern English *skate* and *skare* for Modern English *scare* being recorded.

- o *Skull* and *squall* may also belong with this group; the words' Scandinavian origins are disputed.
- o Spellings with SC-, SK- are, however, not uniquely of old Scandinavian origin: *scar* (= 'mark of injury'), *skirmish*, for instance, are from French; *scorpion, skeleton* are ultimately from Greek; and *scoop, skipper* are from Dutch.
- o Words beginning with SCR- are often included in this group (e.g. *scrape, scream, scree*), but as noted in the *Oxford English Dictionary* (at SCR-), there are no necessary grounds for the usual assumption of a Scandinavian origin for such words. *Scrape*, for example, had corresponding forms in both Old English (*scrapian*) and Old Norse (*skrapa*); Old English *screade* survives in the two Modern English words *screed* and *shred*.
- Scandinavian offered the spelling *knif* where Anglo-Saxon English had *cnif* for Modern English *knife*. This development suggests a possible Scandinavian influence on all Modern English spellings with initial KN- which had CN- in Old English.

## Modern English Scandinavian-derived vowels

It is sufficient to note a couple of points here:

- The digraph EE occurs frequently in words of Scandinavian origin, as in *fleet* 'speedy' (probably < Old Norse *fliotr*), *keel* (< Old Norse *kjolr*), *meek, seem* (< Old Norse *sóma*), *teem, wheeze*; EA occurs less often: *steak* (< Old Norse *steik*), *weak* (< Old Norse *veikr*).
- Sometimes a silent final E indicating a preceding 'long' vowel in Modern English, as in *mire, raise, same, snare* (and with a different vowel quality, *are*) derives from an E that represents an earlier fully pronounced vowel (as in Old Norse *reisa, snara, erum*, etc.).

# The End of Old English

Old English was, of course, increasingly eclipsed by French after the Norman Conquest in 1066, although texts continued to be written in English for some time after that date. The Old English period may be considered to have definitely reached its end in 1154, with the writing of the final entry of the *Anglo-Saxon* or *Peterborough Chronicle*,[18] although the entries from 1122, and more especially those from 1132, increasingly show differences from the West Saxon standard of the earlier entries, and these late entries may justifiably be considered as examples of Middle English.

In the Middle English period, we see the rise of English again and its return to use in the spheres of both administration and literature in which it had for a time been supplanted by French. This we will examine in more detail in Chapter 4. In the next chapter, though, we will first give our attention to the Old English contribution to Modern English spelling.

## Notes

1 Jackson (1953: 76–121) reviews the evidence for the continued use of Latin in post-Roman Britain.

2 In accordance with common usage, 'Anglo-Saxons' will denote the Germanic settlers in England and 'Old English' their language. The exact tribal composition of the invaders need not concern us in this study.

3 For a more detailed introduction to runes, see Page (1987); Elliott (1989).

4 Two further runic symbols are known, but only from manuscript sources, not found in carved inscriptions.

5 Campbell (1969: 12).

6 Crystal (1988: 153).

7 Campbell (1969: §§54, 55).

8 Toon (1992: 417).

9 There are nevertheless indications of other literary standard languages in Anglo-Saxon England, even if they were overshadowed by West Saxon. See Smith, J. (1996: 67).

10 From Whitelock (1967: 181–2) and Wakelin (1988: 20) respectively, with some minor alterations (e.g. <ȝ> for <g>, <þ> for <w>, the dotless <ı>, *modȝeþonc* for *modeþonc*).

11 The angle brackets are here used to indicate a particular letter-form.

12  The letter-form w is first attested in an English place-name *writolaburna* and in the word *triow* 'tree' in a late-7th-century charter (Hogg 1992b: 76), and was introduced to wider use on the Continent by Anglo-Saxon missionaries. It was not until the Normans reintroduced it to England after 1066 that it began to supplant the runic letter ƿ.

13  Scragg (1974: 12, fn1).

14  Pyles and Algeo (1982: 295).

15  Some other words of Latin origin are *cetel* 'kettle' (< *catillus*), *cycene* 'kitchen' (< *coquina*), *peall* 'wall' (< *vallum*), *pin* 'wine' (< *vinum*) and *ynce* 'inch' (< *uncia*). Old English adopted few words from the Celtic language of the Britons. Among those which survived into Modern English are *bannock* 'round, flat loaf' < Old English *bannuc* (compare Welsh *ban*, Breton *bannac'h*), *bin* < Old English *bin/binn/binne* (compare Welsh *ben*) and *brock* 'badger' < Old English *brocc/broc* (compare Welsh *broch*, Breton *broc'h*).

16  For further details of the Viking raids on and settlement in England, see for example Strang (1970: 317–20); Baugh and Cable (1993: 90–94). Typical Scandinavian place-name elements are -BY, -GATE, -THORP(E), -THWAITE and -TOFT, as in, for example, *Grimsby, Harrogate, Scunthorpe, Bassenthwaite* and *Lowestoft*.

17  For a more detailed discussion of the Norse elements of Old English vocabulary, see for example Serjeantson (1935); Pyles and Algeo (1982: 299–300); Baugh and Cable (1993: 94–103).

18  The *Anglo-Saxon Chronicle* is a set of annals probably begun in the court of King Alfred around the end of the 9th century. It exists in several versions. The *Peterborough Chronicle* is the version of the chronicle copied or, for the entries from 1121 onwards, composed in the monastery at Peterborough. (For more on the *Chronicle*, see p. 68.)

# 3

# The Old English Roots of Modern English Spelling

Although in this chapter Old English spelling will be looked at as a system in its own right, we will nevertheless be analysing it very much from the perspective of Modern English. We will, therefore, not take account of the multiplicity of forms found over a period of more than 400 years (which would in any case be impossible in a book of this size) but rather concentrate on those forms that have significance for the evolution of Modern English.[1] The examples of Old English spelling given in this chapter are, therefore, mostly chosen for their recognizable affinity to equivalent Modern English words.[2] Where the two forms differ, the Modern English forms will usually be shown after the Old English form (e.g. *ʒod* 'good'). In this way we will see to what extent Modern English spelling patterns can be traced back to Old English. Two important points should, however, be noted:

- Firstly, it must be remembered that, through developments that will be described in Chapter 4, Modern English derives mainly from the East Midlands dialect of Middle English, which derives from Anglian Old English rather than the West Saxon dialect that became the literary standard before the arrival of the Normans and in which the majority of surviving Old English texts are written. With a few exceptions, therefore, West Saxon words are not direct ancestors of the modern forms (for instance, Modern English *cold*, *cheese* and *light* derive from Anglian *cald*, *cese* and *liht*, not the West Saxon forms

*The History of English Spelling*, First Edition. Christopher Upward and George Davidson.

*ceald*, *cyse* and *leoht*), but the West Saxon forms serve adequately for exemplification, the differences between Old English dialects being relatively slight compared to dialect differences that developed later.

- Secondly, it must be kept in mind that similar spellings in Old English and Modern English do not necessarily represent similar pronunciations: Old English *ȝod* 'good' was pronounced with the vowel [o] (therefore like Modern English *goad* in a Scottish, rather than a southern British, accent), not [ɒ] as in Modern English *god*.

Having noted these points, we can now undertake a detailed letter-by-letter consideration of the Old English roots of Modern English spelling. Readers are reminded that long and short values of vowels are not graphically distinguished in the examples in this chapter, although where relevant the examples will be clearly grouped and analysed according to vowel length. Many sound and spelling changes that occurred after the end of Old English, particularly during the Middle English and Early Modern English periods, are discussed in more detail in Chapter 6.

## A

The OE letter A had short and long sound values.[3]

### Short *A*

- OE short A, pronounced /a/, generally leads to A in ModE, with varying sound values: *catt* 'cat', *daȝas* 'days', *hara* 'hare'.
- Short final -A was a common noun ending (e.g. *mona* 'moon'; *tima* 'time'; *stan* 'stone', *stana* 'of stones'). These endings were typically reduced to -E in ME and survive as final silent -E in ModE forms like *time*, *stone*, where they now generally function as indicators of the length and quality of a preceding vowel (compare *pin/pine*, *rod/rode*).
- OE short A may lead to ModE forms with O: OE *camb*, *fram* > *comb*, *from*; also *long*, *song*, *strong*, *thong*, *throng*. Variants with O are found at an early date, e.g. *and/ond*, *hand/hond*, *land/lond*.

### Long *A*

OE long A, pronounced /ɑː/ has ModE reflexes with long O, with several spellings:

- OA in initial or medial position: *ar* 'oar', *rad* 'road'; OE *brad* produces the expected ModE spelling 'broad', but with a different sound value.
- O (+ consonant) + E: *sar* 'sore', *ban* 'bone'. ModE *one*, from OE *an*, is anomalous in its pronunciation (see p. 187).
- Word-final -OE: *da* 'doe', *sla* 'sloe'.
- In a few words, O alone: e.g. *haliȝ* 'holy'.
- A preceding /w/ in OE typically produces ModE O or OO pronounced /uː/: *hpa* 'who', *tpa* 'two', *spapen* 'to swoop'.
  - ModE -HOOD with the vowel /ʊ/ derives from OE -HAD: *cildhad* 'childhood'.
- ModE may have alternative forms from a single OE root, e.g. *loath/loth* from *lað*.
- In compounds, ModE O has a short value: *bonfire* not \**bonefire*, *holiday* not \**holyday* (see p. 40). The OE A is preserved in *tadpole* (not \**toadpoll*).

Æ

OE Æ had short and long sound values.

- The letter Æ and its sound may occur as mutations (that is, alterations in quality caused by a following vowel) of A in different forms of the same word in OE, depending on the following sound: *dæȝ* 'day', plural *daȝas* 'days'; *habban* 'to have', *hæfde* 'had'. Similarly, note, for example, *seȝeþ/sæȝeþ* 'sayeth, says'.

### Short Æ

- OE short Æ leads to ModE A: *æfter* 'after', *bæþ* 'bath', *fæder* 'father', *þæt* 'that'; with a preceding /w/: *hpæt* 'what', *pæter* 'water'.
- OE short Æ generally merged with A in ME; ModE forms give no indication whether their OE antecedents were spelt with A or Æ: OE *catte/rætt*, ModE *cat/rat*.
- Short Æ followed by ȝ results in ModE AI, thus *bræȝn* 'brain', *fæȝer* 'fair', *tæȝl* 'tail'.

### Long Æ

- Examples of OE long Æ and its ModE reflexes are: *clæne* 'clean', *dæd* 'deed', *hælan* 'to heal', *læce* 'leech', *lædan* 'to lead', *sæd* 'seed'.

As can be seen, some of these OE words give rise to ModE EA spellings and some to EE. The choice was not arbitrary: the Anglian dialect from which ModE ultimately derives distinguished two different vowels among the words for which WSax had only long Æ.[4]

- In the words *æmerȝe* 'embers', *ærende* 'errand', *flæsc* 'flesh' and *-læcan* (> -LEDGE in *knowledge*), OE Æ has produced ModE E.
- Dialect variations have given rise to the anomalous sound–spelling correspondences in ModE *any*, *many*, *Thames*: the forms *æniȝ*, *mæniȝ*, *Tæmese* were characteristically northern, while the ModE pronunciation is of southern origin. In ME the forms were (Southern) *eny*, (Midland) *any* and *ony*, (Northern) *ony*.
- Other developments are seen in *hlædel* 'ladle', *hær* 'hair' and *mæst* 'most'.

## B

The letter B usually occurs with the same sound value in OE as in ModE; it is never silent.

- Initial B: *bacan* 'to bake', *bæc* 'back', *bed*, *biddan* 'to bid', *blis* 'bliss', *brecan* 'to break'.
- Final B was pronounced in OE after M in *camb* 'comb', *dumb*, *lamb*, *pamb* 'womb' (also *climban* 'to climb') where it is usually silent in ModE.
  - OE had no B in *crume* 'crumb', *lim* 'limb', *þuma* 'thumb'; the B was added later at various times, e.g. in *thumb* in the 13th century, in *crumb* in the 16th.
- Some ModE words contain a pronounced B after medial M where OE lacked it: *æmerȝe* 'embers', *numol* 'nimble', *scæmel* 'shamble(s)', *þymel* 'thimble', *slumere* 'slumber'; this is due to a natural tendency to pronounce a /b/ after /m/ in such positions (OE already had *bræmbel* 'bramble' and *timber*, although there was no /b/ in the earlier Germanic forms).
- Medial B could be geminated (i.e. written and sounded as a double consonant): *habban* 'to have'.
- In one case, final B > P: OE *ȝodsib* > ModE *gossip*.
- There was some blurring of the distinction between the consonants /b, v, f/, especially in early OE texts. For instance, in the Northumbrian version of Cædmon's hymn (see p. 21) the word for *heaven* occurs once as *hefaen* and once as *heben*.

## C

OE C had two main values, /k/ and /tʃ/, and some subsidiary values. However, the distinction between its two values was not entirely systematic: *cin*, for instance, could represent the equivalent of *kin* or *chin*, pronounced as in ModE, and the two different values of C were not systematically distinguished in OE manuscripts. In comparison to ModE C, however, the pronunciation of OE C was fairly predictable.

### *C pronounced /k/*

- Before a consonant C always had the value /k/: *clif* 'cliff', *cneo* 'knee', *cnif* 'knife', *cradel* 'cradle', *cpen* 'queen'. ModE has kept C before L and R (*cliff*, *cradle*), but uses silent K instead of C before N, and QU (introduced by Anglo-Norman scribes) instead of Cꝥ.
- C usually had the value /k/ before and after A, O, U: OE *cam* 'came', *corn*, *curs* 'curse'; *sac* 'sack', *boc* 'book', *buc* 'buck'.
- C could be found doubled: *racca* 'rigging' (contrasting with *raca* 'rake').
  - The OE source (*acursed*) of ModE *accursed*, however, did not have the double consonant, consisting rather of a compound of *curse* with the prefix A- (compare *across*); spellings with CC, attested from the 15th century, arose by analogy with Lat-based forms such as *accuse*.

### *C leading to ModE CH*

- OE C pronounced /tʃ/, typically leading to ModE CH, usually occurred before E, I, Y: *ceapen* 'to chew', *ceorl* 'churl', *cild* 'child', *cyse* 'cheese'.
  - OE CEA- may give rise to ModE forms with initial CHA-: e.g. ModE *chary* < OE *ceariȝ*, *chaff* < OE *ceaf*, *chalk* < OE *cealc*. (CHA- is an unusual spelling for words of OE origin, ModE words beginning with CHA- generally being of Fr derivation.)
- C = /tʃ/ also often occurred in final position, where it typically anticipates ModE TCH after a short vowel: *dic* 'ditch', *pic* 'pitch', *þæc* 'thatch'. ModE final CH from OE C = /tʃ/ occurs regularly after L, N, R: *ælc* 'each', *hpelc* 'which', *benc* 'bench', *berc* 'birch'.
  - The CH of ModE *rich* (rather than *\*ritch*) may be influenced by Fr *riche*.
  - Note also *bishopric* with final C (< OE *bisceoprice*); -RIC has also been spelt -*rick* and -*ricke* (16th–18th centuries).

- Medial c = /tʃ/ could be doubled after a short vowel: *streccan* 'to stretch', *picca* 'witch', *precca* 'wretch'.

## Exceptions and variations

- The OE adjectival/adverbial suffix -LICE became ModE -LY: *freondlice* > *friendly*; similarly *ic*, *bærlic* > *I, barley*.
- OE *ciecen* 'chicken' should have given ModE *\*chichen*. It is not certain why the ModE form has /k/.
- In *drencan* 'to drench', *ræcan* 'to reach', *streccan* 'to stretch', the influence of a pre-OE /j/ following the c causes c to become a palatal consonant (essentially like the /k/ in *kit* as opposed to the /k/ in *coot*) and later the value /tʃ/.
- The value of c could vary within the same root: e.g. c in *boc* 'book' = /k/ but in *bec* 'books' = /tʃ/. Such /tʃ/ and /k/ values could also alternate according to dialect or in later development, resulting in such ModE cognates as *bake/batch, break/breach, drink/drench, dyke/ditch, leak/leach, make/match, speak/speech, stink/stench, wake/watch, wreck/wretch*. (See also p. 29.)
- Before a front vowel that had mutated from a back vowel (that is, had become a front vowel under the influence of a following front vowel), c remained /k/: e.g. *cyninȝ* 'king' < a Germanic root *\*kuning-*.
- The above rules notwithstanding, Anglo-Saxon scribes sometimes clarified the pronunciation of c using two devices still familiar in ModE:
  - One device was to show the /tʃ/ value where it might otherwise not be apparent by inserting an E or I after the c; thus *þencan* 'to think' (/'θɛntʃən/) could also be written *þencean*.
  - The other device was to replace c by K to show its /k/ value before a front vowel: *cyn* 'kin', *cyninȝ* 'king', *cycen* 'kitchen' were sometimes written *kin* (so contrasting with palatalized c in *cin* 'chin'), *kyninȝ*, *kicen*. Likewise the genitive case of *folc* 'people' could be either *folces* or *folkes* 'of the people'.
- Some 70 per cent of instances of TCH are found at the end of words of Germanic origin (e.g. *watch, stretch*; *kitchen* is exceptional in having medial TCH). Such OE-derived words saw considerable variation in ME (e.g. being spelt with CC, CCH, CHCH, etc.) before achieving their present spelling with TCH typically by about 1600.

## D

The use of D in OE is essentially as in ModE:

- Word-initially: *dæȝ* 'day', *deofol* 'devil', *dohtor* 'daughter', *drincan* 'to drink', *dust*.
- Medially: *cildra* 'children', *bodiȝ* 'body', *ende* 'end'; doubled: *biddan* 'to ask, bid'.
- Finally: *bed*, *ȝlæd* 'glad', *speord* 'sword'; (widely in past participles) *ȝeendod* 'ended'.
- ModE *alder*, *elder* (= 'species of tree'), *lend*, *spindle*, *thunder* have acquired an intrusive D not present in OE *aler*, *ellærn*, *lænan*, *spinel* or (usually) in *þunor*. Compare also early ME *cunredden*, ModE *kindred*.
- In early texts there was some ambiguity in the pronunciation of medial and final D, which varied between the values of /d/ and /ð/. With the increasing use of *eth* (Ð, ð) and *thorn* (Þ, þ) for the TH values /θ, ð/, this ambiguity was in principle overcome in later OE, but pronunciation sometimes also changed before ModE from /d/ to /ð/, with a corresponding spelling switch from D to TH: *fæder* 'father', *ȝaderian* 'to gather', *hider* 'hither', *modor* 'mother'. (The reverse switch, from *thorn* or *eth* to D, also occurred, e.g. *berðen* > *burden*; see under 'TH'.)

## E

The letter E had short and long sound values, and also occurred in unstressed final syllables with the value /ə/. It was a common noun ending (e.g. *ende* 'end'; *finger*, dative *fingre*). These E-endings for nouns have since disappeared entirely from pronunciation and, mostly, spelling (e.g. *spere* 'spear'), but may survive as final silent -E in ModE forms like *sieve* < OE *sife*.

### Short E

- Short E in OE generally produces short E in ModE: *bed*, *betera* 'better', *helpan* 'to help', *hnecca* 'neck'.
- Short E before N in OE tends to produce ModE I: *hlenc* 'link', *menȝian* 'to mingle', *strenȝ* 'string', *þencan* 'to think'.

- ○ In the case of *enȝlalond* 'England', *enȝlisc* 'English' the change in sound to /ɪ/ has not in the end been marked by a change in spelling, leaving ModE with a sound–symbol anomaly. Spellings with initial I and Y (e.g. *Ingland*, *Yngelond*) were found in ME.
- ○ Where a modern CH or TH follows the N, neither the sound nor the spelling of the vowel has changed from OE: *benc* 'bench', *stenc* 'stench', *lenȝð* 'length', *strenȝð* 'strength'.
- Modern I also develops from OE E when R precedes: *hreddan* 'to rid', though *prettiȝ* 'pretty', like *enȝlisc*, keeps its E despite the change of vowel sound to /ɪ/.
- Short E in OE could also lead to other vowels in ModE:
  - ○ EA, as in *beran* 'to bear', *tredan* 'to tread', and /iː/ spelt EA in *bicpeðan* 'to bequeath', *etan* 'to eat', *mete* 'meat', *pefan* 'to weave'.
  - ○ ModE /iː/ spelt IE: *feld* 'field', *ȝeldan* 'to yield'.
  Further variations are seen in *secȝan* 'to say', *peȝ* 'way'.
- The contrasting long/short vowels in the ModE pair *break/breakfast* represent a recurrent pattern, whereby an OE-derived word (in this case *brecan* 'break') appears with a short vowel in the first element of a compound, although the ModE base form has a long vowel. In many cases this is reflected by the spelling. Other examples, with various vowels, are *bone/bonfire*, *Christ/Christmas*, *coal/collier*, *dear/darling*, *goose/gosling/gossamer*, *good/gospel*, *holy/holiday*, *house/husband*, *moon/Monday*, *nose/nostril*, *old/alderman*, *sheep/shepherd*, *throat/throttle*, *toad/tadpole*, *wild/wilderness*, *wind* ('to coil or twist')/*windlass*, *wise/wisdom/wizard*.
- In a number of words, spellings with OE ER subsequently changed to AR, and have kept that spelling into ModE (the letter name itself has changed from '*er*' to '*ar*'). The HAR- of ModE *harbour* derives from OE *here* 'army', *bern* (< earlier *berern*) > *barn*. There were similar changes in later words derived from Fr, e.g. *ferme* > *farm*.

## Long E

- Long E, pronounced /eː/ in OE, typically produces ModE long E, now pronounced /iː/ and most often spelt EE: *cepan* 'to keep', *cpen* 'queen', *ȝrene* 'green', *metan* 'to meet', *sped* 'speed'; plurals *fet* 'feet', *ȝes* 'geese', *teð* 'teeth'; and, with mostly single E, the personal pronouns *me*, *ȝe* 'ye', *he*, *þe* 'thee', *pe* 'we'.
- OE *periȝ* 'weary' has EA in ModE.
- ModE *here* (< OE *her*) shows yet another spelling development.

*EA*

EA represented a diphthong in OE, with short and long variants. In a number of words it coincides with ModE EA.

- Long EA with the value /iː/: *beacen* 'beacon', *beam, bean, beatan* 'to beat', *east, leaf, stream*; but in *bread, deaþ* 'death' ModE EA has acquired the value of short E, /ɛ/, and in *earn* < *earnian* EAR has the value /ɜː/.
- In ModE *cold, hold* (verb), *old, sold, told*, the O derives from Anglian forms in A (*ald*, 'old', *cald*, 'cold', etc.) as opposed to WSax forms in EA (*eald, ceald*, etc.); see pp. 33–4.
- A wide range of other ModE vowels also result from EA in OE, some again clearly reflecting non-WSax forms (e.g. ModE *sheep* < Anglian *scep*, WSax *sceap*): *bearn* 'bairn', *ceas* 'chose', *eaȝe* 'eye', *eahta* 'eight', *eall* 'all', *ȝear* 'year', *ȝeard* 'yard', *ȝeat* 'gate', *heard* 'hard', *mearh* 'mare', *sceaft* 'shaft', *seah* 'saw', *pearm* 'warm'.
  ○ OE suffix -LEAS > ModE -LESS.
- After C and G, the digraph EA was used instead of Æ, e.g. to show palatalization of C or a /j/ value for G: *ceaf* 'chaff', *ȝeaf* 'gave', *sceal* 'shall'.
- The addition of the noun *hirde* to *sceap* has produced a change of vowel between ModE *sheep/shepherd* (see above, p. 40, for *break/breakfast* and similar length variations involving other vowels).
- ModE *shade* < OE *sceadu*; ModE *shadow* < the inflected form *scead(u)we*.

*EO*

- Long EO has led to ModE EE in many words: *beo* 'bee', *beor* 'beer', *cneo* 'knee', *deop* 'deep', *treo* 'tree', *hpeol* 'wheel'; with single E, *beon* 'to be'.
- There are, however, ModE words with other spellings corresponding to OE EO:
  ○ A in *ceorfan* > *carve*, *deorc* > *dark*, *deorling* > *darling*, *steorfan* > *starve*, *steorre* > *star*;
  ○ E in *cneop* > *knew*;
  ○ EA with various pronunciations in *deor* > *dear*, *eorl* > *earl*, *eorþe* > *earth*, *heorte* > *heart*;
  ○ long I (/aɪ/) in *feohtan* > *fight*, *teoȝeða* > *tithe*;
  ○ IE (with various values) in *feond* > *fiend*, *freond* > *friend*, *ȝeleofan* > *believe*, *leoȝan* > *to lie*, *þeof* > *thief*;

41

- ○ long O in *aceocan* > *to choke*;
- ○ OO in *ceosan* > *choose*, *sceotan* > *shoot*;
- ○ OU in *feoper* > *four* (but just O in *feopertiʒ* > *forty*);
- ○ long Y in *fleoʒan* > *to fly*;
- ○ WOR in several words such as *speord* > *sword*, *peorc* > *work*, *peorð* > *worth*.
- Note that *deor/deorling* have produced different vowels in ModE *dear/darling* (see p. 40 for *break/breakfast* and similar pairs involving other vowels).

**F**

OE had only one letter, F, to serve for the sounds [f] and [v], which were not contrasting speech-sounds in OE, the speech-sound /f/ being pronounced [f] or [v] depending on its position in the word (compare ModE *fine/vine*, *safe/save*, in which /f/ and /v/ are contrasting speech-sounds).

- Word-initial F: *fæder* 'father', *feccan* 'to fetch', *fisc* 'fish', *fleax* 'flax', *folc* 'folk', *frost*, *ful* 'foul', *fyr* 'fire'.
  - ○ F occurred initially before N in a few words in OE. One example is *fneosung* 'sneeze' related to an unattested verb *\*fneosan* 'to sneeze'. In ME the verb existed in the form *fnese*, but went out of use in the 15th century, being replaced by a probably related verb *nese*. ModE *sneeze* is first attested in the 16th century, possibly based on *nese* and reinforced by confusion between *<f>* (= F) and *<ſ>*, the former long form of s.
- Between vowels or between a vowel and a voiced consonant, single F was pronounced [v] (FF was always [f]), and typically leads to ModE V: *æfre* 'ever', *ceorfan* 'carve', *deofol* 'devil', *endleofan* 'eleven', *hærfest* 'harvest', *lufu* 'love', *ofer* 'over', *yfel* 'evil'.
- Medially, F is seen before T in *æfter* 'after' and *oft*; and pronounced as a double consonant, as in *offrian* 'to offer', *pyffan* 'to puff'.
  - ○ The F of *ʒefurðian* > *afford* was doubled by analogy with Lat-derived words such as *affect* (compare the similar doubling of C in *accursed*, L in *allay*, N in *anneal*).
- A voiceless F at the end of a word such as *fif* 'five', *tpelf* 'twelve' became voiced when a voiced ending such as a vowel was added, as in the variants *fife*, *tpelfe*, and if the ModE form derives from the voiced variant, it is spelt with V: thus *five*, *twelve*.

○ In one set of words, however, where OE has a singular noun with
F pronounced [f] (*pulf* 'wolf') but the corresponding plural with
F pronounced [v] (*pulfas*), ModE writes F for /f/ in the singular
(*wolf*) and V for /v/ in the plural (*wolves*): so OE *cealf* but ModE
*calf/calves*, *cnif* but *knife/knives*, *elf* but *elf/elves*, *half* but *half/halves*,
*hlaf* but *loaf/loaves*, *leaf* but *leaf/leaves*, *lif* but *life/lives*, *self* but *self/
selves*, *sceaf* but *sheaf/sheaves*, *þeof* but *thief/thieves*, *pif* but *wife/wives*.
For *hof* 'hoof', *hpearf* 'wharf' and *turf*, ModE has alternative
plurals with V (*hooves*, *wharves*, *turves*) and F (*hoofs*, *wharfs*, *turfs*).
*Roof* is anomalous in that *roofs* is the only written form now considered correct (*rooves* is attested in the 15th century), but *roofs*
may be pronounced with /f/ or /v/.

• In some cases, OE F has no counterpart in ModE spelling: *hæfde* 'had',
*hæfð* 'hath', *heafoc* 'hawk', *heafod* 'head', *hlafdiȝe* 'lady', *hlaford* 'lord',
*pifman* 'woman'.

• The lack of a letter V caused OE some difficulty in spelling Lat loanwords with initial U pronounced [v]. In the case of Lat *uannus/
vannus*, OE used F, producing *fann*, which has been retained as ModE
*fan*; and Lat *Eua*, *uersus* (*Eva*, *versus*) were similarly spelt as OE *efa*,
*fers*, though V was later restored to give ModE *Eve*, *verse*.

## Anomalies

• F is voiced in the preposition *of* /ɒv/, the form with the voiceless
equivalent /f/ eventually coming to be distinguished as *off* with FF.
Historically, the [v] and [f] pronunciations reflect uses of *of* with different degrees of stress: OE *of*, originally an unstressed preposition,
began to be used as an adverb, and as such was often in a stressed position in a sentence. Although the word, whether stressed or unstressed,
continued to be written *of* even into the early part of the ModE period,
from about the beginning of the 15th century the *off* spelling began
to be used more and more frequently for the stressed adverb form,
and the separation of the two spellings was gradually established.

• The initial V of *vixen*, despite F in *fox*, arose in the 16th century from
respelling OE *fyxen* according to a southern dialect pronunciation
with /v/.

○ Similarly ModE has *vial/phial* (ME also *fiol*), with alternative /v/
and /f/ pronunciations, to designate essentially the same object.

○ Similar, but not evidently anomalous in ModE, is the V in *vane*, *vat*
which derives from a southern dialect pronunciation of OE *fana*, *fæt*.

# G

In late OE times ɢ appears to have had four different sound values, depending on its phonological environment: velar [g] and [ɣ], and palatal [ɟ] pronounced further forward in the mouth (but developing into [j]) and [dʒ]. Late northern Eng rune-masters devised a new rune to enable the palatal and velar values to be distinguished, and when <g> was introduced beside <ȝ> in ME the Eng alphabet too was able to make that distinction.

- In general, Eng has continued to use simple ɢ from OE to ModE in words only where it was pronounced as [g], e.g. before A, O, U and L, N, R: *ȝaȝel* 'gale', *ȝlæs* 'glass', *ȝold* 'gold', *ȝos* 'goose', *ȝræs* 'grass', *ȝut* 'gut'.
  - Although initial ɢ is silent before N in ModE, GN implies the full /gn/ value of both letters in OE: *ȝnætt* 'gnat', *ȝnaȝan* 'gnaw'.
- OE ɢ had the value [g] when written and pronounced double between back vowels: *doȝȝa* 'dog', *froȝȝa* 'frog', *staȝȝa* 'stag'.
- In ModE, NG can be pronounced either /ŋ/, as in *long*, or /ŋg/, as in *longer*, but always had the latter value in OE: *brinȝan* 'bring', *enȝlisc* 'English', *lanȝ* 'long', *lenȝþ* 'length'.
- Before the front vowels E, I, Y, OE initial ɢ mostly did not persist into ModE. In those environments it developed the value [j], and is represented in such positions by the modern consonantal Y: *ȝear* 'year', *ȝeard* 'yard', *ȝeolu* 'yellow', *ȝeonȝ* 'young', *ȝese* 'yes', *ȝieldan* 'to yield', *ȝinian* 'to yawn'.
  - In some circumstances this ɢ left no trace at all in ModE, as when the following stressed vowel was (or became) I, and the OE [j] was assimilated to it: *ȝif* 'if', *ȝyccan* 'itch', *is-ȝicel* 'icicle'.
  - Similarly, the OE past participle prefix ȝE-, being unstressed, was progressively lost through the ME period: OE *ȝeboren* 'born', ME *iboren*, ModE *born*. Elsewhere the prefix was reduced to an unstressed vowel: A in *ȝelice* 'alike', *ȝelanȝ* 'along', *ȝemonȝ* 'among', *ȝepær* 'aware'; E in *ȝenoȝ* 'enough'; I in *handȝepeorc* 'handiwork'.

## Scandinavian preservation of ɢ

ModE contains a number of spellings which appear to conflict with the above patterns, by which one would have expected that OE *ȝietan* 'to get', *ȝiefan* 'to give' would produce ModE *\*yet*, *\*yive*. Although those words were sometimes written with initial Y in ME, it appears that Scandinavian influence on northern Eng speech resulted in velar [g] eventually (by 1500) becoming the standard pronunciation, with G therefore retained in the spelling.

## G *replaced by* GH

The H in *ghost* (ME *gost* < OE *gast*) was introduced by Flemish printers on the basis of Flemish spelling (*gheest*); the spelling of *ghastly* is influenced by *ghost*. *Aghast* (< *agast* 'to frighten') first appears in Middle Scots (the ME dialect of lowland Scotland) in the early 15th century and in Eng in the 16th.

- After the introduction of the GH spelling of *ghost* we see this spelling used to indicate /g/ in other words,[5] e.g. *gherle* 'girl', *ghoate* 'goat' (also in the plural forms *gheate* and, in Caxton, *gheet* 'goats'). Between the 14th and 17th centuries we see examples of GH- for /g/ where ModE has GU, as in *ghess*, *ghest(e)*, and even GHU-, as in *ghuest*.
- There is no H in the Dutch word from which is derived *gherkin*, first recorded with H in Eng in the 19th century.

## *Medial and final* G *leading to ModE* W, I/Y *or* GH

Particularly between back vowels, G was typically pronounced [ɣ] in OE. This G has typically developed either to W or to I/Y in ModE, generally depending on the phonetic environment.

- OE G non-initially before and/or after A, O, U normally becomes ModE W: *aȝan* 'owe', *draȝan* 'draw' (contrast its Scandinavian-influenced cognate 'drag'), *ȝnaȝan* 'gnaw' (Scandinavian cognate 'to nag'), *laȝu* 'law', *boȝa* 'bow' (as in 'bow and arrow'), *ploȝ* 'plow' (American spelling[6]), *sloȝ* 'slew' *fuȝel* 'fowl'.
  - Similarly in two-syllable words in ModE: *feoloȝa* 'fellow', *folȝian* 'to follow', *ȝalȝa* 'gallows', *halȝian* 'to hallow', *sorȝian* 'to sorrow', *spelȝan* 'to swallow'.
  - Where there was no word-ending in OE, the G also becomes modern -ow: *belȝ* 'bellows', *mearȝ* 'marrow'.
  - OE *druȝaþ*, *neaȝan*, by contrast, have GH in ModE *drought*, *neigh*.
- After the front vowels Æ, E medial G typically fell silent or became incorporated into a vowel by the time of ModE, written AI: *fæȝer* 'fair',

*hæʒel* 'hail' (also *hæʒl*), *læʒde* 'laid', *leʒer* 'lair', *mæʒden* 'maiden', *næʒ(e)l* 'nail', *ræʒ(e)n* 'rain', *sæʒde* 'said', *seʒ(e)l* 'sail', *slæʒen* 'slain', *tæʒ(e)l* 'tail'. The form *æʒpæðer* on the other hand has produced ModE EI in *either*. An example of loss of G after I is *stiʒrap* 'stirrup'.

- In final position this G led to ModE Y after OE front vowels: *cæʒ* 'key' (commonly written and pronounced 'kay' until the 18th century), *clæʒ* 'clay', *dæʒ* 'day' (contrast the development to W after the back vowel in related *daʒian* 'to daw = become dawn'), *græʒ* 'grey/gray', *hieʒ* 'hay', *pleʒan* 'to play', *peʒ* 'way', *driʒe* 'dry', *bodiʒ* 'body', *haliʒ* 'holy', *maniʒ* 'many'.
  - OE *byrʒan* > *bury*.
  - ModE Y is found with a following E (perhaps to avoid spelling these words with only two letters) in *dye* < *deaʒ*, *eye* < *eaʒe*, *rye* < *ryʒe*.
  - Final G after back vowels produces some instances of modern -OUGH: *boʒ* 'bough', *daʒ* 'dough', *ploʒ* 'plough', *hreoʒ* 'rough', *troʒ* 'trough', while *peʒan* 'to weigh' provides a solitary parallel after a front vowel.
  - In the case of *dpeorʒ* 'dwarf', the final consonant has from the 14th century increasingly been written F in accordance with a pronunciation changed to /f/ (see p. 183).

### Palatalized G leading to ModE DG

The fourth possible value of G in OE was [dʒ]. Typical are geminated ('doubled') forms written with the digraph CG (later GG), which can be seen as the precursor of modern DG: *brycʒ* 'bridge', *cycʒel* 'cudgel', *ecʒ* 'edge', *hecʒ* 'hedge', *hrycʒ* 'ridge', *mycʒ* 'midge', *secʒ* 'sedge', *pecʒ* 'wedge'.

  - Another development, typically in verbs, is ModE Y: *bycʒan* 'buy', *lecʒan* 'lay', *licʒan* 'lie', *secʒan* 'say'.

### H

- In initial position before a vowel H normally survives into ModE: *ham* 'home', *help*, *hund* 'dog, hound'.
- H has been lost from initial position before a consonant:
  - *hlædel* 'ladle', *hlæder* 'ladder', *hlaf* 'loaf', *hlud* 'loud';
  - *hnæʒan* 'neigh', *hnecca* 'neck', *hnut* 'nut';
  - *hræfen* 'raven', *hrinʒ* 'ring', *hrof* 'roof'.

H disappeared before L, N, R long before it could be fixed by printing. It appears that it was already falling silent in this position in the OE period, as it was sometimes omitted in writing, and it is rarely attested after the 11th century, though there are occasional instances of reversal (similar to HW becoming WH) in the ME period: *lheape* 'leap', *nhicke* 'neck', *rhof* 'roof'.

- In ME HW was reversed to WH: *hpæl* 'whale', *hpit* 'white', *hpy* 'why'.
  - The letter sequence WH has been extended to *whole*, *whore* (< *hal*, *hore*) where it is justified neither by word-origin nor by current sound value.
- In two common words, initial H before a vowel has disappeared entirely: OE *hit*, *hem* have become ModE *it*, *'em*, the latter in representing elided colloquialisms as in expressions like *get 'em* (*them* is of Scandinavian origin).

## OE *h* leading to ModE GH, etc.

- H following a back vowel was pronounced [x]; after a front vowel, [ç]. Especially in final position, H could alternate with G, as in *burʒ/burh* 'borough', *sloʒ/sloh* 'slew'. In many cases, H was respelt GH during the ME period and has usually persisted in this form into ModE, although no longer pronounced: *burh* 'borough' (though now written -BURY in numerous place-names), *heah* 'high', *neah* 'nigh' (also in *neahʒebur* 'neighbour'), *þeoh* 'thigh', *þeah* 'though', *þruh* (or *þurh*) 'through', with variant *þuruh* as the source of *thorough*.
  - Many examples of this OE H are found before T (or sometimes OE Þ): *ahte* 'ought', *bohte* 'bought', *brohte* 'brought', *bryht* 'bright', *dohtor* 'daughter', *eahta* 'eight', etc. The OE variants *nopiht*, *napiht* foreshadow the variants *nought/naught*.
  - Not every ModE GH has its origin in OE; some were created under the influence of words in the above categories: *delight* (< OFr *delit* + *light*), *haughty* (< Fr *haut*), *slaughter* (< ONorse *slatr*), and similarly *caught*, *distraught*, *fraught*, *freight*, *furlough*, *inveigh*, *onslaught*, *naughty*, *sleigh*, *sprightly*.
- OE H could be written and pronounced doubled in a medial position: *crohha* 'crock', *hliehhan* 'to laugh'.
- Final H may not be represented at all in ModE: *fah* 'foe', *scoh* 'shoe'.
- ModE *anchor* (OE *ancor*) has taken the H from *anchora*, a misspelling of Lat *ancora*.

## I

OE I had short and long values. The long value changed its quality dramatically in the course of the Great Vowel Shift around the 15th century (see pp. 176–8): the OE distinction is as heard in *tin*/*routine*, whereas in ModE it is as in *din*/*dine*.

- OE short I: *biten* 'bitten', *brinʒan* 'to bring', *drinc* 'drink', *fisc* 'fish', etc.
- OE long I: *bitan* 'to bite', *lif* 'life', *min* 'mine', *hpit* 'white'.
- Different forms of the same word, such as the infinitive and past participle of verbs, may show alternation between long and short sound values of I, a variation much more striking in ModE than in OE in terms of both pronunciation and spelling: ModE *bite*/*bitten*, *drive*/*driven*, *hide*/*hidden*, *strike*/*stricken*, *write*/*written*, etc. In OE, by contrast, both *riden* 'ridden' with short I and *ridan* 'to ride' with long I have a single D; see also *bitan*/*biten* in the above examples.
  - Other cases of related long/short pairs in ModE echo the OE length differences, but often arose at a later date: *child*/*children*, *Christ*/*Christmas*, *drive*/*drift*, *five*/*fifteen*/*fifth*, *white*/*Whitsun*, *wide*/*width*, *midwife*/*midwifery*, *wild*/*wilderness*/*bewilder*, to *wind*/*windlass*, *wise*/*wisdom*/*wizard* (see p. 40 above for *break*/*breakfast* and similar pairs involving other vowels); also by analogy *strive*/*striven*, despite its derivation from OFr. There is some evidence that *give*, *live*, *sieve* for a time had long vowels, but today their vowels are short. In *drive*, *white*, etc. the long /aɪ/ value is distinguished in ModE by final E, which is therefore now anomalous after the /ɪ/ of *give*, *live*, *sieve*.
- In one case a double transmutation has taken place: *pifmann* has variously changed both its vowel sound and vowel letter to become ModE *woman*.

## K

The letter K was rarely used in OE, although it occasionally served to disambiguate C before a front vowel, e.g. *Kent* rather than *Cent*. It has retained this function in ModE (e.g. *cat*, *kitten*).

- K was not used in OE to 'double' C, as in ModE CK; thus ModE *sack* corresponds to OE *sacc*, or simply *sac*. Samuel Johnson was therefore wrong when he insisted on the final CK in *musick, critick, historick*, etc. on the grounds that the Eng spelling should 'always have the Saxon *k* added to the *c*'.[7] There never was a 'Saxon K' in this position in OE.


## L


In OE the letter L had essentially the same value as L in ModE:

- It is seen before vowels in *land, læs* 'less', *leðer* 'leather', *leac* 'leek', *leoht* 'light', *lifer* 'liver', *los* 'loss', *lytel* 'little'.
- It can follow other consonants: *blind, clif* 'cliff', *flyht* 'flight', *ȝlæd* 'glad', *plume* 'plum', *slippan* 'to slip'.
  - OE differs from ModE in that L can follow H and W: *hlid* 'lid', *plispian* 'to lisp'.
- L occurs before other consonants: *meolc* 'milk', *eald* 'old', *ælf* 'elf', *elm, cyln* 'kiln', *help, meltan* 'melt'.
- The letter L could be geminated (i.e. written and pronounced doubled): *sellan* 'sell', *tellan* 'tell'; but in final position both LL and L are found: *eall/eal* 'all'.
  - The OE source of *allay* (*alecȝan*) did not have a double L, but consisted rather of the verb *lay* with the prefix A- (compare *alight*); spellings with LL, attested from the 15th century, arose by analogy with Lat-derived forms such as *allegation* (compare *accursed, afford, anneal* at 'c', 'f' and 'n').
- L could be syllabic after another consonant at the end of a word: *æpl* 'apple', *midl* 'middle', *nædl* 'needle', *seȝl* 'sail', *tæȝl* 'tail', also written *æppel, middel, nædel, seȝel, tæȝel*.
  - The ModE spellings with final -LE (e.g. *middle* rather than *middel*) arose in ME by analogy with Fr-derived words like *people*.
- L was pronounced in words where in ModE it has fallen silent: *cealc* 'chalk', *pealcan* 'walk', *folc* 'folk', *sceolde* 'should', *polde* 'would' (the word from which ModE *could* derives had no L in OE), *cealf* 'calf', *healf* 'half', *palm, psalm*.
  - In a few cases the L fell silent before it became fixed in the spelling (forms without L were well established 200 years before printing began to stabilize spelling), and is therefore not seen in the ModE forms; such cases typically involve the non-appearance of L before or after ModE CH: *hpilc* 'which', *spilc* 'such', *ælc* 'each', *mycel* 'much', *pencel* 'wench'.

## M

- M was generally used in OE as in ModE:
  - Before vowels: *mænan* 'to mean', *mann* 'man', *menn* 'men', *mearc* 'mark', *meos* 'moss', *middel* 'middle', *modor* 'mother', *murnan* 'mourn', *mys* 'mice'.
  - Before final /b/: *lamb*.
  - Initially after s: *smæl* 'small'.
  - Finally after the consonants L, R: *helm* 'helmet', *pyrm* 'worm'.
  - Syllabically after other consonants: *blostm* 'blossom', *bosm* 'bosom', *fæðm* 'fathom'.
- M could be written and pronounced doubled: *spimman* 'to swim'.
- In *æmete* 'ant', the medial vowel was eroded, leaving the consonant sequence /mt/, which became /nt/, as in ModE *ant*. In other cases /mt/ became /mpt/: OE *æmtiჳ* > ModE *empty*. A similar intrusion of P after M is seen before s in ModE *glimpse*, and in *sempstress*, beside *seamstress*.

## N

- N was generally used in OE as in ModE, though it could be preceded by a pronounced C, F, G, H in words where the preceding consonant is silent, lost or changed in ModE: *cneo* 'knee', *fneosung* 'sneeze', *ჳnæt* 'gnat', *hnutu* 'nut'.
- It could occur as in ModE before vowels: *næp* 'neep', *nama* 'name', *nest*, *niht* 'night', *nu* 'now', *nypele* 'nipple'; and with consonants: after initial s, as in *snap* 'snow', and before D (*and*) and T (*minte* 'mint'), as well as after L (*cyln* 'kiln') and R (*corn*).
- As in ModE, it was assimilated to [ŋ] before /k/ and /g/: *þanc* [θaŋk] 'thank', *sinჳan* ['sɪŋgən] 'to sing'. However, if the following C or G was palatalized (i.e. pronounced further forward in the mouth), the N may retain its [n] value: *þencan* (['θentʃən]) 'to think', *senჳan* 'to singe'.
- Like L and M, the letter N could be used to indicate a syllabic /n/, often alternating with non-syllabic spellings: thus *hræfn* 'raven' and *hræfen*, *ofn* 'oven' and *ofen*, *ræჳn* 'rain' and *ræჳen*, *pæჳn* 'wain, wagon' and *pæჳen*.
- Like other consonant letters, N could be written and pronounced doubled: *spinnan* 'to spin'.

○ The form *anneal*, however, derives from OE *ancælan*; spellings of this word with NN are first attested in the 17th century, by analogy with Latinate forms such as *annex* (compare similar doubling of C, F, L in *accursed*, *afford*, *allay*).

## Subsequent loss of N

Many OE words have seen the N subsequently lost or changed:

- Loss of N has occurred word-finally from OE *beforan* 'before', *butan* 'but', *bufan* 'above', *piðutan* 'without' and *holen* 'holly'. Loss of N from *min* 'my, mine' is seen in the ModE possessive adjective *my*, but not in the pronoun *mine*. Also in unstressed word-endings: e.g. *brinʒan* 'to bring'.
  ○ In some cases, however, a form with an N word-ending has become the ModE standard: *written*, *ridden*. Sometimes alternative forms of words have persisted into ModE: *druncen* 'drunk, drunken'.
- With the loss of the second vowel in *henep* 'hemp' (compare cognate *cannabis*), the final /p/ caused the preceding N to be pronounced /m/, with the consequent spelling change to M in ME, whence ModE *hemp*.
- The N of the indefinite article has transferred from article to noun in several words: in ME, *a naddre* (OE *næddre*) was wrongly redivided as *an addre*, whence ModE *adder* rather than *\*nadder* (compare dialect *nedder*); similarly OE *nafoʒar* becomes ModE *auger*. The reverse occurred with OE *efeta* which attracted N from the article to give ModE *a newt* rather than *\*an ewt* (compare dialect *eft*).
- A simple elision of N (and other letters) has also sometimes occurred, as in OE *endleofan* 'eleven', *andlonʒ* 'along'.

## O

- OE short O is seen generally as in ModE: *coc* 'cock', *doʒʒa* 'dog', *mopþe* 'moth'; and with modification to /ɔː/ before R in ModE: *corn*, *morʒen* 'morn'.
- The ModE spelling *daughter* for OE *dohtor* first appeared in the 16th century.
- Long O in OE typically led to OO in ModE, with a range of sound values: *blod* 'blood', *boc* 'book', *broc* 'brook', *brod* 'brood', *dom* 'doom' (but single O in *kingdom*, etc.), *flod* 'flood', *flor* 'floor', etc.; OE *to* has led to both *to* and *too* in ModE.

- In several cases there is a short vowel in ModE when a suffix follows, contrasting with a long vowel in the base word: *collier/coal, gosling/goshawk/goose, gospel/good, Monday/moon, nostril/nose, throttle/throat* (see p. 40 for *break/breakfast* and similar long/short pairs involving other vowels).

- In a few words, o has changed in quality and length: *sceolde, polde > should, would*; in *3lof* 'glove', *oþer* 'other' the vowel is shortened as well as assuming the value /ʌ/.

- ModE final -ow often derives from a different vowel altogether: *cnapan* 'to know', *nu* 'now'; in other cases o was already present in OE: *3ropan* 'to grow'.

## P

- P was used in OE as in ModE: *panne* 'pan', *pluccian* 'to pluck', *prut* 'proud', *specan/sprecan* 'to speak', *apa* 'ape', *help, heop* 'heap'.

- It could be written and pronounced as a double letter, as in *æppel* 'apple', *clyppan* 'to clip'.

- From OE *loppestre*, the P has become ModE B in *lobster*.

- See under 'M' above for intrusive P after M, as in *empty, glimpse*.

## Q

- Q was rarely used in classical OE; but the Lat loanword *reliquias* 'relic' is found in OE writing.

- The letter sequence cp was generally written for /kw/ in initial position in OE (though QU is sometimes found in early texts), but in words that have survived into ModE cp was respelt QU under the influence of Norman Fr after 1066, as in *cpen* 'queen'. For further examples of this cp/QU substitution, see under 'w' below.

## R

- The letter R was used in OE as in ModE, and was pronounced in all positions: *ridan* 'to ride', *3rene* 'green', *tredan* 'to tread', *duru* 'door', *corn, fæder* 'father'.
  - R could occur after initial H: *hrof* 'roof'. (See under 'H' above for further details.)

- Several words were spelt with R and a vowel in OE in the opposite order from ModE: *þærscan* 'to thrash, *þridda* 'third', *þrittiჳ* 'thirty', *brid* 'bird', *pyrhta* 'wright', *porhte* 'wrought', *nosterle* 'nostril'.
- R could be written and pronounced as a double consonant, as in *steorra* 'star'.
- Like L, M and N, a syllabic R could alternate in OE with a spelling with a preceding vowel: *hriþr/hriþer* 'head of cattle'. But forms with vowels predominate: *fæჳer* 'fair', *winter, wundor* 'wonder'.

## S

- Similarly to F and Þ, OE S represented both voiceless [s] and voiced [z] pronunciations of a single /s/ speech-sound.
  - The voiceless value [s] occurred at the beginning and at the end of words and after voiceless consonants: *sapl* 'soul', *slef* 'sleeve', *smercian* 'to smirk', *snæჳl* 'snail', *spætan* 'to spit', *strang* 'strong', *spat* 'sweat', *acsian* 'to ask', *mus* 'mouse'.
  - The voiced value [z] occurred medially between vowels or between a vowel and a voiced consonant: *bosum* 'bosom', *cese* 'cheese', *nosu* 'nose', *husbonda* 'husband', *clænsian* 'to cleanse'.
  - When written and pronounced as a double consonant, as in *cyssan* 'to kiss', S was always voiceless [s].
- Two isolated anomalies may also be mentioned here:
  - One is the later insertion of S in OE *iჳland* 'island', by false analogy with Fr-derived *isle*.
  - The other is the insertion of C in *scythe* < OE *siðe*. *Scythe* is first attested in the 17th century, based perhaps on the mistaken belief that the word was related to Lat *scindere* 'to cut'.

### *Loss of the clear voiced/voiceless distinction in ModE orthography*

Unlike [s] and [z] in OE, /s/ and /z/ are contrasting speech-sounds in ModE (compare *cease* and *seize*). While ModE generally satisfactorily exploits the voiced and voiceless values of F and V respectively, the same success has not been achieved with S for /s/ and Z for /z/ (compare *loose* and *lose*). Moreover, the additional facility of Fr -CE has been applied to introduce widespread random spelling variations and pronunciation ambiguity (compare *mouse* and *mice*, *advice* and *advise*).

The reason for the failure is mainly grammatical, arising from massive changes in the language in ME. Final s occurred far more often as an inflection in ME than in OE, and in that position it came to be voiced in many instances where it had previously been voiceless – final s became voiced where it terminated an unstressed syllable while generally remaining voiceless in stressed syllables. ModE s-inflections are pronounced with /z/ in about 80 per cent of occurrences, after vowels and voiced consonants (e.g. in *sees, hears, bushes, dogs*), and are voiceless /s/ only after voiceless consonants (e.g. in *cats, clips*). On the other hand, many non-inflected words end in /s/ in ModE, and spelling therefore often needs to distinguish /z/ in inflections (e.g. *peas, sins*) from /s/ in similar non-inflectional positions (e.g. *peace, since*). The Eng alphabet as it developed through ME offered several devices for making the voiced/voiceless distinction which were neither needed nor available in OE: voiced s could be respelt as z or sE, and voiceless s could be respelt as cE or ss or sE. We see all these devices in use in ModE forms deriving from OE words spelt with simple s:

- In OE the final s of *bræs* 'brass', for instance, was predictably a voiceless [s], while the medial s in *bræsen* 'brazen' was predictably voiced [z]. ModE, by contrast, has to distinguish the voiced plural s of *bras* from the voiceless s of *brass*, and uses ss for the latter; but although the voiced medial s could still have been used to give ModE *\*brasen* (as in *risen, chosen* rather than *\*rizen, \*chozen*), the letter z was substituted to give *brazen*. Similar patterns are seen in *glass* (OE *ȝlæs*)/*glaze* and *grass* (OE *ȝræs*)/*graze*. But ModE does not apply z consistently for OE voiced s: it has z in *dizzy* (< OE *dysiȝ*), but for the parallel OE form *bysiȝ* it keeps the s, giving *busy*, not *\*bizzy*. It changes s to z in *freosan* 'to freeze', *fneosan* 'to sneeze', *pisnian* 'to wizen', and *hæsel* 'hazel', but writes *cheese, weasel*, not *\*cheeze, \*weazel*.

- If the conversion of voiced s in OE to z in ModE is inconsistent, the ModE device of adding E to distinguish voiced and voiceless s in words derived from OE also leaves ambiguity. The ModE noun *house* (OE *hus*, ME *hous*) has voiceless /s/, although the s is not final and might therefore be taken as voiced by analogy with *arouse*. In the plural *houses* (late OE *husas*, late ME *houses*) and the verb *to house* (< OE *husian*), on the other hand, the medial s is voiced. Consequently, if the purpose of adding E is to distinguish voiced and voiceless values, it is self-defeating in the case of *house*.

- Another pattern is found in ModE *louse, mouse* with their plurals *lice, mice* (these c-endings were not fully established before ModE), from OE *lus, mus* with plurals *lys, mys*. The use of final -ce for the sound /s/ derives from Fr and shows unambiguous voiceless /s/; but the se/ce distinction might then seem to imply that *louse, mouse* had voiced /z/ (by analogy with *advice/advise*). Thus if -ce were used consistently to show voiceless /s/, *louse, mouse* should be written *louce, mouce*. Meanwhile *lousy* has /z/ but *mouser* retains /s/ and *delouse* has pronunciations with either /s/ or /z/.
- Modern respelling with final -ce, pronounced as /s/, is found in a number of other words of OE origin:
  ○ There is a group of particles (mostly first attested in ME, though of OE stems): *once* (< *ones*), *twice* (< *twies*), *thrice* (< *thries*), *since* (< *syns*), *hence* (< *hennes*), *thence* (< *þannes*), *whence* (< *whennes*).
  ○ There are several nouns that now have -ce for a former plural inflection -s (which today would otherwise be voiced as /z/): *bodice* (originally a plural of *body*), *pence* (< *pens*, a contracted plural of OE *peniȝ*), *truce* (as a plural of *true*), as well as a number of words of Fr derivation (see Chapter 5, p. 97). The form *dunce* is derived from the name of the 13th-century churchman *Duns Scotus*.
- Further sound–symbol discrepancies in ModE arising from varying developments of OE s are seen between *cyse/cese* 'cheese', *fleos* 'fleece', *ȝes* 'geese', *is* 'ice', *to lose* contrasting with the adjective *loose*, *to choose* and its past tense *chose*. These problems were further aggravated in ME with the influx of Fr vocabulary leading to pairs such as *lease/please*, *practice/practise*, etc.
- We find voiceless s with added e in ModE *else* (< *elles*), *worse* (< *wiers*), *horse* (< *hors*).
- A single case of OE initial s changing to c is *sinder* which was influenced by the unconnected Fr *cendre* to become ModE *cinder*.

## SC

The letters sc were probably pronounced /sk/ in early OE as they were in Lat; but they were then palatalized, first before front vowels and by 900 generally, to take on the value /ʃ/, as spelt sh in ModE: see the comments on *bishop*, p. 10, and note other examples such as *scacan* 'to shake', *sceaþ* 'sheath', *sceofan* 'to shove', *scip* 'ship', *scoh* 'shoe', *scur* 'shower', *scyld* 'shield', *þæscan* 'to wash', *enȝlisc* 'English'.

- ModE words of Germanic origin beginning with /sk/, whether spelt with SC or SK, are often of Scandinavian origin, their OE cognates having been respelt in ME times with SH: *screopan* 'to scrape', for example, would have been pronounced with initial /ʃr/ in OE, as a ME form *shrape* attests, but ModE *scrape* derives from Scandinavian *skrapa*.
  - This split between words of OE and Scandinavian origin gives rise to pairs of ModE words with different meanings, pronunciations and spellings, although ultimately from a common Germanic root: *shabby/scabby, shell/scale, shirt/skirt, shrub/scrub.*
  - The pair *screech/shriek* are hybrids (SK, K are typical of Scandinavian derivations, but SH, CH typically derive from OE), while *shatter/scatter* reflect southern/northern dialect differences, with no Scandinavian connection attested.
  - An oddity is ModE *ask*, which in OE had many different forms, including *ascian, acsian*; the modern form implies OE pronunciation with /sk/ rather than /ʃ/ (see also under 'x' below).

## T

- OE T was used as in ModE: *ta* 'toe', *tin, to* 'to, too', *treo* 'tree', *tunʒe* 'tongue', *tpentiʒ* 'twenty', *tyrnan* 'to turn', *storc* 'stork', *cetel* 'kettle', *betra* 'better', *æfter* 'after', *heorte* 'heart', *mæst* 'most'.
- T could also be geminated (i.e. written and pronounced as a double letter): *settan* 'to set'.

## Þ, Ð (TH)

The letters Þ, known as *thorn*, and Ð, known as *eth*, normally lead to TH in ModE (for their origin, see pp. 22–3). In OE, *thorn* and *eth* were used more or less interchangeably for both [ð] and [θ], though with some preference for *thorn* in initial and *eth* in final position. As with F and S, OE Þ and Ð could be voiced or voiceless – voiceless in initial and final position and when double medially, but voiced when single medially between vowels or voiced consonants:

- Initially: *þæc* 'thatch', *þancian* 'thank', *þeaht* 'thought', *þencean* 'think', *þeof* 'thief', etc.

- Finally (voiceless as final TH also usually is in ModE): *bæð* 'bath', *bræð* 'breath', *broð* 'broth', *clað* 'cloth', *deað* 'death', *fylð* 'filth', *forð* 'forth', etc. This -TH ending came to be even more widely used in later centuries: *breadth, dearth, depth, girth, growth,* etc.
  - ○ In some cases a voiceless final -TH in ModE derives from a voiced medial consonant in OE where a following vowel has been lost, making a previously medial consonant final: *beniðan* 'beneath', *eorðe* 'earth', *piða* 'pith', *priða* 'wreath'. Most of the -TH endings of ModE ordinal numerals derive from a voiced non-final OE consonant: *eahtoða* 'eighth'.
- Base words with a voiced medial consonant are numerous, nearly all having either a ModE long vowel and final -E or a ModE (usually) short vowel and final -ER: *baðian* 'to bathe', *bliðe* 'blithe', *claðian* 'to clothe', *laðian* 'to loathe', *seoðan* 'to seethe', etc.; *æȝðer* 'either', *broðor* 'brother', *feðer* 'feather', *fyrðra* 'further', *hpæðer* 'whether', etc. Note also *fæþm* 'fathom' and *hæðen* 'heathen'.
  - ○ Many ModE forms which follow this pattern of medial TH voicing are first attested in later centuries, sometimes in ME, sometimes in ModE: *bother, breathe, farther, heather, neither, slither, tether, wither.*
- With a double medial letter representing a voiceless consonant: *cyþþo* 'kith', *moþþe* 'moth', *præððu* 'wrath', *sceþþan* ('to scathe, injure'). In the first three instances ModE has lost the OE ending but the voiceless value remains. ModE *scathe* and *unscathed* are of Scandinavian rather than OE origin, and the TH represents the voiced consonant /ð/.

### TH *anomalies in ModE*

The simplicity of the above sound–symbol correspondences is undermined in many cases in ModE:

- Initial TH has become voiced in the 'grammatical' words *this, that, there, then, thou, thee, though,* etc. probably as a result of frequent occurrence in unstressed positions; the OE equivalents – *þes, þæt, þær, þonne, þu, þe, þeah,* etc. – all began with [θ].
- While the normal positional contrast between voiced non-final and voiceless final TH is shown in ModE in several pairs of words (*bath/bathe, breath/breathe, cloth/clothe, heath/heathen, loath/loathe, north/northern, sheath/sheathe, smith/smithy, sooth/soothe, south/southern,*

*teeth*/*teethe*, *worth*/*worthy*, *wreath*/*wreathe*), the voiceless non-final TH in ModE *earthen*, *earthy*, *filthy*, *frothy*, *lengthen*, *stealthy*, *strengthen*, *wealthy* is anomalous.

○ The following are also anomalous: *smooth* (< OE *smeðe*, yet not spelt *\*smoothe* in ModE) and *to mouth*, both with /ð/, and *booth* which may be pronounced with final /ð/ or /θ/; by analogy with *wreathe*, one might expect the OE verb *becpeðan* to give ModE *\*bequeathe* rather than *bequeath* which, like *booth*, may have final /ð/ or /θ/. *With* (< OE *wið*), like other common grammatical words such as *of* and *is*, is in ModE usually pronounced with a final voiced consonant corresponding to one which had been voiceless in OE (although a voiceless /θ/ pronunciation may also be heard in ModE).

○ In some words the ModE plural inflection -s may restore to a final -TH its OE voiced value: in *baths*, *mouths*, *oaths*, *paths*, *truths*, *wreaths*, *youths* the TH may have the same /ð/ value as in *bathe*, *wreathe*, etc. But elsewhere this does not happen: *breaths*, *broths*, *cloths*, *deaths*, *hearths*, *heaths*, *lengths*, *months*, *smiths*, *strengths* all have /θ/.

○ There are a few words in ModE where medial TH is voiceless, a noticeable contrast being that between *brother* and *brothel*. ModE never doubles TH, and so a form *\*broththel* showing the voiceless value is impossible. (If ModE had kept the letter *thorn*, however, the anomalous sound–spelling correspondence of *brothel* could have been avoided by writing *\*broþþel*.)

### TH *alternation with other spellings*

Þ, Ð in OE and TH in ModE do not always correspond:

• A number of ModE words such as *father* had D rather than Ð in OE *fæder* (see under 'D' for other examples).

• The reverse shift from *thorn* or *eth* to D, perhaps under the influence of Norman Fr, is seen in the OE *berðen*, *morðor*, *ruðor*, *spiþra*, *ʒeforðian* > ModE *burden*, *murder*, *rudder*, *spider*, *afford*; forms with TH – *burthen*, *murther*, *ruther*, *afforthe* – were in use until at least the 16th century.

• In ModE *hustings*, *nostril*, a former *thorn* (Scandinavian *husþing*, OE *nosþyrl* 'nose-hole') has become T. For OE *hiehþo*, *sihþ*, ModE has *height*, *sight*.

U

In OE, the letter U could have short or long values, pronounced respectively /ʊ/ and /uː/.

## *Short U*

The short value in OE typically led to short U in ModE, though a variety of spellings and sound values in ModE, overlapping with other vowel sources in OE, confuses the equivalence:

- Examples of OE short U with the original pronunciation are seen in *ful* 'full', *pullian* 'pull' and *\*putian* 'put' (not itself directly attested, but implied by the related noun *putung*).
- The pronunciation is retained but the U replaced by o in *pulf* 'wolf' and by oo in *pul* 'wool', *pudu* 'wood'. The purpose of this change from U to o was not to reflect any change in pronunciation, but to clarify scribal writing in ME (see p. 75). OE, like ModE, used four distinct letters to spell *pulf* 'wolf', but when in ME the letter *wyn* (ƿ) was replaced by UU (the early form of w), the effect was that such a word would have appeared as *uuulf*, with U three times in succession. When, furthermore, one takes into account that the 'Gothic' style of scribal writing reduced many non-capital letters more or less to short vertical strokes ('minims'), one can see how difficult the reading of *uuulf* could be. If, on the other hand, the vowel is respelt o, then the form *uuolf* is less likely to confuse readers.
- The letter U is retained, but with pronunciation in ModE changed (except in northern Eng accents) to /ʌ/: *butere* 'butter', *cuppe* 'cup', *dust*, *hunʒor* 'hunger', *hnutu* 'nut', *sunne* 'sun', *þus* 'thus', UN-, *under*, *uppe* 'up'.
- In yet another group of words both the sound and letter are changed, the sound to /ʌ/, and the letter U to o (many of these words would otherwise have had a proliferation of minims): *burh* 'borough', *cuman* 'to come', *huniʒ* 'honey', *lufu* 'love', *munuc* 'monk', *sum* 'some', *sunu* 'son', *tunʒe* 'tongue', *pundor* 'wonder'.
- Before R in *turf* the pronunciation of U is modified to /ɜː/ in ModE.
- *Duru* 'door' had an alternative spelling *dor* from OE onwards. In ME, we find the forms *dure* and *dor*, but also *dur* and *dore*. The spelling *door* first appeared in the 16th century and eventually supplanted *dore* in writing, though the ModE pronunciation remains that of the latter.

## Long ʊ

The long value of ʊ in OE has generally undergone regular change of both sound and spelling in its development to ModE: e.g. *hus > house*. The ModE vowel is usually spelt ou in medial position and ow in final position: *hus > house*, *cu > cow*, and similarly *druʒað* 'drought', *ful* 'foul', *hlud* 'loud', *hu* 'how', etc. (Compare Franco-Lat 'ou', 'ow', p. 145.)

- Sometimes ow occurs medially in ModE: *brun* 'brown', *crudan* 'to crowd', *scur* 'shower', *tun* 'town', *ule* 'owl'; and exceptionally ou is final in *þu >* 'thou'.

## Length change

Some words have shortened the long ʊ or lengthened the short ʊ between OE and ModE:

- Shortening, along with a change from /ʊ/ to /ʌ/, has taken place in the following: *duce* 'duck', *plume* 'plum', *sucan* 'suck', *þuma* 'thumb', *uder* 'udder', *us*.
- The following have acquired the long diphthong spelt ou/ow: *fuʒel* 'fowl', *ʒrund* 'ground', *hund* 'hound'.
- Two related cases have a short vowel in ModE when a suffix follows, contrasting with a long vowel in the base word: *house* but *husband*, *husting* (see p. 40 for *break/breakfast* and similar variations involving other vowels). Note also the long ʊ in *ut* 'out' but short ʊ in cognate *utter*.

## w/ƿ

In early manuscripts (and in the Northumbrian dialect more generally), OE used the letter ʊ for the sound /w/, as it had been used in classical Lat; so *uard* and *uundra* in the Northumbrian version of Cædmon's hymn (pp. 20–1). During the 8th century, the runic letter ƿ was increasingly used.

Words with w in ModE are predominantly of OE origin: of the 100 most commonly occurring ModE stems containing w, nearly 75 per cent can be traced back to OE forms with ƿ; about half the rest were spelt with G, H or U in OE; a few, like *power*, *view*, *war*, were words of Fr derivation which became established in the ME period.

- The sound /w/ occurred mostly in initial position in OE, as it does in ModE: *pæpn* 'weapon', *peorc* 'work', *pif* 'wife', *poruld* 'world', *pulf* 'wolf'.
  - Like w in ModE, initial p could also precede R in OE; both letters were pronounced. The w eventually fell silent, but not until printing had fixed the w spelling: *præð* 'wrath', *precan* 'wreak', *prist* 'wrist', *pritan* 'write', *priðan* 'writhe', etc.
  - Initial p also occasionally preceded L in OE, but fell silent in ME times before being fixed by the spelling conventions of print: thus *plisp* for 'lisp' is last attested from the 14th century.
  - The w in ModE *whole* (OE *hal*) began to be inserted in the 15th century; the w in ModE *whore*, OE *hore*, became common in the 16th. Similar spellings, such as *wholy*, *whood*, *whord* (= 'holy', 'hood', 'hoard') were introduced but dropped out of use again.

## w after consonants

- OE p was found after initial C, D, H, S and T:
  - The sequence CP was replaced after 1066 by QU, but in OE was found as in *cpacian* 'quake', *cpellan* 'quell', *cpæþ* 'quoth', *cpen* 'queen', *cpic* 'quick'; and after a prefix in *becpeðan* 'bequeath'.
  - P occurred after initial D as in *dpeorȝ* 'dwarf', *dpellan* 'stay, dwell', *dpinan* 'waste away'.
  - Initial H is seen before OE p as in *hpæt* 'what', but the two letters have since been reversed, giving WH in ModE – see under 'H' (p. 47) for further discussion and examples of this pattern.
  - ModE forms with initial sw dating back to OE include *spete* 'sweet', *spearm* 'swarm', *spelȝan* 'to swallow', *sperian* 'swear' (also *andsparian* 'to answer'), *spin* 'swine'.
  - Initial T before p is seen in words relating to *two* (*tpa*, *tpeȝen* 'two', *tpelf* 'twelve', *tpentiȝ* 'twenty') and in *tpiȝ* 'twig', *tpiccian* 'twitch', *tpin* 'twine', *tpinclian* 'twinkle'.
- In three cases, *andsparian* 'to answer', *speord* 'sword', *tpa* 'two', the w, though written, is no longer pronounced in ModE. In other cases, the original OE p is no longer written: OE *spilc* > ModE *such*, OE *spa* > ModE *so*.

## w after vowels

- When ModE words with final w correspond to OE words with p, the latter typically have a suffix, as in *feape* 'few', *nipe* 'new', or verb-endings such as the *-an*, *-ian* infinitive in *breopan* 'to brew', *sceapian* 'to show'.

- Some ModE words with a medial and final w are not of OE origin (e.g. *pawn*, *pewter*, *powder*, *flaw*, *Jew*, *allow*), and the w of many others relates to a G, H or U in OE (e.g. *laʒu* 'law', *furh* 'furrow').
- In a few words, OE ƿ yields ModE U(E): *clipen* 'clue', *hiep* 'hue', *hreop* 'rue', *treope* 'true'. In ME, -EW was the normal spelling for such words and also for words spelt with -UE or -EU in Fr: e.g. *blew*, *crew*, *glew*. In the 16th century, Richard Mulcaster (see p. 296) states his preference for -EW over -U at the end of words, giving examples such as *trew* (< OE *treope*) and *vertew* (< OFr *vertu*). When some of these words were later again spelt with final -UE, this spelling was extended to some of the -w words of OE origin, such as *hue* and *true*.
  - ○ ModE exploits the spelling difference for lexical and semantic differentiation in *clew/clue* (< OE *clipen*).
- ƿ was not doubled in OE, nor is w found doubled in ModE.

## X

The letter x, pronounced /ks/ or perhaps /hs/, was used in OE in spelling a small group of words in which it has persisted into ModE: *eax* 'axe', *fleax* 'flax', *fox*, *oxa* 'ox', *siex* 'six', *pæx* 'wax'.

- The archaic verb 'to wax' (= to grow) showed the OE variants *peaxan*, *peacsan*, *peahsan*.

## Y

In OE the letter Y originally represented the rounded front vowel /y/, with long and short values. However, from about 800 onwards Y progressively lost its rounding and its sound merged mostly with the values of I, until by ME it ceased to have a distinctive sound value of its own at all. In OE manuscripts of certain periods, notably the 8th century and the 10th century onwards, it was customary to dot Y, just as later it became customary to dot I, presumably to distinguish Y from other similar letter shapes, though the evidence is unclear.

- OE short Y generally leads to ModE short I: *brycʒ* 'bridge', *crypel* 'cripple', *cycene* 'kitchen', *cyninʒ* 'king', *cyssan* 'to kiss', *dysiʒ* 'dizzy'.

OE long Y generally leads to ModE long I: *bryd* 'bride', *fyr* 'fire', *hyden* 'to hide', *hyf* 'hive', *lys* 'lice', *mys* 'mice'.

- The correspondence OE Y > ModE I reflects the vowel development in the Anglian dialect (see further p. 80). A number of OE Y spellings lead to other vowel letters in ModE, generally because the direct source of the ModE form is in another dialect. The mixing of dialect forms and pronunciations also underlies the occasional surprising ModE sound–spelling correspondences:

  ○ A few words follow WSax in respelling Y with U: *crycc* 'crutch', *cycȝel* 'cudgel', *dystiȝ* 'dusty'; also ModE *blush*, *burden*, *church*, *clutch*, *hurdle*, *much*, *shut*, *shuttle*, *thrush*, *thrust*.

  ○ Some follow Kentish pronunciation with E: *cnyll* 'knell', *hymlice* 'hemlock', *lyft* 'left' (= opposite of right), *myrȝe* 'merry'; also ModE *fledge*, *kernel*, *pebble*, *shed*, *merry*.

  ○ Two words combine a U-spelling with a pronunciation from elsewhere: *bury* and *busy* have the spelling characteristic of the West Midland and Southern dialects, but the pronunciation of *bury* (rhyming with *merry*) is Kentish and that of *busy* comes from the East Midlands.

  ○ ModE *dent* and *dint* are both reflexes of the same OE word *dynt*, but reflect developments in different dialects.

  ○ ModE *evil* (WSax *yfel*) derives from an East Midland (Anglian) form *ivel*.[8]

  ○ The development of Y to O in *pyrm* 'worm', *pyrȝan* 'to worry', *pyrsa* 'worse', *pyrt* 'wort' may be due to considerations of legibility, as described under 'U' (p. 59) in connection with *wolf*.

  Following the usual pattern of development, ModE forms would perhaps have been *\*lift*, *\*mirry*, *\*biry*, *\*bisy*, etc.

- In sets of related words OE Y may be a mutation from another vowel (i.e. a variant caused by the influence of a nearby vowel): *cu* 'cow', plural *cye*; *ȝold* 'gold', adjective *ȝylden* 'golden' (compare ModE *gold/gild*); *ful* 'foul', *fylð* 'filth', *afylan* 'defile'.

## Z

The letter z was scarcely used in OE, and then mainly in loanwords such as *bæzere* from Lat *baptista*, and the name *Elizabeth*, ultimately of Gr origin. It was probably pronounced /ts/, as implied by the variant OE spellings *milze*, *miltse* 'mildness'. z has, however, been introduced, sadly inconsistently, in place of voiced s in a number of ModE words descended from OE: *brazen, freeze, furze, glaze, graze, hazel, ooze, sneeze, wizard, wizen* (see discussion under 's' above).

# Notes

1  Readers who want a complete picture of the spelling development of any particular word in English should consult the *Oxford English Dictionary.*

2  The Modern English words are not necessarily equivalent in *meaning* to the Old English words from which they derive (for example, Old English *cniht* 'boy' > Modern English *knight*), but this is irrelevant to a discussion of the development of Modern English spelling.

3  In this analytical section, the abbreviations OE, ME and ModE will be used instead of Old English, Middle English and Modern English.

4  For a map of the Middle English dialect areas, see p. 77.

5  Scragg (1974: 67, note).

6  *Plow* and *plough* derive from different parts of the Old English noun and verb; the former became the standard spelling in American English, the latter in British English.

7  Boswell (1934: 31). Boswell expresses in a footnote the hope that Johnson's authority will put a stop to the 'curtailing innovation' of *critic, public,* etc. for *critick, publick,* etc.

8  Wyld (1936: 207).

# 4

# The Decline and Revival of English in the Middle English Period

## The Arrival of the Normans and its Effect on English Society

In terms of power and political control, Anglo-Saxon England, which had lasted, with a few ups and downs, for some 600 years, came to an abrupt end with the regime change that followed the death of the Anglo-Saxon king Harold and the victory of Duke William of Normandy at the battle of Hastings in October 1066 and William's coronation as king of England on Christmas Day of that year.

Norman nobility and senior clergy soon replaced almost all of their Anglo-Saxon counterparts, so forming a French-speaking bureaucracy in both state and church. Some statistics indicate the extent of the change in the power structure in England in the twenty years after the Norman Conquest:[1]

- By 1087, all 190 barons in England were Norman; not one Anglo-Saxon earl survived William's suppression of the Anglo-Saxon nobility.
- Of the 21 bishops who signed the decrees of the Council of London, a church council held in 1075, 13 were Anglo-Saxon; by 1087, only three bishops were of English birth.

It must be emphasized that this change of regime only affected the upper levels of society. The Norman victory at Hastings did not lead

*The History of English Spelling*, First Edition. Christopher Upward and George Davidson.
© 2011 Christopher Upward and George Davidson. Published 2011 by Blackwell Publishing Ltd.

to a flood of French-speaking Normans into England.[2] Estimates of the numbers of Normans in England suggest that while they might have made up some 10 per cent or more of the population, a more probable figure is no more than 5 per cent and might perhaps be as little as 2 per cent.[3] Although, as noted above, the English barons were all Norman, only about half of the 10,000 or so lesser land-owners were; the other half, therefore, must still have been Anglo-Saxon. And working the land for these land-owners, Norman and Anglo-Saxon alike, were the English peasantry, forming 80 to 90 per cent of the total population of the country. In fact, for the mass of the people, who would have little or no direct contact with the Norman aristocracy in their everyday lives, Norman England was probably not very different from Anglo-Saxon England.

## The Linguistic Significance of the Norman Conquest

Statistics like those given above show that it would be quite wrong to assume a sudden and significant change in the linguistic behaviour of England as a whole after 1066: there simply were not enough French-speakers in the country to make any change in language use over the whole population either probable or necessary. Moreover, there was clearly no intention among the Normans to suppress English in favour of French: William himself tried to learn English (though he gave up due to pressure of other commitments), and the early writs he issued were in English and Latin, not French. The Norman upper classes were not hostile to English but had little need of it. It would only be some of their retainers and officials, such as estate managers, who would have to have been able to communicate in both languages – in French with their superiors and in English with the people they had to supervise or have everyday business dealings with. And while, as we have seen, increasingly many of the senior clergymen were French-speaking, most of the lower-ranking clergy would be English, and preaching to the people would have to have been in English.[4] In the centuries that followed the Norman invasion, there was never a time when the majority of the people of England did not speak English. French never became the everyday language of Norman Britain; it was first the language of the ruling class, and later the language of prestige and culture.

Nevertheless, the English language spoken and written at the end of the Middle English period in the mid-15th century was very different from what one finds in the 11th. The massive changes that arose were due above all to the incorporation of the language and writing practices (both French and Latin) of the Norman invaders. How this came about need not concern us in detail, but certain points are worth noting, firstly with regard to vocabulary and secondly with regard to writing:

- As time passed, French came to be no longer the language of an ethnic group but rather the marker of a social class. There was doubtless an ever-increasing number of people who were competent, to varying degrees, in both French and English. A knowledge of French became a necessary criterion for membership of the upper-middle class, and Williams suggests that from the late 12th century onwards Norman French was strongly influencing upper-middle-class English speech.[5] John of Salisbury, a 12th-century English scholar and churchman, remarks in his writings that by the middle of the century it was considered fashionable to use French words in English conversation. Williams further proposes that bilingual Normans who were looking for a word associated with government, culture, entertainment and so on would be likely to use French words in their English speech, and that, equally, any Englishman trying to operate within an upper-middle-class social setting would not only be sure to have learned some French but would also imitate the Frenchified English of the bilingual speakers.

  How far members of the upper social levels of the English population were actually bilingual is a matter of debate. Lass, for example, suggests that it is not necessary to assume widespread active bilingualism, arguing that, while all educated Englishmen in the 12th and 13th centuries could doubtless read French, they perhaps only spoke it to some extent, and that it was probably from written texts that French words first entered English – borrowing through passive knowledge of the language rather than active use.[6] This matter need not concern us further here: it is sufficient to note that as many as 10,000 words of French origin were adopted into English during the Middle English period, although about 90 per cent of them are not attested until the second half of the 13th century or later. Many are quite technical or literary, and although some embodied new concepts introduced by the Normans, others replaced already existing and perfectly adequate Old English vocabulary. Some examples from the field of government are *baron, crown, empire, government, sceptre*; in the religious sphere, *abbey, convent, religion*; from culture, cookery and entertainment *adorn, dress, fashion, luxury, robe, beef, mutton, pork, veal, minstrel, juggler.*

• Of more concern to the subject of this book is the effect the Normans had on the writing of English. Although power had rapidly passed to a French-speaking elite after 1066, with French-speaking scribes being brought in as part of the Norman administration, English continued to be written. Old English as a written tradition did not come to an end until 1154, with the final entry in the *Peterborough Chronicle* (see p. 32, n. 18) though latterly the *Chronicle* itself is already beginning to show French influence: in the record for the year 1137, for example, are found for the first time in English words of French origin such as *tresor* 'treasury', *Canceler* 'Chancellor', *prisun* 'prison' and *justice.*[7] Moreover, after 1066, the well-developed scribal organization which had produced the West Saxon spelling standard lost its place in the power structure, and decay progressively set in: Donald Scragg notes with regard to the *Chronicle* that 'in spelling, at first the West Saxon standard (as it had developed by 1100) was well maintained, but gradually the scribes' lack of training reveals itself, until the final entry shows only an imperfect grasp of the orthography',[8] further noting the gradual infiltration of Latin conventions such as CH for /x/, TH for /θ/ and UU for /w/ and confusion in the use of the vowel graphemes Æ, E, EA and A. The replacement copy of the *Chronicle* seems to have been made around 1121, and is in the classical West Saxon orthography; the language in the entries for 1122 onwards reflects the dialect of the East Midlands in the 12th century.

## Norman French and Parisian French

Although William and many of his followers hailed from Normandy, the invaders also included, as already noted, Picards from the north, speaking another of the major French dialects of the time, and others from western France, where different dialects again prevailed. The language brought to England by the Normans was, nevertheless, predominantly the Norman dialect of Old French. In England, it was therefore Norman French that, as Anglo-Norman, became the language of culture and prestige and of law and administration. In the centuries following the Norman invasion, however, one French dialect gained steadily in prestige over the others in France and emerged as the basis for an eventual French standard. It was not Norman or Picard, but rather the dialect of the Île de France, with Paris at its heart, which began to dominate, through the prestige afforded it by the French royal court and its administration and the university of Paris. This emerging standard is referred to as Parisian French or Central French or by the French term *francien*. In France, therefore, the language and spelling of the Normans were eventually relegated to the status of a mere provincial offshoot from this main line of development of French.

The same was to happen in England, for various historical and social reasons. Anglo-Norman had largely ceased to be a spoken language by the beginning of the 13th century, although it continued as the language of law and bureaucracy. The loss of Normandy in 1204 broke an important tie that had existed between the two territories. And *francien* was increasingly the language of French literature, and therefore the form of French that was gaining status in England at the same time as Norman French was losing its position of prestige. It was, therefore, Parisian French rather than Norman French which in later centuries became the source of French loanwords into English, with Norman-derived forms dating from the earlier, relatively short-lived period of Norman dominance in the development and use of French in England.

## Some differences between Norman and Central French

Words which derive from Norman French can be distinguished by their form from words that derive from Central French. While we have no need of a detailed analysis of the differences between the dialects,[9] the following points of difference are worth noting for the effect they have had on Modern English vocabulary:

- Latin /k/ and /g/ before /a/ become /tʃ/ and /dʒ/ in Central French (> /ʃ/ and /ʒ/ in Modern French) but remain /k/ and /g/ in Norman French. This produces doublets (i.e. pairs of words that derive from the same root) in English such as *catch* (< Norman French *cachier*) and *chase* (< Central French *chacier*; Modern French *chasser*), both from a probable Late Latin form *captiare 'to seize'. Similarly, we have *cattle* (< Norman French *catel*) and *chattel* (< Central French *chatel*), both from Late Latin *captale* 'property'; and from a supposed Vulgar Latin word *gaviola we have Modern English *gaol* (via Norman French *gaiole*) and *jail* (via Central French *jaiole*) – notice that, regardless of spelling, the Modern English pronunciation is that of the J-form. Other examples of /k/ and /g/ in English that have come down to us via Norman French are seen in *candle, castle, escape, gammon* and *garden* (compare Modern French *chandelle, château, échapper, jambon, jardin*).

- The TCH of *catch* and S of *chase* show another difference between Norman and Central French, one which is similarly to be seen in doublets such as *launch* (< Norman French *lanchier*) and *lance* (< Central French *lancier*; Modern French *lancer*), both from Latin *lanceare*.

- A third dialect difference which we may note here is in the treatment of initial /w/ in words of Germanic origin: Central French altered an originally Germanic initial /w/ to /gw/ (later reduced to /g/) while Norman French kept the initial /w/. This has given rise in English to doublets such as *warder* and *guardian, warranty* and *guarantee*. Similar doublets also occur with words that derive from Old English and words of Germanic origin that entered English via Central French, such as -WISE (as in *clockwise*) and *guise*, and probably *wile* and *guile*.

## Latin

Old English already had a number of words of Latin origin (e.g. *castel, candel, biscop*), some words perhaps even pre-dating the Anglo-Saxon invasion of England. However, the biggest influx of Latin into English began, along with the adoption of much French vocabulary, in the Middle English period.

Latin early had a place in Anglo-Norman bureaucracy. In the first hundred and fifty years or so after the Conquest, it was Latin, not Norman French, that accompanied or replaced English in official documents. The earliest Norman writs in England were written in English and Latin, not French, and in the last decades of the 11th century, laws were written in Latin alone. It was not until the 13th century that French began to replace Latin as the language of official documents such as charters, deeds and wills. The Latin of these documents was, however, quite different from the classical Latin of university texts. Many words were borrowed from Anglo-Norman, and many Latin documents therefore appear to be little more than superficially Latinized Anglo-Norman texts, because so many of the words and formulae used in them have been taken over from the vernacular language.[10]

Of much greater importance in the development of English, however, is the classical Latin that was studied in the universities. In the 12th century, there began a renewed interest in the study of Latin, and as English replaced French in the 14th and 15th centuries, thousands of Latin words were adopted into the English language just as thousands of French words were. In fact, since many of the terms that English was borrowing from French had themselves been borrowed into French from Latin, it is not always possible to identify which of the two languages is the real source of some Modern English words. Words ending in *-ioun* are a case in point: medieval French *processioun* was borrowed from medieval Latin *processionem*. Middle English *processioun* reflects the form of the French word, but in cases such as this (similar examples would be Middle English *possessioun, regioun*) it is difficult to distinguish between Latin and French sources. Similarly, to take as examples some words beginning with F, the following Modern English words could be equally well derived from Latin as from French: *favour, federal, felicity, feminine, festival, fiction, fiscal, flavour, fluid, form, fossil, fraction, fragment.* But much of our Modern English vocabulary is clearly derived from Latin rather than French. That the mining of Latin to add items of vocabulary to English got rather out of hand from the late 15th century onwards does not concern us here, since it has no separate bearing on the Latin contribution to English spelling, though the introduction of Latin-influenced spellings such as *doubt, debt* and *scissors* will be discussed at a later point (p. 191).

## The English Revival

From the middle of the 13th century, we see English begin gradually to regain the status it enjoyed before 1066, although it is an English very different from the old West Saxon written standard of pre-Norman England and the *Anglo-Saxon Chronicle*. A number of factors underlie the rise of English at the expense of French, among which we will note the following:

• War between England and France resulted in England's loss of Normandy in 1204, weakening the link with that part of France with which English nobility still had close ties. In the decades that followed, families with land in both England and France increasingly gave up either their English or their French possessions. Indeed, in the end they had no choice: about 1243, Louis IX of France decreed that those nobles still holding territory in both countries had to decide once and for all which king they owed allegiance to and relinquish

71

either their French or their English lands. Their connections with the Continent now severed, the nobility of England had less reason to continue to speak French.

- Along with the loss of the French connection, French-speakers in England were faced with the loss of status of the Anglo-Norman variety of French most of them still spoke, the prestige dialect of French now being that of Paris. The court of Henry II (1154–89) spoke Parisian French, and during the reigns of John (1199–1216), Henry III (1216–72) and Edward I (1272–1307) there were influxes of French-speakers whose presence and behaviour, particularly during the reign of Henry III, caused great resentment throughout the country and an upsurge in English nationalism. It has been suggested that this may have served to boost the use of English as a badge of true Englishness amongst those who resented and opposed the incomers.[11]

- The 13th and 14th centuries saw the rise of an increasingly powerful and prestigious English-speaking middle class of merchants and craftsmen in the growing towns of England.

- And finally we may note that the high mortality level during the plague (the Black Death) which spread across England between 1348 and 1350 caused a labour shortage which significantly raised the bargaining power and thus the status of the labouring class, and with it the status of the language they spoke.

## The Use of French and English in Society

From what we are told by contemporary writers, it is clear that by the 14th century everyone in England could speak English, and that to reach the widest possible readership writers were aware that they had to write in English rather than French or Latin, as not everyone who might read their works knew these latter languages. Many members of the nobility could now speak no French at all.

While French long remained the main language of administration and the law, the situation gradually changed in favour of English from the mid-13th century onwards. Out of many significant dates and events, the following indicate the trend:[12]

- In 1258, Henry III is the first English king for almost two centuries to issue a proclamation, the Provisions of Oxford, in English (as well as French).

- By 1295, there is clear evidence that English is considered the language of England. A summons to Parliament issued that year warns of the French king's supposed intention to wipe the English language from the face of the earth. The same argument is used several times during the 14th century.
- In 1337, Edward III's claim to the French throne is explained to Parliament in English.
- In 1345, the London Pepperers Guild begins to use English in its records, the first guild to do so.
- In 1356, an order is made that proceedings in the sheriff's court in London must be conducted in English. In the Statute of Pleading of 1362, Parliament issued the same decree with regard to legal proceedings in England, because litigants could no longer understand French. While these statutes were not actually enforced, that they were enacted at all clearly demonstrates the general trend from French to English.
- The year 1363 sees the first official opening of Parliament in English.
- By 1385, according to John of Trevisa, all grammar schools in England have abandoned teaching in French in favour of English.
- From its inception in 1394, the Court of Chancery conducts most of its proceedings in English.

By the time Geoffrey Chaucer (d. 1400) was writing in the second half of the 14th century, the English court was certainly English-speaking, though still French-speaking as well. Of particular importance to the development of a new standard written English in the 15th century is Henry V's use of English in nearly all his official correspondence between 1417 and his death in 1422 (prior to 1417 he had used French). Henry's use of English can be said to mark a turning point in establishing English as the national language of England.[13] In 1422, the Brewers Guild states that it is changing over to keeping its records in English; one of the reasons given for this is that the king now writes in English.

In literature too, there was a significant change in practice over the period in question. Up to about the middle of the 13th century, most literature produced in England was written in French. It was generally only works of a religious nature, such as the *Ancrene Riwle* and the *Ormulum* (see below), that were written in English, though there are exceptions such as Layamon's *Brut* dating from around the end of the 12th century and possibly *The Owl and the Nightingale* (though some now date this to the late 13th century). But from the mid-13th century onwards, more and more literature, in a variety of genres, appears in English, a trend which continues into the next century. The second half of the 14th century sees the appearance of some the most important works of Middle English literature, such as *Sir Gawain and the Green Knight* (in which, it has been calculated, almost a quarter of the words are of French origin), Langland's *Piers Plowman* and of course Chaucer's *Canterbury Tales*.

## *The* Ormulum

The *Ormulum*, a versified English translation of the Gospels by a 12th-century Augustinian canon whose name was Orm, is of some interest in the history of English spelling because of the unique phonetic spelling system Orm devised for it. One feature of Orm's system was his use of a double consonant after a short vowel but a single consonant after a long vowel, as in the following two lines of the poem:

> Þiss boc iss nemmnedd Orrmulum
> Forrþi þatt Orrm itt wrohhte.

('This book is called the Ormulum, because Orm made it.')

Orm is the first English writer to devise and adopt a systematically reformed spelling. However, although his spellings tell us a great deal about his Middle English pronunciation, they play no direct part in the development of Modern English spelling. It is worth noting, nevertheless, that Orm's use of single and double consonants to indicate vowel length is reflected, though in a less thorough and systematic way, in Modern English spelling: e.g. *diner/dinner*, *later/latter*, *ruder/rudder*. Other features of Orm's spelling system are the use of accents to mark long vowels where consonants alone are insufficient to indicate the vowel length; three separate letters for the sounds /j/, /g/ and /dʒ/, hitherto not clearly distinguished in writing; and, for the first time in English documents, WH and SH for earlier HW and SC.

# The End of West Saxon Dominance and its Consequences for Middle English

We must now turn our attention back again briefly to England before and after the arrival of the Normans. By the late 9th century, the kingdom of Wessex under King Alfred had achieved a dominant position in Anglo-Saxon England, and in the period before the Norman Conquest, the West Saxon dialect of Wessex (or something very close to it) had come to be accepted as the standard written form of English. While local dialects were still spoken in Wessex and elsewhere, and were without doubt undergoing changes in grammar and pronunciation (Old English did not suddenly change into Middle English in the mid-12th century), most English writings of this period conform to this West Saxon written standard (though there is evidence of other standards). After the Norman Conquest, however, as English was replaced by French and Latin as the languages of officialdom, West Saxon increasingly lost its position of linguistic prestige and became merely one of several Middle English dialects of equal status. It is for this reason that most 12th-century writings appear quite different to those of the 10th or 11th centuries. In 12th-century writings, writers show changes in the language that had almost certainly already occurred in the spoken language late in the Old English period but of which there are only occasional traces in the writings of the time, standard written languages tending to remain conservative and conventional and slow to acknowledge on-going change in the spoken language (a phenomenon we will encounter again in the late Middle English and Early Modern English periods; see Chapter 6).

In Middle English, no one dialect had the prestige to dominate over the others. Middle English writers, unlike their Anglo-Saxon predecessors, customarily employed whichever form of English they spoke, and scribes who copied their work either preserved the original form of language or else more or less consistently substituted their own local forms. Writing about 1385, Chaucer writes in *Troilus and Criseyde* of the 'gret diversité in Englissh'. What gives rise to this 'diversité' is the absence of any accepted national standard for written English in the early part of the Middle English period.

The absence of a national written standard means that the same word may be spelled in a variety of ways. However, the writing of Middle English was by no means totally uncontrolled: individual scribal training centres seem to have taught their own spelling rules, and the usage of a scribe can often be shown to be quite strictly determined by the practice of a local school. But the usage of the schools prevailed only in particular areas and for limited periods of time, and in general there is a good deal of inconsistency in scribal writings.

Although scribes wrote Middle English in different ways, their spelling generally keeps closer to pronunciation than does that of Modern English.

Middle English writing was not phonetic in the sense of having one and only one written symbol for each sound, but there are relatively few words in which a letter has no corresponding sound in the spoken language, and Middle English spelling, being more fluid than that of Modern English, was better able to adapt to changes in pronunciation as they occurred, until the advent of printing fixed the written language in forms which were or came to be no longer representative of the spoken word.

## The Middle English Dialects

The dialects of Old English were described on p. 15. By the Middle English period, the dialect boundaries have altered slightly and a new north–south division has arisen in the centre of the country, as indicated in Figure 3:

- The *Northern* dialect is spoken north of a line drawn between More-cambe Bay and the River Humber.[14] Geographically, this corresponds more or less to the area covered by Northumbrian in the Old English period, though at its western end the boundary between the Northern and Midland dialects now lies further north than the Northumbrian/Mercian boundary did in Old English.
- The Mercian area of Anglian has split into an East Midland and a West Midland dialect, this split reflecting the fact that much of what is now the East Midland area had been in the Danelaw and therefore subject to Norse influence, while the West Midland area had not:
  - The *West Midland* dialect is spoken in those English counties, and also in parts of the Welsh ones, between Morecambe Bay and the Bristol Channel, extending as far east as the middle of Staffordshire, Warwickshire and Gloucestershire.
  - The *East Midland* dialect is spoken between the Humber and the northern Thames estuary, and in an area extending westwards to mid-Oxfordshire and Derbyshire, and also including the southern part of the West Riding of Yorkshire. East Anglia is often treated as a separate dialect area. The dialect of the Central East Midlands area (that is, of present-day Northamptonshire, Bedfordshire and the western part of Cambridgeshire) is, as we will see, of particular importance in the history of modern English.
- The *Kentish* or *South-eastern* dialect is spoken in Sussex, Surrey, Kent and east Hampshire.

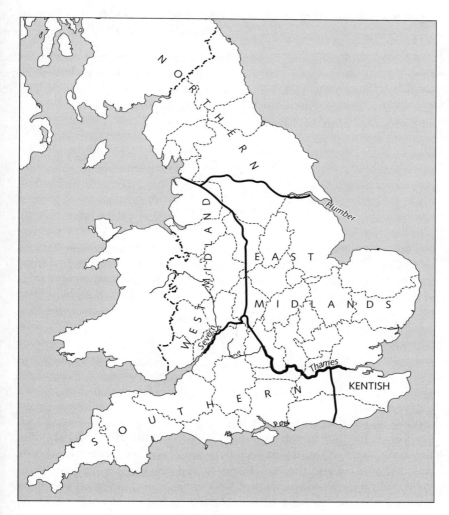

**Figure 3** Map of Middle English dialects.

- The *Southern* or *South-western* dialect, spoken in the counties to the south and west of a line running from north Gloucestershire to the Isle of Wight, occupies much the same area as the West Saxon dialect of Old English. While to the east of the River Severn it has advanced northwards into former Mercian territory, in the east it has given way to the South-eastern dialect deriving from Kentish Old English, which has pushed its way southwards and now covers the whole of the south-eastern corner of England south of the Thames.

As with Old English, it is instructive to look briefly at some differences between Middle English dialects as seen in the following two versions of the touching little 13th-century poem *Three Sorrowful Things*.[15] The first version is probably from the south-west Midlands, the second possibly from the East Midlands.[16]

(i)  *Wanne ich þenche þinges þre*
*ne mai neure bliþe be:*
*þat on is ich sal awe,*
*þat oþer is ich ne wot wilk day.*
*þat þridde is mi meste kare,*
*i ne woth nevre wuder i sal fare.*

(When I think of three things / I can no longer be blithe (= 'happy'): The one is, I shall [go] away / The second is, I do not know which day. The third is my most ('greatest') care, / I do not at all know whither I shall go.)

(ii)  *Þanne i ðenke ðinges ðre*
*ne mai hi neure bliðe ben:*
*ðe ton is dat i sal apei,*
*ðe toþer is i ne pot pilk dei.*
*ðe ðridde is mi moste kare,*
*i ne pot þider i sal faren.*

Notice that the lines 1 and 2 and lines 5 and 6 rhyme correctly in version (i) but not in version (ii); version (i) is therefore probably the original. Some of the differences between these two versions, such as *meste, wuder, ich* and the verb-forms *be* and *fare* in (i) as against *moste, þider, i* and the verb-forms *ben* and *faren* in (ii), reflect differences between the two dialects. The use of Þ versus Ð, and of w versus þ, however, are simply a matter of differing scribal practices.

## New Standard Written Englishes

Although at first no Middle English dialect had the prestige to establish itself as a new standard for the whole of England, a number of more localized written standards did evolve in the course of the 14th century. In a study by M. L. Samuels,[17] four such standards are distinguished.

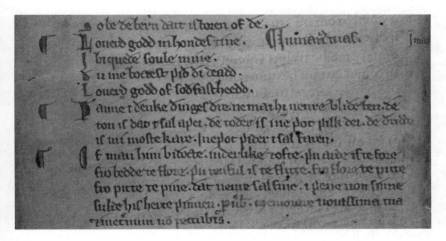

**Figure 4**   *Three Sorrowful Things.* © The British Library Board, ms. Arundel 292 f3v.

Three of these are London-based, while one originates in the southern East Midlands.

The East Midlands-based standard was the variety of English used, though not devised, by the Lollards (followers of the theologian John Wycliffe, d. 1384) in their sermons and religious tracts. Based on the language of the central East Midland area, the Lollard standard was used in the composition or copying of Lollard literature throughout large parts of England – even as far from the Midlands as Somerset, Dorset and Devon. Still found in use in the late 15th century, it was used for secular as well as religious works, both Lollard and non-Lollard. Close to becoming a real national standard form of writing, in the end the Lollard standard could not compete with the standardized written languages originating in London (perhaps also because it was associated with a heretical group that was being hunted down and driven underground).

Before examining the three London-based standards, we must first take a more general look at the language of London.

## Dialect and Spelling in London Writing

Throughout the 14th century, the ranks of the successful, and doubtless also the unsuccessful, in London were constantly being added to by immigration, especially from the Midlands and the North. Given this inflow of people from other parts of the country, and the fact that many of them rose to positions of high status, it is not surprising that the shape and sound of London language was anything but fixed and unchanging: established forms were constantly being replaced by new forms, generally of Midland origin. London English began in early Middle English as a Southern dialect but over time became essentially a Midlands dialect (though with some linguistic features originating in other parts of the country).

Already at the end of the 13th century, Henry III's proclamation known as the Provisions of Oxford (see p. 72) had East Midland as well as Southern features, as did the London charters of the 14th century, these latter also having some specifically Kentish forms. Throughout the 14th century, East Midland characteristics increase as Southern characteristics decrease. In the second half of the century, for example, Chaucer's works include more East Midlands and fewer Southern elements than do earlier documents. By the 15th century, Caxton's printed works have lost almost all distinctively Southern features, as have official documents originating in London. Modern English, deriving as it does (as we will see) from one of the London standards, is therefore chiefly descended from the East Midland dialect of Middle English.

To take just one example of the way in which the change in dialect influenced spelling in documents written in London, we may consider a number of words written with E, U or I:[18] *bregge/brugge/brigge* 'bridge', *hell/hull/hill* 'hill'; *bregge* and *hell* are Kentish spellings; *brugge* and *hull* are West Midland and Southern; *brigge* and *hill* are East Midland forms. A similar pattern is seen in *berie(n)/burie(n)/birie(n)* 'to bury', *kesse(n)/kusse(n)/kisse(n)* 'to kiss' and *senne/sunne/sinne* 'sin'. All these are found in 13th-century London documents, but the E and U spellings gradually decline in frequency over the Middle English period in favour of the East Midland I spellings, although the possibilities afforded by the E ~ U ~ I variation was exploited by poets for the purposes of rhyme: among variants seen in Chaucer, for example, are *kesse/kisse*, *knette/knitte*, *leste/liste*, *mery/mury* and *truste/triste*.[19] (For more on this, see under 'Y', p. 63.)

# The London-Based Standards

The first of the London-based standardized forms of writing is found in a number of 14th-century manuscripts from London and the surrounding area, containing works of various genres.

Another standard based in London is particularly associated with the best manuscripts of Geoffrey Chaucer (d. 1400) and other notable writers of the time. It is less consistent in spelling 'than it is in matters of grammar. In spite of the prestige this standard gained from its asso- ciation with Chaucer, it did not form the basis of the standard written language that developed in the 15th century.

Samuels' third London standard is the language of the English Court of Chancery, especially from about 1430 onwards. Of all three, it is of the most interest to the study of the development of English spelling, as it is from this standard that modern written English developed.

## The Chancery Standard

The term 'Chancery Standard' denotes the official written language that developed in the government offices – the Signet Office, the Court of Chancery, the Office of the Privy Seal and Parliament – during the first half of the 15th century.

Although named after the Court of Chancery, this style of language originated in the Signet Office of Henry V (by whose clerks the king's personal letters were written). The use of English in an increasingly standardized orthography independent of spoken dialects passed to the Chancery Office, and thence in legal documents throughout England. The first use of an official written standard can be dated to August 1417, when Henry V began to communicate with government officials, town councils, guilds, abbeys and other institutions in English rather than French. Although his Signet letters were written by a number of scribes, they have a uniformity of style and language, with spelling that clearly points towards that of modern written English. Analysis suggests that what became the Chancery Standard was primarily based on the Central East Midland written standard of the Lollard writings we have already dis- cussed, with some features from the local London standards. This is hardly surprising: among the large numbers of immigrants into London from the Midlands in the early part of the 15th century, there would undoubtedly be scribes familiar with the Central East Midlands ortho- graphy. There is also evidence from letters written by Henry himself that the usage of his Signet clerks was based on his own personal style.[20]

Given the prestige of Chancery English and its use in official documents that were sent to all parts of the country, it is not surprising that this 'official' English spelling was then copied by professional scribes and others across the country and by 1460 had established itself as a national written norm for official English. Letters from the regions addressed to the lord chancellor in London increasingly used Chancery Standard forms and spellings rather than those of the locality in which the scribes were writing. Spelling in private writing remained less standardized, however.[21]

## Chancery Standard spelling

It must not be thought that, because Chancery spelling became standardized, there was absolute uniformity of spelling, with any given word spelt in one and only one way. Chancery spelling still included variant forms, but what is key is that the variations no longer represented dialect differences in pronunciation and that the favoured form among the variants is already usually the form, or something close to a form, that we see come down to us in modern written English: for example, *any* is found more often than *eny* or *ony* (the latter being the standard Lollard form) and similarly *many* rather than *meny* or *mony*, *muche* or *moche* more than *mych/myche* (Lollard *mych*), *such/suche* rather than *sich/sych/swich*, etc. (Lollard *sich*), and *not* much more often than *nat* or *noght*. Among other aspects of Chancery English spelling,[22] some of particular interest to the history of Modern English spelling, are the following:

- Words spelled with EA in Modern English, such as *appear, feast, reason*, are spelt without A in the Chancery documents: e.g. *appele, appere, fere, fest, grete*, etc. *Treason* in the specimen letter below is one of the rare exceptions.
- Words spelled with A before N in Modern English, such as *command* and *grant*, are generally spelt AU in the Chancery documents: *commaund, graunt*.
- Þ and TH are in free variation, as are I and Y, Y being preferred beside letters with downstrokes: e.g. *knyght, nygh* rather than *knight, nigh*.
- In words corresponding to Modern English *father, mother, gather, together*, etc., we find D rather than TH: *fader, moder*, etc.
- Although probably not pronounced, H is generally written in words of French origin such as *homage, honour, horrible*. There are examples of hypercorrection or error, such as *habundant* for *abundant* (< Old French *abundant/abondant* < Latin *abundant(em)* 'overflowing', forms with H- being found in both French and English of this period due to incorrect etymology relating the word to Latin *habere* 'to have').

- Elision of the vowel of the definite article is standard before a word beginning with a vowel: e.g. *þarchebisshop* 'the archbishop', and in the letter below *thexecucion* 'the execution'; similarly with prepositions: *teschewe* 'to eschew'.

- There is often Y corresponding to a Modern English G: e.g. *ayeinst* 'against', *yeuen* 'given' in the letter below. (For G, see p. 44.)

- In unaccented syllables, E, I/Y, O and U all appear in unstressed syllables: e.g. *fader/fadir/ffador/fadur* 'father'. Similarly in noun- and verb-endings: *costis/costes* 'costs', *kyngis/kynges* 'king's', *askith/asketh* 'asks', etc. The trend in Chancery documents is towards a standard use of E. O and U appear more often in non-Chancery documents.

- Among prefixes, we may note that words which are spelt in Modern English with the Latin prefix AD-, such as *advise* and *advice*, are often spelt with the French A- rather than the Latin AD-: *avis*, *avauntage*, etc.

- Phonetic spellings such as *hey/hye* for *high*, *thow* for *though*, indicative of new pronunciations developing from the 14th century onwards, were characteristic of non-Chancery writing during the first half of the 15th century. Chancery scribes are inclined to maintain spellings that do not reflect the new pronunciations. This has, of course, had an immense effect on the sound–symbol correspondences of Modern English spelling. There are occasional examples of hypercorrection, such as *wythought* with a non-etymological GH for *without*.

We will end this section on Chancery spelling with part of a letter of pardon sent by the king in 1452:[23]

> *By the king*
> *Trusty and welbeloued. we grete yow wel. And albe it that oon Thomas Beneste of Solihille taylour. for certain greete offenses crimes and treasons by him doon ayeinst our Royal personne. was after the due processe of our lawe endited and therupon arained and atteint and Iugement yeuen. which Iugement as ye knowe wel shuld be put in execucion as to morwe* [tomorrow]. *in the town of warrewyk / yet natheles* [nevertheless] *we stured* [stirred] *of pite and mercy by our own mocion haue graunted and yeuen him grace of thexecucion of the said Iugement / and ouer þat haue pardonned him alle his trespaces and crimes & treasons of which he was endited trusting þat he neuer wol offende ayeinst our Royal maieste herafter/*

So close is the language and spelling to that of present-day English that this letter needs few glosses to clarify its meaning.

## The Influence of Printing in the Further Fixing of English Spelling: The Beginning of Modern English

In 1475 William Caxton published in Bruges (now in Belgium), where he had been a merchant for over 30 years, the *Recuyell* (= 'compilation') *of the Historyes of Troye*, the first book to be printed in English. In 1476 he brought the first printing press to England,[24] establishing himself at Westminster. By the time of his death in 1491, he had published about a hundred popular works of various kinds – romances, books of history, philosophy and devotion, and an encyclopedia.

It was this new method of book-production that made both possible and necessary the fixing of the previously more fluid and varied spelling of Middle English, in that books were no longer written in the dialect spoken by a scribe or the scribe's patron but in the dialect of the printer, and most printers were established in or close to London. In addition, printers knew it was in their own interest to adopt forms of language that would have wide acceptance, and once printing was established, there was naturally a tendency to use forms of language that had already appeared in earlier printed books. Just as the Chancery Standard became the standard for official correspondence, so printers came gradually to establish a standard in printed books, though, as Scragg notes,[25] the earliest books printed in England were 'shoddy affairs' compared with the best of contemporary manuscript works, and in most of them the spelling is very irregular. Although there were some differences between the language of the printers and the Chancery Standard, it was the latter form of English that printing eventually served to confirm as the national standard. Caxton's role in this process was crucial: as Strang has said: 'It is hardly too much to say that the range of devices subsequently used in English spelling was largely determined by Caxton's practice (i.e. his selection from existing conventions).'[26]

In Chapter 6 we will look in some detail at the development of English spelling during the Middle English and Early Modern English periods, but before that we will turn our attention to the Franco-Latin contribution to our Modern English vocabulary and spelling.

### Notes

1  From Williams (1975). For more on England after the Conquest, see for example Baugh and Cable (1993), Lass (1987), Strang (1970), Williams (1975).

2  In fact, not all of William's forces were Norman. The 14th-century chronicler Robert Mannyng says that William granted English lands to 'Frankis', 'Normanz', 'Flemmynges' and 'Pikardes' who had fought for him at Hastings. We will nevertheless use 'Norman' as a convenient label for all those who came to England with William.

3  Lass (1987: 56); Blake (1996: 107); Williams (1975: 84).

4  There is, nevertheless, evidence of non-English-speaking priests holding English livings (Strang 1970: 242). This may have been the impetus for Orm writing the *Ormulum* (see p. 74) in a carefully phonetic spelling.

5  Williams (1975: 84).

6  Lass (1987: 57, 59).

7  Hughes (2000: 111).

8  Scragg (1974: 17).

9  The classic description of Norman French, especially as it was used in England, is Pope (1952).

10  Blake (1996: 134).

11  Baugh and Cable (1993: 131).

12  For a detailed chronological outline of the changing use of Latin, French and English in administration, law, the church, literature and personal life, see Williams (1975: 71–80), from which much of the information in this section is taken.

13  Fisher (1996: 22).

14  In Lowland Scotland, the corresponding dialect is known as Middle Scots.

15  Reproduced from Brown (1932).

16  Lass (1987: 62).

17  Samuels (1963).

18  Examples from Burnley (1989: 109–10) and Wyld (1956: 9).

19  For further examples, see Burnley (1989: 128).

20  Richardson (1980).

21  See Sönmez (2000), Smith, J. (1996: 76).

22  For a detailed study of Chancery English, see Fisher et al. (1984), from which much of the information in this section is taken.

23  From Fisher et al. (1984: 143).

24  The end of Middle English and the beginning of Early Modern English is usually placed between 1450 and 1500. If one is looking for one particular significant date to mark a dividing line between these periods, one could well choose 1476, the year in which, by bringing printing technology to England, Caxton laid the foundations for the printers' contribution to the process by which English grammar, vocabulary and spelling became increasingly homogeneous.

25  Scragg (1974: 64).

26  Strang (1970: 158).

# 5

# The Franco-Latin Element

As one might gather just from the length of this chapter, French and Latin have made large contributions to English vocabulary and English spelling.

Specific borrowings from Old French and Latin are analysed alphabetically below according to the sound–symbol correspondences involved, to show the results they produced in Middle and Modern English. The developments shown can only be taken as broadly indicative, since absolutely fixed, standard spellings were unknown in the Middle and Early Modern English periods. For instance, Modern English *pain* appears in Middle English as *peine*, *peyne*, *paine*, *payne* as well as *pain*, but usually only one such alternative form (or occasionally two) will be given below, as it would be impossible to include more variants in a book of this length.[1] One must also remember that it is not always possible to make a rigid distinction between forms of Old English origin and those introduced by the Normans, as some French words were known in English before 1066, and some French words were themselves of Germanic derivation and thus of the same origin as Old English forms. For example, Modern English *waste* can be traced to Old French *waste*, but its absorption into Middle English was no doubt facilitated by its close resemblance to Old English *peste*, with lexical integration in English further supported by the related Latin stem *vast-*. The supporting influence of Latin is even more evident in the case of *chalice*: here Latin *calix* (itself from Greek *calyx*) had been borrowed into Germanic, giving

*The History of English Spelling*, First Edition. Christopher Upward and George Davidson.
© 2011 Christopher Upward and George Davidson. Published 2011 by Blackwell Publishing Ltd.

Old English *cælic* or *calic*, which after 1066 gave way first to Old French *calice* and subsequently to Central French *chalice*. Such was the degree of intermingling of languages in the development of Middle English.

# Doublets, Triplets and Quadruplets

One feature of Modern English vocabulary is the many pairs or groups of words (doublets, triplets and even quadruplets) that have the same ultimate origin in Latin (or in some cases Greek but entering English via Latin) but different forms in English due to their having come into the language by different paths and at different times. The following sets of words exemplify this phenomenon:

- *chief* < OFr *chief*; *chef* < Fr *chef* < OFr *chief*.[2]
- *faction* < Fr *faction* < Lat *factionem*; *fashion* < OFr *façon*, Norman Fr *fachon* < Lat *factionem*.
- *blame* < Fr *blâmer* < OFr *blasmer* < Graeco-Lat *blasphemare*; *blaspheme* directly from the same Lat source.
- *hospital* < OFr *hospital* < Medieval Lat *hospitale*; *hostel* < OFr *hostel* < Medieval Lat *hospitale*; *hotel* < Fr *hôtel* < OFr *hostel*. (Note the circumflex accent in ModFr marking where the *s* used to be: compare Eng *roast*/Fr *rôtir*, Eng *beast*/Fr *bête*, etc.)
- *gentile* (15th century) < Lat *gentilis*; *gentle* (13th century), *genteel* (16th century), *jaunty* (17th century) < Fr *gentil* < Lat *gentilis*.

The reasons for vocabulary sets such as these will be seen in the analysis that follows.

## A

## *Lat and/or Fr A > ModE A*

- *Act* (< OFr *acte*, Lat *actum*), *family*, *carry*; *car* (< LLat *carra*[3]), *argument*, *part*; *quality*, *quantity* (already sometimes with the ModE sound value in Chaucer's time), *squad* (17th century; < Fr *escouade*); *cage* (< OFr *cage* < Lat *cavea*), *alias*, *face*; *declare*, *scarce*; *accuse*, *adventure*.
- OFr did not distinguish short and long A, but A in ANorm was sometimes given a long value perhaps under the influence of OE.[4] The /aː/ changed to /eɪ/ in the Great Vowel Shift (see p. 177): *blasme* > *blame*, *masle* > *male*.

87

- There can be A/E variation in cognate words: *amend* (< OFr *amender* < Lat *emendare*), *emend* (< Lat *emendare*); *ambassador* (formerly also *embassador*; < Fr *ambassadeur*, ultimately < Medieval Lat *\*ambactiator*) but *embassy* (formerly also *ambassy*; < OFr *ambassée* < Lat *\*ambactiata*).

## *Lat and/or Fr A in ModE word-endings*

**-ABLE:** In Lat the choice between -ABIL- and -IBIL- depended on the inflectional vowel of the verb (e.g. Lat *mirari* 'to wonder at', *tangere* 'to touch', *audire* 'to hear' have the derivatives *mirabilis, tangibilis, audibilis* > ModE *admirable, tangible, audible*). The A-stem replaced the I-stem in many words in post-classical Lat and OFr; OFr often wrote -ABLE as an alternative to -IBLE, and in Fr loanwords ME showed the same variability: OFr *faisable/faisible*, ME *fesable/fesible* > ModE *feasible*, ME *pesable/pesible* > ModE *peaceable*.

**-AGE:** The ModE word-ending -AGE (with various pronunciations: *massage, garage, village*) comes from Fr -AGE (< Lat -ATICUS 'related to something': e.g. *villaticum* > OFr *village*).

- In a few derived forms the -A- of the base word has changed to -EN-: *messager, passager, scavager* > *messenger, passenger, scavenger*; such variants were appearing already in ME.
- Words with a final -EGE (*college, privilege, sacrilege*), -EDGE (*knowledge*) and -IDGE (*cartridge, partridge, porridge*) were formerly sometimes also spelt -AGE. Word-origin often appears to have determined the outcome: e.g. *college, privilege, sacrilege* < Lat *collegium*, etc.

**-AL:** The most common examples of ModE -AL all correspond to Lat -AL-: e.g. *capital* (< Lat *capitalis*), *central, final, real, total*. With few exceptions (e.g. ME *naturel, plurel, usuell*), the Eng forms have had -AL consistently from their earliest attestations.

**-AN:** The ending -AN (*Roman, Christian, republican*) derives from the Lat word-ending -ANUS (e.g. *romanus*). EModE hesitated between various endings (*africane, romayn, italien*) but -AN was dominant.

- *Foreign, sovereign* (< OFr *forain, soverain* < Lat *\*foranus, \*superanus*) appeared in ME spelt -EN, -EIN, -AIN, etc.; spellings with G are attested from EModE.

**-ANT/-ANCE/-ANCY:** Lat distinguished present participle endings of verb-stems with A and E/I: ModE *protestant, opponent, obedient* derive from Lat *protestare, opponere, obedire* respectively. ModE words ending in -ENT usually reflect the Lat vowel, but OFr harmonized the present participle endings as -ANT, and words borrowed into Eng from Fr typically have this spelling even where their Lat source would have given -E-: compare Lat-based *renascence, crescent* with the Fr equivalents *renaissance, croissant*.

- Thanks to these variations, cognate ModE words may sometimes have the Fr ending, sometimes the Lat ending: *resistant* but *persistent, attendant* but *superintendent*.

**-AR, -ARY:** These derive, directly or ultimately, from Lat -ARE, -ARIS, -ARIUS, -ARIUM: *altar* (< Lat *altare*), *familiar* (< OFr *familier* < Lat *familiaris*), *particular, peculiar, regular, similar; military* (< MFr *militaire* < Lat *militaris*), *necessary, ordinary, secretary*.

- When stress in Eng shifted back from word-final, the A-vowel became centralized, and in ME the spelling changed from -AR to -ER: e.g. *alter, particuler, peculier, scoler, viker*. With the growth of etymological knowledge from the 16th century, the -AR ending began to be restored, but did not become fully established in some words until the 20th century (*briar/brier, pedlar/peddler* are still alternatives).
- A typical -ARY development is Lat *salarium* > OFr *salaire*, ANorm *salarie* > ME *salarie* > *salary*, with -ARIE the typical ending down to the 17th century.
  - With the -AIRE ending come ModFr borrowings such as *millionaire, questionnaire*. (See p. 90.)

## Lost A

- The second A in OFr *paralisie* (from Gr *paralysis*) was lost in ME: *parlesie > palasy > palsy*. *Paralysis* re-entered Eng in the 19th century.
  - Similarly *fantasy > fantsy > fancy* and Lat *quinancia* > ME *qwinaci/quinasi > quinsy*.
- *Fray, mend, stray* < *affray, amend, astray; penthouse* (EModE *pentice*, etc.) < OFr *apentis*.

## AE

The digraph AE usually occurs in ModE in direct loans from Lat, often in the nominative (= subject case) plural or genitive (= possessive case) singular of Lat nouns ending in -A: *Caesar, algae, curriculum vitae*.

## *Lat A > OFr AI > ModE AI*

In certain phonetic contexts, a stressed Lat /a/, spelt A, became OFr /aɪ/, spelt AI. From Fr, this AI digraph entered ME: LLat *adjuta* > OFr *aide* > ModE *aid*. The value of AI in OFr changed to /ɛɪ/ (/ɛ/ in western France), with widespread respelling of AI as EI: thus Lat *granum* > OFr *grain/grein* > ME *grayn/greyn* > ModE *grain*; *saint* (< Lat *sanctus*) was also spelt *seint*, and entered Eng in that form; *aid* was early spelt *eide* in Eng (15th century). Similarly with *bail, claim, traitor, tailor; captain, certain, fountain*.

- In most cases AI has since been restored, but the doublet *villain/villein* remains.
- A few words derived directly from Lat have acquired a 'Fr' AI spelling: e.g. *prevail* < ME *prevayle* < Lat *praevalere* and *explain* < ME *explane* < Lat *explanare*.
- Modern forms in -AIR have various sources: *affair* < Lat *ad+facere*; *chair* < Lat *cathedra*; *pair* < Lat *paria*; *air* < Lat *aer* < Gr.
  - In some cases, EModE forms with final -AIR changed to ModE -ARE: Lat *declarare* > OFr *desclairier* > ME *declair* > *declare*; and similarly *pare, prepare*. *Repair* 'to mend' < OFr *reparer* < Lat *reparare* may have retained its spelling under the influence of *repair* 'to go' < OFr *repairer* < Lat *repatriare* 'to return to one's country'.
- ModFr/ModE -AIRE < Lat -ARIUM: *doctrinaire, legionnaire, millionaire, questionnaire*. (See also '-ARY' above.)

## *Lat A > ModE EI/EY*

Alternation between A and E in ME (often already in OFr) sometimes led to an original A giving rise to E in ModE: VLat *\*foranus* > OFr *forain* > ME *forayn/foreyn* > *foreign*; similarly VLat *\*superanus* > *sovereign*; Lat *factum* (past participle of *facere* 'to do') > Fr *fait* > ModE -FEIT in *counterfeit, forfeit, surfeit* (but EA in cognate *feat*). Similarly Lat *abbatia* > *abaie/abeie* > *abbaye/abbeye* > *abbey*.

## *Lat A > ModE AY*

A typical development of Lat A to ModE AY is Lat *pacare* > OFr *paie* > ME *paye* > *pay*; similarly *bay, decay, essay, portray*.

## Lat *A* > OFr *AI* > ModE *EA*

Lat A and/or OFr AI > ModE EA, usually pronounced /iː/, is seen in Lat *rationem* > OFr *resun* > ME *reison* > *reason*; and similarly in *ease, clear, feature, peace, plead, please, treat*; also *peasant* (late ME *paissaunt,* ultimately < Lat *paganus* 'of the country').

- In some cases, Lat A had already become E in OFr: *fesan* > ME *fesaunt* > *pheasant, plesir* > ME *plesir* > *pleasure.*

## ModE *AI/AY* from other sources

Some Fr-derived words spelt with AI/AY in ModE did not originate in words with Lat A, but acquired AI/AY by analogy around the 16th century:

- *Maintain* (< Lat *manu+tenere*): OFr and early ME preserved the contrasting vowels: *mainteyne,* etc., the two vowels perhaps being still distinguished in speech as /aɪ, eɪ/. Pronunciation and spelling merged in subsequent centuries, with forms like *meynteyn* typical of the 14th–16th centuries. From the 16th century, spellings with AI began to prevail. Similarly *abstain, contain, detain, entertain, obtain, retain, sustain.*
- *Disdain* and *deign* < Lat *dignare*; both had AI and EI forms in ME.
- *Faint* and *feint* < OFr *faint/feint* (from *feindre* < Lat *fingere* 'to shape, form').

## Lat/Fr *AU* > ModE *AU*

- Especially from the 15th century, numerous Lat words containing AU were borrowed into Eng: *auction* < *auctionem*, and similarly *audible, author, exhaust, inaugurate, pauper, raucous.*
- Some words originated in Gr, passing through Lat and sometimes Fr: *austere* < Lat *austerus* < Gr *austeros*, and also *aura, authentic, caustic, nausea, nautical, pause.*
- Some may owe their ModE forms as much to Fr as to Lat: *applaud, audience, augment, cause, caution, fraud, gaudy, plausible, restaurant.*

Throughout their history in Eng, these words show little variation from AU except an occasional AW (e.g. *cawse, plawsable*).

## Lat *AL* > ModE *AU/AUL/AL*

The AU digraph often arose from A preceding L: Lat *alburnus* > OFr *auborne* > ME (15th century) *aborne* > *auburn*; similarly *causeway*, *daub*, *sauce* (also *saucer*, *sausage*).

- In some cases the Lat L was restored in EModE (at first silently, now pronounced): ME *asaut* > *assault* (similarly *somersault*), ME *caudron* > *cauldron*, ME *faut* > *fault*.
- Some words have since lost the U: *falcon*, *false*, *herald*, *realm*.
- With U lost and L restored, though still silent, are *balm*, *palm* (of the hand), *psalm*, *salmon*.
  - For *calm* the 16th century occasionally saw forms such as *caulme*, *cawme*.
- Both L and U are lost from *safe* (< OFr *sauf* < Lat *salvus*) and *chafe*, though EModE had forms like *salf*, *saulf*.
- *Haughty* is ultimately from Lat *altus*; the H, GH and Y are alterations based on the spelling of Germanic words.

## ME *AU+N*

AU before N was common in both Norman Fr and Central Fr, hence widely used in ME in words of Fr origin (so much so that words of OE origin like *answer*, *hand* were occasionally written *aunswar*, *haunde*, etc., in ME). The history of AU+N in Eng is erratic:

- In many words AUN was continuously used from ME onwards: Lat *amita* > OFr *aunte* > ME *aunte* > *aunt*; similarly *gauntlet*, *haunt*, *launch*.
- In many other words AUN was commonly (but not consistently) written in ME, but then reduced to AN: *daunce* > *dance*; similarly *advantage*, *ancestor*, *branch*, *command*, *grand*, *slander*, *strange*.
- In yet other cases the U was not inserted until the 17th or 18th century: *hanch* > *haunch*, *vant* > *vaunt*.
- In a few (mostly now rare or dated) instances ModE still hesitates between AUN or AN: e.g. *gantry* (for which some dictionaries allow an alternative spelling *gauntry*), and *staunch/stanch*.

## ME *AU+M*

In ME AU was often written before M where there is no U in ModE: ME *chaumber* > *chamber*; similarly *champion*, *flame*, *lamp*.

## *ModE AU not from Lat A*

ModE AU in Lat-/Fr-derived words occasionally originated from vowels other than A: *gentilem > jaunty; domitare > daunt, volta > vault.*

## *Other sources of ModE AU*

Some ModE words of Germanic derivation are spelt with AU: *daughter, draught, laugh, naughty, slaughter, taught* and *taut* (formerly also spelt *taught*). Since they were not normally spelt with AU before the 13th century (and most of them not for a century or two after that), it is reasonable to claim that in these words the ModE AU is in origin a Fr-based spelling device.

- The AU grapheme spread spasmodically to other words of Germanic origin during the ME and EModE periods, especially before L, but the U did not become established in *caulf > calf, haulf > half, taulk > talk, staulk > stalk*; compare ModE *balk/baulk, calk/caulk*.

### *AW+N*

In some words ME AU corresponds to AW in ModE: *launde > lawn* 'grass', *paun > pawn* 'deposit goods', *tauny > tawny*.

- Some words ending in ModE -AWN derive from OFr -AON: *brawn, fawn, pawn* (in chess) < OFr *braon, faon, paon*.

## B

### *Lat and/or Fr B > ModE B*

- Word-initially: *battle* (< OFr *bataille*, VLat *battalia*), *beauty, bottle, butcher; blank, brief.*
- Medially, preserved from Lat through OFr: *labour, member, trouble.*
  - Lat intervocalic B generally became V in Fr, and hence in Fr loans in Eng: *deliver* < Lat *deliberare*.
- In final position B is rarer: *daub* (< OFr *dauber* < Lat *dealbare* 'to whiten'), *barb, curb.*

### *Silent B*

The B is silent in *aplomb, bomb, catacomb, plumb, succumb, tomb* (as also in OE *dumb, lamb*, etc., where the B was probably not pronounced after the

13th century). In ME and EModE most of these Fr loans could be spelt without B: *bome, plomme, towme*; the Fr spelling ensured ModE forms with B.

## Double or single B?

The development of earlier B into ModE BB in Fr-derived words often accompanied a shift of stress to the first syllable in the 16th and 17th centuries, but in ME and late ANorm there had already been a tendency to double consonants to indicate a preceding short vowel: *bobine* > *bobbin, caboche* > *cabbage, riban* > *ribbon*.

## Loss of B

Lat B is lost in *sudden* < Lat *subitanum, rage* < Lat *rabiem* (compare ModE *rabies*).

- The B of SUB-/SUBS- had already been lost in Lat compounds: *succeed* (< *sub-+cedere*), *suffer, suggest, summon, support, surrogate; sustain* (< *subs-+tinere*), *susceptible, suspend; suspect* (< *sub-+specere*).

## Acquired B

B was inserted between M and a following consonant (especially where a vowel dropped out): Lat *rememorari* > OFr *remembrer* > ME *remembre* > *remember*, Lat *numerus* > ANorm *nombre* > *number*; similarly, Lat *camera* > *chamber*, Lat *humilis* > *humble*.

## Restoration of B

In three words a Lat B was lost in OFr and ME, but then restored, unpronounced, in deference to the original Lat forms: Lat *debitum* > OFr *dete* > ME *dette/debte* > *debt*; similarly Lat *dubitare* > ME *doute* > *doubt, subtilem* > ME *sotill* > *subtle*.

# C

## Initial and medial c in words of Fr and Lat derivation

- Initial C: *candle* (OE *candel* < Lat *candela*), *castle, cancel, calm, common, coat* (< OFr *cote*), *court, cover, current, clear*.

- In a few cases there has been some alternation of c with K: *kerchief* already attested in ME as alternative to *curchief* (< OFr *couvrechief* 'cover-head'); *kerb* (first attested in the 17th century)/*curb* < Fr *courbe*.
- Medial c: *second, particular; increase* (< OFr *encreistre* < Lat *increscere*), *subject.*
  ○ Where -CA- occurs medially in Eng, as in words like *political, indicate* (typically first attested in EModE), the derivation is usually more directly from Lat (in these examples < *politicus, indicare*) than from Fr.

### c restored

- The ModE pronunciation of *victuals* /'vɪtlz/ reflects such OFr and ME spellings as *vitaile*; EModE restored the c from Lat *victualia.*
- The ModE pronunciation of *indict*, /ɪn'daɪt/, is anticipated by such ME forms as *endyte, indite*. The spelling *indict* is first attested in the early 17th century, and reflects a supposed Lat derivation, e.g. a LLat verb *\*indictare.*

### ModE final c

Lat-derived word-final c has had various competing spellings:

- It occurs in the ending -IC in numerous words (e.g. *economic, music*), some two-thirds of which derive from the Gr ending -IKOS via Lat -ICUS.
  ○ In ME and later times this ending saw alternative spellings such as -ICK, -IC, -IKE and -IQUE. From EModE times into the 19th century such words were commonly spelt -ICK (Samuel Johnson's *Dictionary* published in 1755 gave its support to -ICK, as in *magick, musick, publick*, etc.; for a comment on this, see p. 49). The American lexicographer Noah Webster (1758–1843) recommended dropping the K, since when -IC has become general, first in America and then worldwide.
- Fr *estomac* (< Lat *stomachus*) led to such forms in EModE as *stomac, -ak, -ack, -ok*; an H reflecting the Lat spelling was added in the 16th century, producing ModE *stomach.*
- From Fr/Lat come *arc* (< OFr *arc* < Lat *arcus*), *disc.*
- Other c-endings are found in modern loans from Fr: *bivouac, bric-a-brac, bloc, chic, cul-de-sac, franc, havoc, tic*; silent in *charabanc.*

## Changing word-final C to K

Eng has absorbed from Fr other words ending in /k/ which do not now have final C:

- In one group spelt with a consonant plus final C in OFr, the C has changed to K in Eng, sometimes as early as ANorm times, sometimes as late as the 18th century: e.g. *tronc > tronk > trunk* is an early development, *parc > park* later; similarly *blank, flank, frank, rank, pork*; also *clerk*, although OE already had *clerc*.
- To indicate that a vowel was not short, Fr -C came to be replaced by -KE in some instances: *lac > lak > lake, duc > duk > duke* (compare *bec > bek > beak*).
- When final /k/ follows a short vowel, ModE typically has -CK: *trac > trak > track*; similarly *check, truck*. (Word-final -CK in words entering Eng from the 13th to the 17th centuries may derive from Fr equivalents with -QU-: e.g. *attack < attaque, mock < moquer*. Recent Fr loans retain the Fr ending -QUE: *boutique, critique*.)

## CC and CQ = /k/

- Double C occurs mainly in polysyllabic words of Franco-Lat origin, generally after short vowels:
  - from Lat: *desiccate, impeccable, succulent*;
  - from Fr: *buccaneer, succour*.
- Double C occurs where a prefix (AD-, OB-, SUB-) has been assimilated to a following stem in Lat (e.g. *ad-+cumulare > accumulare*): *accommodate, accompany, accurate, acclaim, occasion, occupy, succour*, etc. OFr typically spelt such words with single C, and spellings like *acont, acord, acuse, ocupie*, etc. are common in ME and/or EModE.
  - A few Eng words have /k/ spelt CQ, mainly from assimilation of the Lat prefix AD- to words beginning with Q: *acquiesce* (< *ad-+quiescere*), *acquire, acquit*. OFr spelt such words with AQU-, leading to ME and EModE forms such as *aquiess, aqwere, aquite*.

## C before E, I, Y

By the time of the Fr influx into Eng, Fr C before E, I, Y had the value /s/, as it normally has in ModE. (The pronunciation of C as /ʃ/ as in *ocean, social* arose after ME; see p. 185.)

- Word-final -CE, as in *place*, was a feature of the OFr spelling system, and entered Eng in numerous loanwords, e.g. *avoidance, confidence, disturbance, entrance.*
- In ModE word-final -CY, the Y was first introduced in Eng. In ME and EModE, alternative spellings such as -CIE, -CYE were common (e.g. *primacie, primacye*), as was S or T for C (e.g. *secresy, secrety* for ModE *secrecy*).
- Many Gr loans with initial CY- were transmitted through Lat and Fr: *cycle, cylinder, cymbals,* etc.

## T/C *variation in Lat-derived words*

The letter C with the value /s/ before E and I in OFr had two main sources. One was Lat C: Lat *certanus > certain.* The other was Lat T, which before unstressed E, I acquired the same value, /ts/, as C had in LLat. Medieval Lat commonly alternated T and C in such cases: *nacionem* or *nationem*, whence the widespread use of forms such as *nacion* in OFr and ME. The C adopted in LLat, OFr and ME for classical Lat T has sometimes survived into ModE: Lat *spatium > space; platea > place*. Elsewhere, a later preference for classical Lat etymology has led to the restoration of T in place of C, as in the -TION endings: ModE *nation*.

- Two -CION spellings remain in ModE: *coercion* and *suspicion*.
- In general, classical Lat spelling determines the choice between -TIAL and -CIAL: *spatial/facial* (< Lat *spatium, facies*), *inertial/commercial, initial/beneficial, substantial/provincial*.

## Replacement of S by C

Some words of Fr derivation originally written with S have, after a period of vacillation in ME, come to be spelt in ModE with C:

- In late ME and EModE -CE often replaced a simple word-final S: *ace < Fr as, juice < jus, lattice < lattis, pace* (as well as *pass*) *< pas, palace < palais*.
  - Some ME replacements did not last: *cace, cource, falce, responce, sence* (ModE *case, course, false, response, sense*).
- In other cases the -CE replaced plural -S: *dice* arose as a plural of *die; quince* as a plural of *quine/coyn*, etc.; *trace* (= 'part of a harness') as a plural of *trait; invoice* probably as a plural of *invoy*, typically pluralized in ME as *invoyes*; also in words of OE origin, such as *lice, mice*. (See also p. 55.)

## Replacement of c by s

Examples of c replaced by s include Lat *despicere* > *despice* > *despise,* Lat *exercitium* > *exercice* > *exercise.*

- *Raisin* originated in Lat *racimus;* c-forms like *racyn* were among many ME and EModE variants, until the ModFr form *raisin* became dominant from the 16th century.
- A following back vowel may have prevented the use of c in Eng: Lat *lectionem* > *lecon* > *lesson.*
- Two words replaced initial c with s: OFr *cerchier* > *cerche/serche* > *search;* OFr *cirurgien/serurgien* > ANorm *surgien* > *surgeon.*
- Some ME forms with s for palatalized c did not take hold permanently: *sentre, serteyn* (= certain), *fase, sercle* (= circle), *counseil* (= council), *deside, symbal, mersy, voys* (= voice).

## The development of some c/s alternations in ModE

- *Advice ~ advise*: Throughout ME and EModE the -CE, -SE spellings were not consistently distinguished. *Advice* developed from the 13th to the 16th centuries through the stages *avis, advis, advise, advice,* while the verb *advise* was always written with a final E.
  - *Device/devise, peace/appease* show a similar history.
- *Practice ~ practise*: Now identical in sound; the latter formerly rhymed with *advise*. In British usage they represent the noun and verb respectively (Samuel Johnson's 1755 *Dictionary of the English Language* made that distinction), but in American usage *practice* is dominant for both noun and verb, with *practise* an alternative for both.
- *Licence ~ license*: In modern British usage *licence* is a noun, *license* a verb, but Johnson had *license* for both noun and verb; in modern American usage they are interchangeable. The form *license* has no precedent in either Lat (*licentia*) or Fr (*licence*), and originated in Eng (e.g. *licens,* 1493), reinforced by spelling book compilers in the 17th century by analogy with *advice/advise*.[5]
- *Prophecy ~ prophesy*: In British usage, c indicates a noun and s a verb (Johnson already made this distinction); American usage allows *prophesy* for both noun and verb, but *prophecy* only for the noun. Lat *prophetia* > OFr *prophecie* > *prophecy; prophesy* originated as a spelling variant with no etymological basis.
- *Defence ~ defense, offence ~ offense*: The -CE endings are already attested, alongside s-forms, from the ME period, but have no etymological

basis in Lat (*defensio, offensio*) or Fr (*défense, offense*); they appear anomalous beside the ModE adjectives *defensive, offensive*, and it was to avoid such anomalies that Noah Webster in the early 19th century recommended *defense, offense*, now standard in America.

○  *Fence* is standard in both British and American usage, although the word derives from *defence/defense* and appeared in ME as *fens, fenss, fense*, etc.

•  *Pretence ~ pretense*: British and American usage also diverges over *pretence/pretense*. C and S forms both occur in EModE.

•  *Council ~ counsel*: These two forms have different meanings in Eng. The Lat words from which they derive originally had a similar distinction in meaning (*concilium* 'assembly', *consilium* 'advice'), but the meanings came to overlap in Lat usage and merged entirely in Fr *conseil*. In ME and EModE spellings with C and S were virtually interchangeable, but Johnson made a clear distinction, based on the Lat derivations, which has been maintained ever since.

### SC *anomalies*

•  *Ascertain* is by derivation *a+certain*, the S perhaps surviving from EModE *assertain*.

•  *Scent* (< Fr *sentir* 'to smell') did not acquire its C until the 17th century.

•  The spelling of *scissors* (< Lat *cisoria*, OFr *cisoires*) was highly uncertain before the 20th century, with over 40 variants attested, including *cysors, scizzors, sesours, sizars, sycers*. ModE *scissors* only appeared in the 17th century, with SC- from Lat *scissor* 'tailor', *scindere* 'to cut'.

•  Lat *scindere* may be the model for the SC in *scythe* (< OE *siðe*). Johnson has *sithe* as the preferred form but allows both.

### C *and* K *pronounced /k/ before front vowels*

The letter K was used in Norman Fr to replace a C with the value /k/ before a front vowel. OE had made limited use of K for a similar purpose (e.g. *king*) and the example of K in Norman Fr provided a model for its wider use in ME. As a result, a number of words entered Eng from OFr with the sound /k/ before a front vowel variously spelt with C, K, QU, etc. but increasingly all written with K in ME:

•  OFr *soc* with the suffix -ET changed the C to K for ME *soket*, > ModE *socket*. Similarly *buquet/buket* > *bucket*, *coquille/cokille* > *cockle* 'shellfish', and also *cuckoo, cricket, jacket, pocket, ticket*.

## CH

The Eng value of CH as /tʃ/ originated in OFr and was integrated into Eng after the Norman Conquest. A typical development is Lat *cantare* > OFr *chanter* > ME *chaunte* > *chant*. Other examples are *bachelor, brooch, butcher, chair, chamber, chance, exchequer, franchise, merchant, treachery*.

- The sound /tʃ/, spelt C, was already common in OE before front vowels: *cild* (ModE *child*). Since this OE use of C to spell /tʃ/ entailed some ambiguity, inasmuch as C could also be used for /k/ before front vowels, it is understandable that when Norman Fr offered the digraph CH to represent /tʃ/, it was rapidly adopted for Fr loanwords and native Eng vocabulary alike. The great majority of words of OE origin that are spelt with CH in ModE are attested consistently written with CH from the 13th century onwards (some from the 12th century); the OE C-spelling is scarcely attested after 1100.

### Central Fr CH, Norman Fr C

- Lat C = /k/ before A developed to CH /tʃ/ in Central Fr but in Norman Fr it remained /k/. Some Norman loans entered Eng with CA- soon after the Norman Conquest, while their Central Fr equivalents entered ME with CHA- a century or two later. Sometimes both forms have survived into ModE: *cancel/chancel, cant/chant, catch/chase, cattle/chattel*.
- Word-final CH is slightly different. The doublet *pocket/pouch* shows the usual Norman Fr/Central Fr /k ~ tʃ/ divergence. In several other words, by contrast, ModE final CH (or TCH after a short vowel) derives from Norman Fr, with Central Fr having the sound /s/, spelt S, SS, C or ç: *catch/chase, launch/lance, pinch/pincer*.

### CH pronounced /ʃ/ in ModFr loans

CH with the ModFr sound value /ʃ/ is found in more recent borrowings: *brochure, chalet, champagne, chateau, chef, chic, cliché, moustache, nonchalant*, etc.

### Fr CH anglicized to SH

Sometimes Fr CH has been anglicized as SH:

- The commonest example is Fr *choc, choquer,* borrowed into Eng in the 16th century: competing forms such as *chok, shok, chock, chocke, shocke,* etc. were eventually rejected in favour of *shock.*
- Other examples are *chantez > (sea-)shanty, escarmuche > skirmish, fetiche > fetish, hache > hash, peluche > plush,* etc.


### D

ModE D generally reflects Lat and/or Fr D:

- Word-initially: *danger* (< OFr *dangier* < LLat \**dominiarum*), *develop, different, doctor, dress, during.*
- Medially: *evidence* (< Lat *evidentia*), *immediate, student, tremendous*; and with the prefix AD-, as in *admit.*
  - Lat AD- attached to a stem beginning with D results in Lat and ModE -DD-: *add* (< Lat *addere*), *addiction, address, adduce.* (OFr and ME often wrote such words with single D.)
  - D has been doubled in developments from Fr where there has been a stress shift to the first syllable in ModE: *boudin > podyng > pudding, sodein > sodayn > sudden.*
  - Some words with single medial D (e.g. *hideous, medal, model, study*) were occasionally written with DD in EModE.
- Word-finally: *aid* (< OFr *aide* < LLat *adjuta*), *record, void*; *demand* (< Fr *demander* < Lat *demandare*), *legend, round, second.*
- Occasionally, ModE D derives from Fr T: *carte > card, diamant > diamond, jeu parti > jeopardy.*


### Insertion of D

A D has been added in some words of Franco-Lat derivation, especially after N:

- In some cases, the D had already appeared in OFr, e.g. Lat *pulverem* > OFr *puldre* > *powder*; similarly *meddle, remainder, tender.*
- In other cases, the D originated in Eng: Lat *sonum* > OFr *son* > ME *soun* > *sound*; and similarly *jaundice* < *jalnice, jaunice.*
  - A past participial -ED may have encouraged the eventual fixing in EModE of final D, e.g. *expound* < ME *expoun* (past participle *expouned*); perhaps similarly for *astound,* from *astone.*

## Insertion of true or spurious etymological D

A D was inserted after initial A in a number of words, particularly before J and V, to reflect a real or supposed Lat root with the prefix AD-, although OFr had often dropped the D and borrowings entered ME without it:

- Before J: EModE *ajoine, ajourn, ajudge*, ModE *adjoin, adjourn, adjudge*.
- Before V: ModE *adventure, advertisement, advice, advocate*; compare ModFr *aventure, avertissement, avis, avocet*. EModE also had *aduayle, aduenge* but the D failed to become established, hence ModE *avail, avenge*.
- Non-etymological D is seen in *advance, advantage*. The Lat prefix in these cases was not AD- but AB-, whence OFr A- (e.g. ModFr *avantage*).
- Medieval Lat introduced the D in *admiral*, by analogy with Lat *admirari* 'to wonder at', so creating the form *admiralus* as an alternative to *amiralus* < Arabic *amir-al(-bahr)* 'commander of the (sea)'.

## Loss of D

- Lat *manducare* > Fr *manger* 'to eat' > *manger, mangy, blancmange*.
- Lat *diurnum* 'day-long' > ModFr *jour* 'day', whence Eng *journal, journey*.
- In a few cases D was lost in Eng: *laund* (still used in the 17th century) > *lawn* (= 'grass'); *scand* (still used in the 18th century) > *scan*.

### E

## ModE short E from Fr and Lat

- Lat and/or Fr E > ModE E (often through ME): *cent* (< Lat *centum*), *debt* (< Lat *debitum*), *dress* (< OFr *dresser* < VLat \**directiare*), *direct* (< OFr < Lat *directus*), and also *accept, attention, mental, sex, success*, etc.
- Franco-Lat E from other Lat vowels:
  - Classical Lat Æ > E: *pæne* 'almost' > Eng PEN- as in *peninsula, penultimate*; PRÆ- > PRE- as in *president*.
    - Some words had Æ forms in the 16th–18th centuries, based on the Lat spellings: e.g. *æsteme* (ModE *esteem* < Lat *æstimare*), *ædifice, hæsitation, præsent*.
  - Similarly, Lat Œ > E: Lat *œconomicus* > *economic*.

○ Lat I, A, O > E: *desk* < *discus, letter* < *lit(t)era*; *hotel* < Lat *hospitalis* (via OFr *hostel*); *develop* < Lat *volupare* (via Fr *développer*).

## *Stressed E before R > ER, AR*

- Franco-Lat-derived words with ModE -ER- are *certain* (< OFr *certain* < Lat *certus*), *concern, confer, deter, perfect, person, service*, etc.
  ○ In some cases, ER > AR: *arbour* (< ME *erber* < OFr *erbier* < LLat *herbarium*), *farm* (< OFr *ferme* < Medieval Lat *firma* 'fixed payment'), *marvel, parsley, partridge, parson, quarrel, varnish*.
  ○ In some cases ME or EModE AR spellings reverted to ER: Lat *perfectum* > OFr *parfet* > ME *parfit* > *perfect*, Lat *perfumare* > OFr *parfumer* > ME *parfume* > *perfume*.
  ○ Two ModE relics of those changes are *varsity* ~ *university*, and *varmint* ~ *vermin*.

## *E followed by N or M > A*

Occasionally E > A before N and M: OFr *frenetique* > *frantic* (compare *frenetic*), Lat *exemplum* > ModE *example*, MFr *pensée* > *pansy*.

## *Franco-Lat E or Æ > ModE long E usually spelt E or E–E*

Among Franco-Lat derivations containing long E, usually stressed, are *adhere* (< Fr *adhérer* < Lat *adhærere*), *complete* (< Lat *completus*), *concrete, equal* (< Lat *æqualis*), *extreme, immediate, legal, material, period, previous, recent, secret, series*, and words with the suffix -ESE (< OFr *-eis* < Lat *-ensis*).

- A few of these words had EE/EA spellings in EModE: *compleat/ compleet, extream/extreem*, etc.
- Verbs ending in -CEED/-CEDE derive from Lat -CEDERE or Fr -CÉDER: *exceed, proceed, succeed* but *cede, accede, concede, intercede, precede, recede, secede*. The first ME or EModE forms of all these words were written -CEDE. Forms such as *interceed, preceed, recead/receed*, found mainly in EModE, did not prevail.
- The two spellings *discrete/discreet* (< Lat *discretus*) came to be used for separate meanings.
- Spellings were sometimes altered in EModE to match Lat spelling: thus, around the 16th century, *adhære, æqual, prævious* for *adhere, equal, previous*.

## Franco-Lat E > ModE EA

EA typically represents the long E sound /iː/ in ModE; it was commonly pronounced /ɛː/ in EModE. The EA spelling is found in many words of Franco-Lat derivation: Lat *bestia* > OFr *beste* > ME *beste* > *beast*; Lat *impedicare* > OFr *empechier* > ME *empeche* > *impeach*.

- ModE spellings with EA are often first attested in the 16th century: *appeal* (earlier *apeel, apele*), *beak* (earlier *bek, beke, beeke*), *cease, conceal, cream, decease, feast*, etc. *Seal* (= 'closure'), on the other hand, appeared in the 13th century.
- ME often saw alternative forms, for instance with EE as in *beest* (although in general EE and EA had different pronunciations; see pp. 176–7).

In a few cases, Franco-Lat E has led to ModE EA = /ɛ/. This resulted from vowel length variation in the 16th and 17th centuries, the EA spelling indicating a former long value while the pronunciation eventually settled on the short value: *measure* (< OFr/ANorm *mesure* < Lat *mensura*), *endeavour, jealous* (compare *zealous*), *treachery, treasure*; also *pearl, rehearse, search* now with /ɜː/.

## Franco-Lat E > ModE EE

In ModE, EE generally has the same /iː/ value as long E, E–E and EA, but in ME it generally represented /eː/. However, overlap in spelling was frequent (e.g. *complete* saw EModE alternatives *compleat/compleet*), and confusion has persisted to the present day: e.g. *speak/speech* < ME *speke/speche*. Similar E+consonant+E patterns changing to EE+consonant are *chere* > *cheer, pele* > *peel, splene* > *spleen*.

## Suffix -EE

The suffix -EE is mostly derived, directly or indirectly, from the Fr past participle ending -É: *absentee, employee, escapee, referee, trainee*. This -EE suffix first arose in ME legal language, but today's most common forms nearly all date from EModE or later (e.g. *trustee* in the 17th century, *detainee* in the 20th).

- In ME, the -EE ending was not yet established, early forms often being first spelt -E, some being subsequently anglicized with Y (in EModE *committee* had endings ranging across -E, -EE, -IE, -EY, -Y); -EE forms introduced later give such doublets as *entry/entree, levy/levee, medley/melee*.

- Some -EE words that have entered Eng in the past 200 years keep the Fr acute accent and pronunciation: e.g. *matinée, soirée*. There is often uncertainty about how Frenchified the spelling should be: *negligee/ negligée/negligé, melee/mêlée, puree/purée*. (See also p. 113.)

## Franco-Lat E > ModE EI

The digraph EI from Franco-Lat E has two main values: /eɪ/ as in *vein*, /iː/ as in *deceit*. There was a great deal of overlap in both pronunciation and spelling between AI, AY, EI and EY in ME and EModE, when a common pronunciation /eɪ/ (or possibly /aɪ/) may be assumed. Many words deriving from an E-base with both EI/EY and AI/AY spellings in EModE eventually became established with AI in ModE (e.g. Lat *preciare* > *preyse/ prayse* > *praise*); a much smaller number of words have EI: Lat *regnare* > OFr *regne* > *reign/raign* > *reign*, and similarly *rein, veil, vein, heir*.

- The verbs *conceive, deceive, perceive, receive* and the related nouns *conceit, deceit, receipt* derive from classical Lat forms -CIPERE for the verb, -CEPTUM for the noun. OFr had verb forms such as -CEVEIR, -CEIVRE, which in ME and EModE saw numerous variations, including -CEVE, -CEAVE, -CEIVE, -CIEVE, -SAVE, -SAIVE (the last two showing the older /eɪ/ pronunciation). The -CEIVE spellings were generally established by the 17th century, by which time the pronunciation was changing to modern /iː/.

## Franco-Lat E > IE

The spelling rule 'I before E except after C' testifies to the ModE use of the IE digraph to represent the same /iː/ sound as EI: *relieve* but *receive*. A typical pattern is Lat *brevem* > OFr *bref* > ME *bref* > *brief*, where the I was first written in Eng in the 16th century, though it occurred earlier as an OFr variant. Other words with a similar development are *achieve, chief, fierce, grief/grieve, niece, piece, relief/relieve, retrieve, siege*, all of which were commonly written without I until the 16th century. The simple ME E spelling represented a close /eː/, but by 1500 that value had generally changed to the /iː/ of ModE.

## EO for long and short E

The OE digraph EO typically developed into ModE EE: *deop* > *deep*. It was occasionally adopted by ANorm scribes,[6] specifically, it has been suggested by Jespersen,[7] to represent the then variously spelt vowel corresponding to the EU of ModFr *peuple, jeu parti*, so giving ModE *people, jeopardy* (the pronunciations with long and short E respectively arose in the EModE period). However, the development is uncertain:

- The form *peple* was in use from the 13th to the 16th centuries, but *people* first in the 15th.
- The word *leopard* is attested throughout the ME period with simple A, E, I, U, and Y spellings (e.g. *lepard*) as well as intermittently with EO, the EO spelling apparently based on the Lat spelling (compare Lat *leo* 'lion').

## *Fr -E/-EE/-IE > ModE -EY and -Y*

In ME and EModE there were many possible spellings for the -EY/-Y ending, with, for instance ModE *journey* attested between the 13th and 16th centuries with the endings -AY, -AYE, -E, -EE, -EIE, -EY, -EYE, -IE, -Y.

- A substantial group of ModE words have spellings ending in -EY derived from OFr -EE, often related to a participle spelt with A in Lat: e.g. Lat *caminata* > OFr *cheminee* > ME *chimeney* > *chimney*; similarly *alley, attorney, covey, journey, medley, valley, volley*. ModE also has words of parallel development whose ending has been reduced to -Y: *army, country, destiny, embassy, entry, jelly, puppy*, etc. Several words from these groups had alternative ME and EModE spellings, e.g. *contray*.
- Nouns (mainly abstract) with -Y endings are from Fr -E: e.g. Lat *qualitatem* > OFr *qualite* > ME *qualite* > *quality*; and similarly *ability, activity, authority, city, community, county, difficulty, duty, facility, opportunity*, etc. The -E spelling was by the 15th century often extended to -EE (*qualitee*); by the 16th century the endings -IE, -YE were common, but by the early 17th century ModE the ending -Y (*quality*) was generally established.
  - Words of the *quality* type do not normally show ME and EModE alternative forms with -AY or -EY.
- A few -EY words stem from a Fr -IE ending, e.g. *comfrey, curts(e)y, pulley, stor(e)y*.
- A commonly occurring development originated in Lat -IA and led via Fr -IE to ModE -Y: Lat *phantasia* > OFr *fantasie* > ME *fantasye* > *fantasy*.

○ Although words of the *fantasy* type have the same ending as *country*, etc., in ModE, their EModE alternative forms are distinct, typically ending in -IE, -YE, but not -AY, -EY.

## *ModFr loans with* E + *accent*

- A number of modern Fr loans optionally retain the Fr accent (*élan, élite, crème, fête*), but may anglicize pronunciation and/or spelling (e.g. *crêpe* /kreɪp/ ~ /krɛp/, *crape* /kreɪp/).

## *Franco-Lat initial* DE-/DES-/DI(S)- *variations in Eng*

The Lat prefixes DE- and DI(S)- both suggested negativity, DE- originally implying 'down' and DI(S)- 'apart'; in compounds, their meanings readily overlap. As their use developed through Fr and into Eng, some of their forms merged and separated again, further blurring the distinction between them:

- In Lat DIS- lost its S before various consonants, giving rise to ModE *difficult, digest, dilute, diminish, direct, divert, divide, divorce.*
- OFr typically converted Lat DIS- to DES-. ME often adopted Fr forms with DES-, but in almost every case the prefix has since been re-Latinized to DIS- even when the stem to which it is attached clearly derives from the Fr rather than the Lat form: e.g. Lat *displicare* > OFr *despleier* > ME *desplay/dysplay* > *display*, OFr *desloger* > *deslodge/dyslodge* > *dislodge*.

## *Franco-Lat* EN-/IN-, EM-/IM- *in Eng*

Variations similar to the above are seen between the prefixes IN- (typically of Lat origin) and EN- (as in Fr), which become IM-/EM- before B (*imbibe, embroil*), M (*immune*), P (*empower, impotent*); EModE, however, sometimes had N in these positions too (e.g. *enboss, inpression*). The variability of these prefixes is seen in the alternation of EN- in *enforce* with IN- in *reinforce*.

- In both ME and ModE there has been fluctuation in spelling between the Lat I and Fr E (e.g. ME and/or EModE *imbrace, ingen* 'engine', *intire, emprove, enclude*), with occasional further variation using A (e.g. *anpyre* for *empire*, and the development Lat *inungere* > *enoint* > *enoynt*

> *anoint*). Typical developments of the EN-/IN-, EM-/IM- variations may be seen in Lat *increscere* > OFr *encreistre* > ME *encrese/increse* > *increase* where ModE has reverted to Lat IN- from ME EN-, and conversely Lat *implicare* > *employer* > *employ/imploy* > *employ*, where ModE preserves the Fr E.

  ○ Occasionally the two spellings have allowed a distinction of meaning to arise: in British English at least, *ensure* 'make certain' but *insure* 'take out insurance on'.

  ○ In some cases where British spelling prefers EN-/EM-, many American dictionaries offer IN-/IM- as an alternative: *imbed*, *imbitter*, *inclose*, *incumber*, etc.

- In the case of INTER-/ENTER- 'among, between', where again a Lat IN- form often yielded EN- in Fr and originally also in Eng, almost all ME ENTRE-/ENTER- forms have reverted to Lat INTER- in ModE (e.g. EModE *enterest*, ModE *interest*); exceptions are *enterprise* and *entertain*.

## *Sources of Eng -EL/-LE*

Several hundred words spell their final syllable with -LE (e.g. *bubble*, *cycle*, *idle*, *middle*, *table*), nearly a hundred with -EL (e.g. *angel*, *camel*, *cancel*, *laurel*, *morsel*, *panel*, *travel*), some with both (*duffel/duffle*, *mantel/mantle*).

- In most words now ending in -EL, that syllable formerly carried the main stress, whereas ModE -LE usually derives from historically unstressed syllables. The tendency in EModE to shift the stress to the first syllable of the -EL words has resulted in the two spelling patterns merging with regard to sound, so that today there is no clear basis for -EL/-LE to be distinguished.
- The commonest examples of both endings derive from OFr: e.g. *people*, *level* (though many words, especially with -LE, are of OE or other Germanic origin, e.g. *little*, *middle*).
- The development of *people* offers a good paradigm for many words ending in -LE: Lat *populum* > OFr *poeple* > ME *peple* > *people*. The final syllable of *people* and similar words was commonly spelt in ME with a wide variety of vowel letters, as -EL, -IL, -UL, -YL, etc. In EModE, printers showed a growing tendency to prefer the Fr -LE spelling in many words of both Franco-Lat and OE descent.
- Most ModE -LE spellings ultimately derive from Lat -IL-, -OL-, -UL-, fewer from -AL-, -EL-:

- ○ VLat *battalia* > *battle* by the 16th century, though *battel* was found up into the 19th; Lat *capitalem* > OFr *catel* > ModE *cattle* (another development, from Central rather than Norman Fr, produced *chattel*).
- ○ EModE reversed a Lat -EL- to -LE in three words where the Lat -EL- had already passed into OE: Lat *castellum* > OE *castel* > *castle*; similarly *candle*, *mantle*.
- ○ *Mettle* originated as an EModE spelling variant of *metal*, with the separate sense of *mettle* encouraging the differentiation of spelling, which became established in the 19th century.
- ○ *Principal* < Lat *principalem*; *principle* < Lat *principium*, OFr *principe*, with the L inserted in ME.
- ○ A large number of -LE words arose from an unstressed Lat -IL- in adjectival forms: *able* (< Lat *habilem*), *gentle*, *humble*, *noble*, *possible*, etc. In many cases a form with -LE already existed in OFr before the word entered Eng (e.g. *noble*, *possible*), but occasionally the -LE is an anglicization of a Fr -IL-/-ILLE ending: *gentle* < *gentil*, *myrtle* < *myrtille*.
- ○ *Bottle* arose from OFr *bouteille*, < Lat *boticulam*, leading to ME forms like *botel* and, with the stress shifted from the second to the first syllable, EModE *bottle*.
- ○ With -LE from Graeco-Lat -OL-: *apostle*, *epistle*, *parable* (compare cognate *apostolic*, *epistolary*, *parabola*).
- ○ Many Fr-derived -LE endings originated in Lat -UL- which often survives in a cognate ModE form: *angle/angular*, *article/articulate*, *circle/circular*, *constable/constabulary*, *miracle/miraculous*, *people/population*, *table/tabular*, etc.
- ○ In some cases Lat had no intervening vowel: ModE *ample*, *double*, *example*, etc. < Lat *amplus*, *duplus*, *exemplum*, etc.
- ○ In *chronicle*, *participle*, *syllable*, etc., the L first appeared in Norman Fr or Central Fr.
- Unlike words now spelt with -LE, few ModE -EL spellings vacillated between the two endings in ME.
  - ○ Some ModE -EL endings originated in Lat -AL which was modified to -AIL in OFr and saw ME variations such as -ALE, -AYL, -AYLLE, as well as forms with E such as -EIL, -EYL, -ELL, -ELLE, -ELE, and eventually unstressed ModE -EL. Examples (with their Lat sources) are *channel* (< *canalis*), *fuel* (< *focalia*), *minstrel* (< *ministerialis*), *vowel* (< *vocalis*). *Travel* and related *travail* (< Lat *trepaliare*) saw all the above endings in ME, and others.

- ○ Short stressed -ELL- in Lat and (often) OFr led typically to final -ELL in ME (with variants -ELE, -ELLE, and others) and then to unstressed -EL in ModE: Lat *cap(p)ella* > OFr *chapele* > ME *chapel* (also *chapell/chapelle/chapaile/chapyll*) > *chapel*, and similarly *bowel*, *chisel*, *damsel*, *duel*, *level*, etc.
- ○ A third group (*barrel*, *counsel*, etc.) originated in stressed Lat -IL- or -ILL- (as in *barillum*, *consilium*, etc.). They show no consistency in ME: *barrel* was sometimes *barylle* and even *barayl*; *counsel* was widely conflated with *council* and commonly spelt with -AIL, -EIL, etc.

## Sources of Eng final -EN

- Some words have -EN unchanged from Lat: *abdomen*, *gluten*, *omen*, *pollen*, *semen*, *specimen*, *stamen*, etc.
- Another group of Franco-Lat derivatives has -EN typically reduced from a long vowel spelt -EYN, -AYN in ME and deriving from Fr and Lat forms based on A, e.g. Lat *subitaneum* > OFr *soudain* > ME *sudayne* > *sudden*.

## Sources of -ENT, -ENCE, -ENCY

The unstressed word-endings -ENT, -ENCE, -ENCY often overlap with the endings -ANT, -ANCE, -ANCY (see p. 88).

## Sources of Eng final -ER

Unstressed -ER has a number of sources in Fr- and/or Lat-derived words:

- Final -ER is seen from Lat onwards in *cancer*, *character*, *alter*, *consider*.
- The -ER may have arisen by reversal of Fr -RE, as in *number*, *order*, *letter*, *chapter*, *offer*, *member*, etc. (These words were typically written with final -RE in ME, but in EModE switched increasingly to -ER.)
- The -ER may have originated as -ER in Fr, in many cases with variation at some point to -IER. The spelling -IER was sometimes used in ME where ModE writes -ER: occasionally in *litter*, *manner*, *quarter*, somewhat more often with *matter*, *officer*.
- The -ER may have developed from Lat -ATOR through MFr/ME -OUR to ModE -ER: e.g. Lat *portator* > OFr *porteour* > ME *portour* > ModE *porter*. Similar histories underlie *controller*, *counter*, *recorder*, *turner*, and partially also *waiter* (< OFr *waitour*).

110

## *Fr-derived* -ERY

- In ModE words, such as *battery, grocery, imagery, nursery, robbery, scenery,* the ending -ERY has a variety of sources. Some -ERY words derive from Lat or Graeco-Lat, such as words in which Eng -ERY derives from Lat -ERIA or -ERIUM: e.g. Lat *miseria* > OFr/ME *miserie* > *misery*; Lat *mysterium* > OFr *misterie* > ME *misterye* > *mystery*; other examples are *adultery, artery, cemetery, dysentery, monastery, periphery, presbytery.* Later formations are *confectionery, slavery.*
- ME and EModE could vary the spelling considerably: for instance, *mystery* is attested as *mystyrie, mistirie, mistrie,* and *treachery* as *trechory, trechury, trecchry.* The E-less form has sometimes become standard in ModE (e.g. *ministry*; see also below, pp. 115, 126).

## *Franco-Lat* -ESS

The feminine -ESS suffix is of Fr (-ESSE), ultimately Lat (-ISSA), origin: *actress, countess, duchess, goddess,* etc.

## *Fr-derived* -ET, -ETTE

- In many words, the ending -ET derives from the Fr diminutive suffix -ETTE carrying the main stress (e.g. *tablet* < Fr *tablette*). This stress pattern is suggested by frequent EModE spellings with -ETT, -ETTE (e.g. *pockett, pockette*), but as with many other words derived from Fr, the stress later moved to the beginning of the word and the ending was reduced to unstressed -ET: *basket, blanket, bracket, bucket, budget, bullet,* etc.
  - With similar EModE forms ending in stressed -ETT, -ETTE, but ultimately deriving from a Fr source ending in -ET, are *banquet, bonnet, brisket, claret, closet, cornet, corset, cricket,* etc.
- Words ending in -ET in ModF (such as *ballet, beret, bidet, bouquet, buffet, cabaret*) have silent T, a feature increasingly retained in ModE for loans from the 18th century onwards.
  - *Ballet* is first attested as *ballette* with final syllable stress in the 17th century, but the Fr form *ballet* now established.
  - Early anglicized (16th and 17th centuries) as *vallet* or *valett,* ModE *valet* has first-syllable stress and final T optionally silent.
- A couple of dozen words are usually written with Fr -ETTE: *brunette, cassette, etiquette, omelette, palette, roulette, serviette, silhouette.* Most are

direct loans from Fr, but the suffix can also be added to non-Fr words, e.g. *kitchenette, leatherette.*

○ The earliest occurrences of such words in Eng sometimes showed some anglicization (e.g. 17th and 18th-century *omelet, roulet*), but the Fr ending subsequently became established. A few of these words may reduce the ending to -ET in American Eng (*cigaret, epaulet, omelet*).

## Final silent E

In words of Franco-Lat derivation, final silent E often represents the vestige of a Lat word-ending that was reduced to [ə] in OFr. Sometimes pronounced in ME (variably in Chaucer), it had fallen silent before the 16th century, while it came to indicate some other feature of pronunciation, such as the value of a preceding vowel or consonant (compare *note/not, tense/tens*).

- Fr- and/or Lat-derived final silent E often occurs after C and G: *lace, chance, force, office*, etc.; *age, change, college, huge, large*, etc.
- Lat endings reduced to ModE E are:
    ○ -A: e.g. *note* (< Lat *nota*), *page* (< Lat *pagina*) and similarly *cause, couple, culture, figure, nature.*
        ▪ While, for example, the E of *note* was pronounced in OFr, alternative spellings such as *not, noot, noat* show it to be silent in ME and EModE.
    ○ -(I)UM: *centrum* > *centre, exercitium* > *exercise, votum* > *vote* and in a number of words ending in -CE/-GE (e.g. *college, price, service, silence, space*).
    ○ -EM: *criminem* > *crime, decadem* > *decade* along with various words ending in -CE (e.g. *peace, voice*).
    ○ -UM: Lat *casum* > OFr *cas* > ME *caas/cais* > *case*; the ending was typically lost altogether in Fr, and the -E acquired in Eng.
- In *despise, exercise, rinse*, final -SE arose from Fr -CE; but final -SE in ModE often replicates -SE in OFr and/or ModF: *ease* (OFr/ModFr *aise*), *excuse, expense, immense, noise, please, refuse, response, suppose, surprise, use.*
    ○ Particularly common in British spelling is the suffix -ISE, as in *realise*, from the Fr verb ending -ISER, as in *réaliser* (the z of the alternative -IZE derives from Lat and ultimately Gr).

112

○ In other cases silent final E after S originated in Eng, as in Lat *casus* > OFr *cas* > ME *caas/cais* > *case*; and similarly *base* (adjective), *compromise, paradise, close* (adjective). Source words have no final E in Fr and the E in ModE indicates a preceding long vowel or diphthong or, after another consonant, a voiceless value for the S (e.g. contrasting *tense* with *tens*); similarly, earlier Fr-style spellings without E give way to ModE -SE in *cours* > *course*, *puls* > *pulse*, *sens* > *sense*, etc.

## Final silent -E after E, I, O

- In a few modern loans the second E indcates a feminine noun or adjective, as in the distinction *fiancé/fiancée*; other examples of a silent E (here given, as commonly in Eng, without an acute accent) are: *allee* (Fr *allée*), *entree, levee, lycee, matinee, melee, negligee, puree*. (See also pp. 104–5.)
- Final -IE is found in modern Fr loans: *folie*, contrasting with Eng *folly*, and similarly in *bonhomie, bourgeoisie, calorie, genie, lingerie, menagerie, patisserie, prairie, reverie, sortie*.
- With a final -OE, only *hoe* derives from Fr (< OFr *houe*).

## Ambiguity of final silent E after U

The great majority of words ending in -UE derive from Fr:

- In nearly two-thirds of the words concerned, the final -UE is silent, especially after G and QU: *fatigue, unique*.
- The others typically pronounce the -UE as /uː/ (e.g. *blue*) or /juː/ (e.g. *value*). This pattern has been extended to *clue, hue, rue, true* of OE origin (see p. 62).
  ○ The words *ague, argue* belong to this sound pattern despite the preceding G (contrast *ague/vague, argue/morgue*).
- In some cases the E may indicate a typically Eng quality in the preceding long vowel or diphthong: *opaque* (compare *make*), *plague, vague*, etc. In other cases, the Fr value of the preceding vowel has persisted: *plaque* (contrast *opaque*), *antique* (compare *bike*), *boutique, clique, fatigue, intrigue*, etc.
  ○ The anomalous form *tongue* (OE and ME *tunge*) appears to have -UE to show the G was not palatalized, as in ModE *lunge*, and to distinguish *tongues* from *tongs*.

- A group of words ultimately of Gr origin, which are spelt with final -OGUE in Fr and in British convention, were sometimes spelt with just final -OG in ME or EModE (e.g. *catalog, prolog*), as they are in current American Eng.

## Final consonant plus pronounced -E

In ModE there are a small number of words from Lat in which the final E is fully pronounced: *aborigine, pace* 'deferring to', *recipe, simile, vice* 'in place of' (/ˈvaɪsiː/, but also /vaɪs/).

## Loss of final E

A large number of words first entered Eng with a Fr form ending in -E, which in the course of time ceased to be written.

- Among words borrowed from Fr forms with final E and in most cases often written with E in ME and/or EModE are *act, aid, alarm, bank, bomb, branch, cabin, campaign, class, cup, debt, drug, guard, gulf, herb, hour, lamp, merit, model, oil, parish, risk, stuff, tax, touch, triumph.*
- Originating in Gr but reaching Eng via Fr, and often written with final E in the early centuries of their use in Eng (ranging from ME to as late as the 19th century), are *acrobat, comet, democrat, diplomat, epitaph, magnet, metaphor, method, myth, nymph, oxygen, paradox, parallel, period, planet, problem, symbol, syntax, system.*
- Numerous words ending in ModE -ER formerly had final -ERE (e.g. *manere, matere* for ModE *manner, matter*). So strong was the tendency to write final -RE in EModE that even words lacking -E in Fr were often written with it, e.g. Fr *papier*, EModE *papire*, ModE *paper*; similarly *dinere, powere*.

## Lost initial E

A widespread pattern involves the loss, or absence, of initial E from Lat words beginning either with SC-, SP-, ST- or with EXC-, EXP-, EXT-. As these two patterns developed from Lat (or other sources) through OFr and/or Spanish, their spellings merged: SC-, SP-, ST- acquired an initial E to become ESC-, ESP-, EST-, while initial EX- was simplified to ES-, so also producing ESC-, ESP-, EST- (these examples are marked by ⁺ below). The effects on Eng are varied:

- In a few cases the initial E has survived into ModE: *eschew,* ⁺*escort,* ⁺*esplanade.*
- More often, a word with initial E co-exists with a cognate word that has lost it: ⁺*escape/scapegoat, escalope/scallop, escarpment/scarp, especial/ special, espy/spy, espouse/spouse, estate/state,* ⁺*estranged/strange.* Among these, the form without E sometimes derives more directly from the original Lat (e.g. *status > state*), while the E-form derives from Fr (OFr *estat > estate*). In other cases, the E was written in ME or EModE, but is no longer current, thus *escallop > scallop.*
- In the largest number of cases the E has never or only rarely been attested in Eng, though the words concerned clearly derive from E-forms in OFr or ANorm: ⁺*scaffold* (< OFr *eschafalt*), ⁺*scald* (< OFr *eschalder*), *spine* (< OFr *espine*), *stage* (< OFr *estage*), *stew* (< OFr *estuve*), *study* (< OFr *estudie*). *Squire* strictly belongs with these, *esquire* being a later loan from Fr.

### *Loss of medial* E

- A substantial number of words ending in -ERIE in Fr have equivalents in ModE ending in -RY with no preceding E:
  - Instances of an original -ERY with the E lost at some stage between OFr and ModE are: *ancestry, bigotry, carpentry, chivalry, foundry, forestry, gallantry, hostelry,* etc.
  - Sometimes, as with OFr *ribaulderie,* ModE *ribaldry,* the E is not attested at all in Eng.
  - In other cases, like *cavalry* from Fr *cavalerie,* forms with -ERY were common up into the 17th century; *jewellery* and *jewelry* are current in 20th-century BrE and AmE respectively.
- Sometimes an unstressed medial E was lost from the stem of a word: *canvas, chestnut, constable, curts(e)y, empress, enmity, fortress,* etc. from earlier *canevas, chesten, conestable, cortesie* (compare *courtesy*), *emperess, enemity, forteresse,* etc.

### *Lat* EL *> ModFr/ModE* EAU

The ModFr trigraph EAU has entered Eng in modern loans such as *beau* (ModFr/OFr *beau* < earlier OFr *bel* < Lat *bellus*), *bureau, chateau/ château, gateau/gâteau, plateau, tableau.* Also in older loans: *beauty* < OFr *beaute* (< Lat *bellus* beautiful).

## F

### *Franco-Lat initial and medial* F > *ModE* F

- Word-initially: e.g. *face, family, fine, flavour, flour/flower, fluid, force, fragment, front, frustrate, future*.
  - OE *fann* (ModE *fan*) < Lat *vannus* (OE did not have [v] in initial position).
- In medial position, mostly in stems beginning with F after a prefix or other element (*inferior* is one exception): *conform, deform*, etc.; *comfort, infant, manifest, profound, refrigerator, surface*.
  - Lat *facere* 'to do, make' has various derivatives: *manufacture, perfect, scientific*; also Fr-derived forms: *affair, benefit, defeat, signify*.
  - Other Lat F-stems are -FEND, -FER, -FESS, -FIDE, -FIL(E), -FIN(E), -FIRM, -FLAT(E), -FLECT, -FLICT, -FLU-, -FUGE, -FUM(E), -FUS(E).

### *Franco-Lat final* F

Final single F does not arise in direct Lat derivations, but is seen in certain Fr loans. The following were mostly acquired in ME: *beef, brief, chief, grief, gulf, mischief, proof, relief, scarf, serf, waif*; also *safe, strife* with -E marking a preceding diphthong.

  - ModFr loans with final F are *aperitif, chef, massif, motif*.

### *Double* F

- Unlike ModFr loans with final -IF (*motif*, etc.), older loans have -IFF in ModE: *bailiff, mastiff, plaintiff, pontiff*.
- Some modern loans have ModFr medial FF: *bouffant, buffet* (= 'meal'), *chauffeur, chiffon, coiffure, gaffe, soufflé*.
- Older loans may have had single medial F in both Fr and Eng, but ModE now writes FF: *muffle, raffle, ruffian, saffron, scaffold, traffic*.
- A few ModE words with single F were sometimes written with FF in EModE: *deffence, deffend, reffuge*.
- *Coffer* and *coffin* (< Lat *cophinus*) were commonly spelt with single or double F in OFr and ME; EModE saw learned variants with PH. Perhaps the classical and biblical connotations of *prophet* caused the PH form to prevail over such EModE alternatives as *proffet, proffit*.

116

## Double F *by assimilation*

Lat prefixes AD-, DIS-, EX-, OB-, SUB- change their final consonant to F before stems beginning with F, producing an -FF- that persists from Lat into Eng: e.g. *affect, afflict, differ, difficult, effect, efficient, offend, offer, suffer, suffice.*

# G

## Initial and medial G = /g/

Examples of G = /g/ from Lat and/or Fr G are *neglect* (< Lat *neglegere*), *agree* (< OFr *agreer* < LLat *aggratare*), and also *argue, disgust, fragment, gradual, ignore, magnificent, regular, single, vulgar.*

- Some Fr-derived words are of Germanic origin: *gain, garage, gay, engage,* and (with Lat prefix RE-) *regard, regret.*
- In a few words, the Normans brought forms with /g/ into Eng: ModE *gallon, gammon, garden, garter, gauge* (compare ModFr *jambon, jardin,* etc. from Central Fr).
- Lat C and Q > /g/ in Lat *credentare* > OFr *greanter/granter* > ME *graunt* > *grant, acuta* > *agu* > *ague, acrem* > *aigre* > *eager, draco* > *dragon, aquila* > *aigle* > *eagle.*
- Fr C > ModE G: *flacon* > *flagon, sucre* > *sugar.*

## Final G = /g/

Word-final /g/ is rare in words of Franco-Lat origin: *drug* < Fr *drogue, fig* < *figue* < VLat *fica;* also *wig* from *periwig* < *peruke* < MFr *perruque.*

- Words ending in -OGUE in BrE, such as *dialogue* (< Lat *dialogus*, OFr/ME *dialoge*), *catalogue, monologue,* are commonly written with final -OG (*dialog,* etc.) in American usage.

## Initial and medial G = /dʒ/

- Word-initially: *general* (< OFr *general* < Lat *generalis*), *genius, gentle, germ, gesture.*
- Medially: *dungeon* (< OFr *donjon*), *pageant* (< ANorm *pagin/pagent*), *agitate, eligible, imagine, legend, magistrate, origin, regiment, region, tangible.*

117

- ○ Most examples with GY are ultimately of Gr origin: *gymnasium, gyration, energy, strategy*; also words formed with -LOGY (e.g. *technology*).
- In some words of Fr origin, the G arose from the assimilation of a consonant and a following /j/ during the development to OFr: e.g. Lat *aetaticum* > OFr *edage* > ME *eage/aage* > *age*; Lat *sedicum* > OFr *sege* > *siege*. Similarly Lat *bullicare* > *budge*, Lat *cambiare* > *change*, Lat *caveam* > *cage*, Lat *dominionem* > *dungeon*, Lat *fabricare* > *forge*, Lat *servientem* > *sergeant*.

## Final G = /dʒ/

Since the palatalized value of G depends on a following front vowel, it cannot occur word-finally. The ending -GE produces the effect of a final palatalized G:

- This -GE may arise from the reduction of Lat word-endings to Fr -E: *collegium* > *college* and similarly *refuge, vestige*; *spongia* > *sponge* (ModFr *éponge*).
- Lat verbs ending in -GERE gave rise to *indulge, (sub)merge, surge, urge, verge*.

### GG

- Doubling of G occurs in Lat when the prefixes AD- or SUB- are assimilated to a stem beginning with G; GG is seen in ModE derivatives: *aggravate, aggregate, aggression, suggest*.
  - ○ Forms with single G (e.g. *agrauate, agregate*) were quite frequent in EModE.
- A few words spelt with medial single G in Fr were borrowed into ME. As happened with the medial consonant of numerous premodern disyllabic loans, the G was doubled in EModE to reflect the shift of the Eng stress from the second syllable to the first syllable: *baggage, bugger, faggot, haggard, juggle, nigger* (compare ModFr *bagage, bougre, fagot*, etc.).
  - ○ EModE saw other forms of the GG type (e.g. *flaggon, suggar*) which have not become standard.

### DG

The digraph DG begins to appear, especially in monosyllables, in ME and more often in EModE, in words of both Germanic and Franco-Lat origin. The latter often retained the Fr single G (e.g. *juge*) through ME, until they adopted the -DG- pattern (*judge*) in EModE. A following E (as in *judge*) was sometimes omitted in EModE (*judg*).

○ *Alledge, pidgeon* were common up to the 19th century, but failed to become standard.

GH

• GH is chiefly associated with words of OE or other Germanic derivation, but its popularity in EModE infected vocabulary of Franco-Lat derivation by analogy: e.g. *delite > delight* by analogy with Germanic *light, distract > distraught, inveie > inveigh*.
  ○ *Sprightly* is the adjectival form of *spright* which itself is a spelling variant (by analogy with GH forms like *right, sight*) of the more usual *sprite* < Fr *esprit* < Lat *spiritus*.
  ○ *Haughty* derives from Fr *haut* 'high'; in EModE it had alternative forms such as *hautie* and *haltie*.
  ○ *Caught* results from the conflation of the OE verb *læccen* 'grasp' and ANorm-derived *cacche(n)*; the past tense *læhte/lahte* offered a model for ME *cahte*.

GU

• Initial GU arose in Fr when OFr altered an originally Germanic initial /w/ to /gw/. Germanic cognates spelt with initial W sometimes occurred in OE, but those that survive into ModE arose more often as a Norman variant on GU,[8] forming ModE doublets: *ward/guard, warranty/guarantee, wile/guile,* -WISE (as in 'clockwise')/*guise* (see also p. 69). Before perhaps the end of the 12th century, this /gw/ became /g/;[9] as the U fell silent, it was omitted in Fr spelling before A (thus ModFr *garde, garantie*) but retained before E, I (ModFr *guide, guêpe* 'wasp'). In ME these words were commonly written without U regardless of the following vowel: *garde, gide, gile, gise*. It was not until EModE that texts began regularly marking the /g/ value of G with a following U (compare the use of H for the same purpose in forms like *gherle* 'girl', *ghess* 'guess', *ghoos* 'goose'; see p. 45). From around the 16th century U was increasingly restored after G: thus *guard* (also *reguard*, though this form did not become standard), *guide, guile, (dis-)guise*, and by extension certain Scandinavian-type words such as *guess* (ME *gessen*), *guest*.

119

- In some other cases GU originated in Lat where the U had the value /w/ which ModE usually retains: *distinguish, languid, languish.* ME vacillated between forms, writing *langage,* for instance, as well as *language.*
- Numerous words ending in -GUE with silent -UE have entered Eng from Fr. The U indicates a preceding velar G before the otherwise palatalizing E, but as ME and to some extent EModE had not yet adopted this diacritic use of U, we find spellings such as *fuge, plage, vage, voge* (ModE *fugue, plague, vague, vogue*), with variants including *plaage/plag.* Similarly *colleague, league* had EModE variants without U (e.g. *college, leag*).
  - *Renege* had earlier forms with final -GUE.

### GN

The G of the Lat string GN is silent in some words that have been influenced by Fr (e.g. *sign*). The ModFr value /ɲ/ for GN is a 17th-century development: prior to this, Fr *signe* was simply pronounced /siːn/, and was adopted with silent G in Eng (ME and EModE forms without G, e.g. *syne,* are attested).

- *Deign* and *reign* have a similar development, with GN in Lat *dignare, regnare* and ModFr *daigner, régner,* and with various ME and EModE forms without G (one of which survives in *disdain*).
- Other Eng words have an equivalent GN in Fr, but not in Lat: Lat *campania* 'expanse of open country' > ModFr *campagne* (via Italian) and, by a separate development, *Champagne*; whence ModE *campaign, champagne.*
- ME had a few forms with G that have not survived into ModE, e.g. *capitaign, certaigne.*
- Why G should have been retained in *foreign, sovereign* from among various EModE alternatives is unclear; neither has G in its VLat (\**foranus,* \**superanus*) or Fr (*forain, souverain*) antecedent.

### GM

Words ending in GM (with silent G) are ultimately of Graeco-Lat origin: *diaphragm, paradigm, phlegm.* These three all end in -GMA in Lat and -GME in Fr, and had various forms in ME and EModE, e.g. *diafragma, paradigme, fleum.*

## Lost G

In various words Lat G was lost during its passage through Fr: *entire* (ModFr *entier*) < Lat *integrum*; *flail* < Lat *flagellum*; *frail* < Lat *fragilis*; *rule* < Lat *regula*; similarly *loyal, royal* < Lat *legalis, regalis*; *ally, rely* < *ligare* 'to tie'; *deny* < *negare* (compare *negate*).

## H

Apart from its use in digraphs such as GH and PH, the letter H generally occurs only before vowels, and generally at the beginning of words. It generally has the sound value /h/ in ModE though it may be silent in words of Franco-Lat origin: *habit, history, honest, hospital, hotel, hour, human*. (It is, of course, found silent in final position in the written forms of exclamations such as *oh* and *ah*, and in words borrowed from other languages, such as *shah* (< Persian) or *cheetah* (< Hindi), which will be discussed in Chapter 8.)

## Medial H

- Non-initial Franco-Lat H occurs most often after a prefix: *inhuman, dehumanize, exhale, inhalation, coherent, adhesive*, etc.
- Occasionally an H occurred between vowels in the middle of a word or word-root in Lat, e.g. *vehere* 'to carry', *vehementem* 'impetuous', *nihil* 'nothing' (whence ModE *vehicle, vehement, annihilate*).

## Loss of /h/

The /h/-value was lost from Lat in the early centuries CE. H generally remained silent in successor languages such as Fr, and was often dropped in writing:

- In OFr, loss of initial H was frequent: Lat *habitare* > OFr *abiter* 'inhabit', and similarly *herba* > *erbe* 'herb, grass', *hominem* > *om* 'man', *hospitalem* > *ospital* 'hospital', *hora* > *ore* 'hour'. Many such forms entered ME and EModE, which often had H-less spellings such as *abit, armonie, eir, erbe, onest, onur, orrible, our, umble, umo(u)r* contemporaneously with equivalent H-forms.
  - Lat *historia* lost the H in OFr; *story* is first attested in Eng with the entire first syllable of the Lat form lost.

- Some Franco-Lat derivatives entered Eng too late to be affected by H-loss, e.g. *hesitate, hilarity.*

## *Restoration of* H

As knowledge of and respect for the classical languages grew from the 15th century, forms with Lat H were normally preferred. In most cases the H-forms became dominant in EModE, and by the 18th century had mostly displaced the H-less alternatives. Over that period, the H began to be pronounced, at an earlier date in some words than in others: 16th- and 17th-century writings on spelling and pronunciation indicate no /h/ in words such as *habit, harmonious* and *heritage*, and in his 18th-century *Dictionary* Johnson records the lack of initial /h/ in *heir, herb, honest, humour* and certain other words. That some of these words have acquired an /h/ in their current pronunciations is due to their spelling.

- Certain words that had entered ME from OFr with silent or lost H were still heard without /h/ as late as the 19th and 20th centuries, e.g. *human, humour.*
- Some words still have silent H: *heir, honest, hono(u)r, hour* (and in America *herb*).
  - The still occasional use of *an* before words beginning with H = /h/ which are not stressed on the first syllable, e.g. *heretical, historical, hotel, humane*, suggests that they too were until recently generally pronounced without the /h/, and indeed in some instances may still be.[10]

## *Non-restoration of* H

In a number of words, etymological H did not re-establish itself:

- *Able, ability* < Lat *habilem, habilitatem*: OFr had forms with and without H, as did ME and EModE (e.g. *abill, hable, hablete*, etc.).
- *Arbo(u)r* < Lat *herbarium*: OFr wrote *(h)erbier* with or without H; Eng took the H-less variant, reinforced by false analogy with such words as *arboreal*.

## *Etymologically unfounded* H

An H unjustified by the origin of a word may have persisted into ModE:

- Lat *eremita* was sometimes spelt with initial H in medieval Lat and OFr; whence ModE *hermit*.
- The H of ModE *hostage* appears to have been added to an H-less Lat stem in OFr by association with *host*, and so entered ME; forms without H also occurred.
- ModFr *haut* 'high' (< Lat *altus*) attracted initial H from Germanic; derived from *haut* are ModE *haughty* and *enhance* (< ANorm *enhauncer*, OFr *enhaucer*).

## Frankish H

OFr had a considerable number of non-Lat (mostly Frankish) derivatives in which H was still pronounced, and continued to be widely pronounced in Fr up to the 16th–17th centuries. The H in these words was pronounced in ME and was not omitted in writing: *hanche* > *haunch*, *hanter* > *haunt*; similarly *hamlet*, *harbinger*, *harness*, *harp*, *harpoon*, *hash*, *haste*, *hatchet*, *haul*, *hideous*, *hue* (as in 'hue and cry').

## I

## Lat I and Eng I/ʒ

Lat I had three sound values: it could be a long vowel rather as in ModE *machine*, a short vowel rather as in ModE *chin*, and a semi-vowel as in ModE *yes*.

- There is no systematic correspondence between ModE and Lat vowel length but this has no effect on spelling: the first I of Lat *filius* 'son' is long but is the short I, /ɪ/, in ModE *filial*; in ModE *miser* the originally short Lat I is pronounced as a long I, /aɪ/.
- The Lat semi-vowel /j/ at the beginning of a stressed syllable corresponds to ModE J: *iustitia* 'justice'.

## Lat and/or Fr I > ModE long I written I–E

- Among many examples are *describe* (< Lat *describere*), *tribe* (< Lat *tribus*), *arrive*, *combine*, *compromise*, *despise*, *divide*, *exercise*, *fragile*, *inspire*, *sacrifice*, *spite*, *title*, etc.; -ISE/-IZE from Graeco-Lat -IZARE, as in *organise*, *realize*, etc.

- The long value of ɪ may be marked in ModE by a following silent consonant that in various ways reflects the word's actual or supposed derivation: *sign* < Lat *signum*, *isle* < Lat *insula*, and similarly *delight*, *indict*, *sprightly*, *viscount*.
- Certain features arising in the ME and EModE period may be noted:
  - Most words could be written with ʏ: *byble*, *combyne*, *cryme*, *descrybe*.
  - Many words now written with the split digraph -ɪ–ᴇ were also written without final ᴇ, a distinction often being made between nouns or adjectives without ᴇ and related verbs with ᴇ. This difference corresponds to distinctions made in Fr, as between nouns *avis*, *déclin*, verbs *aviser*, *décliner*, giving ME *avis* 'advice' often without ᴇ but *avise* 'to advise' always with ᴇ, and similarly *declyn/declyne*, etc.
  - Three less common EModE variations are:
    - -ɪᴇ- for -ɪ–ᴇ: *aspier*, *desier*, *paradies*, *sacrifies* = ModE *aspire*, *desire*, *paradise*, *sacrifice*.
    - The -ɪɢʜᴛ spelling that became fixed in *delight* (from earlier *delite*, etc.) also attested for *appetite*, *despite*, *indict*, *quite*, *site*: thus *apetyght*, *despight*, etc.
    - A double ɪ representation of the long value (also found in OE), also found as ɪȷ: *paradijs*, *sacrifijs*.

### Franco-Lat *i* > ModE long *i* written *i* before another vowel

Examples are *dialogue* (< OFr *dialoge* < Lat *dialogus*), *alliance*, *client*, *diary*, *diet*, *piety*, *pious*, *prior*, *quiet*, *triumph*, etc. In most of these words, the ɪ remained unchanged from Lat onwards (apart from the ʏ-alternation mentioned above).

- Some cases do not derive from Lat ɪ: *lion* < ANorm *liun* < Lat *leonem*.

### Fr *i* in Eng

More modern loans from Fr have the Fr /iː/ value for ɪ: *antique*, *artiste*, *bourgeoisie*, *chemise*, *critique*, *fatigue*, *machine*, *magazine*, *mystique*, *physique*, *police*, *prestige*, *routine*, *unique*.

- Loans in the 16th and 17th centuries were often given anglicized variants without final ᴇ, some of which survive with other meanings today, e.g. *antic*, *artist*, *critic*, *mystic*, *physic*.

- In some cases, the stress has moved back to or closer to the beginning of the word (as often happened with older Fr loans in Eng), at the same time altering the phonetic value of the final vowel: *calorie, camaraderie, prairie*. The majority of these words entered Eng in the 19th century, and some were at first alternatively written with an anglicized final Y: *geny, menagery, sorty* = 'genie, menagerie, sortie'.
  - In *guarantee* and *repartee*, the -IE (Fr *garantie, repartie*) has been anglicized to -EE.

## Fr and/or Lat I > ModE medial IE

*Tier* originated in Fr *tire*, *frieze* in Fr *frise*, Lat *frisium*, and *mien* partly in Fr *mine*. There were alternative spellings in EModE, e.g. *tear/teer/tere, freese*.

## Franco-Lat I > ModE Y

*Style* was originally spelt with I in Lat *stilus*, though sometimes as *stylus* by analogy with Gr *stylos*. *Style* was often written *stile* before the 20th century.

## Lat or Graeco-Lat -IA/-IUM/-IUS > ModE Y

Some ModE forms retain Lat -IA, e.g. in Graeco-Lat loans (*hysteria, nostalgia*; also plurals: *bacteria, criteria*). Normally, however, Lat -IA has become ModE -Y, often through varying intermediate developments in Fr:

- Gr words ending in stressed -IA borrowed into Lat developed into ModE as follows: *energia > energie/energye > energy*. Similarly *agony, allegory, category, comedy, economy, fantasy, harmony, irony*, etc., and words ending in -LOGY.
- Certain Graeco-Lat-based ModE forms ending in -CY, such as *aristocracy, democracy, prophecy*, reflect a LLat respelling of -TIA as -CIA, with OFr -CIE providing the model for Eng; forms with the original T (e.g. *democratie*) were sometimes used in EModE.
  - Non-Graeco-Lat *accuracy, delicacy, intimacy, literacy, privacy* derive (mostly mid-17th century) from Lat-based Eng adjectives: thus *accuracy* derives from *accurate* (< Lat *accuratus*) with no corresponding form in Fr or Lat.
- Some Lat words ending in -IA had a similar outcome, ModFr -IE/ModE -Y: *century, ceremony, copy, envy, industry, library, penury*. In some cases ModE derives its -Y from OFr -IE via ME -YE: Lat *gloria* > OFr *glorie* > ME *glorye* > *glory*.

- ○ Where no OFr -IE form existed and/or the Lat form was a late medieval creation, Lat -IA may have been converted to Eng -Y directly by analogy:
  - From classical Lat -ANTIA/-ENTIA (LLat -ANCIA/-ENCIA) come ModE *agency, efficiency, frequency, infancy, tendency.*
  - Lat -RIA gives rise to *history, injury, luxury, memory, misery, usury, victory.*
- In numerous instances, ModE prefers a Fr form with final -E to a Lat-derived alternative with -Y: thus *experience*, not *\*experiency* (< Lat *experientia*, ModFr *experience*) though EModE forms such as *experiensie, experiensy* are attested.
  - ○ Sometimes Lat-derived and Fr-derived forms co-exist in ModE: *competency/competence, despondency/despondence, emergence/emergency, excellence/excellency.*
- Many ModE words ending in -ERY (e.g. *mockery*) are built on the Fr suffix -ERIE. Although in principle this ending originates in Lat -ARIA or -ERIA, as in Lat *cancellaria* > OFr *chancelerie* > ME *chauncelrie* > *chancellery/chancery*, many ModE examples are Fr coinages (e.g. *flaterie* > *flaterye* > *flattery*) and some Eng (e.g. *battery, machinery, bakery, cookery*).
  - ○ The -ERY ending is often reduced to -RY in ModE: *citizenry, foundry, pantry, rivalry.*
  - ○ Occasional forms with other preceding vowel letters parallel this pattern: *burglary, infirmary, armoury, treasury.*
- In addition, Lat -RIUM > ModE -RY: *estuary* (< Lat *æstuarium*), *cemetery* (< Lat *cœmeterium*), *diary, dictionary, mystery, dormitory, factory*, etc.
  - ○ Lat -ARIUM is preserved in direct loans: *aquarium, crematorium, delirium*, etc.
- Furthermore, Lat -ARIUS > ModE -ARY: nouns *actuary, anniversary, secretary*; adjectives *arbitrary, contemporary, literary, military, necessary, ordinary*, etc.
  - ○ Similarly from -ORIUS: *compulsory, contradictory, introductory, mandatory, obligatory, satisfactory*, etc.

### *Franco-Lat I to final -Y in ModE verbs*

- *Study* and *vary* show straightforward development from Lat I to ModE Y: Lat *studiare* > OFr *estudier* > ME *studye* > *study, variare* > *varier* > *varye* > *vary*. Similarly *carricare* > *carier* > *carye* > *carry, maritare* > *marier* > *marye* > *marry*.

- In monosyllabic verbs with two preceding consonants – *cry, fry, ply* of Lat origin, plus *spy* (and *espy*) and *try* which did not originate in Lat – ME and EModE saw variation between Y and I, e.g. *cri, crie, criy* (also *crij*).
  - A verb such as *vie* (possibly < Fr *envier*) with only one preceding consonant is spelt -IE rather than -Y in accordance with the ModE tendency to avoid spelling nouns, verbs and adjectives with fewer than three letters (e.g. *awe, eye,* etc.).
- Verbs of two or more syllables ending in Y = /aɪ/ consist, at least in origin, of a prefix plus monosyllabic Franco-Lat stem: *ally* (< OFr *alier* < Lat *alligare* < *ad+ligare*), *apply* (< ANorm *ap(p)lier* < Lat *applicare* < *ad+plicare*), *defy, imply, multiply, rely, reply.*
  - In *deny, supply* the -Y originates in Lat E: *deny* is cognate with *negate, supply* with *supplement.*
- Many polysyllabic Y-verbs end in -(I)FY from Lat *facere* or related -FICARE 'do, make', reduced in Fr to -FIER (e.g. *satisfy* < OFr *satisfier* < Lat *satisfacere; justify* < OFr *justifier* < LLat *justificare*). Some (e.g. *beautify*) were created in Eng.

## *Franco-Lat I to ModE short I*

- Numerous ModE words have a short I of Fr and/or Lat origin: *city* (< Lat *civitatem*), *risk* (< Fr *risque*), *estimate, family, figure, history, image, prince, rich, simple, vicar, university.*
- Some recurrent elements are:

**-MIT, -FLICT, -SIST:** *Admit, commit, dismiss, emit, omit,* etc. < Lat *mittere* 'to send', *missum* 'sent'); *afflict, conflict, inflict* < Lat *flictere* 'to strike'; *assist, consist, desist, exist* (= *ex+sist*), etc. < Lat *sistere* 'to cause to stand upright'.
**DIS-, DI-, IN-, IM-, INTER-, INTEL-:** For DI(S)-, see p. 107. For IN-, see pp. 107–8. Among words having the prefix INTER- (Lat 'among, between') in ModE are *interact, intercept, intercourse, interdependent, interest, interfere, interpret, interrogate,* etc. (Before a stem beginning with L, the R is assimilated: *intellect, intelligent.*)
**-ICTION/-INCTION/-ISION/-ISSION/-ITION:** These words typically descend from -IO stems inflected as -IONEM in Lat, the -EM being lost by the OFr period, and later formations (e.g. *benedictionem* > ModFr *bénédiction*): *contradiction, distinction, decision, permission, definition,* etc.
**-IBLE:** The ending -IBLE typically represents a Fr reduction of Lat -IBILEM: *credible, possible, visible,* etc.

○ The ending -ABLE is sometimes used in ModE alternatively to -IBLE, e.g. *collectable* beside *collectible*; such variation was more common in EModE, with forms such as *horrable, terrable*.

**-IC:** The ending -IC is seen in nouns and adjectives: *basic, economic, music, public*, etc. Its immediate source is typically Lat -ICUS, but most examples originate in Gr -IKOS/-IKE. ANorm generally had forms in K: e.g. *publik, musik(e)*.

**-ICE:** The ending -ICE is mostly found in nouns, pronounced /ɪ/, /aɪ/ or /iː/: *edifice, office, service; advice, device, sacrifice* (also the verbs *entice, suffice*); *caprice, police*. Nearly half of the forms with /ɪ/ originate in the Lat endings -ITIA/-ICIA, -ITIUS/-ICIUS, -ITIUM/-ICIUM: e.g. *service* < Lat *servitium*. A few come via Fr from inflections of Lat words ending in X: *accomplice* (< OFr *complice* < Lat *complex*, accusative *complicem*), *cornice, chalice*. Several are adapted from OFr forms, often with -IS: *apprentice* (< OFr *apprentis*), *coppice, jaundice, liquorice*, etc.

○ *Practice* was adapted from *practise*, and *poultice* from Lat *pultis*; *bodice* is a ME respelling of *bodies* (see p. 55); *crevice* is from ME/OFr *crevace* (ModFr/ModE *crevasse*).

**-ID:** The ending -ID mostly originates in the Lat adjectival ending -IDUS/-A/-UM, but often comes more directly from Fr -IDE: *liquid, rapid, solid, splendid, stupid*. Several nouns are of Lat or Graeco-Lat origin: *hybrid, pyramid*.

**-IER:** ModE examples of this ending are found in words deriving at various periods from Fr, corresponding to Fr words with the endings -IÈRE (*barrier, frontier, glacier, rapier*) or -IER (*brigadier, brazier* 'coke heater', *cashier, soldier*).

○ More recent loans may retain distinctively Fr forms and pronunciations (*croupier, dossier, métier, papier mâché*).

**-IL:** The ending -IL has, usually via Fr -IL, -ILLE, various Lat sources:

○ the adjectival ending -ILEM: *April, civil, fossil*;
○ the noun ending -ILIUM: *council*;
○ the noun/adjective ending -ILLUM: *pencil, pupil, tranquil*;
○ the noun ending -ICULA/-UM: *lentil, peril*;
○ the verb endings -ILLARE/-ILLARI: *cavil, instil(l)*.

**-IN:** The ending -IN mostly derives from Fr, often also from Lat:

○ A good number of examples derive, via Fr, from Lat -INUS: *assassin* (originally Arabic), *basin, chagrin, coffin, cousin, dolphin, satin*. EModE often had variants of these forms with final E, but sometimes reflected the nasalization of the Fr pronunciation by adding G: thus *basin/bassine/basing/bassyng, satin/satine/satyng*.

- Other Eng -IN words derive from Fr -INE, often with a Lat antecedent in -INA: *cabin, javelin, muslin, resin, ruin, vermin*; some of these were often written with -INE in EModE: *cabine, ruine*.
- A large group of chemical substances have names, many coined in Eng, ending in -IN (in origin a form of -INE < Fr -IN(E), Lat -INUS/-INA): *aspirin, h(a)emoglobin, insulin, heroin, paraffin* (first coined in German), *penicillin, saccharin, tannin, toxin, vitamin*. A few of these words can be written with final -E: e.g. *adrenalin/ adrenaline, gelatin/gelatine*.
- The -IN of *margin, origin, virgin* < Lat -INEM.
- The -IN of *bulletin, florin, mandolin, poplin, violin* came (mostly via Fr) from Italian diminutive ending -INO.
- -IN from other Fr vowels: *griffin* (OFr *griffoun*), *maudlin* (Fr *Madeleine*), *pumpkin* (OFr *pompon*), *urchin* (formerly *hurcheon*, from Norman Fr *herichon*).

**-INE:** Common examples, with endings from various sources, include nouns *discipline* (< Fr *discipline* < Lat *disciplina*), *doctrine, engine* (< OFr *engin* < Lat *ingenium*), *ermine* (< OFr *ermine*), *heroine, medicine*; verbs *determine* (< OFr *determine* < Lat *determinare*), *destine, examine, imagine*; and adjectives *genuine* (< Lat *genuinus*), *feminine, masculine*.

- In many of these words, EModE vacillated between forms with and without final E (e.g. EModE *doctrin, examin, feminin*); that variation is still occasionally seen in ModE, as in *adrenalin(e)*, *gelatin(e)*.

**-IOUS:** The ending -IOUS simply represents the suffix -OUS attached to a stem ending in I: *glorious* < ANorm *glorious* < Lat *gloriosus* < *gloria* 'glory', *obvious* < Lat *obvius* < *via* 'way'.

**-IS:** Words ending in -IS fall into several categories:

- The majority are of Graeco-Lat origin: *basis, cannabis, chrysalis, crisis, emphasis*, etc.; compounds based on -ITIS (e.g. *arthritis, hepatitis*), -LYSIS (e.g. *analysis, paralysis*), -OSIS (e.g. *diagnosis, symbiosis*), -POLIS (e.g. *metropolis, Minneapolis*) and -THESIS (e.g. *antithesis, hypothesis*).
- There are words of pure Lat origin: *axis, pelvis, penis*.
- A few are older anglicized loans from Fr: *daïs* (< OFr *deis*), *marquis* (< ANorm *marchis*), *portcullis* (< OFr *porte coleïce*), *tennis* (< Fr *tenez*), *trellis* (< OFr *trelice*).
- A few are modern loans from Fr with silent -S: *chassis, debris, précis*.

**-ISE:** The ending -ISE, pronounced /ɪ/, /aɪ/ or /iː/, as in *practise, premise, promise, treatise, precise, devise, expertise*) arose from various Fr and Lat

sources: e.g. *precise* < MFr *precis* < Lat *praecisus*; *promise* < ANorm *promesse*/
-*isse* < Lat *promissum*; *devise* < OFr *deviser* < LLat *divisare*; *expertise* < ModFr
*expertise*.

○ The form *practise* arose from a late medieval switch of endings
from c as in *practical* to the s of OFr *practiser*; in EModE both
*practise* and *practice* are attested as *practis*.

○ The form *premise* reflects ANorm *premesse*/-*isse*, while the alternative *premiss* reflects Lat *praemiss*- and ModFr *prémisse*. Similarly
EModE spellings of *promise* with I and E reflect vacillation
between Lat *promiss*- and Fr *promesse*.

○ *Treatise* was sometimes written with final -IS in EModE (and before),
sometimes with other endings including -ICE, -ICE, -YCE, -YSS,
-ESSE.

**-ISH:** Apart from the OE adjective suffix -ISC (as in *Englisc* 'English'),
the main source of ModE -ISH is the inflected form of Fr -IR verbs
(e.g. *finish* from FINISS-, a stem of the verb *finir*), and similarly *establish*,
*polish*.

○ *Fetish* < ModFr *fétiche* (18th century).

**-ISM/-IST:** The endings -ISM/-IST are of Graeco-Lat origin, and early
manifested in the Christian terms *baptism*/*baptist*. Both endings have pro-
liferated in ModE, with loans from Fr -ISME/-ISTE (e.g. *impressionisme*,
*impressioniste*) and numerous 20th-century Eng coinings (e.g. *ageism*,
*leftist*).

**-IT:** Lat past participle endings -ITUS/-ITUM > (often via Fr) -IT in *audit*,
*credit*, *debit*, *decrepit*, *explicit*, *habit*, *implicit*, *illicit*, *merit*, *solicit*, *tacit*.
EModE saw -ITE, -ITT spellings (e.g. *creditt*, *merite*).

○ A few ModE -IT forms derive from the Lat verb *ire* 'to go', either
from third person singular *it* (*exit* 'he/she goes out') or from the
past participle *itum* (*ambit*, *circuit*, *transit*). Third person singular
present tense endings of other Lat verbs are seen in *affidavit* and
*deficit*.

○ The following nouns also originate in Lat: *limit* (< *limitem*), *orbit*
(< *orbita*), *pulpit* (< *pulpitum*).

○ *Esprit* and *petit* are from ModFr.

**-ITE:** The ending -ITE, pronounced with /ɪ/ (*definite*, *favo(u)rite*, *hypocrite*,
*infinite*, *opposite*) or /aɪ/ (*invite*, *polite*, *parasite*, *satellite*), originates in Lat
-ITUS (e.g. *definitus*, *politus*) or -ITARE (e.g. *invitare*, via Fr *inviter*).

○ Forms without final E (e.g. *definit*, *favorit*, *hipocrit*, *infinit*, *opposit*)
were sometimes seen in EModE.

**-ITY:** Lat -ITATEM > Fr -ITÉ > ModE -ITY: *city* < OFr *cité* < Lat *civitatem*.

o After I, the ending changes I to E in Lat, Fr and Eng: thus *society* (not *\*sociity*) from ANorm *societe*, Lat *societatem*.

o In the case of *plenty*, the I of Lat *plenitatem* was already lost in OFr.

**-IVE:** Lat suffix -IVUS/-A/-UM > noun and adjective ending -IVE: *active, adjective, alternative, conservative, detective, directive, expensive, effective*, etc.

o The ending -IVE is occasionally found in adjectives reaching Eng via Fr: *costive* (< Lat *constipatus*), *naïve, plaintive*.

o The ending -IVE was used fairly consistently in Eng adjectives from ME onwards, except that in the early centuries the Fr masculine ending -IF was sometimes preferred to feminine -IVE (e.g. *actif, nominatyf*).

**-IX:** The ending -IX comes directly from Lat or Graeco-Lat: *appendix, cervix, matrix, helix, phoenix*.

## The *I*-glide after *L* and *N*

• ModE -L(L)I- corresponds to a ModFr LL/ILL spelling in e.g. *battalion/ bataillon, brilliant/brillant*. When such words entered Eng (most first attested in EModE), they had alternative forms, one closer to ModFr and one closer to ModE: e.g. *bataillon/battaillion, brilliant/brillant*.

o In *parliament* the I is an Eng innovation (among several alternative spellings); *parlament* was common until the 17th century and *parlement* (as in Fr) until the 18th.

• The case with -NI- is similar. ME and EModE variants of *companion, minion, onion, spaniel* include forms with G (as in Fr, e.g. *compagnon*) and/or without I: *compainoun, mynon, oynon, spaignol*. EModE variants for *miniature* include *minature, mignature, miniture*.

## Assimilated *I*

In ModE the letter I before another vowel in an unstressed final syllable has frequently become assimilated with a preceding C, D, G, S, T, X: e.g. *special* /'spɛʃl/. Most of the ModE spellings follow Lat spelling (with the usual loss of inflections): e.g. Lat *productionem* > ModFr/ModE *production*. Words that had a clear Lat source generally preserve the I in ME and EModE (though with common substitution of Y for I, and also C for T and OU for O: *condicyoun, pacyent, relygyon, specyal, visyon*; but the assimilations are attested from the mid-15th century with spellings such as *prosesschchon* 'procession' and *oblygaschons* 'obligations'.[11]

## Other sources of ModE ɪ

- Lat A > E in Fr > ModE ɪ: (Lat *caballus* 'horse' >) OFr *chevalerie* > ME *chivalerie* > *chivalry*; *caminata* > *cheminee* > *chimenee* > *chimney*; *comparationem* > *compareson* > *comparysoun* > *comparison*; *datum* > *de* > *dee* > *die/dice*; *mister* and *mistress* are ultimately from Lat *magister*.
- Lat ɪ > Fr E > ModE ɪ: VLat *\*frimbria* (< Lat *fimbria*) > OFr *frenge* > ME *frenge* > ModE *fringe*; the ModE spelling follows the normal sound change from /ɛ/ to /ɪ/ before /n/, as also in OE-derived *hinge* and *singe* (see pp. 39–40).
- Lat/Fr O(U) > ModE ɪ: Lat *parochia* > OFr *paroche* > ME *paroch(e)* > *parish*. Another example is ModE *cartridge* from Fr *cartouche*.
- Lat/Fr (O)U > ModE ɪ: two words with initial Eng SQUI- originated in Lat SCU-: *scutarius* 'shield-bearer' > *(e)squire*, *scurellus* > *squirrel*; *stifle*, *trifle* developed from ME *stufle*, *trufle* (probably from OFr *estouffer* and *trufle* respectively). *Brisk* may derive from Fr *brusque*.

## Lost ɪ

- Unstressed ɪ has sometimes been elided: Lat *capitaneus* > OFr *capitaine* > ME *capitain/capteyn* > *captain*; Lat *capitulum* > *chapitre* > *chapiter* > *chapter*; Lat *caminata* > *cheminee* > *chimenee/cheminey* > *chimney*; Lat *clericus* > OE/OFr *clerc* > *clerk* (ModE *cleric* dates from the 17th century).
- In a few cases, an original Lat ɪ became OFr EI, and converted to final Y in ModE: *convey* < Lat *via* 'way', *purvey*, *survey* < Lat *videre* 'to see'.
- The Lat ɪ of *maior* was retained in Fr *maire* and ME *mair*, but re-Latinized in EModE to give ModE *mayor*.
- Fr ɪ > ModE EE or EA: *breeze*, *canteen*, *esteem*, *genteel*, *lees*, *marquee*, *redeem*, *tweezers*, *veer*, *veneer* and *league* (compare ModFr *brise*, *cantine*, *estimer*, *gentil*, *ligue*, etc.).
  - *Intreague* is found for *intrigue* in EModE.
- Fr -IE(U)R > ModE -EER: *buccaneer*, *career*, *engineer*, *pioneer* (compare ModFr *boucanier*, *carrière*, *ingénieur*, *pionnier*).

## Silent ɪ after U

The silent ɪ in words spelt -UI- has various sources:

- Some derive from Fr spelling:
  - In *fruit*, the C of the Lat source *fructus* (OFr *fruit*) was restored in such MFr and EModE forms as *fruict*, but ME spellings such

as *frut, frute* suggest that the I was perhaps never pronounced in Eng.

○ With *suit* (Lat *sequita*, OFr *siute*), ME spellings without I, e.g. *sute*, suggest that the I was never pronounced in Eng but was restored to the spelling by analogy with Fr *suite* (first attested in Eng from the late 17th century). The same applies to *pursuit*.

○ *Nuisance* is first attested in EModE with precisely that spelling, as in Fr.

• Several other words have UI with silent I in ModE, but it appears in varying degrees to originate in Eng:

○ *Bruise* (< OE *brysan* and OFr *brisier/bruisier*, ANorm *bruser*) has a complex and uncertain history. ModE *bruise* may be a compromise influenced by Eng dialects and/or by the Fr variants.

○ The I of *juice* originated in ME, the Franco-Lat source *jus* having no I; forms with and without I competed throughout ME and EModE, until ModE *juice* emerged in the 17th century.

○ *Recruit* came from the Fr dialect form *recrute* in the 17th century. At first both *recruit* and *recrute* were used; the preference for *recruit* may be due to analogy with *fruit*.


# J

For the Romans the letter J was merely a variant of the letter I with no independent alphabetic status. In due course, this I/J came to be pronounced as a consonant, /dʒ/, the value it had in OFr and has today in ModE in words acquired from Lat and OFr (e.g. *judge*). In Fr J came to be pronounced /ʒ/, as in ModE/ModFr *bijou*.

• The process by which the letters I and J became separated in the alphabet is described in Chapter 6 (pp. 184–5).


## Franco-Lat ʒ in Eng

• Among ModE words with initial Franco-Lat J are *janitor, jovial, jurisdiction, just, juxtapose.*

• Franco-Lat-derived J after prefixes occurs in derivatives of:

○ Lat *iacere* 'to throw' (past participle *iectus*): *abject, adjective, conjecture, dejected, ejaculate, subject, trajectory*, etc.;

○ Lat *iacere* 'to lie recumbent': *adjacent*;

133

- ○ Lat *iugum* 'yoke' and *iunctus* 'joined': *adjunct, conjugal, conjugation, conjuncture, disjunctive, subjugate*;
- ○ Lat *iuvenis* 'young': *juvenile, rejuvenate*;
- ○ the roots IUD-, IUR-, IUS- relating to law: *adjudicate, judicial, prejudice, conjure, injure, perjury, justificatory*, etc.
- The Lat prefix AD- occurs before stems beginning with J (e.g. *adjacent, adjective, adjust*). Some of these words were written without D in EModE (*ajoine, ajourn, ajudge*).
- Examples of J between vowels are *major* (< Lat *maior* 'bigger'), *pejorative* (< Lat *peior* 'worse').
- Other ModE J-words relate less directly to Lat forms, having undergone more radical changes through Fr or having reached Fr from languages other than Lat: e.g. (with the Fr precursor in brackets): *jet* (*jet*), *jetty* (*jetée*), *join* (*joindre*), *judge* (*juge*), *juggle* (*jongler*), *jury* (OFr *juree*), *jubilee* (*jubilé*).

### I/ʒ and G

One effect of the vowel I/J becoming a consonant in post-classical Lat was to create a sound–spelling ambiguity, as the new value /dʒ/ was also the value acquired by G before E, I, Y.

- In OFr a number of words containing either G or J in Lat were spelt alternatively with either J or G, a variation that led to some ModE forms with G or J that in Lat and/or Fr used the other letter:
  - ○ Lat *gesta* > OFr *geste/jeste* > EModE *gest/jest* (or *ieste*) > ModE *jest*.
  - ○ Lat *gentilis* > OFr/ME *gentil, jentil* > EModE *gentle, jentle*, and finally *gentle, jaunty* in ModE.
  - ○ The switch from G to J in *jelly* (< Fr *gelée*) occurred relatively late (the spelling *gelly* was still in use into the 19th century).
- The opposite development, from Lat I/J to Fr/Eng G, is seen in the following:
  - ○ Lat *iacere* 'to lie recumbent' > OFr *gesir* (present tense *gist*), whence ModE *gist* and *joist* (the latter entering ME in the form *giste*).
  - ○ Lat *iuniperus* > ModE *juniper*; however, *iuniperus* > OFr *genevre* > Dutch *genever*, whence *gin*, a drink flavoured with juniper berries.
- A few ModE words have alternative spellings: e.g. *gibe/jibe* (possibly < OFr *giber*).
- In Central Fr (but not Norman Fr), /g/ in Lat words beginning with GA- became /dʒ/ and were then respelt with J: Lat *gaudia* > *joie* > *joy*;

Lat *galbinus* > OFr *jalne/jaune* 'yellow', whence ModE *jaundice*; Lat *gamba* > *jambe* 'leg' whence *jamb* (compare ModE *gammon* from Norman Fr *gambon* < *gambe*).

○ ModE *gaol/jail* derives from VLat *\*caveola/\*gaviola*. The G-form is from Norman Fr, the J-form from Central (Parisian) Fr. Regardless of spelling, the ModE pronunciation is that of the J-form.

## ModE ʒ from other Lat sources

- *Jealous* is a doublet of *zealous*, the z being the original Graeco-Lat spelling; but its pronunciation, probably /dz/ in Graeco-Lat, split between the values /z/ and /dʒ/ to give separate spellings with z and J for the separate modern meanings; forms with G (*gelos, gelus*, etc.) were normal in OFr and common (beside *ielus*) in ME. The ModE spelling *jealous* became established in the 17th century.
- The J in *adjourn, journal, journey, sojourn* derives from DI- in Lat *diurnus* 'daily'.

# K

The sound /k/ was normally represented in Lat by C or Q. K was later introduced sporadically in Romance languages, chiefly before the front vowels E, I, Y where C would have wrongly suggested a palatal value. In OE K was sometimes used before E, I, Y for the same reason (see p. 48), but C was the usual spelling for /k/ in all positions. However, from around the 13th century the use of K increased in words of both Franco-Lat and OE origin. For the change from C to K in ME, see 'C' above (p. 96).

In many words the ModE K took several centuries to become established. Thus an old (12th-century) word like *duke* also saw forms such as *duc, duk, duck* and many others during the ME period; and a more recent (17th-century) borrowing like *risk* was often written *risque* (as in ModFr) up into the 19th century.

There are several patterns by which spellings with K developed in ModE in words of Fr derivation:

- ModE K replaced Fr C after a long vowel or diphthong or a consonant: *beak, duke, lake; blank, rank, trunk, clerk, park, pork, risk*.
- After a short vowel, CK is now usual: *attack, brick, mock, shock, track*.

- In some words the K was found already in OFr (especially Norman) usage: *cloak, kennel, market, plank, pocket, provoke, rebuke.*
- A number of words ending in ModE C had -CK until the 19th century (e.g. *musick > music*); see pp. 49, 302.
  - Such words restore the K before suffixes beginning with a front vowel (e.g. *traffic, trafficker, trafficking*).
- ModE K may derive from a (sometimes post-classical) Lat C: *damask* (< *Damascus*), *desk* (< *desca*), *disk* (< *discus*).

## L

The letter L occurs in most positions in words of Franco-Lat origin, corresponding to an L in Lat and/or Fr, e.g. *large* (< Fr *large*, Lat *largus*), *rule* (< OFr *reule*, Lat *regula*):

- Word-initially, before vowels: *letter, line, lodge, luxury.*
- Medially between vowels: *palace, elect, military, colo(u)r, stimulus*; between long A, I, O, U and silent E: *pale, mile, role.*
- Before and after consonants: *album, calculate, calcium,* etc.; *blame, clear, flower, glory, place.*
- Word-finally: *appeal, control*; in adjectives ending in -AL (*actual, final,* etc.).
  - The ending -LE occurs in numerous ModE words: *noble, uncle, single, people,* etc., and in -ABLE, -IBLE, etc.

### Double L

Double L arises where Lat prefixes have been assimilated to stems beginning with L:

- AD-: *allege, allow, alloy, ally*;
- CON-: *collapse, colleague, collect*;
- IN-: *illegal, illicit*; *illuminate, illustrate*;
- INTER-: *intellect, intelligent*;
- PER-: *pellucid.*

### Double or single L

Lat-based words may contain LL (in most cases transmitted through Fr, often with earlier spellings with single L): *collar* (ME *coler* < ANorm *coler* < Lat *collum* 'neck'), *valley* (< OFr *valee* < Lat *vallis*), *million, pollute, rebellion, village;* inherited from Gr: *parallel, syllable,* etc. ModE medial LL often corresponds to Franco-Lat L, and conversely ModE final L may correspond to Franco-Lat LL. Such changes typically reflect a shift of stress to the beginning of the word (compare ModE *folly* with first-syllable stress, Fr *folie* with final-syllable stress):

- ModE LL, Fr (and Lat, if Lat is the source) L: *gallery* (ModFr *galerie,* medieval Lat *galeria*), *jolly* (ME *joly/jolyf* < OFr *joli/jolif*), *pillar* (ModFr *pilier*), *roll* (ModFr *rouler*). (Where ME has single L, EModE increasingly sees forms with LL.)
  - ○ Some (mainly two-syllable) words, sometimes written with LL from EModE onward for two or more centuries, were, however, finally standardized with the original Franco-Lat single L: *balance* (earlier *ballance/ballaunce*), *colonel* (earlier *corronel/collonel*), *colo(u)r, palace, value.*
- Franco-Lat LL becoming L in Eng is seen in words typically with final -LLE in ModFr but final single L in ModE, with the stress moving from the final syllable in Fr to the first syllable in ModE. Many of these words first appear in ME with the modern -EL ending, or else -ELE, a form often used in OFr: e.g. *chapel* (OFr/ME *chapele,* ModFr *chapelle*), *damsel, libel, marvel* (ModFr *demoiselle, libelle, merveille*); also *family,* ModFr *famille.*
  - ○ For nouns, -LLE is typically a feminine ending, and a group of Eng words whose Lat and OFr sources had masculine gender derived their -EL from OFr -EL, which in ModFr has typically become -(E)AU: *bowel* (OFr *boel,* ModFr *boyau*), *camel* (OFr *chamel,* ModFr *chameau*), *chisel, jewel, morsel,* etc. (ModFr *ciseau, joyau, morceau*).

### L *lost and acquired*

- In some words, Lat L was lost after A in both spelling and pronunciation in developments through Fr and/or ME, though often restored in writing in EModE and subsequently also in speech, in deference to the Lat form: e.g. Lat *adsaltus* > OFr/ME *asaut* > (early) ModE *assault* with L restored in both writing and pronunciation. Similar developments are seen in *ca(u)ldron, falcon, false, fault, herald, realm.*
  - ○ However, L restored to the written form was not always restored in speech: *almoner, balm, calm, palm, psalm, salmon.*
  - ○ In certain other cases an original Lat L lost in OFr was never re-established in Eng: e.g. *chafe, safe, save* (< Lat *calefacere, salvus*).

- In a few words, an L first arose in OFr and/or ME: *participle* (< Lat *participium*), *chronicle* (< ANorm *cronicle*, OFr *cronique*), *principle*, *syllable*, *treacle*, *truffle*, *turtle*.
- There are instances of alteration from R to L: e.g. Lat *marmor*, *purpura* > *marble*, *purple*.

## M

The letter M occurs in most positions in words of Franco-Lat origin, corresponding to an M, or sometimes MM, in Lat and/or Fr:

- In initial position: *machine*, *member*, *modern*.
- Medially, between vowels: *damage*, *domain*, *promise*, *human*; following (silent) L and R: *salmon*, *normal*; preceding B, P and PH: *member*, *assumption*, *triumph*; at the boundary between two parts of a word: *dismiss*.
- In final position, in a number of borrowings from Lat: *quondam*, *item*, *tandem*, *interim*, *passim*; *minimum*, *optimum*; preceding ModE silent E indicating a preceding long vowel: *blame*, *crime*, *volume*.
  - In many words, M is final due to the loss of a following (Old) Fr and/or Lat ending: e.g. *norm* (< Lat *norma*), *sum* (< OFr *summe*, Lat *summa*). A vestige of these endings can be seen in the final E with which these words were first written in Eng, in some cases (e.g. *farme*, *calme*) throughout the ME and EModE period.
  - Final /m/ may be followed by a now silent B or N: *tomb* (< LLat *tumba*), *aplomb*, *bomb* (as also in Germanic words, e.g. *dumb*, *lamb*); *autumn* (< Lat *autumnus*), *damn*, *hymn*, *solemn* (but compare *autumnal*, *solemnity*, etc.).

### Single and double M

- M occurs where the Lat prefixes CON- and IN- are assimilated before bilabial consonants such as /p/ and /m/: *combat*, *combine*, *imbibe*, *impulse*, etc. With stems beginning with M this creates a double M: *command*, *commit*, *immense*, *immigration*, etc.
  - In *summon*, the B of the Lat prefix SUB- has been assimilated to the M of *monere* 'to warn'.
- Some instances of Eng MM originate in Lat MM: *inflammation* from *flamma* 'flame'; *mammal* from *mamma* 'udder'; *consummate*, *summary*, *summit* from *summus* 'highest'.

- Some words spelt with MM in ModE had a single M in the source languages: *ammunition* < obsolete Fr *amunition* < *la munition*; *pommel* < OFr *pomel* < Lat *pomum* 'fruit'.
  - A few words today with single M were sometimes written with MM for two or more centuries from the EModE period: *camel, comedy, damage, homage, lemon*. The earliest attestation of nearly all these words in Eng has single M, with MM increasingly used in EModE.
- Some words spelt with M in ModE had MM in the source languages: *flame* < OFr *flamme*, Lat *flamma*; *sum* < OFr *summe*, Lat *summa*. OFr and ME also had spellings with MB: OFr *flambe*, ME (e.g. in Chaucer) *flaumbe*.
- The MM of *gammon* 'joint of ham' originated in MB (Norman Fr *gambon*).

### M *from* N

A switch from original N to M sometimes occurred, notably in word-final position:

- *Anthem* < Graeco-Lat *antiphona*, reduced to *antefn* in OE; an M first appeared in ME, and ModE *anthem* emerged in the 17th century.
- EModE forms of *flotsam* and *jetsam* with both M and N are attested (compare related *jettison* with N).
- *Pilgrim* derives from the OFr *pelegrin* but was almost always spelt with M from ME onwards.
- *Random, ransom* are found with both M and N in late ME and EModE.

### N

ModE N originating in a Fr and/or Lat N:

- In initial position: *nation, niece, normal*.
- Medially between vowels: *general, final, honest*.
- Medially, after L and R: *vulnerable, govern*; before C, D, S, T: *experience, punctual, demand, round, immense, response, fragment, plant*; in derivatives of Lat and/or Fr present participles, such as *vibrant* (

*vibrantem*), *imminent*, *torrent*; in derivatives of Lat gerunds (verbal nouns) and gerundives (verb forms expressing necessity), such as *legend* (via Fr < Lat *legenda* 'things to be read'), *memorandum*, *tremendous*.

## Word-final N or /n/

- Word-final N often arises from the loss of Lat word-endings (e.g. ModE/ModFr *action* < Lat *actionem*): *education, corrosion, possession*; also in nouns ending in -MEN: e.g. *specimen* (< Lat *specimen*), *abdomen*, etc.).
- Final N preceded by a silent G: *benign, sign*, etc. Some words have cognates without G: *deign/disdain* (< Lat *dignus*), *feign/feint* (< OFr *feindre, feign-, feint*), *line/align* (< Fr *ligne*).
- Silent word-final N following M: *autumn, column, condemn, damn, hymn, solemn* (< Lat *autumnus, columna*, etc.). In EModE this pattern was sometimes extended to words in which the immediate source word had no N: *volumn* for *volume* (< OFr *volum* < Lat *volumen*).
- A final silent E in Fr may be lost after N in ModE: OFr *persone* > ModE *person* (though often spelt with -E in ME). Conversely, a Fr form ending in N may appear with final -NE in Eng: e.g. OFr *ton* > ModE *tone* (with various ME forms including *ton, toon*), and similarly with *decline, pine*, from *déclin, pin*.
- A number of adjectives appear in Eng with the feminine form of their Fr antecedent: e.g. *fine* from Fr *fin* (feminine *fine*), and similarly *canine, divine*, etc.

## Double or single N

- ModE may have a double N where Lat prefixes AD-, CON- and IN- precede Lat stems beginning with N: *announce* (< OFr *anoncer* < Lat *adnuntiare*), *annul, connect, connotation, innocent, innate*. Most of the above words are first attested with NN in EModE or later; the few that appeared earlier were sometimes written with single N: *anounce, inocent*.
  - A few instances of NN in Lat-derived words are from roots with NN: *annual, anniversary*, etc. from Lat *annus* 'year'.
  - Some instances of NN originated in EModE as the stress shifted to the first syllable (a procedure observable with many consonants): *bonnet* < OFr *bonet*, *channel* < OFr *chanel*, *dinner* < OFr *diner*, and similarly *cannon, cranny, fennel, kennel, manner, tennis*. Most of these

words are first attested in ME with single N, the NN typically not occurring until the 16th century.

- ◦ More recent Fr loans may or may not show a reduction of Fr double N to single N in Eng. Most are first attested in the 19th century, with both single and double N, as in *colon(n)ade*, *legion(n)aire*, *marion(n)ette*, *million(n)aire*; but the following appear always with Fr NN: *ennui*, *mayonnaise*, *personnel*, *question-naire*; while *maisonette* is not attested with Fr NN.

## N *lost and acquired*

- Some ModE words have lost an initial N by its transfer to a preceding indefinite article: *an apron* (< EModE *a napron*), *umpire* (< ME *noumpere*); compare *adder* and *newt*, p. 51.
- Eng has gained an N in a few words:
  - ◦ The N of *messenger, passenger* was first attested in late ME (compare the similar insertion of N in *harbinger* < OFr/ME *herbergere*, *scavenger* < *scavager*).
  - ◦ *Banister* is a corruption of *baluster* (compare *balustrade*). *Enhance* derives from OFr *enhaucier* < Lat *altus* 'high'.
  - ◦ M and N sometimes switched in their passage to ModE: *aunt* < OFr *aunte*, Lat *amita*; *count* ('add numbers') < OFr *conte* < Lat *computum*; *tense* (as in 'past tense', etc.) < OFr *tens* < Lat *tempus*.

## O

### Lat *and/or Fr* O > *ModE* O

The vowel O had short and long values in Lat. They do not systematically correspond to the same quantities in Eng: e.g. Lat *moralis* with long O, ModE *moral* with short O; Lat *socialis* with short O, ModE *social* with long O.

- ModE O has various pronunciations, but most ultimately derive from Lat O: *occupy* (< ANorm *occuper* < Lat *occupare*), *order* (< ANorm *ordre* < Lat *ordinem*), *move* (< ANorm *mover* < Lat *movere*), *money* (< ANorm *moneie* < Lat *moneta*), *depot* (< ModFr *dépôt* < Lat *depositum*); and similarly *office, horror, abhor, décor, pork, host, role, droll, provoke, actor, history, commit, prove, cover, exception*.

## *Lat* U > *ModE* O

There are cases of Lat U > ModE O: LLat *tumba* > ANorm *tumbe*/OFr *tombe* > ME *toumbe*/*tumbe* > *tomb*; Lat *gubernare* > *govern*, Lat *unionem* > *onion*. *Costume*/*custom* both originated in Lat *consuetudinem*.

## *ModE* O *in Lat-derived prefixes*

- COM-: *combat*, *commit*, *compound*, *accommodate*; with assimilation to a following consonant in the root: *collect*, *correspond*; with N before other consonants: *conflict*, *connect*, *console*, *contaminate*; also as CO- before vowels, H and GN: *coalesce*, *coerce*, *coherent*, *cognate*.
  - In *comfort* and *comfit*, the CON- was altered in Eng to COM-: *comfort* < OFr *cunforter* < Lat *confortare* 'to strengthen'; *comfit* < ME *confyt* < OFr *confit*.
  - CON- often lost its N before V in OFr/ANorm: e.g. ANorm *covent* 'convent' < OFr *convent* < Lat *conventus*). Such words entered ME in N-less forms: ME *covent*, *covenant*. The Lat N was restored in some words in Eng (16th-century *convent*) but not in others (ModE *covenant*).
  - Before B and P, OFr normally wrote CUM-: *cumbatre* 'to combat', *cumpagnie* 'company'. Although this was later altered back to the Lat COM- spelling, Eng retained the pronunciation related to CUM-, whence the /ʌ/ vowel of *comfort*, *company*, *compass*, etc.
- OB-: *obedient*, *object*, *oblige*, *obscure*, *obtain*, *obvious*; with assimilation to a following consonant in the root: *occupy*, *offer*, *oppose*; also as O before M: *omit*.
  - Forms with single C, F and P were found in ME/EModE (some reflecting OFr forms): *ocupy*, *oficer*, *opose*, etc.

## *Doubling of consonant to indicate short* O

ModE has a double consonant following short O in a number of words where the consonant was typically written single in ME/EModE: *cotton* (ME *coton*), *folly* (ME *foli*), and similarly *bobbin*, *bottle*, *jolly*, *lottery*, *pottery*, *volley*.

- EModE often wrote *hono(u)r* with double N. Other words sometimes written with a doubled consonant after short O in EModE include *copy* (*coppy*), *model* (*moddel*), *proper* (*propper*), while others of a similar sound pattern are not attested as ever having been so written (e.g. *modern*, *modest*).

## Long O written O–E, OE

Long O is most often indicated in ModE words of Franco-Lat origin by means of the split digraph O–E: *code* (< Fr *code*), *dome* (< 15th-/16th-century Fr *dome*), *envelope, globe, note, provoke, role, tone.*

- A number of O-words in ModE derive, usually via Fr, from Lat AU: e.g. *close* 'shut' (< OFr *clore/clos-*, Lat *claudere*), *explode* < Lat *explodere/explaudere* (compare *clause, applaud*).
- *Abhor* is unique in having a stressed -OR, similar verbs in ModE having a following E (e.g. *adore, explore, ignore*); the explanation is that the -ORE words all had single R in Lat (e.g. *ignorare*), while *abhor* derives from Lat *horrere* with RR and was sometimes written *abhorre* in EModE.
- Of words in which the digraph OE represents long O, only *hoe* derives from Fr although of Germanic origin. The -OE spelling first appeared in the 18th century; earlier spellings had W (e.g. *howe*).

## ModE OA for long O

ModE also represents long O by means of OA, which came into use in the 16th century. While most ModE words spelled with OA are of Germanic origin, a dozen (*approach, boast, cloak, coach, coast, coat, encroach, moat, poach, roach, roast, toast*) came from Fr, all of which were spelled -O–E in EModE (*approche, boste, cloke, coche*, etc.). Both OA and O–E spellings are encountered in 16th- and 17th-century texts.

- It is not certain why these words came to be respelt with OA, while a much larger number kept their O–E spellings. We find various representations of long O in EModE: *noat/not, roase/roose, stoan/stoon* for *note, rose, stone*. Few of the OO spellings were used after the 16th century and few of the OA spellings after the 17th.

## Franco-Lat O in affixes

**-OR, -OUR:** The ending -OR was originally Lat, and many of the words with that ending in ModE are exact Lat forms: *actor, doctor, professor, operator, error, horror, senior, superior,* etc.

- Many other words with -OR may have it modelled on the Lat ending, but derive more directly from Fr forms with other endings which were often used in ME or EModE:

143

○ *Ambassador, author, emperor, governor, tailor* were often written with -OUR in EModE.

○ *Bachelor, chancellor* were often written with -ER in ME and EModE.

○ *Councillor* was formerly not distinguished from *counsellor.* Both derive from Fr *conseiller* and were often written *counseller* in ME.

○ *Warrior* (OFr *werreor,* ModFr *guerrier*) was in ME generally spelt -IOUR.

○ *Ancestor, anchor, traitor* have ModFr equivalents ending in -RE (*ancêtre,* etc.) and were often spelt with -RE in ME.

○ *Mayor* was adopted in EModE as a more Latinate form (compare *major*) in preference to ME *mair(e)* from Fr *maire.*

• The Anglo-American -OUR/-OR difference (*colour/color,* etc.) arose from the recommendation of the American lexicographer Noah Webster (see p. 302) that all such words be standardized with the same ending. The British endings are leftovers from a general reduction of -OUR to -OR in the 18th century, giving forms such as *interior, emperor* today which were formerly written *interiour, emperour,* etc.

**-ORY:** The word-ending -ORY has two sources in Lat:

○ Lat adjective ending -ORIUS, which became OFr -OIRE, ANorm -ORIE: *advisory, contradictory, peremptory, retaliatory, statutory,* etc.

○ Lat noun ending -ORIA, which also became OFr -OIRE, ANorm -ORIE: *dormitory, purgatory, oratory, victory,* etc.

### *OI, OY*

The digraph OI and the diphthong /ɔɪ/ arose most often through changes to Lat vowels in OFr (the source of many ModE OI-words typically first attested in ME, 13th–14th centuries): Lat *directum* > OFr *dreit* > *(a)droit* > *adroit;* Lat *vocem* > OFr *voiz* > *voice;* similarly Lat *punctum* > *point.* Other examples are *choice, cloister, exploit, join, moist, noise, poison, toilet.* From ModFr come *bourgeois, memoir, repertoire, connoisseur, mademoiselle, turquoise,* etc.

• The suffix -OID (as in *celluloid, paranoid, typhoid*) is derived from Graeco-Lat -OIDES.

• Until the 17th century, *choir* was generally spelt with QUI-; the ModE CHO- was apparently adopted in deference to the Graeco-Lat source word *chorus* and/or ModFr *choeur.*

- Until the 17th century OI was often written OY (e.g. *coyne, moyste, noyse, poysun* for ModE *coin, moist, noise, poison*). ModE kept OY in final position: *convoy, coy, employ, joy*, etc.
  - The medial OY in *oyster* is anomalous. EModE had spellings with OI: *oistre, oister.*
  - The OY digraph occurs medially before a vowel in a few words whose form is identical to that of ModFr: *doyen, flamboyant, foyer, loyal, royal, voyage, voyeur.*

### OO

Not many OO-words are derived from Fr, and all originally had a different vowel:

- The largest group end in stressed -OON corresponding to ModFr forms ending in -ON: *balloon, cocoon, harpoon, lampoon, saloon* (ModFr *ballon, cocon*, etc.). In most cases the earliest Eng spellings (EModE) ended in -ON or -ONE. *Mushroom*, from Fr *mousseron*, was first spelt with final N in Eng.
- A few other words of Fr derivation containing OO are:
  - *boot* (ME/EModE *bote*) from OFr *bote*;
  - *cuckoo* from either ME *cucu* or Fr *coucou*;
  - *fool* (ME also *fol, fole*) from Fr *fol*;
  - *poor* (also *pover, pour* in ME) from OFr *povre* (ModFr *pauvre*);
  - *troop*, an anglicized EModE variant on *troup* (OFr *trope*, ModFr *troupe*).
- Both *brooch* and *broach* entered ME from Fr as *broche*.

### OU, OW

The digraph OU occurs in many words of Franco-Lat origin, with various pronunciations: *country, courier, course, group, poultry, round, hour, serious, tour, journal*. In EModE there was uncertainty over the pronunciation of many words containing OU/OUR in ModE, with a corresponding variety of spellings; the spelling that has become established has not consistently reflected the pronunciation that has become established.

- The digraph OU originated in early OFr to represent a diphthong /ou/ that arose from Lat O and U (e.g. Lat *florem* > OFr *flour* 'flower'),

145

reduced by the end of the 12th century to /uː/. OE /uː/ had been represented by U, but this became ambiguous: since U was not distinguished in shape from V, it could be read as /uː/, /ʊ/ or /v/. The digraph OU introduced by Fr scribes provided a way of representing long U which avoided the ambiguities of U: Fr words spelt with OU entered ME with that spelling for /uː/ (as with *doute* 'doubt'), and OE words containing long U, such as *hus* 'house', were respelt with OU, giving ME *hous(e)*. See OE 'U' (p. 60).

- Fr words containing OU taken into Eng after the Great Vowel Shift were unaffected by the pronunciation change of OU from /uː/ to /aʊ/: e.g. *group* from Fr *groupe*, which first appeared in Eng in the late 17th century. *Blouse* is exceptional as a 19th-century loan in which the vowel-pronunciation has been anglicized.
- In several words Fr-derived OU came to be pronounced as short U in ModE: *country, couple, courage, cousin, double, flourish, nourish, touch, trouble*. Most of these words were spelt with O or U in ME and slightly later with OU.
- In a few words OU before L has the value of long O: *mould* (American *mold*) 'to shape', *moult* (American *molt*), *poultry, poultice*.
- A following R affects the value of OU in various ways: *hour, bourbon* 'whiskey', *courtesy, course*; in modern loans: *bourgeois, gourmet, tour, tourniquet*.
- The ending -OUS originated in the Lat adjectival ending -OSUS (e.g. *famosus*), which became -OS or -US in OFr and -OUS in ME, though at first with alternative spellings such as -OS, -OUSE, -OWS, -US.
- In certain cases there is an overlap between OW and OU, most obviously between *flower* and *flour* (both derived from OFr *flour/flor/flur*, Lat *florem* and not distinguished in spelling in ME or EModE) and the cognates *renown/noun*.
  - More usually, there is a positional distinction between OW and OU, with OW used at the end of a syllable and OU in mid-syllable: *allow, endow, prow, vow* (OU in this position occurs exceptionally in the ModFr loan *chou*).
  - Between vowels we find OW in *bowel, coward, dowager, flower, power, prowess, towel, tower, trowel, vowel*; and before consonants that begin the next syllable we find it in *chowder, dowry, powder*.
  - OW also occurs before final N in Fr-derived *crown, frown, gown, renown*, though OU is normal before N when a further consonant follows (*announce, count, round*, etc.); note the anomaly of *renown/noun* < Lat *nominem*.

## O *lost*

O may be lost by elision: *crown* < Lat *corona*, Fr *couronne* (forms with O, e.g. *coroun*, were common in ME and EModE); *curts(e)y* < *courtesy*.

- Loss of O is seen in certain American forms, e.g. *esophagus* for British/Graeco-Lat *oesophagus*.

## P

### P *in words of Franco-Lat origin corresponding to Lat and/or Fr* P

- Initially and medially: *part, people, pity, place, present, special, rapid, culpable, discipline, collapse*; in words beginning with the prefixes PER-, POST-, PRE-, PRO-.
- In final position: *carp, develop, equip, map, pomp, usurp*; also with a final unpronounced E indicating a long value for the preceding vowel: *cape, rape, tripe*, etc.
  - In such words Fr typically has a final -E (*carpe, pompe*, etc.) or -ER in the case of verbs (e.g. *développer*); Lat nouns often had a final -A (*carpa, mappa*, etc.).

### Double or single P

- Lat PP occurs where prefixes are assimilated to the P of a following stem:
  - AD-: *apparent, appeal, appear, approach, appropriate*;
  - OB-: *opportunity, oppose, oppress*;
  - SUB-: *supplant, supplement, support, suppose*.
  Spellings with single P were common in ME: *apere, aproche, apele, oportunite, sopose* (= 'appear, approach, appeal, opportunity, suppose').
- As with many other consonants, EModE tended to double a former single P in disyllabic words where the Fr second-syllable stress of shifted to the first syllable in Eng: *coppice, puppet, supper, supple* (compare ModFr *couper* 'to cut', *poupée, souper, souple*).
  - Certain words could be written with PP in EModE, but the doubling did not become established; ModE forms have the original single P: *chapel, copy, proper*.

## P *lost*

- Lat P was lost in Eng in words in which it was softened to V in OFr: *achieve* (also *chief*) < OFr *achever* (also *chef*) < Lat *caput* 'head', *arrive* < *ariver* < *arripare* < Lat *ripa* 'shore', *travail*/*travel* < *travail* < LLat *tripalium* 'torture implement'.
- Deriving from verbs ultimately going back to Lat *capere* 'to take', with its vowel variations CEP- and CIP-, we have *receipt* but *conceit*, *deceit*. In EModE, all three words were sometimes written with and sometimes without P, the P being inserted in deference to its being in the Lat words from which they derive (perhaps also under the influence of Fr, where *recepte* was a standard form through much of the 16th and 17th centuries).
- Lat *tempus* 'time' was first reduced to *tens* in OFr. Throughout EModE, the word was variously spelt *tens*, *temps* and *tense*, the latter (as in *present tense*) eventually becoming standard.

## P *acquired*

A single example of P originating in Eng is seen in *purse* (< Lat *bursa*), which already had the form *purs* in OE.

### PH

PH occurs predominantly in words of Gr origin. There are, however, some Lat-derived words spelt with PH in ModE whose connection with Gr are tenuous or non-existent: *lymph*, *pamphlet*, *sulphur*, *triumph*, *trophy*.

- The spelling *nephew* with PH appears as a conflation of several factors: OFr *neveu* was pronounced with /v/, and the same pronunciation is clearly indicated by EModE *nevew*. However, the tendency for both Eng and Fr around the 16th century to insert etymological letters led to forms such as *nepveu*, *nepvew* (from Lat *nepotem*); Eng melded the P into the digraph PH. The PH was and may still be pronounced /v/, but is being displaced by a spelling pronunciation /f/.

## Q

OE scarcely used Q at all, /kw/ being regularly spelt CP. Norman scribes, who used Q in writing Fr and Lat, were by the 12th century beginning to apply it to such OE words as *quake, queen, quell, quick* and *bequeath*, so that by the 13th century all these words are attested spelt with both CW (sometimes also KW) and QU, and by the 14th spellings with QU had become the norm. When Norman Fr words with Q began to be included in Eng texts, their spelling sometimes varied between QU and CW (e.g. *cwite/quit*), and other variants, especially QW, were not uncommon up into EModE.

## Positions of QU

QU corresponding to Lat and/or Fr QU:

- Word-initially and medially: *quality, question, square, squirrel, bouquet, liquid, lacquer, banquet, marquis.*
  - Several words derive from OFr with loss of initial E (*square, squash, squeamish, squire, squirrel*); more recent is *squad* (ModFr *escouade*, 17th century).
  - Pre-18th-century loans were often written with C, CK, K (e.g. *licor, pickant, marketry*); 18th-century *etiquette* has a much earlier doublet in *ticket*.
- Word-finally, phonologically rather than orthographically, in -QUE: *boutique, technique, grotesque.*
  - Words that entered the language in the 17th century or earlier were often written with K (e.g. *antike, opake, arabesk, brusk*).

## Doubling of Q

Q is not doubled by assimilation of a Lat prefix (compare *accede, affect*, etc.), but the conversion of the prefix AD- to AC- in Lat-derived words has much the same effect: *acquiesce, acquire, acquit.* In ME such words were typically written without C.

## Q lost and acquired

Generally, where Lat has QU, so does ModE.

- In a few cases VLat or OFr converted classical Lat QU to C, and the word entered Eng with the Fr spelling: *cry* (verb) < Lat *quiritare*, VLat *\*critare*; *coy* < Lat *quietus*, reduced to *coi* in Fr, often spelt with K in EModE (*koie, koy*).

- A larger group of words had C in Lat which was respelt QU before E and I in Fr and hence quite widely in EModE, until the ModE spelling with C, K or CK became established. Spellings with QU and/or CQU pronounced /k/ (often alongside alternatives using K, CK, etc.) were particularly common in the 17th century, but are attested for a number of words for a century or two before and/or after that time, e.g. *attaque, banque, embarque, magique, musique, pique-nique, remarque, risque, zodiaque.*
- In some words the QU originated in Eng: e.g. *quilt* < Lat *culcita*, OFr *cuilte*; *quince* < ME *coyn/quine* < OFr *cooin* < Lat *cotoneum*.
- When final /k/ immediately follows a short vowel, ModE typically has -CK, as in the development *trac* > *trak* > *track*, and similarly with Fr-derived *check, truck*. Word-final -CK developed between the 13th and 17th centuries; most ModFr equivalents have QU: *attack* (*attaque*), *barrack(s)* (*baraque*), *brick* (*brique*), *mock* (*moquer*), *shock* (*choquer* verb, but *choc* noun).
  - Some recent Fr loans retain the Fr -QUE: *plaque, cheque* (anglicized in America as *check*), *clique, brusque, discotheque, grotesque, opaque, unique,* etc.

## R

### *Lat and/or Fr R > ModE R*

- Word-initially and medially: *reason, round; parent, spirit; branch, create, front, strange; argue, order, pork, search, urban*; words with the prefix RE- (*remember, report, research, result, return,* etc.); words ending in -ARY, -ERY, -ORY (*necessary, machinery, history*).
- Word-finally: *appear, chair, matter, occur, particular,* etc.; also phonologically final and absorbed into diphthongs ending in /ə/ before silent E: *rare, severe, require, ignore, pure.*

### *Double or single R*

- Lat RR > ModE RR: *current, error, horror, narrate, territory, terror,* etc.
  - Some of these words could be written with single R in EModE, e.g. *current* < Lat *currentem* 'running', previously *corant* (< OFr *corant*).
- Doubling arises after a prefix ending in R, or with assimilation of a prefix ending in other consonants, when R is the first letter of the following stem:

- ○ INTER-: *interrogate, interrupt*;
- ○ AD-: *arrest, arrogant*;
- ○ CON-: *correct, correspond, corrupt*;
- ○ IN-: *irrational, irrelevant*; *irrigate*;
- ○ SUB-: *resurrection, surreptitious, surrogate.*
  - ▪ Some Eng words beginning with SURR- (e.g. *surround, surrender*) originate in Lat SUPER-, reduced to OFr SUR-.

Some of the above words already in use in ME (chiefly those beginning with ARR-) tended at first to be written with single R, as they had been in OFr (e.g. *areste, arive, soronde*). Typically with the development of classical learning in EModE, Lat-derived spellings with RR (including some etymologically incorrect, e.g. *surround* < Lat *super+undare*) established themselves as standard.

- A good number of words written with single R in Lat and Fr came to be written increasingly with RR in EModE to reflect, as with many other consonants, the shift of stress to an initial syllable with a short vowel: *barrel, carry, cherry, currant, garrison, marry, mirror*, etc.
- In a number of words ModE has the original Lat single R, although RR was also commonly written in EModE: *baron, carol, forest, merit, moral*, etc.
  - ○ Spellings of *very* with RR (e.g. *verray*; OFr *verai*/ANorm *verrai* < Lat *verum*) were dominant in ME; the form *very* is not attested until the 15th century.

### Loss of R

- The complete loss of R is rare. Two instances are the fish *dace*, in EModE *darce* < OFr *dars*; and *palsy*, ultimately from *paralysis*.
- Where R occurred twice in successive syllables, there are instances of one R being lost, e.g. *surgeon* < ANorm *surgien*, OFr *sirurgien*.
- R may be converted to L:
  - ○ This occurred already in Lat when the prefixes INTER- and PER- were assimilated before a stem beginning with L, as seen in ModE *intellect, intelligent, pellucid.*
  - ○ In several words there has been conversion of Franco-Lat R to L in Eng: *glamour, laurel, marble, purple.* In *colonel*, we have a case of L > R > L in spelling (Ital *colonello* > Fr *coronnel* > EModE *coronel/colonel*) with the pronunciation stopping at /r/.

## R *acquired*

- R from L or T:
  - ○ Lat L > OFr R: Lat *capitulum* > OFr *chapitle* > OFr *chapitre* > ME *chapiter* > *chapter*; similarly Lat *cartulam* > *charter*; Lat *lavandulam* > *lavender*; Lat *scandalum* > *slander*.
  - ○ *Potage* > *porage* in EModE, whence *porridge*.
- R inserted:
  - ○ Lat *perdix* > OFr *perdriz* > ME *partrich* > *partridge*; Lat *thesaurus* > VLat (in Gaul) *tresaurus* > OFr *tresor* > ME *tresor* > *treasure*.
  - ○ *Parsnip* acquired its R in EModE (ME *passenep* < Lat *pastinaca*).
  - ○ The origin of R in *sentry* is unclear, but compare 16th-century *centrinel* for *sentinel*.

## S

The letter S is found in Lat- and/or Fr-derived ModE words in most positions:

- Word-initially: *second* (< Fr *second* < Lat *secundus*), *sure* (< OFr *seure* < Lat *securus*), *spirit* (< ANorm *spirit*, OFr *espirit* < Lat *spiritus*), *slave*, *strange*, *square*, (Graeco-Lat) *scene*; in the Lat prefix SUB- and its variants (*subject*, *success*, *suffice*, *suggest*, *summon*); in the prefix SUPER- (*superficial*, *supervision*) and its Fr derivative SUR- (*surface*, *surprise*, *survive*).
- Medially: *nasal*, *present*, *blasé*, *hospital*, *industry*, *adolescent*: before M in words of Graeco-Lat origin: *enthusiasm*, *mechanism*; before -ION and -TION: *occasion*, *cohesion*, *vision*, *question*, *exhaustion*; before -QUE in ModFr loans: *grotesque*, *picturesque*.
- Word-finally (other than in inflections):
  - ○ In Lat *alias*, *habeas* and Graeco-Lat *atlas*, *pancreas*; in Fr-based *alas*, *bias*, *canvas(s)*.
  - ○ In Lat singular forms *series*, *species*; and plurals of Graeco-Lat base words ending in -IS: *analyses*, *bases*, *crises*, *theses*, etc.
  - ○ In Lat or Graeco-Lat words ending in -IS: *axis*, *pelvis*, *chrysalis*, *paralysis*.
  - ○ In mostly Graeco-Lat words ending in -OS: *asbestos*, *chaos*, *cosmos*, *ethos*, etc.
  - ○ In the suffix -OUS (mostly relating to Lat adjectives ending in -OSUS): *cautious*, *frivolous*, *hideous*, etc.

152

- In the Lat suffix -US: *bonus, cactus, census, circus, nucleus*; in words ending in -PUS (the Lat transcription of Gr *pous* 'foot'): *octopus, platypus.*
- Before a final silent E as in *false, sense, lapse, verse*; between long A, E, I, O, U and silent E: *base, obese, exercise, close, use.*
- Silent in ModFr words and phrases: *chassis, debris, faux pas, fracas, précis, à propos, rendezvous, s'il vous plaît.*

## Inflectional -s

As an inflection, word-final s has three different functions in ModE:

- as the normal plural ending (e.g. *words*);
- as the ending of the third person singular of the present tense of verbs (e.g. *makes*);
- (with an apostrophe in ModE) as indicating possession (e.g. *John's*).

In OE s served as a plural inflection only for a minority of nouns, was not yet used for the third person singular present tense verbal inflection, and was used to show the possessive form only of some nouns. However, s was being more widely used as a plural marker in the Northumbrian dialect of OE[12] and was spreading southwards, though it was far from dominant in the southern dialects. s as a plural inflection in ModE, however, also has Franco-Lat antecedents: its seeds were present in OE, but it became standard with the influx of Fr nouns into ME. The use of s as a plural marker in Fr stems from Lat accusative plural forms, e.g. *poetas, populos*. Just as many other unstressed Lat syllables were compressed and eroded during their evolution into Fr, so the distinction between the Lat plural inflections -AS, -OS was lost (and often even the vowel itself, as in Lat *muros* 'walls' > OFr/ModFr *murs*), and the Lat accusative plurals *poetas, populos* appear as *poètes, peuples* in ModFr, and through Fr as *poets, peoples* in ModE.

## Double or single s

- ModE ss is already present in Lat (occasionally Graeco-Lat) stems: *class, essential, fossil, mass, necessary, pass, possible*; also in derivatives from Lat past participles: -PRESSUM: *compressor, expression, impressive*: -CESSUM: *process, concession, predecessor*; -CUSSUM: *discuss, percussion*, etc.

153

- s is found doubled by assimilation of the prefix AD- to a Lat stem beginning with s: *assent* (< AD-+*sentire* 'feel'), *assert, assign, assimilate, assist,* etc.
  - To these may be added several other words whose stems have been influenced by Fr en route from Lat: *assail, assault, assemble, asset, assize, assuage, assure* (words that were used in OFr and ME were generally written with single s: *asail, asaut, asemle, asise, asuage, aseure*).
- s is found doubled in words beginning with the prefix DIS- before a stem beginning with s: *dissuade* (compare *persuade*), *dissect, dissident, dissimilar,* etc.

*Double s from Fr*
- In final position ss occurs in the feminine suffix -ESS < Fr -ESSE < Lat -ISSA: *abbess, empress, duchess, countess,* etc.
- Word-final -ss occurs in some words of Fr derivation that may have no direct Lat precursor:
  - In some cases they have lost a following E: *caress, embarrass, harass, fortress, prowess* < ModFr *caresse, embarrasser, harasser,* OFr *forteresse,* ANorm *prowesse.*
  - In other cases the OFr word ends in a single s which entered ME but has been doubled in ModE: *burgess, chess, compass, harness, mattress, trespass* < OFr *burgeis, esches, compas, harneis, materas, trespas.*
- In a number of words, ModE ss represents the phonetic simplification of a Lat consonant group, mostly with intermediate forms spelt with ss in Fr: *lesson* < OFr *lecon* < Lat *lectionem* 'reading'; *dress* < OFr *dresser/drecier* < VLat *\*directiare; mussel* < Lat *musculus, assay/essay* < Lat *exagium* 'weighing'.
- Certain words with medial ss are direct loans from ModFr, most without immediate Lat antecedents: *casserole, cassette, connoisseur, dossier, finesse,* etc.
- In ME and EModE, spellings of most of these words with final -CE, -SE, -SSE, -S were common, often predating the present ending with -SS.

*Double/single s variation*
The distinction between *canvas* 'fabric' and *canvass* 'seek votes' (both from Fr *canevas*) is recent. *Pastime* was often written as two words, e.g. *passe tyme,* in EModE).

- In ME and EModE, some 40 different spellings for *scissors* were attested, such as *cisers* (< OFr *cisoires*, from Lat *caedere* 'to cut'); forms with SC- did not emerge until the 16th century, reflecting a supposed origin in or connection with Lat *scissor* (< *scindere* 'to cut').

## Silent and superfluous *s*

A few ModE words are spelt with a silent medial s:

- Early OFr *isle* (< Lat *insula*) became *ile* and so entered ME; however, 16th-century Fr restored the s spelling in deference to the Lat form, and that spelling was copied in EModE, eventually becoming standard. Both *aisle* (< Lat *ala*, ModFr *aile* 'wing') and *island* (< OE *iȝland*) acquired s by analogy with *isle*.
- *Ascertain* entered EModE with variant spellings such as AC-, ACC-, ASC- and ASS-, of which only the first has a historical basis (< OFr *acertener* < *a* 'to' + *certain*).

## Loss of *s*

### Loss of *s* at prefix/stem boundaries
- The Lat prefix DIS- often lost its s, as seen from such ModE derivatives as *difficult, digest, dilute, dimension, direct, disperse* (< *dis-+spersum*), *divide*. The s is retained in compounds created after the classical Lat period such as *disfigure, disgust, dislocate, dismember, disrupt*.
- The prefixes EX- and TRANS- assimilate the initial s of a following stem: compare *execute* and *persecute, exist* with *insist, extinct* with *instinct, transcribe* with *inscribe, transpire* beside *inspire*, etc.
  - Occasionally a double s is written in ModE, typically as an alternative spelling (*transsexual* as an alternative to *transexual*), or with the prefix separated by a hyphen (*trans-sonic* as an alternative to *transonic*).
  - Lat wrote such words with both single and double s (*transcendere* or *transscendere, transcribere* or *transscribere*). Spellings with SS are sometimes found in EModE.

### Loss and substitution of final *s*
- A few words that historically ended in s were misconstrued as plural forms at various times, and a new singular was created by removal of the s:

155

- *Asset(s)* originated in OFr *asez* (ModFr *assez* 'enough'), spelt *asetz* in ANorm, and by EModE written *assets*; a new 'singular' form *asset* without s had emerged by the late 19th century.
- The singular *cherry* arose in ME by loss of s from earlier forms such as OE *ciris*, Norman Fr *cherise*.
- Similar developments are seen in *sherry* (< the Spanish place-name *Xerez*, now *Jerez*), first attested in Eng in the 16th century as *sherris* or *sherries*; in *pea*, from *pease* (< Lat *pisa*); *sash* (window) from Fr *châssis* 'frame'.

- Conversely, some real plural forms were not recognized as such, and their s inflection was respelt -CE. Examples of Fr derivation include *dice, quince, trace* ('part of harness'), *invoice, accidence*.
  - Fr (more often OFr than ModFr) or Lat s was replaced by Eng -CE in many non-plural words: *ace, advice, choice, device, juice, pace, palace, peace*, etc.
- Non-word-finally, an original Lat s was replaced by C in OFr to give Eng *(salt-)cellar, cider, grocer*.

## s lost in Fr

The letter s, pronounced /s/ or /z/, was regularly suppressed before other consonants in OFr. This development occurred first in the south of France, but did not reach the north until after the Norman invasion of England, with the consequence that it left the ANorm dialect largely unaffected, but overtook Central Fr during the 12th and 13th centuries (though the s was subsequently restored at least in writing in many words of noticeably Latinate form in the 15th and 16th centuries, only to be deleted again if silent in the 18th century. As a result there are large numbers of ModE words containing s that have ModFr equivalents without s, though its absence has since the 18th century commonly been marked by an acute or circumflex accent (e.g. *stage*, ModFr *étage*; *arrest*, ModFr *arrêt*). Some Eng words were nevertheless affected by this loss of s: e.g. Lat *adaestimare* > OFr *aasmer* > *aemer* > ME *ame* > *aim*; Lat *blasphemare* > OFr *blasmer* > *blame*; Lat *disjunare* > OFr *disner* > *dine*.

## ModE z in place of s

Between vowels the letter s came to be pronounced /z/ in post-classical Lat and hence in Fr. In most cases ModE has taken over such spellings with s, but in a number of words z or even zz began to be substituted in EModE: e.g. *breeze, buzzard, frieze, hazard, lozenge, magazine, razor, seize.*

## *s acquired*

- Lat -TIONEM produced the ending -SON in Fr, whence also in Eng: Lat *comparationem* > OFr *comparaison* > ModE *comparison*, and similarly Lat *jactationem* > ModE *jettison/jetsam*, *potionem* > *poison*, *rationem* > *reason*, *traditionem* > *treason*. Similarly, involving the reduction of D: Lat *obedientia* > (via ANorm) ModE *obeisance*.
- In a number of words, ModE writes s where historically (variously in Lat, OFr, ME) there had been a C: e.g. *despise, exercise, hearse, mason, raisin, rinse, sausage*, etc.
- Another example of acquired s is *tennis* < Fr *tenez* 'hold'.

### SH

The spelling of /ʃ/ showed a great deal of variation throughout the ME and EModE period, with ModE *ship* attested as *chip, scip, schip, sip, ssip*, as well as *ship*, and ModE *English* as *Englisc, Englisch, Englis, Engliss, Englissh, Englissch, Inglisc*, etc. Of these spellings, the most commonly used in ME was SCH, but there were marked regional differences.[13] The digraph SH is first attested in the early 13th century in the work of the Augustinian canon Orm,[14] who experimented with a new regularized orthography of his own (see p. 74). SH was becoming established especially in London (e.g. in Chaucer) by the 14th century, was generally accepted by the mid-15th, and by the 17th century the alternatives listed above were scarcely used any more. The SH digraph was widely applied to words of Fr, and occasionally Lat, derivation:

- A few cases were already listed under 'CH' above (see p. 101), where Fr CH has been anglicized as SH: e.g. *fetiche* > *fetish, hache* > *hash, choc* > *shock*.
- Much more widespread was the adoption of SH in word-final position to replace Fr SS: e.g. *finish*, from the Fr verb *finir* with its inflected form *finiss-* (e.g. *finissent* '[they] finish'). Parallel cases are *abolish, accomplish, banish, brandish, cherish, nourish, perish, polish*, etc.
- OFr SS led to ModE SH in a number of other words: *brush* (compare ModFr *brosse*), *cash* (ModFr *caisse*), *crush, leash, push, quash, anguish, parish, cushion, mushroom*.

## T

### *Franco-Lat T > ModE T*

- Word-initially: *table, total, turn, train, trouble*; in the Lat prefix TRANS-: *transport, transfer.*
- Medially: *data, complete, politics; title, metre, actor, enter, certain, question, extra.*
  - Word-final -TY is typically a sign of Franco-Lat derivation: *city, pity*; and words ending in -ITY (ME -ITE < Fr -ITÉ < Lat -ITATEM): *activity, intensity, necessity.*
- Word-finally: *combat, secret, visit, pilot, hut, defeat, float, trout, doubt, act, result, front*; in words ending in -ANT, -ENT: *important, different.*
  - Orthographically medial but phonologically final: *rate, compete, invite, note*; preceded by S: *chaste, haste, paste, taste.*
  - A number of modern loans from Fr end in silent T: *ballet, bouquet.*

### *Double or single T*

- Eng TT from Lat TT, chiefly in words derived from the verb *mittere* 'to send': *admittance, committal, intermittent*; also where there has been assimilation of the Lat prefix AD- to a stem beginning with T: *attempt, attend, attention, attract, attribute.*
  - Also in orthographically similar Fr-derived forms: *attach, attack, attain, attitude, attire, attorney* (generally written with single T in OFr and ME: e.g. ME *ateyn* 'attain', *atende, atire, atorne* 'attorney').
- Eng TT from Fr T:
  - A larger number of words spelt with TT in ModE derive from OFr forms with single T which, like many other consonants, was doubled in EModE to reflect a stress-shift from the final syllable in Fr to the first syllable in Eng: *battle* (ME *batayle*, ModFr *bataille*), *bottle* (ME *botel*, ModFr *bouteille*), *button* (ME *botoun*, OFr *boton*), *mattress* (ME/OFr *materas*, ModFr *matelas*), *pattern* (ME/Fr *patron*).
    - *City, pity* and *metal* were sometimes written with TT in EModE, but in these cases the single T has persisted as the ModE standard; *mettle* originated in EModE as a spelling variant of *metal*.

### *Eng TT in other word-endings*

Few words in ModE end in TT:

- Two senses of *butt,* 'barrel' and 'shooting target', are of Fr derivation, and both were sometimes also written *but, butte* in EModE; the ModE preference for *butt* may be due to a wish to make a distinction with the conjunction *but.*
- The form *nett,* as an alternative to *net* 'free of deductions' (EModE *net, nett, nette*), avoids confusion with the noun *net.*
- A number of words (not all of Fr origin) have the Fr diminutive ending -ETTE (e.g. *brunette, cassette, cigarette,* etc.).

### T before CH

Most instances of ModE TCH are found in words of Germanic origin (e.g. *watch, stretch*). A smaller number of words of Romance (mainly Fr) derivation are also written with TCH: *crotch, match* 'for lighting', *butcher, hatchet.* Most entered ME with the Fr digraph CH (e.g. MFr spellings such as *boucher, hachet, huche* 'hutch').

- Certain other words of Fr derivation began to be written with TCH in EModE (e.g. *atchieve, batcheler, dutchess, toutch*), but these forms failed to become established.
  - The letter-name *aitch* is unusual in having TCH preceding by a long-vowel digraph; it arose as a 19th-century respelling of the ambiguous form *ache.*

### T lost or altered

- Classical Lat T was subject to variation with C in later Lat and alteration to C in Fr, as in *space* < OFr *espace* < Lat *spatium* (post-classical Lat also *spacium*).
- Lat -CT- produced Fr and Eng s/ss in *ambassador, dress, lesson, stress,* from Lat stems AMBACT-, DIRECT-, LECT-, STRICT-.
- There is a group of words in which an original Lat T has become s in Fr and Eng: thus Lat *comparationem* > ModFr *comparaison,* ModE *comparison,* and *potionem* > *poison* (see also p. 157).

### T acquired in Eng

Eng has added a final T to some words that previously (in OFr and sometimes in ME) ended in N: *ancient* (ME *auncien*), *pageant* (ME *pagyn*), *parchment* (ME *parchemin*), etc. This is due to hypercorrection: the final T having frequently been dropped in words such as *giant* in which it was etymologically correct (< VLat *gagantem* < Lat *gigantem* < Gr), it was frequently added to words in which it did not belong. A final T was occasionally added to words in which it has not survived: e.g. *margin, orphan, sermon, surgeon, vermin* (compare *varmint*).

- A case of inserted T in Eng is ModE *tapestry* (EModE *tapesry/tapissery*).

*TH*

The Eng digraph TH originated as a Lat transcription of the Gr letter *theta*, and was used in Lat, and hence widely in Fr and Eng, in the spelling of words of Gr derivation (e.g. *theory, method, rhythm*). Through the ME period this TH was increasingly adopted in place of the OE symbols Þ and Ð to represent the native Eng voiced and voiceless sounds /ð, θ/. Since Lat and Fr lack the sounds /ð/ and /θ/, the digraph TH is not normally found in Eng words of pure Lat (as opposed to Graeco-Lat) or Fr derivation. There are, however, a few exceptions:

- *Faith* is the sole survivor of several words in which western OFr (including Norman) developed intervocalic Lat D and T to /ð, θ/, so reducing Lat *fidem* by the 11th century to more or less the pronunciation of ModE *faith*, with the spellings *feið, feiþ, feith* attested in Eng from the 13th century.
- The TH of *author, authority*, by contrast, owes nothing to the Fr treatment of Lat (Lat *auctor*, OFr *autor*, ModFr *auteur*): the H first made its appearance in the 16th century in forms such as *aucthor*, and it is not until 1617 that any suggestion of the TH being pronounced /θ/ is recorded.[15]
- The form *anthem* is uniquely Eng, resulting from a progressive simplification of Lat *antiphona* from OE onwards, until by late ME/EModE it achieved the form *antem*; the insertion of H with pronunciation change from /t/ to /θ/ then paralleled that of *author*.
- The TH of *thyme* is of genuinely Graeco-Lat origin, but appears always to have been pronounced /t/ in Eng (*tyme* was a common spelling into the 18th century).

# U

## Sound values of U

OE U had one short value /ʊ/ (as in *ful* 'full') and one long value /uː/ (as in *fūl* 'foul'). In ModE, there are four sound values: short /ʊ/ as in *put* and /ʌ/ as in *but*; long /uː/ as in *truth* and /juː/ as in *duke* (though not all Eng accents observe these distinctions).

- The split in the sound value of short U between the original /ʊ/ and the new value /ʌ/ appears to have come about around the mid-17th century,[16] and therefore affected words of both Franco-Lat and Germanic origin.
- The development of long U is more complex:
  - OE long U was respelt OU in ME (see p. 176); then, following the Great Vowel Shift in the 15th and 16th centuries (see p. 177), its sound value became /aʊ/: *out*, etc.
  - The great majority of ModE words containing long U derive from Fr and/or Lat and when they entered Eng in ME or later gave long U the value /iuː/, subsequently reduced to /juː/, although many words later lost the /j/ (e.g. *rule*, *sugar*).
  - Some ModE words with long U are of OE origin: *clue, hue, true, Tuesday*. These were typically spelt -EW (e.g. *clew, Tewisday*); this spelling pattern survives in such words as *brew, chew, dew, few, new*, etc., and in EModE it was also applied to Fr loanwords: e.g. *view* < OFr *veue*, *dew* (ModE *due*) < OFr *deu*. (See also p. 62.)

## Lat U, Fr U/OU/O > ModE short U

The short values of U typically occur before two (or more) consonants, a consonant digraph, and x:

- In initial and medial position, almost always with the value /ʌ/: *drug* (< ModFr *drogue*), *sum, ultimate* (< LLat *ultimatus*), *usher, abundance* (< OFr *abundance*), *discuss, button* (< OFr *boton*), *public, muscle, luxury, product, adult, result, judge*; in the Lat prefix SUB- (and variants): *subject, success, suggest, supplement*.
  - In a few words, U is pronounced short when followed by only a single medial consonant: *bunion, pumice, punish, study* (compare *human, studious*). Spellings with double letters are attested: *bunnion, punnish*, etc.

161

- ModE *punish* follows the pattern of many other Fr-derived words ending in -ISH (e.g. *vanish, finish, abolish*) which have only a single consonant after a short vowel.
- Also included here are Lat forms such as *minimum, status*.
  - Examples of the short *put*-U: *bullet* (< 16th-century Fr *boullette*), *pudding, fulcrum* (< Lat *fulcrum*), *butcher, cushion* (< OFr *cussin/coissin*).
- Short U does not occur word-finally.

## *Lat and/or Fr* U > *ModE long* U

Long U normally occurs before a single consonant followed by a vowel, or before a vowel, or word-finally:

- Although in general two following consonants indicate a short U, U may have the long value if the second consonant is L or R: *bugle* (< OFr *bugle* < Lat *buculus*), *putrid*.
- Word-initially and medially: *ubiquitous, universe, unite, community, human, music, student, attitude, presume, genuine, suicide*.
  - *Puny* is a respelling of Fr *puisne* 'later born'.
- Word-final U is seen in recent loans (*impromptu, menu* from Fr, *in situ* from Lat).

## *Lat and/or Fr* U > *ModE* UI

In a few words of Franco-Lat origin, medial long U is spelt with the digraph UI, thus in *bruise, fruit, juice, nuisance, pursuit, recruit, suit*. In ME and EModE all of these had alternative U–E spellings: *bruse, frute, pursute, recrute*, etc. The sources of these words show various U-spellings: e.g. *bruise* (< ANorm *bruser*), *fruit* (< OFr *fruit* < Lat *fructus*), *juice* (< Fr/Lat *jus*), *nuisance* (< ANorm *nussance/nuisance*), etc.

## *ModE* UR, URR

The majority of words with UR are Franco-Lat in origin:

- Some derive from UR forms in both Fr and Lat: *absurd* (< Fr *absurde*, Lat *absurdus*), *furtive, murmur, purge, surge, urban, urgent*.
  - *Disturb, occur* derive from Lat *disturbare, occurrere*, with no ModFr equivalents.

- Other UR words have ModFr equivalents with OUR (and were often written with OUR in ME, EModE): *curb* (also *kerb*)/*curve* (ModFr *courbe*), *curtain* (OFr *courtine*), *furnace* (ModFr *fournaise*), *nurse* (ModFr *nourrice*), *purple* (ModFr *pourpre*), *purse* (ModFr *bourse*), *turn* (ModFr *tourner*).
  - Some of these have U in Lat, others O: respectively *curvum*, *cortina*, *fornacem*, *nutricem*, *purpura*, *bursa*, *tornare*.
- The prefixes PUR- and SUR- (e.g. *purpose, pursuit, surface, surprise*) derive from Lat PRO- and SUPER- via ANorm/OFr PUR-/POR-/POUR- and SUR-/SOR-/SOUR-.
- Words with the R doubled may have sources in O and/or U: *currant* < ANorm *Corauntz* = Corinth), *current* (< OFr *corant*/*curant* < Lat *currere* 'run'), *curriculum* (< Lat), *scurrilous* (< Fr *scurrile* or Lat *scurrilis*), *turret* (< OFr *torete*/*tourete* < Lat *turris*).

## Word-final -UE

- Words with silent -UE in -QUE and -GUE are mostly from Fr and/or Lat (*antique* < Fr *antique*, Lat *antiquus*, *vague* < Fr *vague*).
- Nearly all ModE words ending in non-silent -UE are of Fr origin:
  - Some have exactly their ModFr forms: *accrue, argue, avenue, continue, due*, etc. *Hue* (as in 'hue and cry'), *retinue, value* derive from OFr.
  - *Ague* and *blue* derive from Fr *aigu* 'sharp' and *bleu*.
  - Some ModE -UE words have lost following consonants seen in Fr: *sue, ensue, pursue* all relate to the Fr verb *suivre* 'to follow' (OFr *sivre*; ANorm had forms ending in -SUER); *rescue* (ME *rescouse*) < OFr *rescous(s)e*.
- Most words ending in -UE were sometimes spelt with -EW in EModE (e.g. *accrew, argew, continew*); see p. 161.

### EU

- Graeco-Lat EU: The digraph EU originating in Gr was transmitted to Eng via Lat: *neurotic, pleurisy, leuk(a)emia, rheumatic*.
- The long-U value of EU also occurs in a number of words of non-Gr origin:
  - from Lat *feudal, neuter*;
  - from Fr *adieu, deuce, lieu, liqueur, manoeuvre*/*maneuver, oeuvre, pasteurize, queue*; in the ending -EUR: *connoisseur, entrepreneur, amateur, chauffeur, grandeur*.

- The pronunciation of the first syllable of *lieutenant* as /lef/ in British speech goes back many centuries, as is shown by ME and EModE *leftenant*.

## U *in Lat noun/adjective endings*

The endings -US and -UM could terminate both nouns and adjectives in Lat: nouns *campus, census, consensus, circus, focus, genius, genus, onus, status, stimulus, momentum*, etc.; adjectives and past participles: *bonus, primus, detritus*.

- Two -US words are based on Gr *pous* 'foot', transliterated into Lat as -PUS: *octopus, platypus*.
- Some -UM forms have no Lat antecedent: *conundrum, condominium, laudanum, pandemonium, tantrum, valium*; in the names of chemical elements: *potassium, uranium*.
  ○ *Linoleum, petroleum* are based on Lat *oleum* 'oil'.

## U = /w/

The letter U could have the value /w/ in Lat and this has survived into ModE with its original Lat U spelling in many words after another consonant: *conquest, distinguish, extinguish, languish, quality, sanguine, anguish* (< OFr *anguisse*), *language* (< ANorm *langage/language*, the U by analogy with Lat *lingua*).

- The value /w/ for U is also occasionally heard after S: *persuade, suave* from Lat; *cuisine, suite, suede* from Fr; in EModE the form *perswade* was sometimes used.

## V

## *Fr and/or Lat* V > *ModE* V

- Word-initially: *vast, vehement, viable, volume, vulnerable*.
- In medial position: *civil, severe, vivid, prevail, medieval, intervene, invent, revolve*.

## -VE

The sound /v/ is heard in word-final position in a number of ModE words of Franco-Lat derivation spelt -VE: *cave, move, pave, save, slave*.

Whereas after many other consonants ModE often drops a final E that is still written in ModFr (e.g. *modern/moderne, group/groupe*), the E is always retained after V, since the lack of a clear distinction in spelling between the sound values of V and U/W before the 17th century led writers to mark final /v/ with a following E, in words of Germanic origin, e.g. *have, love*, as much as of Franco-Lat.

- Other words ending in -VE deriving from Lat stems include *nerve, deprive, derive, preserve, resolve*; the suffix -IVE: *active*.

## Acquired V

- Lat medial B > V in Fr and hence Eng: *beverage* (ModFr *breuvage* < Lat *bibere* 'to drink'), *cavalry/chivalry* (ModFr *chevalerie*, Lat *caballus* 'horse'); *deliver* (ModFr *délivrer*, Lat *deliberare*), *govern* (ModFr *gouverner*, Lat *gubernare*); *tavern* (ModFr *taverne*, Lat *taberna*).
- Lat medial P > Fr and Eng V: *cover/covert* (ModFr *couvrir*, Lat *cooperire*), *manoeuvre/maneuver* (ModFr *manoeuvre*, Lat *manuoperare*), *poverty* (ModFr *pauvreté*, Lat *paupertatem*), *travail/travel* (ModFr *travail*, Lat *tripalium*).

## Loss/alteration of V

- Lat V > B: Lat *curvus* 'bent' > ModFr *courbe*, Eng *curb*.
- Lat V > F: Lat *brevem* > Fr *bref*, ModE *brief*; similarly *beef, chief, mischief, proof, relief, safe, serf, strife*, etc.
  - Word-initial examples are *fan* (< Lat *vannus*), *ferrule* (< OFr *virol*, Medieval Lat *virola*).
- Lat V > G: Lat *cavea* > Fr/Eng *cage*.
- The first syllable of *curfew, kerchief* derives from OFr *covre* 'cover'.
- *Manoeuvre* has lost its V in EModE *manure*.
- *Stew* < OFr *estuve*.

## W

Since the Lat alphabet had no W, and its daughter languages do not use W in native words, W is not normally found representing /w/ in ModE Franco-Lat derivatives. Instead, such words typically use U: *distinguish, quiet, persuade*. Instances of W = /w/ in ModE words of Fr origin are few:

- Fr U > Eng W: *Swiss* (< Fr *Suisse*) and *tweezers* (< 17th-century *tweeze* < Fr *étui* 'small box').
- Some Eng words with initial W have parallels in words beginning with G(U): *wage/gage*, *ward/guard*, *reward/regard*. The W-forms derive from Norman Fr, the G-forms from the Central Fr from which ModFr derives (compare ModFr *gager*, *garder*, *regarder*). See further pp. 69–70.

### *AW, EW, OW in words of Fr origin*

In ModE words of Fr origin containing one of the digraphs AW, EW, OW (e.g. *lawn*, *jewel*, *flower*), the W typically arose, usually in EModE, by substitution for an earlier Eng and/or Fr U (e.g. *flower* < *flour*; *pewter* < ANorm *peutre*). One reason for the change was to overcome the then ambiguity of the letters U/V: writing *power* rather than *pouer/pover* ensured the latter would not be confused with the first two syllables of *poverty/pouerty*.[17] This alteration was not, however, applied consistently: parallel spellings with AU, UE and OU are not uncommon, and some words have forms using either W or U: hence the variations between such cognates as *accrue/crew*, *noun/renown*, *revue/review* and *flour/flower*.

- ModE AW < Norman or OFr forms (with a variety of spellings): *spawn* < OFr *espandre*, *fawn* < OFr *faon*, *lawn* 'grass' < OFr *launde*, *paw* < ANorm *poue*.
  - Most of these words had spelling alternatives with AU/AW in EModE, the pair *laune/lawne* being typical.
- ModE EW from Fr: *crew*, *curfew*, *nephew*, *pew*, *stew*, *view*, *pewter*, *jewel*, *sewer*.
  - The EW spelling in these words in EModE varied with EU, U(E), UWE, etc. (e.g. *screw/skrue*, *pewter/peuter*; *jewel/iuel*), and a number of ModE forms spelt with UE were formerly also spelt EW (e.g. *argue*, *virtue* as *argew*, *virtew*, *blue* as *blew*, and *sue* as *sew*) – see also pp. 62, 161. Whether a ModE spelling has EW or UE is fairly arbitrary.
- Among ModE OW words of Franco-Lat origin are *allow*, *flower*, *powder*, *power*, *tower*. Forms with OW often formerly had U or OU spellings: *coward/cuard*, *towel/touel*, *allow/aloue*, *powder/pouder*, *tower/tour* for ModE.

166

# X

## Medial x

- The vast majority of examples of medial x in ModE Lat-derived words involve the Lat prefix EX-: *example, exempt, exile, except, excuse, express, exquisite, extend.*
  - When EX- precedes a stem beginning with S, the s is omitted in ModE: compare *execrate* with *consecrate, exist* with *insist.* (See also p. 155.) EModE sometimes shows forms with EXS-, especially before P: *exspect, exspire.*
  - Some EXC- forms saw variants without C in EModE: *exellent, exite.*
  - When EX- precedes a stem beginning with H, the H is silent: *exhaust, exhibit*; it was occasionally omitted in EModE, as in *exale, exort.*
- Other instances of Franco-Lat medial x are relatively few: e.g. *anxious, approximate, auxiliary, axis, luxury, maximum, nexus, noxious, toxic.* Nearly all of these words were first used in EModE (most in the 17th century), only *luxury* being attested in ME.

## Final x

Lat final x > ModE x: *apex, appendix, crux, index,* etc.

- Such words mostly first appeared in Eng with the revival of classical learning around the 16th century or later.
- Other Lat-derived words ending in x in ModE have lost the final syllable of their Lat form, sometimes during passage through Fr: *flux* < Lat *fluxus, lax* < Lat *laxus,* and similarly *fix, flex, mix, sex, tax, vex.*

## -XION *and* -CTION

*Complexion, crucifixion, fluxion* are standard ModE forms, and *connexion, deflexion, inflexion* exist as alternatives to *connection,* etc.

- *Complexion* derives from the past participle *plexum* from the Lat verb *plectere*; although ME and EModE used such alternatives as *compleccion, complection,* ModE is firm on the x-spelling.
- *Crucifixion* derives from the participle *fixum* of *figere* 'to fix'; the form *crucifixion* has been consistently used in the Christian tradition, and *\*crucifiction* is not attested.

- *Fluxion* is similarly determined by the Lat participle *fluxum*; the verb *fluere* offers no -CT- alternative.
- Uncertainty has arisen in the case of *connexion, deflexion, inflexion* because, despite the Lat participles *nexum, flexum* with x, the corresponding infinitives, *nectere, flectere,* have given rise to the Eng verbs *connect, deflect, inflect.*
  - In his *American Dictionary of the English Language* (1828), the American lexicographer Noah Webster (see p. 302) recommended the -CT- forms, which (despite ModFr *connexion, deflexion, inflexion*) are today found much more frequently.

## ModFr –x

- ModFr silent final x: *faux pas, grand prix.*
- Silent or pronounced /z/ in ModE, ModFr final x may be a plural inflection after AU and EU: *bureaux, chateaux, jeux.*

## Loss of x

Lat EX- is sometimes reduced to initial s in ModE: *sample* from *example, scald* from Lat *excalidare, soar* from Lat *ex aura, spend* from *expend,* and *strange* from Lat *extraneus.*

## x from CC/CKS

The x of *cox* 'boatman' arose from *cockswain,* while *pox* (as in *smallpox*) was respelt from the plural of *pock* (as in *pockmarked*). These replacements of CC or CKS by x are first attested in EModE; other examples are 20th-century: *sox* for *socks, fax* from *facsimile. Proxy* < *proc'cy* < *procuracy.*

## Y

The letter Y was introduced into the Roman alphabet to represent the equivalent Gr vowel in words transliterated from Gr. From OE times onward Y has often alternated with I (compare *carry/carries, gypsy/gipsy*), with Y overwhelmingly preferred in final position.

### Initial and medial Y < Graeco-Lat and/or Fr Y

- In words of Franco-Lat origin, initial Y is only found in names (e.g. *Yvonne*).

- In medial position Y as a full vowel usually indicates Graeco-Lat origin (two exceptions being *nylon*, a 20th-century invented term, and *style*, altered from *stile* < Lat *stilus*, often written *stylus*). Many such words have been handed down with similar forms in ModE and ModFr (e.g. ModE *analysis*, *cycle*, *physical*, *psychology*, *system*, *type*, ModFr *analyse*, *cycle*, *physique*, *psychologie*, *système*, *type*). The similarity of the ModE form of such words to their Lat and Fr forms often makes it impossible to say whether they derive more directly from Lat or from Fr.
  - In a few cases the spelling varies between ModE and ModFr, with one using Y and the other I, in most cases the I-form having also been used in ME and/or EModE, e.g. ModE *asylum*, *crystal*, ModFr *asile*, *cristal*, ME/EModE *asilum*, *cristal*.
  - The short and long values of Y are not indicated by spelling, thus *hysteria* with the short value and *hydrogen* the long value. The same stem may vary between the long and short values, e.g. *cycle/cyclical*, *type/typical*.
- Common sources of ModE Graeco-Lat Y are the Gr prefix SYN- and its assimilated variants (e.g. *synergy*, *syllable*, *sympathy*, *system*) and the Gr word-forming elements such as HYDRO-, OXY- and -LYSIS (e.g. *hydrolysis*, *oxygen*). Although pronounced the same as -ISM, -IST (e.g. *criticism*, *communist*), the endings -YSM, -YST (e.g. *paroxysm*, *analyst*) are unrelated and derive from Gr via Lat and Fr.
- Medial Y between vowels derives from Fr: *bayonet*, *buoyant*, *foyer*, *mayonnaise*, *royal*, *voyage*.
  - The Y in *mayor*, *prayer* is an Eng innovation (ANorm *mair*, *praiere*).
  - Medial Y with the /j/ value after consonant letters occurs only occasionally in ModE, as in the suffix -YER (< OFr -IER): *lawyer*, *sawyer*. (Note that the W in both these cases is part of a vowel grapheme AW.)

### *Word-final* Y

- Large numbers of Franco-Lat words have Y in final position after a consonant, where it varies with I (*cry*, *crying*, *cries*, *cried*) and may have long value (*cry*) or short (*envy*).
- Word-final Y also occurs after vowels: *essay*, *obey*, *employ*, *guy*.
  - In medial position ModE generally prefers AI, EI, OI (e.g. *paid*, *vein*, *join*) to AY, etc., though exceptions are found (e.g. *oyster*).

- In Franco-Lat sources ModE Y usually derives from I (see Fr -E/ -EE/-IE > ModE -EY and -Y, p. 106, for words of the type *country*, *quality* where the Y goes back to Lat A and Fr E; for the development of Lat or Graeco-Lat -IA/-IUM/-IUS to ModE -Y, and of Franco-Lat I to final -Y in ModE verbs, see pp. 125–6).

## Z

The letter Z was scarcely used in OE, since /z/ did not arise word-initially or -finally in native words, and S represented it unambiguously between vowels in medial position (see OE 's', p. 53). In OFr, on the other hand, Z served a variety of functions and under Fr influence it came into ever wider, though inconsistent, use in Eng through the ME and EModE periods.

### z/s variations in Fr- or Lat-derived words

- A rare case of Z inherited directly from Fr is *dozen* (< OFr *dozeine*); spellings with S were common in both EModE and MFr.
- There was a marked tendency especially in the 16th century (in Fr as well as Eng) for intervocalic S pronounced /z/ to be respelt Z. Examples of EModE conversion of intervocalic S to Z in words of Fr origin are *blazon*, *brazier* (for burning coals), *breeze*, *buzzard*, *frieze*, *hazard*, *lozenge*, *magazine*, *razor*, *seize*, *size* (compare ModFr *blason*, *brasier*, *brise*, etc.).
  - In a few words (*embezzle*, *frenzy*, *grizzled*, *guzzle*, *muzzle*) with S in corresponding OFr *besillier*, ModFr *frénésie*, *grisaillé*, OFr *gosiller*, ModFr *museau*, the ModE Z is not intervocalic; but these words were formerly spelt with intervocalic S (ME or EModE *enbesyl*, *frenesie*, *grisel*, *gussel*, *mosel*).
- A few Eng Z-spellings came from Graeco-Lat. A small group of Gr derivations with initial Z (*zeal*, *zed*, *zephyr*, *zodiac*) entered ME and have always been written with Z; but in *horizon*, medial Z has varied with S (e.g. ME *horison*).

### The suffix -IZE/-ISE

There are some 200 verbs in general use ending in the suffix -ISE/-IZE, spelt with Z in American usage and S or Z in British usage. The ending

170

originated in Gr with z, which was transmitted through Lat and OFr to Eng beginning in the ME period.

- Three factors interfered with the straightforward adoption of z for all words ending in /aɪz/:
  ○ The increasing variation of z/s in OFr and ME.
  ○ The competing model of words like *surprise,* always spelt with s (-ISE in those words being not the Gr suffix but part of a Franco-Lat stem).
  ○ Developments in Fr which undermined the z-spelling of the Gr -IZE suffix; for example, the 1694 edition of the authoritative dictionary of the Académie Française standardized the spelling of the Gr suffix with s (e.g. *baptiser, organiser, réaliser*) for ModFr in accordance with the general Fr rule for the spelling of /z/ between vowels as s, and the consistent use of -ISE by ModFr from then on gave weight to a widespread preference for it in British usage. American usage, on the other hand, came down steadfastly on the side of -IZE, and BrE now allows either spelling.

# Notes

1  Readers who want a complete picture of the spelling development of any particular word should consult the *Oxford English Dictionary.*
2  In this and following sections, the abbreviations Lat, Fr, ANorm, OE, ME, etc. will be used instead of Latin, French, Anglo-Norman, Old English, Middle English, etc. For a complete list of abbreviations, see p. xi.
3  Latin nouns and adjectives are generally cited in this chapter in their nominative form (= the form indicating the subject of a sentence), e.g. *candela, certanus,* although strictly speaking it is from the Latin accusative case (= the form indicating the object of a sentence), e.g. *candelam, certanum,* that most French nouns and adjectives developed. Only where the form of a French and/or English word requires that its derivation be shown from a Latin accusative case which differs in some significant way from the nominative case is the source word given in its accusative form, e.g. *rationem, pulverem* (nominatives being *ratio, pulvus*): Lat *rationem* > OFr *resun* > ME *reison* > *reason,* Lat *pulverem* > OFr *puldre* > *powder.*
4  Pope (1952: 447).
5  Scragg (1974: 43, footnote).
6  Scragg (1974: 49).
7  Jespersen (1949: 79 §3.25).
8  Pope (1952: §1093).

 9   Pope (1952: §192).
10   Wells (1990: s.vv. **historical, hotel**).
11   Wyld (1956: 293).
12   Baugh and Cable (1993: 155–6).
13   Scragg (1974: 46).
14   Scragg (1974: 29, 31).
15   Dobson (1968: 1008, 1020).
16   Dobson (1968: 720–2).
17   Jespersen (1949: 89 §3.49).

# 6

# Some Sound and Spelling Developments in Middle and Modern English

We have now analysed the Old English and Franco-Latin roots of our present-day English spelling, and in Chapters 7 and 8 we will look at the contributions that Greek and other languages have made to English orthography. However, many of the unpredictable and problematic relationships between the letters and the sounds of Modern English have come about not from the intermingling of the spelling systems of these various and very different languages, but from, on the one hand, alterations to the Old English spelling system, leading to pairs of words such as *sun* and *son*, alike in sound but different in spelling, and, on the other hand, from sound-changes that radically altered the pronunciation of English during the Middle English and Early Modern English periods,[1] leading, firstly, to there being many words in Modern English with silent letters, as in *gnat, high, knee, wring*, etc. (compare German *Gnade* 'mercy', *hoch, Knie, wringen*, in which all the letters are pronounced); secondly, to phonetic realizations of the English vowel-letters very different from those of the corresponding letters in Latin and the continental European languages (compare, for example, English *name*, *dame* with German *Name* /ˈnaːmə/, French *dame* /dam/; English *seen*, *leer* with Dutch *een* /eːn/ 'one', German *leer* /leːr/ 'empty'; English *drive, lime* with Danish *drive* /ˈdriːvə/, French *lime* /lim/; English *school*, *boot* with Dutch *school* /sxoːl/, German *Boot* /boːt/ 'boat'; English *bout* with French *bout* /bu/ 'end, tip'); and thirdly, to pairs or sets of words

*The History of English Spelling*, First Edition. Christopher Upward and George Davidson.
© 2011 Christopher Upward and George Davidson. Published 2011 by Blackwell Publishing Ltd.

that while related by derivation and similar in spelling differ significantly in pronunciation, e.g. *child/children, wise/wisdom, divine/divinity.*

The above examples show the three key ways in which the English language changed in terms of sound–spelling correspondences:

1    a change in spelling without necessarily a change in the sound represented;
2    the loss of a sound without a corresponding loss of the letter which had hitherto represented that sound; and
3    the change in a sound without a change in the spelling which had hitherto represented that sound.

Although with the rise of the Chancery Standard (see p. 81) the 15th century saw a steady movement towards a fixed spelling that very much resembles the spelling of Modern English, and the advent of printing continued this trend, the 15th century was also a time of immense change in the pronunciation of English, and in many cases the spellings which became fixed no longer adequately represented the pronunciation of the day but rather represented the pronunciation of an earlier period. (We have already noted, for example, the Chancery preference for GH spellings in words like *high*, against other possible spellings in use at the time, such as *hye*, that better reflected the then current pronunciation.) In other words, as English spelling became more fixed, it also became increasingly less representative of the sounds of the spoken language. This state of affairs has, of course, continued into Modern English. In general, if a letter or digraph was pronounced at the time it first came to be printed, it is likely to have been preserved in Modern English even if it has since fallen silent (hence *gnat, know, ought*, etc.), while letters that were no longer pronounced and fell out of use before the form was fixed by printing cause no such problems (e.g. Old English *hlaford* > Middle English *loverd* > Modern English *lord*); and if a letter or digraph has changed in pronunciation since the time it was first printed, it is likely to have been retained in English orthography even if it might be confused with another letter or digraph (hence *tale* and *tail, see* and *sea*, etc.).

This chapter is not intended as a full account of the changes that have taken place since the beginning of the Middle English period, but will focus on developments that are of particular relevance to an understanding of Modern English spelling and sound–spelling correspondences. A number of these have been briefly commented on or alluded to in previous chapters.

# The English Alphabet

The basic stock of letters that Old English took from Latin was A, B, C, D, E, F, G, H, I/J, K, L, M, N, O, P, R, S, T, U/V, X, Y, plus the rarely used Q and Z. The use of this set of letters was reinforced by Norman French and by the influx of words from Latin, Greek and other languages in later centuries. The main innovations of the Old English writing system (above all, the letter *thorn*, Þ, for TH) outlasted the Norman conquest for a time, but ultimately they could not resist the impact of the development of printing, with its continental influences, in the 15th century.

At the beginning of the Middle English period, the English alphabet consisted of the following 27 letters:

A, Æ, B, C, D, E, F, 3, H, I, K, L, M, N, O, P, Q, R, S, T, Þ, Ð, U, ƿ, X, Y, Z.

During the Middle English period, a number of changes were made to this inventory of letters, and these will be outlined in this chapter. By the end of the period, we see a slightly different set of symbols, one that is almost identical to that of present-day English:

A, B, C, D, E, F, G, H, I, K, L, M, N, O, P, Q, R, S, T, U, V, W, X, Y, Z.

The only letter of the current English alphabet missing from the above inventory is J (for which, see below, pp. 184–5).

# Spelling Changes Introduced by Anglo-Norman Scribes

After the Conquest, French scribes introduced some new spellings which are reflected in Modern English orthography. They will be mentioned again in the alphabetical section of this chapter, but for convenience we will note a number of them here:

- C(E) replaced S: Old English *mys*, Modern English *mice*;
- CH replaced C: Old English *cild*, Modern English *child*;
- GH replaced H: Old English *liht*, Modern English *light*;
- QU replaced CW: Old English *cwen*, Modern English *queen*;

175

- TH gradually replaced Ð and Þ, finally by about the end of the 15th century;
- V was introduced by Anglo-Norman scribes in the 13th century;
- W (a ligatured double U/V) had essentially replaced Þ by the end of the 14th century, although Þ may be seen in some charters as late as the middle of the 15th;
- EA, borrowed by French scribes from Old English, was later re-introduced into English for /ɛː/: Old English *mete*, Modern English *meat*;
- IE was used to represent /eː/: Old English *feond*, Modern English *fiend*;
- O frequently replaced U in juxtaposition with M, N, V, W: Old English *sunu*, Modern English *son* (but compare Old English *sunne*, Modern English *sun*);
- OU replaced U: Old English *hus*, Modern English *house*.

## The Long Vowels of Middle English and the Great Vowel Shift

There were seven long vowels in Middle English, spelt as shown below:

/aː/ as in *name*, *faas* 'face';
/ɛː/ as in *clene* 'clean', *heeth*, *death*;
/eː/ as in *nede* 'need', *sweete*;
/iː/ as in *fine*, *shyne*, *wiis*;
/ɔː/ as in *holy*, *oon* 'one';
/oː/ as in *mone* 'moon', *foot*;
/uː/ as in *hous*, *clowde* 'cloud'.

Notice that the long vowel could be indicated either by a doubling of the vowel-letter or by a following -E. (Where in fact the length of the vowel was clear from its phonological surroundings, no further indication of length was needed or given: e.g. *child*, in which the vowel is long because of the following consonant group; see p. 178.) Notice also that spelling is not in itself a reliable guide to the pronunciation of some of the vowels.

The Great Vowel Shift (GVS) is the name given to a number of important and related pronunciation changes which affected these long vowels during the 15th, 16th and perhaps early 17th centuries and which resulted both in the differences between the sound–spelling correspondences of the continental European languages and those of Modern English remarked on above (e.g. French *dame* /dam/, English *dame*; French *lime* /lim/, English *lime*) and in the differences in pronunciation of the stressed vowels of pairs of words such as *divine/divinity* and *serene/serenity*, and also ultimately, though not directly, in (i) Modern English words such as *meet* and *meat* being alike in sound, and (ii) the difference in pronunciation of the OO of *food, good* and *blood*, etc.

Neither the exact mechanics nor the exact dates of these changes need concern us here.[2] The GVS and subsequent developments affected the pronunciation of the Middle English long vowels as follows:

Middle English /aː/ > /ɛː/ in the GVS, then > /eː/ and subsequently /eɪ/: Modern English *mate, name*;

Middle English /ɛː/ > /eː/ in the GVS, then subsequently > /iː/: Modern English *beat, tea*;

Middle English /eː/ > /iː/ in the GVS: Modern English *beet, see*;

Middle English /iː/ > /eɪ/ in the GVS, and subsequently /aɪ/: Modern English *bite, time*;

Middle English /ɔː/ > /oː/ in the GVS, then > /oʊ/ and subsequently /əʊ/: Modern English *road, bone*;

Middle English /oː/ > /uː/ in the GVS: Modern English *boot, moon*;

Middle English /uː/ > /oʊ/ in the GVS, and subsequently > /aʊ/: Modern English *house, out*.

Some of the post-GVS developments were not completed until well into the 18th century, and intermediate pronunciations between Middle English and present-day English can be discovered in rhymes allowed or, implicitly, disallowed by poets and playwrights of the intervening period: Shakespeare (1564–1616), for example, does not rhyme words spelt with EE and EA, such as *see* and *sea*, *seek* and *speak*, which make perfect rhymes in present-day English, as in his day EE was pronounced /iː/ and EA /eː/. Alexander Pope (1688–1744), on the other hand, rhymes *tea* and *obey*.

Since English spelling was during this same period becoming ever more fixed, these sound-changes were for the most part not reflected in the spelling system. Attempts were sometimes made to distinguish vowel sounds by spelling – for example, at the end of the 15th century, there was a move towards using EE or IE (as in *deep, thief*) for the long vowel /eː/, which became /iː/ in the GVS, and EA (as in *clean*) for the long vowel /ɛː/, which became /eː/ in the GVS, and subsequently /iː/ – but actual practice was far from consistent.

## Some further comments on the GVS and its effect on sound–spelling correspondences

- In the case of words such as *name, stone* which ended in an E deriving from any of several Old English vowels (e.g. *-a* in Old English *nama* 'name'), the E ceased to be pronounced during the 14th and 15th centuries and became a marker of the length and sound quality of the preceding vowel, as in the examples *name, clene, nede, fine,* etc. given above. This use of the silent E has continued into Modern English – compare *can* and *cane, bit* and *bite, not* and *note* – but not necessarily in all the words that were once spelt with a silent E: compare from the above examples *clene,* Modern English *clean; mone,* Modern English *moon.*
- Words that entered English after the completion of the GVS were not affected by it. Compare, for example, *polite* (first attested in English in 1501) in which the second vowel has undergone the same phonetic change as in *fine* and *wise,* and *police* (first attested as a noun in 1716, though there is an earlier attested use as a verb) in which the word has retained the /iː/ of French (but see the note on *blouse,* p. 188).
- Vowels might be lengthened or shortened in certain phonological environments. The fact that the GVS acted on long vowels, but not short vowels, could thus have an immense, and frequently confusing, effect on sound–symbol correspondences which is still to be seen in present-day English. A few examples will suffice:
  - In late Old English, short vowels were lengthened before consonant sequences such as /mb/, /nd/, /ld/ and /rd/. This lengthening was lost again in many cases by the end of the Middle English period. With the action of the GVS, one sees modern reflexes of the remaining long vowels in words such as *climb, bind, mild, yield, old,* etc. However, in some words there was a subsequent shortening of the vowel, leading to pairs of words similar or identical in spelling in Modern English but with different pronunciations: *wind* (verb, with /aɪ/) but *wind* (noun, with /ɪ/), *fiend* and *friend,* etc.
  - If the short vowel in Old English was followed by three consonants rather than just two, there was no lengthening. Hence, after the action of the GVS, we have *child* with /aɪ/ but *children* with /ɪ/.
  - Vowels were regularly shortened when followed by two unstressed syllables: hence, after the action of the GVS on the long vowel, we have Modern English *wild* but *wilderness* and similarly with words such as *divine* but *divinity, serene* but *serenity,* etc.

178

○ Beginning in the Old English period, vowels that were originally long were shortened when followed by certain consonant sequences: hence, again after the action of the GVS, we have in Modern English *wise* but *wisdom*, *sleep* but *slept*. The same rule underlies Modern English *hide* but *hid* (Old English *hydde/hidde*). There were inconsistencies in vowel-length before /st/, leading for example to Modern English *Christ* but *fist*, *ghost* but *lost*, *least* but *breast*.

## Consonant Doubling

In late Anglo-Norman and in Middle English, there was a tendency to double consonant letters to indicate a preceding short vowel. (Compare the use of double consonants for this purpose in the *Ormulum*, p. 74.) The use of double consonants to indicate short vowels increases in the 16th and 17th centuries, especially accompanying a shift of stress to the first syllable in words of French origin: *baggage, bonnet, cabbage, cotton, jolly, puppet/poppet* (compare French *bagage, bonet, caboche, coton, joli, poupée*). (For further examples, see the letter entries in Chapter 5.)

Having made these general points, we will pass now to a letter-by-letter consideration of some of the sound and spelling developments in Middle and Modern English.[3]

### A

In EModE,[4] words such as *scant* and *want*, *hand* and *wand*, *dash* and *wash* still rhyme. In the 17th century Dryden rhymes *began/swan/crane* and *far/war/care*. Only later do the vowels become rounded by the presence of preceding /w/ to give ModE /ɒ/ and /ɔː/. This change does not happen, however, if the vowel is followed by /k/, /g/ or /ŋ/, as in *wax, wag, twang*.

### AE

Æ dropped out of use during the 12th and 13th centuries, being replaced by A, EA or E: compare OE *æppel*, ME *appel, eappel, eppel*. Æ was reintroduced in the 16th century in Lat- and Gr-derived words (for Lat

Æ and Gr AI: *ægis, anæmia, encyclopædia*, etc.) but has now generally dropped out of use in favour of AE or in many cases, and especially in AmE, a simple E: *encyclopedia, medieval*. See also pp. 219–20.

## AI/A–E/AY

- In early ME, a new diphthong was formed by the vocalization of ʒ after front vowels: OE *sæʒde* > ME *saide* > ModE *said*, and similarly *bræʒn* (ModE *brain*), *fæʒer* (ModE *fair*), *tæʒl* (ModE *tail*).
- AI and A–E, as in *bait* and *bate*, *tail* and *tale*, etc., became identical in sound at least by the 16th and 17th centuries, and perhaps even earlier. The ME origins of the words in this group is generally reflected by the ModE spelling, a ME /aː/ being represented by A–E in ModE, while ME /aɪ/ is represented by AI and AY (as in *hail, day*).
- In northern ME, including Middle Scots, an I was frequently used after a vowel to indicate that it is a long vowel, as in *raid* (< OE *rad*; OE *rad* also > ModE *road*). *Raid* was subsequently borrowed into southern Eng.

## C

- In OE, C represented /tʃ/ or /k/. It was thus ambiguous with regard to pronunciation, and when with the value /tʃ/ was replaced by CH by ANorm scribes: OE *cese, cild* > ModE *cheese, child*. The OE C-spelling is rarely attested after 1100. See also comments at 'H'.
- C represented /k/ in words such as OE *cyn(n)* 'kin', *cyninʒ/cynʒ* 'king'. As is clear from the ModE forms, C in this position was replaced by K, as it had already occasionally been in OE.
- C was also replaced by K before N: OE *cnawan, cniht*, ModE *know, knight*. The K was no longer pronounced by the late 17th century.
- By the time of the French invasion of England, Fr C before E, I, Y had the value /s/ that it normally has in ModE, in words of both Fr and OE origin: ME *cyte* 'city' < OFr, ModE *ice* < OE *is*.
  - In late ME and EModE -CE often replaced a word-final S: *ace* < Fr *as*, *juice* < *jus*, *palace* < *palais*.
  - In some cases, the -CE replaced plural -S: e.g. *lice, mice* < OE *lys, mys* (and compare the plurals *pennies/pence*); *dice* arose as a plural of *die* 'tool' (< OFr *de*). See also pp. 55, 97.

## DG

The digraph DG begins to appear in medial and final positions in late ME, and more frequently in EModE, in words of both Germanic and Franco-Lat origin, replacing earlier GG: e.g. OE *ec3* > ME *egge* > ModE *edge*.

- Words of Franco-Lat origin often retained the Fr single G (e.g. *juge*) through ME, but adopted the DG pattern (as in *judge*) in EModE.

## E

- In ME, a final -E may represent the sound /eː/, as in *pite* 'pity', *cyte* 'city', or an unstressed /ə/.
- E was used to represent an unstressed /ə/ that developed in late OE through the gradual loss of distinctiveness in word-endings and short vowels in unstressed syllables (e.g. OE *tima* > ME and ModE *time*, OE *nacod* > ME and ModE *naked*).
  - The final -E ceased to be pronounced at the end of the 14th century.
  - As an ending, the -E was extended in use to some words in which it had no basis in OE: OE *bryd* > ME and ModE *bride*.
  - An optional final -E was used by scribes and printers to equalize the length of lines.
  - For final -E after V, as in *have, love, sieve*, see pp. 48, 164–5.
  - The loss of E from the -ES noun and verb endings (as in ModE *cats, dogs, walks*, etc., but not in *churches, wishes*, etc.) began in northern ME in the early 14th century, and is seen somewhat later in the Midland and Southern dialects.

### EA

EA represented the phoneme /ɛː/ in ME. ME /ɛː/ developed in two ways: to /eː/ and to /iː/. The /iː/ pronunciation was at first considered less polite, but between the 16th and the mid-18th centuries, it steadily replaced /eː/. Not all words in the EA group made this change, however, hence the current pronunciation of *break, great, steak, yea* as opposed to the more usual pronunciation of EA in *heath, seam*, etc.

- Shortening of the EA vowel in some words in EModE has led to ModE *bread, deaf, death,* etc. An EA spelling for *heavy* (< OE *heviʒ*) is first attested in the 16th century.
- For *break/breakfast,* see p. 40.
- For *speak/speech,* see p. 104.

### EI

A new diphthong was formed in ME by the insertion of /ɪ/ between a front vowel and /x/ (OE *ehta* > ME *eighte*). In late ME, EI and AI became identical in sound (as in *vein, vain*).

### G

- The letter ʒ representing /g/ was replaced by <g> at the beginning of the ME period, as in *dogge* 'dog' (OE *doʒʒe*). In the 14th century, ʒ representing /j/ was replaced by Y, as in *yeer* 'year', and when representing /x/ was generally replaced by GH, as in *bright, brought* (see 'GH' below). The character ʒ disappeared completely shortly after 1500.
  - Word-initial GN (as in *gnat, gnaw*) lost the /g/ sound by the early 17th century.
  - For the loss of the OE prefix ʒE-, see p. 44.
- Spellings of *foreign, sovereign* (< OFr *forain, soverain*) with G from the influence of *reign* are attested from the 14th century.

### GH

- For GH in *ghost,* etc., see p. 45.
- As we have already noted, ANorm scribes frequently replaced the OE H with GH: OE *niht,* ME *night*; OE *brohte,* ME *broughte* 'brought'. (The letter ʒ was also used: *niʒt, brouʒte.*) The GH represented /x/, which was pronounced [ç] after a front vowel and [x] after a back vowel, as in ME *night* and *broughte* respectively (and as also in Modern German). Although, under the influence of Chancery and the printers, this digraph has continued to be written from the ME period to the present day, the sound it represented/represents has undergone many changes. Some of the key points in the complex developments of this set of words are as follows:

○ The /x/ was being dropped from pronunciation as early as the 14th century, as attested by spellings such as Chaucer's *hey/hye* for *high*. On the other hand, there is evidence that it was still being pronounced by some people as late as the early 17th century.

○ In another development, by late ME the /x/ had in northern dialects developed to /f/ in some phonological contexts, hence ModE *laugh, rough*. Forms with -F instead of -GH are also found from the 14th century in words not pronounced /f/ in ModE (e.g. *þof/þowf* for *þohh* 'though', *þurf* for *þurh* 'through'), and in dialect forms (compare *dough* and *duff*). In the case of *dwarf* (< OE *dþeorȝ*), -F has established itself as the standard spelling, therefore causing no sound–spelling problems.

○ The forms *plough/plow* derive from different parts of the noun declension (i.e. the different forms a word takes according to its role in a sentence), e.g. OE *plog*, plural *plogas* > early ME *ploh*, plural *ploȝes* > later ME *plough*, plural *plowes*, whence the two ModE forms *plough/ploughs, plow/plows*. In the case of *plough*, BrE therefore has a written form *plough* with a spoken form corresponding to the alternative written form *plow* which is preferred in AmE. *Enough*/(archaic) *enow* similarly derive from different parts of the declension of the word.

○ When stressed, OE *þurh* > *þuruh* > ModE *thorough*. Similarly OE *burh* > ModE *borough* (*burrough* was the commonest spelling in EModE; the spelling *burgh* became obsolete in England in the 17th century but is the usual form in Scottish Eng.) Unstressed *þurh* > *þurh/þruh* > ModE *through*.

○ Many words ending in -H in OE have ModE spellings with -OW rather than -OUGH, e.g. OE *furh*, ModE *furrow*. In EModE, both spellings were possible, e.g. *furrough, furrow(e)*, just as there were accepted variants *burrough, burrow(e)* for ModE *borough*.

○ With GH no longer being pronounced, after the action of the GVS on long vowels (such as the I of *high*) it became a marker of a long vowel or diphthong. Hence by analogy, a GH spelling was sometimes introduced where it had no justification: e.g. *delight* < earlier *delite* < OFr *delit*. The -GH- spelling is also attested in forms such as *apetyght, despight* for *appetite, despite*, but these spellings did not in the end establish themselves.

○ Notice that the vowels written OU before GH in ModE derive from several different vowels in OE, as can be seen from *bough* (< OE *boh*), *cough* (< ME *coghen* < OE *cohhian*), *dough* (< OE

183

*dah*), *rough* (< OE *ruh*), *though* (< ME *þohh* < ON *\*þoh*), *through/ thorough* (< OE *þurh*), etc. GH is also found after AU in ModE, as in *laugh* (< Anglian OE *hlæhhan*), *taught* (< OE *tæhte*).

## H

- OE H- was lost from initial consonant clusters HL-, HN-, HR-, which were thus simplified to L-, N-, R- during the ME period. H- was apparently already falling silent before L, N, R in OE, as one sometimes finds it omitted in writing of that period; in any case, it had disappeared long before it could be fixed by printing, and there is no trace of it in ModE spelling: OE *hlaf* > ModE *loaf*, OE *hlud* > ModE *loud*, OE *hnecca* > ModE *neck*, OE *hnutu* > ModE *nut*, OE *hræfn* > ModE *raven*, OE *hrycg* > ModE *ridge*.
- In ME HW was reversed to WH: *hpit* 'white', *hpy* 'why'. WH is first attested in regular use in the *Ormulum* (see p. 74).
  - In the early 15th century, the WH letter sequence began to be extended in use to words with an initial /h/ followed by O, where it had no justification from either pronunciation or word-origin. Only *whole* and *whore* have remained; forms such as *wholy*, *whood* and *whoord* 'hoard' have dropped from use again.
- With the adoption of WH for earlier HW, CH for C, GH for H and ȝ, and TH for þ, ME saw the establishment of a set of two-letter spellings for single consonant sounds with H regularly the second letter of the digraph.
  - For /ʃ/, the dominant spelling in the 13th and 14th centuries is SCH, especially word-initially. There were many other spellings in ME, such as SS, SSH, even SZSH. Orm was the first to use SH regularly.

## I, J

- Originally J was simply a graphic variant form of I, used especially as the second or last character in a series of two or more I's: thus *iiij* for '4'. The ModE use of I for the vowel sounds and J for the consonant sound /dʒ/ began around 1630 to 1640, but the treatment of these as fully separate letters of the alphabet took some time to become established: for example, Samuel Johnson in his *Dictionary*

(1755) distinguishes the '*I* vowel' from the '*J* consonant' but treats words beginning with these letters in a single list of entries: thus . . . *jar*, . . . *jaw*, . . . *jay*, . . . *ice*, . . . *idol*, . . . *jealous*, . . . *jerk*, . . . *ill*, . . . .

- In the 17th and 18th centuries there was mutual assimilation of an /ɪ/ or /j/ (often written I) and a preceding /s, z, t, d/ to /ʃ, ʒ, tʃ, dʒ/. Thus we have ModE *ambition, patient, question, soldier, special, vicious, vision*, and with spellings without I, *measure, nature, ocean, sugar, usual*. However, a number of words have reverted to sequences of /s, z, t, d/ + /ɪ, j/: e.g. *bestial, odious, piteous, tedious*.

## I, Y

By the middle of the 13th century, Y came to serve as a convenient means of breaking up a difficult-to-decipher series of letters with short down-strokes (minims) produced by a succession of I, U, N, M: hence spellings *nym, myn* for *nim, min*, etc. This use of Y continued through the ME period and was extended in use, so that in the 16th century I and Y were generally interchangeable, e.g. *king ~ kyng, wille ~ wylle, roial ~ royal, saieth ~ sayeth*. Word-finally the spellings were IE and Y: *cittie ~ citty, famylie ~ family* (compare Richard Mulcaster's suggested distinction between word-final -IE and -Y, p. 296). In the 17th century, spellings become more established in their modern forms.

## K

- Initial K had ceased to be pronounced before N by the early 17th century. Shakespeare (d. 1616) was, for example, able to make a play on words between *knight* and *night*.
- For the spelling -IC/-ICK (as in *music*, formerly *musick*), see pp. 136 and 302.

## L

- There are many examples of a 'silent l' in ModE:
  ○ before F/V: e.g. *half/halve, calf/calve*;
  ○ before K: e.g. *folk, talk, walk, yolk*;
  ○ before M: e.g. *calm, psalm, salmon*.

Evidence of such losses can be seen from the 14th century onwards, e.g. *samon/samoun* in the 14th, *behaf* in the mid-15th. In the 16th century, Richard Mulcaster lists in his pedagogical textbook, the *Elementarie* (1582), a number of words, such as *balm, calm, calf, chalk, talk, walk,* in which, he states, the L is silent. And there is evidence that the loss of L was formerly more extensive than it is today: e.g. *fawkener* 'falconer', *soger* 'soldier'. The process of reinstating some of these lost L's to the written and spoken language had two stages. Firstly, L was often restored on the basis of the Lat source word; for example, in the 15th century ME *faucon* was reformed as *falcon* on the basis of Lat *falco*, and ME *faute* (< Fr *faute* < VLat *\*fallita*) followed Fr practice by adding an L before the T. But even then the L was not necessarily pronounced: Alexander Pope (d. 1744) rhymes *fault* and *ought*, Jonathan Swift (d. 1745) *fault* and *thought*. In a second stage, pronunciation was made to match the spelling – obligatorily in, for example, *soldier*; optionally in *falcon* (though pronunciation with /l/ is now usual).

- L is also silent in *could/should/would* (< OE *cuðe, scolde, wolde*). The L was inserted in *could* in the early 16th century by analogy with *should* and *would*, by which time the L was silent in the latter two words and sometimes not written (e.g. *shudd, shoo'd, wode,* etc.).
- *Shan't* is a contraction of *shall not*. Forms such as *sha'nt* and *shan't*, and also *shannot*, are attested in the 17th century. *Sha't* is written for *shalt* in Congreve's *The Way of the World* (1700). Similarly, *won't* is a contraction of *woll not*, in which *woll* is a variant of *will*. *Won't* is attested from the 17th century, *wonnot* in the 16th.

## N

The final N of *damn, hymn,* etc. was pronounced in ME. Evidence of its later loss comes from written forms such as *dam to deth* 'condemn to death' (1460), *authum* 'autumn' (1526), *hymme/imme* 'hymn' (1530).

## O

- The anomalous O in ModE *woman, women* (ME *wimman, wimmen* < OE *wifman* 'wife-man', *wifmen*) did not arise until the 13th century, first of all in texts in western ME dialects in which the original -I- had become a rounded vowel. There have been a variety of spellings and pronunciations in the past, including, for example, a 16th- and 17th-century pronunciation of *woman* which allowed a play on words between *wo-* and *woe*.

- The expected pronunciation of *one* is seen in *alone* and *atone* (compare *stone*, etc.). The pronunciation of the vowel in *one* and *once* shows a non-standard development from OE long A seen also in dialect forms such as *wuk* 'oak'. An initial /w/ was added to the beginning of *one* and *once* in popular speech during late ME. Forms with /w/ existed alongside forms without the /w/ in EModE, and were adopted as the regular forms in the 17th century, though Christopher Cooper, a schoolmaster and parson, in his *Grammatica Linguæ Anglicanæ* 'Grammar of the English Language' (1685), can still describe the pronunciation /wʌn/ for *one* as 'barbarous'.

*OO*

Three groups of words in which the ModE vowels is spelt oo but pronounced in different ways can be represented by *food* /fuːd/, *good* /gʊd/ and *blood* /blʌd/. That the vowel in all three words was originally a long /oː/ is clear from the oo spelling. This, as we have seen in the discussion of the GVS above, regularly became /uː/. This is the case with *food*, and also with *boot*, *fool*, *moon* and *spoon*. A second group, represented here by *good*, and also including *book*, *foot*, *hood*, *hook*, *look*, *shook*, *stood*, underwent a shortening of the vowel to /ʊ/ in the 17th century. (Not all Eng accents observe these distinctions.) In a third group, *blood* and *flood*, the vowel was shortened in the 15th century and then unrounded to /ʌ/, along with the vowel in other words with /ʊ/ such as *brother*, *come*, *done*, *love*, *month*, *mother*, etc.

Sounds and spellings are more confused with regard to modern reflexes of ME /uː/ before R: compare *poor*, *moor*, *floor*, *pour*, *flour*, *our*, etc. *Floor* and *pour* have the same diphthong in ModE as *bore* and *boar* (which had the vowel /ɔː/ in ME) and *hoard* and *whore* (which had the vowel /oː/ in ME). The unpredictable sound–spelling correspondences in this section of our ModE word-stock have a complex history. In the case of *door*, for example, the spelling *dore* was the dominant form in the 16th century; the oo spelling first appeared in the 16th century, and eventually supplanted *dore* in writing, though *door* is now pronounced as if *dore*.

- OE *to* has led to both *to* and *too* in ModE. *Too* was the stressed form of the word, which in the 16th century began to be spelt with oo.

### OU, OW

- The digraph ou originated in early OFr to represent a diphthong /oʊ/ that arose from Lat o and u (e.g. Lat *florem* > OFr *flour* 'flower'), which became /uː/ by the end of the 12th century. OE /uː/ had been represented by u, but this became ambiguous: since u was not distinguished in shape from v, it could be read as either. The digraph ou introduced by Fr scribes provided a way of representing long u unambiguously: Fr words spelt with ou entered ME with that spelling for /uː/ (as with *doute* 'doubt'), and OE words containing long u, such as *hus* 'house', were respelt with ou, giving ME *hous(e)*.
  - Fr words written with ou that were taken into Eng after the GVS were naturally unaffected by the GVS pronunciation change of /uː/ to /aʊ/: e.g. *group* (< Fr *groupe*), which first appeared in Eng in the late 17th century. *Blouse* is an exception, a 19th-century borrowing in which the vowel-pronunciation has been anglicized to /aʊ/.
- ou and ow have become fixed in spellings mainly according to their position in the word, with ou in initial or medial positions before consonants and ow used syllable-finally before a consonant or vowel and word-finally: thus *our, oust, about, loud, mouse, mouth, shout*, etc. but *chowder, dowry, powder, bowel, coward, flower, prowess, towel, tower, vowel, allow, endow, prow, vow*, etc.
  - ou is nevertheless found word-finally in *you* and *thou*, and in some borrowings from or via Fr: *chou, bayou, bijou, caribou*, etc.
    - The pronunciation of *thou* arises from a stressed form of the word; hence OE /uː/ has developed to /aʊ/ in the GVS. The pronunciation of *you*, on the other hand, derives from an unstressed form /jʊ/, from which a stressed form /juː/ later developed.
  - ow also occurs before final N in Fr-derived *crown, frown, gown* and OE-derived *brown, down, town*, etc., though ou is normal when a further consonant follows N, as in Fr-derived *announce, count, round*, etc. and OE-derived *found, ground, pound*, etc. Note also the anomaly of *renown/noun*, both ult. < Lat *nominem*, via Fr (compare Fr *renom/nom*).
  - When next to /w/, the /uː/ vowel sound may be retained with the ou spelling, as in *wound* 'injury' (as opposed to *wound* 'coiled').

- ModE may exploit the ou/ow distinction for lexical differentiation, e.g. between *flower* and *flour* (both < OFr *flour/flor/flur* < Lat *florem* and not distinguished in spelling in ME or EModE), and also between *foul* (< OE *ful*) and *fowl* (< OE *fuȝel*), both found with ou and ow spellings in the past.

### R

- There have been several cases of metathesis (i.e. a change in the order of sounds in a word) with /r/: e.g. *bird* (< OE *brid*; ME *bryd, byrd*); *third* (< OE *þridda*; *thrid* was the dominant form through ME), *thirty* (< OE *þritiȝ*; initial *thi-* was recorded in the 15th century and this has been the dominant spelling since the 16th); *bird* and *ðirdda* are, however, recorded in Northumbrian dialect in the OE period. Similarly, but with metathesis in the other direction, *thrill* (< ME *thirl* < OE *þyrlian*), *through* (< OE *þurh*).
- The vowels of words such as *fern, fir, fur* merged in the 17th century, followed in the 18th century by the loss of the /r/ after the vowel. From the point of view of sound–spelling correspondences, this loss of /r/ resulted in the coalescing of many previously distinct sounds: e.g. *horse, hoarse* both /hɔːs/. (The vowels of such words remain distinct in accents, such as those of Scotland, in which the R is still pronounced.)

### S

Voicing of intervocalic /s/ to /z/, written s or ss, after an unstressed syllable in words such as *desist, resist* (compare the pronunciation of *consist, insist*), *dessert, possess* occurred in EModE, at first with both voiced and voiceless forms co-existing.

### U, V

- As with I and J, U and V were for a long time treated as variants of the same letter, whether vowel or consonant, v being written or printed for the first letter of a word, u in other positions: thus *vnder, victorie* but *naturall, innouation*. Not until the 17th century were the two letters used consistently as they are today, and some dictionaries continued to enter words beginning with U and V in a single list as late as the 19th century. Johnson is well aware of the vowel/consonant distinction, but in his *Dictionary* (1755) chooses to follow tradition: thus . . . *valid,* . . . *vast,* . . . *udder,* . . . *veal,* . . . *vital,* . . . *ulcer,* . . . *umpire,* . . . *voice,* . . . .

- The use of vv for w prevented the doubling of v in the same way as other vowels doubled after a short vowel: compare *sit/sitting* with *give/giving, pat/patting* with *have/having.* In these cases, the verbs with a silent E behave in spelling like similar words with long vowels: *dive/diving, save/saving.*

UE, EW

For words such as *blue* and *blew,* *clue* and *clew,* see pp. 62, 161, 166.

Y

- For the interchangeable use of I and Y, see 'I, Y' above.
- About the middle of the 13th century Y began to be used instead of ȝ to represent /j/: hence, for example, *year* (< OE ȝear).
- Pseudo-archaic *ye* = 'the' derives from a printers' abbreviation in which Y was substituted for a thorn, Þ, though as early as the 13th century there were scribes who wrote Y and Þ identically. Thus *ye* = 'the'; the pronunciation /jiː/ is now traditional but has no historical justification.

# Etymology-Based Spellings and Spelling Pronunciations

## *Etymology as a source of spelling change*

We have already noted in our chapters on the OE and Franco-Lat elements in Eng several instances of spellings being etymologized (i.e. altered to reflect actual or supposed source words), especially in the EModE period. Some, such as the etymologically incorrect D in *admiral* (< Arabic *amir-al-bahr* 'lord of the sea' with the added D of Lat *admirabilis,* etc.) and the etymologically correct D of *admonish* (earlier *amonest* < OFr *amonester*

< LLat *admonestare*) cause no sound–spelling problems in ModE, but many others do. For convenience we will gather some of these together here:

- B, P
  - *debt, doubt, subtle*: the Lat B's of *debitum, dubitare* and *subtilem* were lost in OFr and are not seen in ME, but are then restored, unpronounced, in deference to the Lat source words: Lat *debitum* > OFr *dete* > ME *dette* (late ME *debte*) > *debt*; Lat *dubitare* > ME *doute* > *doubt*, Lat *subtilem* > ME *sotill* > *subtle*. The B's remain unpronounced.
  - *conceit, deceit, receipt*: all derive from verbs ultimately going back to Lat *capere* 'to take', and in EModE were sometimes written with P and sometimes without, the P being inserted in deference to the Lat. The P is not pronounced.
  - *comptroller*: this erroneous spelling of *controller* (< ME *counter-roller* < ANorm *countreroullour* 'someone who makes a copy of a roll') was due to a confusion with *count* (< OFr *cunter* < Lat *computare*), whence the *compt-* spelling, which has dropped out of use again except in some official titles. The pronunciation is usually that of *controller*, though a spelling pronunciation (see below) with /-mp-/ is also accepted.
- C
  - *indict*: the ModE pronunciation /ɪnˈdaɪt/ is anticipated by such ME forms as *endyte, indite*. The spelling *indict* is first attested in the early 17th century, and reflects a supposed Lat derivation, e.g. the LLat verb \**indictare*.
  - *victuals*: the ModE pronunciation /ˈvɪtlz/ reflects such OFr and ME spellings as *vitaile*; EModE restored the C of Lat *victualia*. Mulcaster (see p. 296) disapproves of the spelling *victuall* for *vitle*.
  - *scythe*: the C in *scythe* (< OE *siðe*) is first attested in the 17th century, based on a mistaken connection with Lat *scindere* 'to cut'. Johnson recommended *sithe* but allowed both spellings. *Scissors* (< ME *cisours* < OFr *cisoires* < LLat \**cisoria* 'cutters') has been similarly affected.
- H
  - *stomach*: Fr *estomac* (< Lat *stomachus*) led in EModE to such forms as *stomac, -ak, -ack, -ok*; an H was added in the 16th century, whence ModE *stomach*.
  - *rhyme*: the spelling reflects an assumed but uncertain connection with Lat *rhythmus* < Gr *rhythmos*.

- s
  - *island, aisle*: the s of *island* (< OE *iȝland*) was inserted by false analogy with Fr-derived *isle* (< Lat *insula*); *aisle* (< Lat *ala*) acquired an s by analogy with *isle*.

*Hiccough* for *hiccup* (earlier *hicket*) attested from the 17th century onwards, apparently from an erroneous assumed connection with *cough*, has merely added to the sound–spelling confusions already existing in the -OUGH words. Many other etymologized spellings have come and, fortunately, gone again, e.g. *sainct* 'saint' < OFr *saint* < Lat *sanctum*, *auct(h)our* 'author' < OFr *autor* < Lat *auctor*.

## Spelling pronunciations

If some spellings have added unnecessary confusion to Eng spelling on the basis of real or imagined word sources, new spelling pronunciations (i.e. pronunciations that reflect spellings) have gone a little way to lessening the confusion as literacy has increased over the past few centuries and people have come to pronounce certain words as they are written. We have already noted above the possible pronunciation of *comptroller* with /-mp-/, reflecting a completely erroneous and etymologically unjustified spelling. Among the various spelling pronunciations that have developed in English, we may note the following:

- H
  - *habit, herb, hotel*, etc.: see p. 122.
  - *forehead*: in a well-known little rhyme by the poet Longfellow, *forehead* rhymes with *horrid*, and this is still a common pronunciation of the word. But the spelling pronunciation /ˈfɔːhɛd/ is also accepted.
  - *author, authority*, etc.: perhaps by analogy with Gr-derived *authentic*, the ME forms *autor, autority* (via Fr < Lat *auctor, auctoritatem*) acquired an etymologically unjustified H in the 16th century, probably influenced by Fr in which H-forms appeared in the 15th and 16th centuries. *Author* and *authority* continued to be pronounced with TH = /t/ through EModE, but eventually developed a pronunciation /θ/ that reflected the spelling. Similarly *anthem* (< OE *antefn* < LLat *antiphona*) acquired the TH spelling in the 16th century; this also led to the present-day pronunciation with /θ/. Other words which have gained a /θ/ pronunciation due to their spelling are *theatre, thesis* and *throne*.

- L

  After an etymological L was inserted in the EModE period to words such as ME *asaut* (> ModE *assault*), *caudron* (> *cauldron*), *faucon* (> *falcon*), *faut* (> *fault*) – see p. 137 – some of these took on pronunciations to match their spelling.

- O

  Words spelt with O formerly pronounced /ʌ/ are now increasingly pronounced with O = /ɒ/: e.g. *colander, combat, comparable, comrade, conduit, constable.*

- W

  Since the 19th century, the /w/ has been restored in *quote, swollen, swore, woman* and increasingly in *towards.*

Other words which, like *forehead,* have gained spelling pronunciations are *clapboard, grindstone, often, waistcoat* and *wristband.* Some which have not are *boatswain, coxswain, forecastle* and *Christmas.* The first D of *Wednesday* is now often pronounced and the D of *husband* always is.[5]

# Notes

1. Görlach (1991: 9) notes various dates that have been suggested for Early Modern English: 1476–1776, 1500–1650, 1500–1700, 1500–1800, 1540–1750. The year of the introduction of printing into England, 1476, is a convenient date for the start of the period. A convenient date for the end of Early Modern English is 1660, the year of the restoration of the Stuarts to the English throne, a date that also marks both the end of a period (beginning about 1530) during which there was the fastest growth in vocabulary in the entire history of English and the beginning of a period (ending about 1760) in which we see the greatest efforts to standardize and 'fix' the language (see Chapter 9 for more on this).

2. For a chart outlining these and other sound-changes affecting English vowels, see Lass (1987: 133–4).

3. For fuller accounts of developments in Middle and Early Modern English, see, for example, Barber (1976), Görlach (1991), Burrow and Turville-Petre (1996, 2005).

4. As in other alphabetical sections in this book, language names are from here on given in abbreviated form.

5. For more examples, see Strang (1970: 81–3).

# 7

# The Greek Contribution

## The Importance of Greek in English

Greek-derived words may constitute over 10 per cent of the total vocabulary of English.[1] However, that figure includes many rare and highly technical words, and the proportion occurring in everyday language is considerably smaller. But while fewer than the Old-English-, French- and Latin-derived constituents of English, Greek-derived words form an important element of the language, contributing a rich assemblage of analytical and technical concepts.

We may look upon the Greek elements of Modern English as having arrived in a series of waves, each of which will be considered in turn in this chapter.

## The First Wave

Most early Gr-derived words associated with Christianity reached OE through Lat:[2] e.g. *alms* (< OE *ælmysse* < VLat *\*alimosina* < LLat *elimosina* < Gr *eleēmosunē*[3] 'compassion'), *angel* (< OE *engel* < Lat *angelos* < Gr *angelos* 'messenger', actually written *aggelos* with a double ΓΓ[4] – for the transliteration of Gr ΓΓ as NG, see p. 209 below; later, *engel* > *angel* under the influence of OFr *angele*), *bishop* (< Lat *episcopus* < Gr *episkopos* 'overseer'), *devil* (< OE *deofol* < Lat *diabulus* < Gr *diabolos*

*The History of English Spelling*, First Edition. Christopher Upward and George Davidson.
© 2011 Christopher Upward and George Davidson. Published 2011 by Blackwell Publishing Ltd.

'slanderer'), *priest* (< OE *priost* < LLat *presbyter*, possibly in a form *\*prebester* < Gr *presbuteros* 'older, elder'). The Gr-derived OE word *cirice* 'church' (< LGr *kurikon* < Gr *kuriakon [doma]* '[house] of the Lord'), however, reached the Germanic languages, including OE, directly from Gr, probably through Gothic. The forms of these words have all been thoroughly anglicized over the years (see for example the remarks on *bishop*, p. 10), and today show nothing of their Gr origin.

## The Second Wave

Further Gr loans arrived during the ME period (via Lat and/or Fr), and were substantially anglicized in form (e.g. Gr *phusikos* > Lat *physicus* > ANorm *fisike* > ME *fisik*), but were then typically respelt (e.g. *fisik* > *physic*) in the EModE period according to the Graeco-Lat patterns of transliteration that will be described below, and therefore can be considered, as far as ModE spelling is concerned, along with the words belonging to the third wave.

One group of loanwords which entered Eng during this period was contributed by Christianity, whose New Testament was first written in Gr (though a Gr somewhat different from classical Gr). Examples are *blasphemy, diocese, hierarchy, orthodox, schism*. As with *phusikos* > *fisik* > *physic*, many of these loans were first adopted in anglicized spellings, but were later respelt in a form more resembling the Gr words from which they derived (or at least the Latinized versions of such words): e.g. Gr *schisma*[5] > ME *scisme/sisme/cisme* > *schisme* (16th century), *schism* (17th century).

## The Third Wave

Especially since the 16th century, Gr-derived words have been added in large numbers to the stock of Eng vocabulary. A few are in common use (e.g. *basis, centre, comic, electric, energy, idea, myth, pause, problem, scheme, theory, type*), but the great majority are more or less confined to specialist technical language. The spelling of this third wave of Gr loans has been only slightly anglicized: they are generally characterized by distinctive spellings and sound–spelling correspondences (such as CH = /k/ as in *character*) which mark them off from the central core of Eng word-forms, and frequently contain letters (such as the P of *psychology* and the G of *phlegm*) whose presence in ModE is explicable only through an account of the origin and history of the words they appear in.

Just as under the second wave, one group of loans entered Eng through the Christian church. Examples are *catholic, ecclesiastic, ecumenical/ oecumenical, theology*. Some are doublets of earlier, fully anglicized loans: beside *alms*, we have the 17th-century new entry *eleemosynary* (both from Gr *eleēmosunē*); beside *bishop, episcopal* (15th century; < Gr *episkopos*); beside *devil, diabolical* (16th century; < Gr *diabolos*). *Presbyter*, like *priest* a derivative of Gr *presbuteros*, entered Eng in the OE period (as *presbiter*), but appears to have been lost to the language and borrowed afresh in the 16th century (with all but the earliest examples spelled with a Y). Specialist Gr-derived vocabulary has also entered Eng in the field of science and medicine, as characterized by such affixes as -GRAPHY, -LOGY, -LYSIS, GEO-, BIO-, HYDRO-. One medical dictionary includes under A the following Gr-derived words:[6] *acetylcholine, achlorhydria, achondroplasia, acromegaly, actinomycosis, adenoid, aerobic, aetiology, allopathy, amblyopia, amenorrhoea, aminophylline*. Yet another field with technical terminology derived from Gr is literary analysis. A dictionary of literary terms lists the following Gr-based forms under A:[7] *acatalectic, acephalous, agon, amphibrach, anacoluthon, anagnorisis, antiphrasis, antonomasia, apocalyptic, apophthegm, aposiopesis, asyndeton*.

## Gr Transliterated into Lat

The stems of many Gr-derived words in ModE were first taken into Lat (for which reason they may equally well be referred to as Graeco-Lat stems), transliterated from the Gr into the Roman alphabet according to certain conventions of letter-equivalence, conventions which still largely determine the spelling of most Gr-derived ModE vocabulary. These correspondences are shown in Table 1.

## Gr Aspiration in Lat and Eng

Classical Gr distinguished two variants of the consonant sounds which Eng writes as T, P and K, one variant being more heavily aspirated than the other, rather like the difference between the T of *hotel* and the T + H of *hothouse*, the P of *upon* and the P + H of *uphold*, and the C of *bacon* and the CK + H of *backhand*. Following the standardization of the

**Table 1**  Transliteration of Greek letters into Roman letters.

| Greek | A | B | Γ | | Δ | E | Z | H | Θ | I | K |
|---|---|---|---|---|---|---|---|---|---|---|---|
| Latin | A | B | G | | D | E | Z | E | TH | I | C |
| Greek | Λ | M | N | | Ξ | O | Π | P | Σ | T | Y |
| Latin | L | M | N | | X | O | P | R | S | T | Y |
| Greek | Φ | X | Ψ | | Ω | | ' | 'Ρ | PP | | ΓΓ, ΓΚ |
| Latin | PH | CH | PS | | O | | H | RH | RRH | | NG, NC |
| Greek | AI | EI | OI | | AY | EY | OY | | | | |
| Latin | Æ/AE/E | E/EI/I | Œ/OE/E | | AU | EU | U | | | | |

The ' symbol indicates aspiration (see 'Gr Aspiration in Lat and Eng').

Gr alphabet in 402 BCE, the aspirated variants /t$^h$, p$^h$, k$^h$/ came to be represented by the letters *theta, phi, chi* (Θ, Φ, X), paralleling their non-aspirated equivalents *tau, pi, kappa* (T, Π, K) for /t, p, k/. Before the standardization of Gr spelling, not all Gr dialects used *phi* and *chi*, and the dialects which did not use them wrote the sounds either as plain unaspirated Π, K or else with an added H; some used TH rather than *theta*. Until about 150 BCE, the Romans wrote both the unaspirated and aspirated Gr consonants as T, P, C, but subsequently marked the aspiration with H: earlier *Corinto, Pilipus, Antioco* > *Corintho, Philippus, Antiocho*. This addition of H after T, P, C gave rise to the widely used Graeco-Lat spellings TH, PH, CH which have entered Eng in large numbers. In the case of a few early Gr loanwords, the spelling became established in Lat before the H was added, giving *calx, purpura* for what would later have been transliterated as *\*chalx, \*purphura*. This historical accident has resulted in the Eng forms *calcium, purple*, rather than *\*chalcium, \*purphle* which their Gr origins might have suggested; compare the geological terms *chalcedony* and *porphyry*, the latter a direct transliteration of the same Gr stem as found in *purple*.

## Assimilated aspirations

Aspirated consonants could arise in classical Gr from sequences of a non-aspirated consonant followed by an aspirated vowel (that is, a vowel preceded by [h]; see further examples below, pp. 215–17), the T + [h], Π + [h] or K + [h] then merging to give the single letters *theta, phi* and *chi*. Examples (all entering Eng via Lat) are:

197

- *cathedral* (< *kathedra* < *kata* 'down' + *hedra* 'seat'), *catholic* (< *katholikos* < *kata* 'throughout' + *holos* 'all'), *method* (< *methodos* < *meta* 'with' + *hodos* 'way'), *authentic* (< *authentikos* < AUTO- 'self' + -HENT- denoting doing);
- *ephemeral* (< *ephēmeros* < *epi* 'on' + *hēmera* 'day'), *hyphen* (< *huphen* < *hupo* 'under' + *hen* 'one').

Despite its origin in a Gr K + [h] merging to give *chi*, however, *leuchaemia* (< *leukos* 'white' + *haima* 'blood') is now written *leukaemia* or *leukemia* (see p. 215 for further discussion).

## The loss of the aspiration

By the beginning of the Christian era, the aspiration that had provided the rationale for the Lat spellings TH, PH, CH was disappearing from the sound system of Gr. *Theta*, *phi* and *chi* /tʰ, pʰ, kʰ/ became /θ/, /f/ and /x/ respectively.

Lat lost its [h]-sound altogether, and with the letter H silent Roman writers were not always certain when to use it, sometimes omitting it when a Gr derivation might have prompted it and sometimes inserting it when no Gr H was involved. A few of these aberrations have left their mark on Eng spelling:

- TH: *Carthage*, in North Africa, should strictly have been written *Cartago* in Lat, not *Carthago*.
- PH: pseudo-Gr PH occurs in Lat *lympha*, ModE *lymph* (compare cognate *limpid*); further examples are *triumph* (Lat *triumphus*, earlier *triumpus*) and *trophy* (Lat *trophaeum*, earlier *tropaeum*, < Gr *tropaion*).
- CH: Roman writers were particularly prone to insert a spurious H when C was followed by R: e.g. Eng *lachrymal*, *lachrymose* (from a Gr-influenced misspelling *lachryma* for correct Lat *lacrima* 'teardrop'); *sepulchre* from a misspelling *sepulchrum* for *sepulcrum*.

# Graeco-Lat TH, PH, CH in Eng

Although OE had letters that could represent the fricative pronunciations of TH, PH and CH (i.e. Þ and Ð for /θ/, F for /f/, ȝ (G) or H for /x/), so great was the influence of Graeco-Lat writing practices that in most cases it is the digraph spellings that have persisted into ModE (e.g. *photograph*, not *\*fotograf*).

*TH*

The post-classical pronunciation of Graeco-Lat TH as [θ] coincided with the [θ] of native OE words (as in ModE *thin*), and was also easily identified with the voiced equivalent [ð] (as in ModE *then*). Although OE Þ and Đ offered advantages over TH (being more economical and not susceptible to misreading as T + H), TH displaced them in the ME period (see p. 176). Even the earliest surviving texts (from the 8th century) show Eng adopting TH in some words, and eventually Eng was to write TH almost everywhere the sound /θ/ occurred, whether in words of Gr derivation (e.g. *thesis*) or not (e.g. *thin*). Among the most common Gr-derived words with TH in ModE are *aesthetic, anthology, anthropology, arithmetic, arthritis, asthma, athlete, authentic, cathedral, catholic, enthusiasm, ether, ethic, ethnic, euthanasia, Gothic, labyrinth, lethal, marathon, mathematics, methane, method, monolithic, myth, orthodox, panther, plinth, polythene, rhythm, sympathy, theatre, theme, theology, theory, therapy, therm, thesis, throne.*

Words of Gr derivation adopted by Eng after the revival of classical learning (i.e. from around 1500) always use TH for Gr *theta*, but some earlier loans were often spelt without H before the 17th century: e.g. *autentik, etik, Gotic, letargie, panter, teatre, teme.* Restoring letters to simplified medieval spellings in order to reflect the original Lat transliterations from Gr (e.g. *Gotic* > *Gothic*) later became widespread, especially in the 16th century.

### Anomalies and non-Gr TH

- Correct sound–spelling correspondence, wrong etymology:
  - ○ Perhaps by analogy with Gr-derived *authentic*, the ME forms *autor, autority* (through Fr < Lat *auctor* 'originator, doer', *auctoritatem*) acquired an H in Eng in the 16th century, probably influenced by Fr in which H-forms appeared in the 15th and 16th centuries. Eventually the forms *author, authority* developed a /θ/ pronunciation that reflected the spelling.
  - ○ The H in *anthem* (< OE *antefn* < LLat *antiphona*) acquired the TH spelling in the 16th century; this also led to the present-day pronunciation with /θ/.
  - ○ The non-Gr-derived H in *Anthony* (< Lat *Antonius*) sporadically produces the pronunciation /θ/ (more often in America than Britain).
- Correct etymology, wrong sound–spelling correspondence:

○ *Thomas* and *thyme* have never been pronounced with initial /θ/, and were formerly commonly written as *Tomas* (compare *Tom*) and *tyme/time*. Their Gr origin with initial *theta* led scholars to restore the H with which they had first been transliterated into Lat, but they have not acquired matching spelling pronunciations.

*Loss of H from TH*

* *Treacle* (< Gr *thēriakē* 'antidote to venomous bite') and *treasure* (< Gr *thēsauros*) lost their H in passing through Lat and Fr.
* *Acolyte* reflects a medieval Lat spelling *acolytus*; Gr *akolouthos* would normally have produced Lat *acoluthus*. Scholars in the 16th century attempted to introduce the form *acoluth* into Eng, but it did not become established.

PH

Graeco-Lat PH did not displace OE F but did gain some ground at its expense. Although the letter F perfectly represents the same /f/ sound as is represented by PH, ModE has in the majority of cases retained, or revived, the Graeco-Lat digraph PH wherever classical Gr had *phi*, as in *philosophy*, *photography*. In particular, from around 1500, PH was adopted for Gr-derived words that in Gr had been spelt with *phi*. While many of these words were new to Eng, others had been part of ME vocabulary, typically spelt with F: ME *fesant*, *olifant* (> ModE *pheasant*, *elephant*), *blasfemie*, *diafragma*, *fantom*, *fenix*, *fisik*, *fleme* and *profet*. *Aspalt* and *spere* added H after their P. (For *phial/vial*, see p. 43.) Some writers took PH even further: *prophane* for *profane* (< Lat *profanus*; the PH spelling appeared in LLat and MFr, whence it entered Eng; it was commoner than the F spelling until the end of the 17th century), *sopha* for *sofa* (< Fr *sofa*, also written *sopha*).

Since this renaissance of PH, there have been occasional reversions to F: *phancy*, *phrenzy*, *phantastic*, *phrenetic* > *fancy*, *frenzy*, *fantastic*, *frenetic* (though medical terms such as *schizophrenia* retain PH).

Among the Gr-derived Eng words spelt with PH are *alpha*, *amorphous*, *amphibian*, *asphalt*, *atmosphere*, *blasphemy*, *catastrophe*, *diaphragm*, *dolphin*, *elephant*, *emphasis*, *epitaph*, *euphoria*, *nymph*, *orphan*, *paraphernalia*, *phallic*, *phantom*, *pharmaceutical*, *phase*, *pheasant*, *phenomenon*, *philosophy*, *phobia*, *phoenix*, *phosphate*, *photograph*, *phrase*, *physical*, *prophet*, *schizophrenia*, *telephone*, *typhoid*.

## Anomalies and non-Gr PH

The popularity of PH in recent centuries has seen it spread somewhat beyond the stock of Gr-derived vocabulary:

- *Lymph* and *triumph* have already been mentioned (p. 198): in Lat *tropaeum*/*trophaeum*, the first form correctly transliterated the original Gr but it was the second that entered Eng as *trophy*.
- *Nephew* (< ANorm *neveu* < Lat *nepos* 'grandson') acquired its PH around the 15th century; the related word *neve* (< OE *nefa*), attested up to the late 17th century, is also found with a PH spelling in the 16th.
- The PH spelling of Lat *sulphur*, an alternative spelling to Lat *sulfur*, is not related to Gr. *Sulphur* is now the standard form in BrE, *sulfur* in AmE.

### CH

The pronunciation of Graeco-Lat CH normally developed in Eng to /k/. CH = /k/ usually indicates a classical Gr derivation, but may reflect Italian CH (e.g. *Chianti*, *gnocchi*). Among common Gr-derived words in ModE are *archaeology*, *archaic*, *architecture*, *bronchitis*, *chaos*, *character*, *charismatic*, *chasm*, *chemical*, *chlorine*, *cholera*, *chorus*, *Christian*, *chrome*, *chronic*, *dichotomy*, *echo*, *hierarchy*, *mechanical*, *melancholy*, *ochre*, *orchestra*, *orchid*, *psychological*, *scheme*, *schizophrenia*, *scholar*, *school*, *stomach*, *technology*.

The CH spelling has been preserved, or revived, in most Gr-derived words in ModE: *chaos*, *chemist*, *chorus*, *technology*, *monarch*, etc. Before the growth of classical learning after about 1500, reflexes of Gr words with *chi* were normally spelt with a C: *caracter*, *Crist*, *cronicle*, *melancoly*, *scoole* (also *skoole*); a K might be used as well as C: *ecko* (also *ecco*), *stomack*; *choir*, *chorister* were regularly spelt with Anglo-Fr QU; and *Mihael* with H alone rather than CH.

- The history of *choir* is interesting. Originating in Gr *choros*, it was transliterated into Lat as *chorus*, and reduced in OFr to *cuer*, with alternative forms such as *queur*, which led to ME and EModE forms such as *quere*. A change in pronunciation in EModE encouraged its respelling as *quyre*, *quier*, *quire*, etc. The original Graeco-Lat CH was restored in the 17th century.

*Anomalies and non-Gr* CH

Like PH, Graeco-Lat CH has gone beyond its etymologically justified bounds in a number of spellings:

- Unetymological CH
  - We have already noted Lat *lachrymose, sepulchre* (see p. 198).
  - The H in *anchor* (< OE *ancor* < Lat *ancora*) is a pedantic error, first attested in the 16th century, mirroring the CH of the equally etymologically incorrect Lat form *anchora*.
  - Samuel Johnson in the 1755 *Dictionary of the English Language* recommended the form *ache* (properly *ake*, from OE *acan*) in the mistaken belief that the word was derived from Gr *achos* 'pain'.
- Anglicized pronunciation
  - ARCH- retains its /k/ pronunciation in *archangel, archetype, architect, archon, anarchy, monarch*; but before a consonant the native Eng value of CH, /tʃ/, prevails: *archbishop, archduke*.
  - The Graeco-Lat CH in *cherub* (orig. < Hebrew *kᵊrub*, and written as *cheroub* in the Gr translation of the Hebrew Bible known as the Septuagint) lost its /k/ value, and assumed the standard Eng /tʃ/ pronunciation.
  - *Conch* (< Gr *cogchē/conchē*; for Gr ΓΧ = Graeco-Lat NCH, see below, pp. 209–10) sometimes anglicizes its CH to /tʃ/ although /k/ is usually given as the more frequent or preferred pronunciation.
  - *Schism, schist, schizophrenia* all derive from a Gr stem with initial ΣΧ-. Before the 16th century *schism* was spelt with initial CI-, SI- or SCI- and pronounced /'sɪzm/. This pronunciation was retained after the Graeco-Lat SCH- spelling was restored, but /'skɪzm/ and /'ʃɪzm/ are also permissible. *Schist* acquired a pronunciation with initial /ʃ/ as it passed through Fr. *Schizophrenia* has the normal Graeco-Lat pronunciation /sk/.
- Spelling confusions
  - *Autarchy* 'absolute power' and *autarky* 'self-sufficiency' are not always distinguished, the latter commonly also being spelt *autarchy*.
  - Confusion often arises between *chord* and *cord*, the respective Graeco-Lat and anglicized spellings of the same stem (should one write 'strike a cord' or 'strike a chord'?).
  - Sometimes the loss of H from CH is due to Fr influence: e.g. Fr-derived *camomile* as against Graeco-Lat *chamomile*, both acceptable

in ModE. But the arbitrary distinction of *acrostic* with -IC and *hemistich* with -ICH (both < Gr *stichos* 'line of verse') is purely Eng, and cannot be laid at the door of Fr (*acrostiche, hémistiche*).

## Consonant Clusters Including *theta, phi* and *chi*

### PHTH, CHTH, STH

*Phi, chi* and *sigma* preceding *theta* in Gr produce the expected transliterations PHTH, CHTH and STH in Eng:

- initially: *phthisic, chthonic, sthenic*;
- medially: *diphtheria, diphthong, naphtha, ophthalmic, autochthonous, ichthyosaurus, asthma, isthmus*.

The pronunciations of such clusters are frequently simplified: e.g. /'tɪzɪk/, /'θɒnɪk/, /'ɪsməs/. And note the frequent /dɪpθ-/ for /dɪfθ-/. This inevitably creates sound–spelling problems and errors in ModE.

### TTH, PPH, CCH

The Gr consonant groups TΘ, PΦ, KX were transliterated into Lat as TTH, PPH, CCH, as in Eng *Matthew, sapphire, bacchanal, saccharine*. In Eng they have the same simple sound values as Graeco-Lat TH, PH and CH, and not, for example, as Eng TTH in *cutthroat*, PF in *helpful* or KC in *bookcase*.

## *Rho*

The Gr letter *rho*, written P and transliterated as Roman R, was also subject to aspiration in Gr (though with a different phonetic result, the loss of voicing). In classical Gr initial *rho* and medial double *rho* normally carried this aspiration, which in word-initial position (but not in medial position) was indicated in the later Byzantine (medieval) spelling system by a reversed apostrophe. One Gr dialect, however, used a preceding H. When transliterated into Lat, these initial aspirated *rho* and medial double *rho* spellings conventionally appeared as initial RH and medial RRH. A single medial or final *rho* was not aspirated and was transliterated as R, as in *character* (< Lat *character* < Gr *charaktēr*).

203

In Gr, when an initial *rho* became medial due to the addition of a prefix, the *rho* doubled, and this is reflected in the Eng spellings of, for example, *rhinoceros* (< Gr *rhis, rhin-* 'nose' ) and *antirrhinum* 'species of flower thought to resemble an animal's muzzle' (< Gr *antirrīnon*), *rhythm* (< Gr *rhuthmos*) and *arrhythmia* 'lack of rhythm' (< Gr *arruthmia*).

A medial Gr-derived RRH can also occur at the end of Eng words where a Gr or Lat suffix has been dropped: *catarrh* (< Fr *catarrhe* < Lat *catarrhus* < Gr *katarrous*), *myrrh* (< Lat *myrrha* < Gr *murra*).

RH and RRH occur much less commonly in Eng than Graeco-Lat TH, PH or CH. Gr-derived words in ModE include *cirrhosis, diarrhoea, haemorrhage, myrrh, rhea, rhesus, rhetoric, rheumatic, rhinoceros, rhizome, rhododendron, rhombus, rhubarb* (ultimately < Gr *rha*) and *rhythm*. Originally, the H was generally omitted (*retorik, reumatike, rinoceros, rubarb, rythm*), but it was revived in the 16th century in accordance with the tendency at that time to alter the spellings of words to reflect the spellings of their Lat and Gr source words.

• The word *rhyme*, which ultimately derives from Lat *rhythmus*, preserved an H-less spelling longer than most, as in Coleridge's *The Rime of the Ancient Mariner* (1798). The *Oxford English Dictionary* has citations for *rime* up into the early 20th century; spellings with H appear from the mid-16th century.

# Non-Aspirated Gr Consonants in Eng

The Gr non-aspirated consonant letters are Β, Κ, Δ, Γ, Λ, Μ, Ν, ΓΓ, ΓΚ, Π, Ψ, Ρ, Σ, Τ, Χ, Ζ and Π. For the standard transliteration equivalences between these and Roman letters, see Table 1 above (p. 197).

## *Graeco-Lat B*

• Graeco-Lat B occurs word-initially: *basilica* (via Lat < Gr *basilikē*), *ballistics, barometer, biology.*
  ○ The initial BD of *bdellium* 'fragrant gum' (via Lat < Gr *bdellion*) is generally pronounced /d/, though /bəd-/ is also possible (and spellings *bid-* and *bed-* are found in ME and EModE).
• Graeco-Lat B occurs medially: *cybernetics* (< Gr *kubernētēs*), *bibliography*, and after a prefix in *parabola* (via Lat < Gr *parabolē* < *para* 'beside' + *bolē* 'throw'), *amphibious, problem, symbiosis.*

- Graeco-Lat B occurs word-finally in *iamb* 'poetic foot' and *dithyramb* 'hymn, song' (via Lat < Gr *iambos, dithurambos*).
  - The final B is generally silent, as is the case with non-Gr-derived words such as *comb* and *lamb*, but it may be pronounced.
- Doubling of B occurs in a few words of Semitic origin transmitted through Gr: *abbot, rabbi, Sabbath, shibboleth*.

## Graeco-Lat c *(excluding* CH*)*

- Graeco-Lat c occurs with the value /k/ chiefly before the letters A, O, L, R:
  - Initially in *cardiac* (via Fr and Lat < Gr *kardiakos*), *caustic, cladistics, colossus, comet, cosmopolitan, creosote, crisis, crystal*; in prefixes and combining forms[8] such as CATA- 'down' (e.g. in *catapult*), CALLI- 'beautiful' (e.g. in *calligraphy*).
  - Medially after prefixes and combining forms in *apocalypse, democratic, eucalyptus, holocaust, iconoclastic, microcosm, protocol,* and in the prefix EC-/ECTO- 'out' (e.g. *ecstasy, ectoplasm*).
- c can be occur doubled: e.g. in *streptococcus,* and where the prefix EC- 'out' precedes a stem beginning with c, as in *ecclesiastic* (ult. < Gr *kaleein* 'to call').
- In rare technical words, c can also precede N (as in *cnidarian* 'jellyfish' < Gr *knidē* 'nettle') and T (as in *ctenoid* 'comb-shaped' < Gr *ktenoeidēs*).
  - In the former, the c may or may not be pronounced; in the latter it is silent.
- The sound group /ks/, which might have been expected to appear as CS, is not usually so spelt, but has its own letter, X, which will be discussed in its turn below. In this respect, *ecstasy* (< Gr *ekstasis*, not *\*exstasis* or *\*extasis*) is anomalous.
- Before the letters E, I, Y, Gr-derived stems which were transliterated into Lat before the change of Lat /k/ to /s/ show that change: *centre* (< Lat *centrum* < Gr *kentron*), *cycle, exorcise* (via Fr < Lat *exorcizare* < Gr *exorkizein*), *solecism*.
  - Lat c may be pronounced /k/ even before the front vowel E. In *cephalic* the c was traditionally pronounced /s/ (compare *encephalitis, hydrocephalus*), but in scientific circles is now generally /k/.

Gr spelt *sceptic, sceptre, skeleton* with SK-, but these words have evolved in different ways in Eng: *sceptre* has followed Fr in reducing /sk/ to /s/, while *sceptic* retains the Gr pronunciation /sk/. (Alongside AmE *skeptic*, note that Dr Johnson gave *skeptick* as his only spelling. The earliest, 16th-century, Eng citations have *skeptik*.) By the 18th century *skeleton* had generally replaced the earlier form *sceleton*.

## Graeco-Lat D

- Graeco-Lat D occurs initially in the words *delta*, *dogma*, *dose* (< Fr < Lat *dosis* < Gr *dosis*), *dragon*, *drama*, *dromedary* (< Gr *dromas* 'runner'; in the combining forms DEMO- 'people', DENDRO- 'tree', DERMO- 'skin', DEUTERO- 'second'; and in the prefixes DECA- 'ten', DI- 'two', DIA- 'through', DYS- 'badly'.
- Medially it occurs after prefixes and combining forms in e.g. *aerodrome* (< Gr *dromos* racecourse; compare *dromedary* above), *antidote*, *epidemic*, *orthodox*, *pterodactyl* (< Gr *daktulos* 'finger'), *rhododendron* (< Gr *rhododendron* < *rhodon* 'rose' + *dendron* 'tree'), *taxidermist*.
- D occurs doubled in a few biblical terms derived from Hebrew and transmitted through Gr: *Armageddon*, *Sadducee*.

## Graeco-Lat G

Gr *gamma* was the source of the Roman letter C, with G a later Roman adaptation of C, but once established in the Roman alphabet G was regularly used to transliterate *gamma*. In classical times G had the sound value /g/, but it was later palatalized to /dʒ/ before front vowels.

- G pronounced /g/ is seen:
  - word-initially in *galaxy* (< Gr *galaxias*), *gonad*, *glossary*, *grammar*;
  - medially in *archipelago* (< Ital < Lat *pelagus* < Gr *pelagos*), *catalogue*, *demagogue*, *dogma*, *ergonomics*, *logarithm*, *magnet*, *oligarchy*, *protagonist*, *sarcophagus*, *stigma*; in combining forms such as MEGA-, PHAGO- 'eat' (as in *phagocyte*); and after combining forms and prefixes, as in *calligraphy*, *diagonal*, *polygamy*, *pentagon*, *telegram*.
- G pronounced /dʒ/ is seen:
  - word-initially in *gypsum*; in combining forms such as GEO-, GEN-, -GEN 'birth' (as in *genetic*, *oxygen*), GERI- 'age' (as in *geriatric*), GYMNO- 'naked' (as in *gymnasium*), GYRO- 'circle' (as in *gyrate*);
  - medially in *energy*, *exegesis*, *haemorrhage* (phonologically now word-finally before a silent E; < Lat *hæmorrhagia* < Gr *haimorragia*), *hydrogen*, *logic*, *nostalgia*, *strategy*.

- The G in GYN- 'woman' was formerly pronounced /dʒ/, both initially in *gynaecology* and medially in *misogyny*, but by the end of the 20th century medical and scientific usage preferred initial /g/ in *gynaecology*.
- When GIGA- is used as a prefix meaning a billion, as in *gigavolt*, the initial G is pronounced /g/ (compare *gigantic*).
- With the loss, in terms of pronunciation, of G in initial GN in OE *gnat*, etc. (see p. 182), the sequence /gn/ no longer accorded with the normal sound patterns of Eng; hence the loss of the initial /g/ of *gnathic* 'of the jaw', *gnomon* 'the pointer of a sundial', *Gnostic*. However, /g/ is retained at a syllable boundary, as in *ag-nostic*.
  - The presence or absence of a syllable boundary also affects the pronunciation of *diaphragm* (< Gr *diaphragma*), *phlegm*, etc.: compare *phlegm* and *phleg-matic*. (However, in the grammatical term *syntagm*, < Gr *suntagma*, the G is pronounced, as it is in *syntagmatic*.) *Phlegm* and *physiognomy* acquired their present spellings after the revival of Gr learning around 1500; previously they had forms such as *fleme*, *fisnomie*. *Physiognomy* is generally pronounced without /g/ in BrE, but with /g/ in AmE.
  - *Cygnet* is derived via Fr from Lat *cycnus/cygnus*, Gr *kuknos*.

In Gr ΓΓ represented the sounds /ŋg/ shown by the Lat digraph NG: see 'Graeco-Lat N' below.

### Graeco-Lat κ

Direct transliteration of Gr *kappa* by Lat K rather than C was very rare, but *calendar* was in earlier times often written with initial K in both Lat and Eng. Modern transliteration of Gr, not mediated through Lat, is on the other hand more inclined to use K, as in *kinetic*, *kleptomania* (see p. 225).

- Note that although KILO-, in origin a Fr coinage (with the introduction of the metric system in 1795) and used to indicate multiples of 1,000 (as in *kilogram*, *kilometre*), is derived from Gr, it is not based on a form with initial *kappa*. The term was derived from or inspired by Gr *chilioi* 'thousand' with initial *chi* (as seen in Eng *chiliad* 'period of 1,000 years'), and by standard Graeco-Lat transliteration would be written *chilo.

## Graeco-Lat L

- Graeco-Lat L is seen word-initially in e.g. *laconic, leprosy, lexical, lithium, logical, lyre, lyric.*
- Graeco-Lat L is seen medially in the stem HOLO- 'all' (as in *holistic, hologram*) and after a combining form or prefix in *dilemma, eclectic, eclipse, epileptic, monolith, ideology, catalyst.*
- Word-finally Graeco-Lat L is found in *beryl* (< Gr *bērullos*), *coral* (< Gr *korallion*), *crystal, idol, metal* (< Gr *metallon*), *sibyl.*
  - Words with final L from Gr ΛΛ often have LL in their derivatives: *beryl* but *beryllium, coral* but *coralline, crystal* but *crystalline, metal* but *metallic, sibyl* but *sibylline; idyl* (AmE spelling; compare BrE *idyll*, which keeps the original Gr ΛΛ) but *idyllic.*
- Doubling is common as in *alleluia, ballistic, phallic,* in the combining forms ALL- 'other' (e.g. *allegory, allergy, parallel*), CALLI- 'beauty' (as in *calligraphy*).
  - Doubling may also arise through assimilation of a prefix ending in N to a stem beginning with L: e.g. *ellipse* < EN- + stem LEP-; *syllable* < SYN- + stem -LAB-.
- Almost all occurrences of the initial consonant string SCL-, pronounced /skl/, in Eng are in words of Gr origin, based on Gr *sklēros* 'hard', as in *sclerosis.* (Other occurrences of SCL in Eng straddle syllable boundaries, as in *dis-close*, or have silent C, as in *muscle.*)

## Graeco-Lat M

- Graeco-Lat M occurs word-initially in *magnet* (< Gr *Magnētis lithos* 'stone from Magnesia'), *mania, mastodon, mathematics* (< Gr *mathēmatika*), *matriarchy, melody, metal, meter, music, myth*; in the combining forms MACRO-, MEGA(LO)-, MELANO- 'black' (as in *melancholy*), MESO- 'middle' (as in *Mesopotamia*), META- 'across' (as in *metaphor*), MICRO-, MONO-.
  - Initial MN not being native to the phonology of Eng, the M is normally silent in *mnemonic*; but where a syllable boundary separates the two letters, the M is pronounced (as in *am-nesty* and *am-nesia*, from the same root – compare Gr *mnasthai* 'to remember' – as underlies *mnemonic*).
- Examples of medial Gr-derived M are *dogma, polygamy* and *theme.*
- M occurs doubled in *ammonia, comma, dilemma, grammar, gamma*, but words derived from the same stems have single M in some derivatives in Eng: *gamma ~ gamut, grammar ~ glamour.*

○ Doubling varies in *gram/gramme, program/programme* (see p. 306).
- M is also doubled where the prefix SYN- is affixed to a stem beginning with M and assimilated, as in *symmetry*, not *\*synmetry*.
- M is never word-final in Gr, but with the loss of a word-ending it
can be in Eng. Characteristic Gr-derived Eng endings with a syllabic
M are -SM, -THM: *enthusiasm* (< Gr *enthousiasmos*), *logarithm, microcosm, paroxysm, rheumatism, rhythm*; and -GM, where the G is silent,
as in *diaphragm, paradigm* (see p. 207 above). Non-syllabic word-final
M occurs in Eng *emblem* (< Gr *emblēma*), *idiom, problem, system,
symptom, telegram.*

## Graeco-Lat N

- Graeco-Lat N occurs word-initially in *narcotic, nautical, nausea,
necropolis, nectar, nemesis, neurotic, nymph*, and in combining forms
NANO- ('dwarf', as in *nanosecond* = one billionth of a second), NEO-
('new', as in *neolithic*).
- Graeco-Lat N occurs medially in words such as *anemone, carcinogenic,
endocrine* 'denoting a type of gland' (now phonologically word-final
in -CRINE; < Gr *endon* 'within' + *krinein* 'to separate'), *pandemonium*
(a coinage of Milton's), and in combining forms such as ANTI- and
PENTA-.
- Graeco-Lat N may occur word-finally in words such as *dragon* (< Gr
*drakōn*), *horizon, hymn* (< Gr *humnos*), *orphan* (< Gr *orphanos*),
*phenomenon* (< Gr *phainomenon*), *python*. As can be seen, many, but
not all, of these words have source words that end in -N in Gr.
- Graeco-Lat N is rarely doubled in Gr-derived words. *Cannabis,
cinnamon, tyranny* are three instances, and further cases are seen in
biblical terms mostly of Hebrew origin: *gehenna, hosannah, manna.*
- Graeco-Lat N may be lost through assimilation to a following consonant: the prefix SYN- 'with' becomes SYL- or SYM- in words like
*syllable, symmetry, sympathy*, or simply loses the N altogether, as in
*system, syzygy* (an astrological term).

## Graeco-Lat NG, NC, NX, NCH

In these spellings, Lat has not applied the normal letter-equivalences
in its transliteration of Gr. If transliterated by the standard letter-
equivalences, ΓΓ, ΓΚ, ΓΞ, ΓΧ would have given Roman GG, GC, GX, GCH,
resulting in, for example, Eng *\*sphiggter* for *sphincter*, *\*sphigx* for *sphinx*,

*melagcholy* for *melancholy*, etc. However, Lat opted instead for NG, NC, NX, NCH, reflecting the pronunciation of these consonant clusters, giving ModE *angel, gangrene, diphthong, sponge, encephalitis, phalanx, larynx, melancholy, bronchitis, conch.*

- In some words the consonant following the N has undergone later palatalization: e.g. *angel, sponge, conch* (when pronounced /kɒntʃ/ rather than /kɒŋk/), *encephalitis* (if pronounced /ɛnsɛf-/).

## Graeco-Lat P (excluding PH, PS)

The letter P transliterates Gr *pi* except before Roman S, in which case the PS together transliterate the Gr letter *psi* (see 'PS' below).

- Word-initially, Graeco-Lat P occurs in *paean* (AmE *pean*; via Lat < Gr dialect *paian*), *panic* (< Gr *panikon*), *pause, plastic, plectrum, poet, political, python*, and in many combining forms and prefixes: PACHY- 'thick' (as in *pachyderm*), PAEDO- (AmE PEDO-) 'child' (as in *paediatrics*), PALAEO- (AmE PALEO-) 'old' (as in *Palaeolithic*), PALIN- 'again' (as in *palindrome*), PAN- 'all' (as in *pandemonium*), PARA- 'beside' (as in *paragraph*), PATHO- 'suffering' (as in *pathetic*), PATR- 'father' (as in *patriarch*), PENTA- 'five' (as in *pentagon*), PERI- 'surrounding' (as in *periscope*), PIEZO- 'to press' (as in *piezoelectric*), PLATY- 'flat' (as in *platypus*), PLEISTO- 'most' (as in *pleistocene*), PLEO- 'more' (as in *pleonasm*), PLUTO- 'wealthy' (as in *plutocracy*), PNEUMO- 'breath' (as in *pneumonia*), POLY- 'many' (as in *polytechnic*), PORNO- 'prostitute' (as in *pornography*), PROTO- 'first' (as in *prototype*), PTERO- 'wing' (as in *pterodactyl*), PYRO- 'fire' (as in *pyromaniac*).
- Graeco-Lat P does not occur word-finally in Gr, but does so medially in numerous stems and combining forms: e.g. *anthropoid, archipelago* (< Gr *pelagos* 'sea'), *catapult, hypnotic, Mesopotamia* (< *potamos* 'river'), *octopus, Olympic, optic, therapy, tropic, type.*
- Doubling of Graeco-Lat P is rare: it occurs in the names of the letter *kappa* and the obsolete letter *qoppa*, and in the stem HIPPO- ('horse') found in *hippopotamus* and *Philip* (see p. 216).
  - *Sapphire* and the personal name *Sappho* do not reflect double *pi* but *pi* + *phi* (see p. 203).
- Graeco-Lat P is silent in word-initial consonant strings unknown in native Eng words: *pneumonia, pterodactyl, ptomaine*. But in non-initial position, when a syllable boundary intervenes, the word may

be re-syllabified, allowing the P to be pronounced: e.g. *helico-pter* > *helicop-ter*, *sym-ptom* (compare *ptomaine*) > *symp-tom*.

○ The P of *ptarmigan* is based on a false etymology, being prefixed by analogy with Gr initial PT- to Gaelic *tarmachan*.

## Graeco-Lat PS

Like *xi*, *psi* represents two consonant sounds together, /ps/. These could perfectly well have been represented by the separate letters *pi* and *sigma*, and the Romans transliterated *psi* by the letters PS.

- Except in initial position, where P + S never occurs in native Lat or Eng words, it is not immediately obvious which Eng words derive PS from Gr *psi*. Thus, while it is clear that such words as *psalm*, *psephology*, PSEUDO-, *psittacosis*, *psoriasis*, *psyche*, etc. contain Gr *psi*, it is not immediately evident that *apocalypse*, *apse*, *autopsy*, *calypso*, *dyspepsia*, *eclipse*, *ellipse*, *epilepsy*, *gypsum*, *palimpsest* and *synopsis* do so (though, of course, the Gr origin of these words may be evident from other word-elements such as DYS-, EPI-, SYN-). Various words of solely Lat derivation such as *capsule*, *lapse* (and its derivatives *collapse*, *elapse*), *solipsism* contain a PS which does not derive from Gr *psi*.
- Word-initially in Eng, the P is silent except in the letter name *psi* itself. A medial syllable boundary, however, may permit the pronunciation of the /p/: e.g. *epsilon*, *upsilon*, structurally *e-psilon*, *u-psilon* (*psilon* = 'bare') have been re-syllabified as *ep-silon*, *up-silon*.

## Graeco-Lat R (excluding RH, RRH)

Unless aspirated, the letter R in Gr derivations is restricted to medial and final position except in clusters with other consonants:

- Gr-derived R occurs in initial consonant clusters in e.g. *bronchitis*, *crypt* (< Gr *kruptē*), *chrysalis*, *dragon* (< Gr *drakōn*), *gram(me)*, *program(me)*, *phrase*, *trauma*.
- Gr-derived R occurs medially between vowels in e.g. *paroxysm*, *perimeter*, *erotic*, *pyre* (now phonologically word-final; < Gr *pura*), and before or after consonants in e.g. *anthropoid*, *Arctic*, *barbarous*, *cardiac*, *ergonomics*, *harmony*, *herpes*, *morphine*, *myrtle*, *orchid*, *ornithology*, *orthodox*, *Persian*, *Terpsichore* 'muse of dancing'.

211

- ○ Graeco-Lat R does not commonly occur before or after L or X in stems of Gr origin (although there is, for example, a rare word *hyparxis* 'subsistence', < Gr *huparxis*).
- ○ Graeco-Lat R also occurs in the string STR (*strategy*, *gastric*).
- Gr-derived R is found word-finally in *aster*, *hector*, *martyr*, *meteor*, *nectar*.

## *Graeco-Lat s*

Graeco-Lat s occurs widely in all positions, sometimes pronounced /s/, sometimes /z/:

- Word-initially the sound value is /s/, as in (before vowels) *satyr* (< Gr *saturos*), *seismic* (< Gr *seismos* 'earthquake'), *sophisticated*, *symphony* and (before consonants) *sceptic* (< Gr *skeptikos*), *scheme* (< Gr *schēma*), *sporadic*, *sphinx* (< Gr *sphigx*; for Gr GX > Lat NX, see pp. 209–10), *stadium*, *strategic*.
- In medial position, the /s/ value prevails before voiceless consonants: *callisthenics* (< Gr KALLI- 'beauty' + *sthenos* 'strength'), *phosphorus* (< Gr *phōsphoros* 'bringing light'), *plastic*, *telescope*; also in prefixes and combining forms, such as ESO- 'within' (as in *esoteric*), ISO- 'equal' (as in *isobar*). /z/ is found before M: *cataclysm*, *chasm*, *microcosm*, *schism*.
  - ○ Final silent E generally shows that a preceding phonologically final s is voiced: *pause* (via Fr < Lat *pausa*, prob. < Gr *pausis*), *phase* (via Fr < LLat *phasis* < Gr *phasis*), *phrase*, *enthuse* (formed from *enthusiasm* < Gr *enthousiasmos*); but *base* (via Fr < Lat *basis* < Gr *basis*) has /s/.
- In final position in a singular word, the sound value is also /s/: *analysis*, *basis*, *crisis*, *hippopotamus*, *neurosis*, *rhinoceros*, *thesis*. However, in the plural, the final s is pronounced /z/ in conformity with other Eng -ES inflections, as in *boxes*, *dishes*, *masses*, *watches*: *analyses*, *bases*, *crises*, *neuroses*, *theses*.
  - ○ In names such as *Hades*, *Socrates*, the sound value is also /z/.
- In other instances the s is arbitrarily voiced or voiceless, as in *hypotenuse*, *mausoleum*, *nausea*. Although in Gr the medial s of the source words from which *museum* and *music* derive is voiceless /s/, in the Eng derivatives it is regularly voiced /z/.
- Doubling occurs occasionally in Gr-derived words: *abyss* (< Gr *abussos*, though one s was lost from *abysm* in its passage through Fr),

*colossus, Colosseum* (but with single s in the Italianized spelling *Coliseum*), *cypress, glossary, narcissus, odyssey, pessary.*

○ Of the alternative forms *dissyllabic, disyllabic* the former was influenced by Fr spelling, which perceived the word as having the prefix DIS-, although clearly the prefix is DI- ('two'), making *disyllabic* the etymologically correct form.

## Graeco-Lat T (excluding TH)

* The letter T occurs word-initially in *tactics* (< Gr *taktikos*), *tantalize, tautology, taxidermy, tomb, trauma, toxin, tropic, type,* and in combining forms such as TECHNO- 'art' (as in *technical*), TELE- 'far' (as in *telegram, telescope*), TERA- 'monster, a million million' (as in *terahertz*), TETRA- 'four', TOPO- 'place' (as in *topography*), TRI- 'three'.
* The letter T is found medially in -TAPH 'tomb' (as in *cenotaph, epitaph*), -TOM 'cut' (as in *atom, appendectomy*) and TROPH- 'nourishment' (as in *atrophy*).
* Doubling is occasionally seen, as in *attic, glottal* (< Gr *glōttis*, the TT here being a dialect variant of SS: compare *glottal/glossary*), *psittacosis* 'disease of birds'.
* The sequence PT is common in Gr-derived words: *eucalyptus, heptagon, sceptic, epileptic.* In initial position the P is silent, as in *pterodactyl*.

## Graeco-Lat X

Like *psi, xi* stands for two sounds, /ks/, but unlike *psi* (which Lat replaced with PS), *xi* passed into the Roman alphabet. Probably the majority of words containing the letter X in Eng are of Gr origin, but in their frequency of occurrence they lag far behind words containing the Lat-derived prefix EX-, which are far more common than all the Gr stems taken together. EX- is, however, itself occasionally a Gr prefix, as in *exegesis* (< Gr *exēgēsis*) and *exodus* (< Gr *exodos*). EX- occurs only before vowels; before a consonant it is replaced by EK-, which becomes EC- in Lat and hence also in Eng, as in *eccentric* (via LLat < Gr *ekkentros*), *eclipse* (via Lat < Gr *ekleipsis*), *ecstasy* (< Gr *ekstasis*).

* Graeco-Lat X is found word-initially in combining forms such as XENO- 'foreign' (as in *xenophobia*), XERO- 'dry' (as in *Xerox*®), XYLO- 'wood' (as in *xylophone*); since word-initial /ks/ is foreign to the sound patterns of Eng, the pronunciation of X in such words is typically /z/.

- Graeco-Lat x occurs medially in *anorexia, apoplexy, asphyxia, axiom, axis, dyslexia, galaxy, lexical, hexagon, oxygen, paroxysm, taxonomy*.
- Graeco-Lat x occurs word-finally in e.g. *anthrax, calx, calyx, climax, coccyx, helix, larynx, onyx, paradox, phalanx, pharynx, phlox, phoenix, sphinx, syntax, thorax*.

### Graeco-Lat z

The letter z at first had no function in Lat at all. Indeed, the Romans omitted it from its Gr position before H in the alphabet (. . . *epsilon, zeta, eta,* . . .) and only added it on at the end of the alphabet again when they later needed it for transliterating Gr.

- Gr-derived z is found word-initially in *zeal* (< Gr *zēlos*), *zephyr, zodiac, zone* and in the combining form ZOO- (< Gr *zōion* 'animal').
- Medially, Gr-derived z occurs in *amazon, azalea, enzyme, horizon, ozone, protozoa, rhizome, syzygy, trapeze*. In these, z is pronounced /z/; in the combining form SCHIZO-, z may be pronounced /z/ but, as in *schizophrenia*, more usually /ts/, in *eczema*, z = /s/ or /z/.
- We find Gr-derived z word-finally in *topaz* (< Gr *topazos*).
- Most important for ModE spelling is the suffix -IZE, first transliterated perhaps for Christian terms like *baptize*, but since extended widely in use. In Fr the suffix was written -ISE, and this was formerly the standard spelling in BrE too. The -IZE spelling is standard in AmE, and is now becoming standard in BrE also.
  - The z spelling was early extended to *analyze* (Samuel Johnson in his 1755 *Dictionary* has *analyze* but *paralyse*); *analyze* and *paralyze* are standard in AmE, *analyse* and *paralyse* in BrE.

# Aspirated and Unaspirated Vowels in Gr and Lat

Word-initial vowels in Gr might be aspirated or unaspirated. Aspirated vowels were indicated by a reversed apostrophe ' (known as a 'rough breathing') above the vowel, while lack of aspiration on a vowel would be indicated by a normal apostrophe ' (the 'smooth breathing'). Lat transliterated the aspirated vowels with a preceding H; if the vowel was not aspirated, Lat, unlike Gr, did not specifically mark this (except by not writing H). Thus Gr *'ērōs* 'hero' would be transliterated into Lat as *heros*, but Gr *'erōs* 'Eros, god of love' as Lat *Eros*.

- H was sometimes wrongly omitted or wrongly inserted, e.g. Lat and Eng *halcyon* < Gr *alcyōn* 'kingfisher' (possibly on the false assumption of a connection with Gr *hals* 'sea').

## Graeco-Lat Vowels in Eng

### *Initial A/HA*

- Non-aspirated A is seen in *angel* (< Gr *aggelos*; for the transliteration of Gr ΓΓ as Lat and Engl NG, see pp. 209–10), *Arctic* (< Gr *arktikos*), *arithmetic*, *athlete*; also in prefixes and combining forms A- 'without', AER- 'air', AMPHI- 'both', ANAO- 'up', ANDRO- 'male', ANTHRO- 'human', ANTI- 'against', ARCH- 'chief', ARISTO- 'best', ARTHR- 'joint', AUTO- 'self'.
- Aspirated A is seen in *Hades, harmony, harpy*, and in the combining forms HAEMO- 'blood' (as in *haemoglobin*, etc.; in American spelling HEMO-), HAGIO- 'holy' (as in *hagiography*), and HALO- 'salt' (as in *halogen*).
  - With non-initial -HAEM-, there has been uncertainty in Eng about how the initial aspiration should be handled after a prefix or combining form:
    - With a prefix not ending in an aspirated consonant, such as AN-, the aspiration has simply disappeared: *anaemia*, not *⋆anhaemia*.
    - With the stem LEUKO- (< Gr *leukos* 'white'), the Gr *kappa* followed by the aspirated initial vowel of -HAEM- would normally become *chi*, so giving the transliteration *leuchaemia*. When the word first appeared in Eng in the 19th century, its spelling varied between *leuchaemia, leucaemia* and *leukaemia*, the now standard form (but compare *leucocyte*, etc.). The K ensures a correct sound–spelling correspondence: the form *leucaemia* would suggest an /s/ pronunciation, as in *glycaemia, septicaemia*; similarly, with the simplification of AE to E in AmE (HEMO- for BrE HAEMO-), K avoids the suggestion of /s/.

### *Initial E/HE*

*Epsilon* and *eta*, the first a short vowel, the second long, were both transliterated into Lat as E. However, their sound value in Eng does not necessarily correspond to their length in Gr: HEPTA- 'seven' was spelt with *epsilon* and HEMI- 'half' with *eta*, but both have /ɛ/ in Eng;

conversely, *Helen* and *helix* were both written with *epsilon* in Gr but have different sound values /ɛ/ and /iː/ in Eng.

- Non-aspirated E is seen in *echo, electric, epic, erotic, ethos, ethnic,* and in a range of prefixes and combining forms such as EC-/ECTO-/EX-/EXO- 'out' (e.g. *ecstasy, ectoplasm, exegesis, exogamous*), EM-/EN- 'in' (e.g. *emblem, enthusiasm*), ENDO- 'within' (e.g. *endoscope*), EPI- 'on' (e.g. *epitaph*), EU- 'good' (e.g. *euthanasia, euphoria*).
- Aspirated E is seen in *hebdomadal, Hebrew,* HECTO-, *hedonism, hegemony, helix, helium, Hellenic, hemisphere, hepatitis, heptagon, hermetic, hero, herpes, heterosexual, hexagon.*
  - *Hermit* (ME *ermyt* < Gr *erēmitēs*) acquired H from medieval Lat and Fr and eventually developed a spelling pronunciation to match; compare *eremite,* from the same Gr source.
  - *Eureka,* cognate with *heuristic,* has lost its H in both sound and spelling.
  - For *economy, ecumenical,* see p. 221.

## Initial *I*/HI

The number of words formed with initial I transliterating Gr *iota* is not very great.

- Non-aspirated I occurs in *idea, idiom, idiot, iodine, ion, iota,* and in the combining form ISO- 'same' (as in *isobar, isogen*).
  - The initial Gr vowels of *icon* and *idol* were spelt with the digraph EI, probably pronounced /iː/ by the time of their first transliteration and so rendered simply by Lat I, which had this phonetic value.
- Aspirated I is seen in *hibiscus, hierarchy, hippopotamus, histogram, history.*
  - Initial HI- in HIPPO- 'horse' lost its aspiration and therefore its H after the combining form PHIL- in the name *Philip* (= 'lover of horses').

## Initial *O*/HO

As with E, Lat O transliterates two Gr vowel letters, short *omicron* and long *omega.* In Eng derivatives from Gr, O it may be pronounced /əʊ/ or /ɒ/ irrespective of its length in classical Gr.

- Non-aspirated initial O is found in *orchestra, orchid, ornithology, orphan, orthodox, osteopathy, ostracize, oxygen,* deriving in all these words from the letter *omicron* (e.g. < Gr *orchēstra, orchidion,* etc.).
- With aspiration O occurs in *hoi polloi, holistic, holocaust, homeopathy, homily, homonym, hoplite, horizon, horoscope,* the O in all but the last of these deriving from *omicron* (e.g. < *hoi* 'the', *holos* 'whole', etc. and *hōroskopos* < *hōra* 'hour').
  - The stem *hodos* 'road' is seen in e.g. *hodograph, hodoscope,* but Fr-derived *odometer* is preferred to *hodometer.* The non-aspirated form is also seen in *anode, diode, electrode,* while residual aspiration is seen in *cathode* (compare *cathedral,* etc., p. 198).

## Initial U

Lat used U to transliterate Gr OY.

- Unaspirated initial OY underlies the initial U of *uranium* and *urine.*
- OY is never aspirated in Gr, so in principle no Gr-derived word should be spelt with initial HU in the Roman alphabet. The form *hubris* (also written *hybris*; < Gr *hubris*) is a 19th-century borrowing directly from Gr, not entering Eng via Lat (see 'The Fourth Wave: New Gr Spellings' below, p. 224).
- The initial U of *utopia* was a pun created by Sir Thomas More in his book (1516) of the same name, and was designed to reflect both the Gr combining forms OU- 'not' and EU- 'good'.

## Initial HY

Lat took the Gr letter Y and added it to the end of the alphabet (Z was added later) specifically to transliterate Gr *upsilon.*

- Initial *upsilon* is always aspirated and initial HY- is characteristic of Gr derivation (though there are a few rare words in Eng of non-Gr origin which begin with HY-, such as the *hyawa,* a tree found in Guyana, and *hyleg,* a term used in astrology): *hyacinth* (< Gr *huakinthos*), *hyena* (< Gr *huaina*), *hygiene, hymen, hymn, hysteria* and in combining forms such as HYDRO- 'water' (as in *hydraulic, hydrogen*), HYGRO- 'wet' (as in *hygroscopic*), HYPER- 'over' (as in *hyperbole*), HYPNO- 'sleep' (as in *hypnotherapy*), HYPO- 'under' (as in *hypochondria, hypocrite*).

- ○ The aspiration is lost from HY in medial position in *clepsydra* 'water clock' (via Lat < Gr *klepsudra*; *-udra* < *hudor* 'water').
- ○ *Hybrid* derives from Lat *hibrida* 'mongrel' with an alternative Lat spelling *hybrida* possibly influenced by Gr.

# Non-Initial Simple Graeco-Lat Vowels

Classical Gr had seven vowel letters: A, E, H, I, O, Y and Ω. *Epsilon* and *omicron* were short vowels, *eta* and *omega* long vowels. Lat had six vowel letters (A, E, I, O, U, Y) with which it could represent these seven in transliterations from Gr; Table 1 above (p. 197) shows the correspondences. (As we have seen in the section 'Initial U' above, Lat used U for transliterating Gr in a way which does not concern us here.)

Vowels in Lat could be long or short, but this was not indicated by any difference in the letter symbols themselves.

The results of transliterating non-initial Gr vowels into the Roman alphabet are essentially the same as those shown in the preceding section for the initial aspirated or non-aspirated Gr vowels, and need little further discussion or exemplification.

In terms of sound–spelling correspondences, the lengths of the vowel letters E and O in Eng do not necessarily correspond to the length of the vowels in Gr (and Lat), as was noted above under 'Initial E/HE' and 'Initial O/HO'. Further examples of this can be seen under 'E' and 'O' below.

## Graeco-Lat and Eng A

Eng *analysis* < Gr *analusis*, *character* < Gr *charaktēr*, -GRAPH < Gr -GRAPHOS, *magma* 'molten rock' < Gr *magma*, *planet* < Gr *planētēs*, *trachea* < Gr *tracheia*.

## Graeco-Lat and Eng E

Eng *eclectic* < Gr *eklektikos*, *epilepsy* < Gr *epilēpsia*, *ethos* < Gr *ēthos*, *genesis* < Gr *genesis*, *geometry* < Gr *geōmetria*, *lexicon* < Gr *lexikon*, *method* < Gr *methodos*, *orchestra* < Gr *orchēstra*, *theory* < Gr *theōria*, *thesis* < Gr *thesis*.

- • The final E is pronounced in *epitome*, *sesame* (< Gr *epitomē*, *sēsamē*), an unexpected sound–spelling correspondence in ModE (compare *tome*, *same*).

### Graeco-Lat and Eng ɪ

Eng BIO- < Gr *bio-*, *crisis* < Gr *krisis*, *critic* < Gr *kritikos*, *ion* < Gr *ion*, *isthmus* < Gr *isthmos*, *logic* < Gr *logikē*, *stigma* < Gr *stigma*.

### Graeco-Lat and Eng ᴏ

Eng *coma* < Gr *kōma*, *comma* < Gr *komma*, *crocus* < Gr *krokos*, *gnosis* < Gr *gnōsis*, *horizon* < Gr *horizōn*, -PHOBIA < Gr -PHOBIA, PHOTO- < Gr PHŌTO-, *problem* < Gr *problēma*, *rhododendron* < Gr *rhododendron*, *zone* < Gr *zōnē*.

### Graeco-Lat and Eng ʏ

Eng *chrysalis* < Gr *chrusallis*, *dactyl* < Gr *daktulos*, *paralysis* < Gr *paralusis*, *platypus* < Gr *platupous*, *pylon* < Gr *pulōn*, *system* < Gr *sustēma*.

• The letter ᴛ before or after ʏ occurs typically in stems of Graeco-Lat origin: *analytical*, *martyr*, *tyrannical*.

## Complex Gr Vowels in Lat and Eng

This section will concern itself with the Gr digraph vowels (apart from OY – see 'Initial ᴜ' above, p. 217). The transliteration of AI, EI, OI, AY, EY and OY into the Roman alphabet was less straightforward than that of the simple vowels; Table 1 above (p. 197) shows the basic equivalences.

### Gr AI transliterated as Æ/AE or ᴇ

Up to the 3rd century BCE, Lat transliterated the Gr digraph AI as AI, but by classical times had adopted AE instead, as in *aegis* < Gr *aigis*. In both Lat and Gr, there developed in subsequent centuries a tendency to reduce the spelling of AI/AE to simple ᴇ, representing a sound /eː/.

Successive changes in spelling and pronunciation over the centuries – for the Eng pronunciation of AE as /iː/, as in *Caesar*, due to the Great Vowel Shift, see pp. 176–9 – have resulted in a legacy of variation in Eng: e.g. *daimon/daemon/demon*, *cainozoic/caenozoic/cenozoic*. *Cainozoic*, for example, is a modern transliteration of the original Gr, with pronunciation of the first syllable as /kaɪn-/ or /keɪn-/); the first syllable of *caenozoic* is pronounced /siːn-/; CENO-, with pronunciation /siːn-/ or /sɛn-/, is more frequent in AmE.

Until the 20th century, the digraph AE was commonly printed as the ligature Æ, which distinguished it from the sequence A + E in, for example, *aerial*, which in Gr had the discrete vowels A + E, not the AI digraph (Gr *aerios*). Until the end of the 19th century, this was reflected in pronunciation, *aerial* being pronounced /eɪˈɪərɪəl/ or /eɪˈeərɪəl/. There was therefore no respelling of the words as *★erial* or *★Pheton*.

The combining form GRECO/GRAECO- was formerly written GRÆCO-, derived from the Romans' normal term for 'Greek', *Graecus*, itself of Gr origin although *Graikoi* was not the word the Greeks normally used to describe themselves. *Diet* entered Eng already reduced from AE, reflecting LLat *dieta* rather than classical Graeco-Lat *diaeta* (Gr *diaita*). *Gangrene* similarly arrived in Eng with Lat E, although Gr spelt the second vowel AI.

Several words used AE for a while (if decreasingly over the centuries after 1500): *enigma* (< Gr *ainigma*) was formerly written *ænigma* in Eng; *æther* was increasingly written *ether* by the 19th century; medieval *heresye* was briefly reformed as *hæresie* on the basis of its etymology, before reverting to *heresy*; early Eng spellings of *phenomenon* for a while followed Lat *phænomenon*; and *sphere* was for a time etymologized to *sphære* before achieving its present form. *Dæmon* has given way to *demon* by the 20th century (though there had previously been some distinction of meaning), while *hyæna* (< Gr *huaina*) enjoyed scholarly preference after the 16th century before reverting to *hyena*.

More recently, the stem PAEDO- 'child' (< Gr PAIDO-) has largely yielded to PEDO- in *encyclopedia*, but in British medical usage *paediatrics* is still usual (AmE *pediatrics*). Slightly more resistant to the modern reduction to E in British usage are *archaeology* and *palaeography*, as well as some forms with initial AE: *aegis, aeon, aesthetic*. Such words commonly have just E in American usage: *archeology, paleography, egis, eon, esthetic*. The reduced American spelling is particularly prevalent among medical terms, such as *etiology, anemia, hemorrhage, gynecology, orthopedic*, where it is perhaps tending to displace BrE *aetiology, anaemia, haemorrhage, gynaecology, orthopaedic*. Also resistant to change is the AE of *Michael*.

### Gr EI transliterated as E or I

Although a digraph, Gr EI perhaps represented a simple vowel sound rather than a diphthong, and was liable to misspelling in classical Gr as just *iota* or *eta*.

Lat transliterated Gr EI as either E or I, not as EI. Direct transliterations from Gr to Eng giving EI, as in *eirenic, kaleidoscope, pleistocene, seismic, protein, Pleiades* typically date from the 19th or 20th centuries, and have therefore not come via Lat. The contrast between such modern transliterations and the older Lat-derived ones is seen in pairs such as *apodeictic/apodictic* 'demonstrably true' (< Lat *apodicticus* < Gr *apodeiktikos*), *cheiropractic/chiropractic, Eirene/Irene*.

Lat gave Eng an arbitrary spelling variation by tending to transliterate Gr EI as E before a vowel and as I before a consonant: thus *panacea, trachea* (< Gr *panakeia, tracheia*) but *icon, idol, lichen* (< Gr *eikōn, eidōlon, leichēn*), and similarly with *crocodile, dinosaur, empirical, idyll, pirate.* Note, however, *angiosperm* (< Gr *aggeion*) with I before O, and *hygiene* (< Gr *hugieinē*) with E before N preventing a repetition of I in *\*hygiine*.

Underlying the Y of *therapy, idolatry* is Gr -EIA (Gr *latreia* 'worship', *therapeia*) whereas Gr -IA underlies the Y of *theory, history* (< Gr *theōria, historia*).

## Gr OI transliterated as Œ/OE or E

Early Lat transliterated OI as OI, but just as classical Lat replaced AI with AE, so it also replaced OI with OE. As with Æ, printers traditionally used a ligature Œ in Graeco-Lat transliterations (e.g. *Œdipus, cœlacanth*), but separate letters are now more usual (*Oedipus, coelacanth*).

In Eng the original Lat transliteration with OE has in its most common occurrences given way in the 20th century to simple E, as in *ecology, economy* (< Gr *oikos* 'house'), *ecumenical* (< Gr *oikoumenikos* 'inhabited'), *solecism. Penal* was sometimes reformed to *poenal* on the basis of its etymology in EModE, but that form did not persist beyond the 17th century.

In scientific, especially medical, terminology, British usage tends to keep OE (*amoeba, coeliac, diarrhoea, oesophagus, oestrogen*) whereas in American usage it has widely been reduced to E (*ameba, celiac, diarrhea, esophagus, estrogen*).

The OE spelling of *Phoebus, Phoenician, phoenix* was recreated on the basis of etymology from *Febus*, etc., before 1500.

Eng *comedy* and *tragedy* have in their time been etymologized as *comoedy, tragoedy*, but these forms never established themselves.

The stem of *poet* originated in Gr as POIE-, but was commonly compressed to POE- and so transliterated into early Lat; an attempt to etymologize the word in Eng as *poiet* failed. The POIE- stem has nevertheless kept its longer form in *onomatopoeia, pharmacopoeia* (AmE -PEIA).

*Paranoia* today has a 'modern' transliteration with OI, but through most of the 19th century it was written in Graeco-Lat fashion as *paranoea*.

The 'modern' transliteration *koine* 'common standard dialect' (< Gr *koinē* < *koinos* 'common') represents the same stem as the Graeco-Lat transliteration *coen-* (as in *coenobite* 'monk living in a community').

## Gr AY transliterated as AU

The Gr digraph AY was transliterated into Lat as AU. Graeco-Lat AU occurs most commonly in the combining form AUTO- 'self' (as in *autism, autobiography*, etc.) but also in *aura, austere, authentic, caustic, cauterize, centaur, dinosaur, glaucous, hydraulic, mausoleum, minotaur, nausea, nautical, pause, tautology, trauma*. (Note that although many compounds with -PHOBIA are of Gr derivation, the stem CLAUSTRO- in *claustrophobia* is from Lat *claustrum* 'lock, bolt'.)

Graeco-Lat AU is generally pronounced /ɔː/ in ModE but *glaucoma* and *trauma* are sometimes pronounced with the classical Gr value /aʊ/.

## Gr EY transliterated as EU

The Gr digraph EY was transliterated into Lat as EU. It scarcely occurred in native Lat (*neuter* originated as a compound *ne-uter* 'not either'), but was common in transliterations from Gr.

In Gr-derived words, EU occurs in the combining form EU- 'good' (< Gr EU-), as in *eucalyptus, eucharist, eugenics, eulogy, euphemism, euphoria, euthanasia*, and in words such as *deuterium, eunuch* (< Gr *eunouchos* < *eunē* 'bed'), *Europe, hermeneutic, heuristic* (with related *eureka* < Gr *heurēka* 'I have found'; *eureka* appears to be a medieval rendering of the Gr word – conventional Graeco-Lat transliteration would have produced *heureca*), *leukaemia, neurotic, pharmaceutical, pleurisy, pneumonia*, PSEUDO-, *rheumatic, therapeutic, zeugma*.

## Gr OY transliterated as U

Gr OY was transliterated as the Roman letter U. Since the letter U occurs commonly throughout the Eng spelling system, the resulting forms do not always appear so characteristically Gr as do many of the derivatives previously discussed.

Graeco-Lat U for Gr OY occurs initially in *uranium* (< *Uranus* < Gr *Ouranos*), *ureter* (< Gr *ourētēr* < *ouron* 'urine'), *utopia* (< Gr OU- 'not') and medially in *bucolic, cynosure, enthusiasm, eunuch, hypotenuse, music, platypus*.

While a few -US endings in Eng are Graeco-Lat transliterations of -OYΣ (e.g. *octopus, platypus* < Gr *oktōpous, platupous*), most are Lat adaptations of the Gr noun-ending -OΣ: *crocus* (< Gr *krokos*), *hippopotamus, oesophagus, phosphorus, sarcophagus, streptococcus.*

A few Gr-derived words diverge from this transliteration pattern:

* *Acoustic* owes its -OU- to its passage through Fr – normal Graeco-Lat transliteration would have produced *acustic* (compare the medical term *hyperacusis*).
* The *bou-* of *boustrophedon* 'ox-turning' is a direct transliteration of the Gr, contrasting with the traditional Lat transliteration seen in *bulimia* 'ox-hunger'.
* *Glucose* arose from a Fr transliteration not of OY, but of Y, which in Eng would otherwise have given the spelling *glycose* (compare cognate *glycerine*).
* *Nous, noumenon* contain direct non-Lat-mediated transliterations of Gr OY, dating from the 17th–18th centuries.

## Y

Lastly in this section we will consider some anomalies and confusions, mainly involving Y:

* *Aneurysm* derives from Gr *aneurusma* (< *eurus* 'wide'), but may be spelt *aneurism* as if formed with the Gr-derived suffix –ISM.[9]
* The prefixes DYS- (< Gr) and DIS- (< Lat) are pronounced identically in Eng, and can have very similar meanings (with generally negative connotations). Misspellings, especially DIS- for DYS-, are common. Where the stem of a word is clearly Gr, DYS- is usually correct: *dysentery, dyslexia, dystrophy* (< Gr *entera* 'bowels', *lexis* 'word', *trophē* 'nourishment'), *dyspepsia* (< Gr *duspepsia*). Some compounds, however, combine Gr and Lat elements: thus we write *disorganize*, not *⋆dysorganize*, although *organ* derives from Gr, and *dysfunction*, not *⋆disfunction*, although *function* derives from Lat.
* The confusions between DIS- and DYS- are further complicated by the Gr-based combining forms DI- 'two' and DIS- 'twice', which themselves occur interchangeably in the forms *disyllabic, dissyllabic.*
* Confusions surrounding the spelling of *style* 'manner of writing, etc.' go back to Lat itself. In Lat, *stilus* meaning 'a writing implement' could also be written *stylus*. The OFr spelling was *stile*. The Y spelling became

dominant under the influence of Gr *stylos* 'column'. (*Stile* = 'steps built into a wall' is of OE origin, < *stigel*.)

- Before the 16th century, various Graeco-Lat transliterations now with Y were spelt with I in Eng (e.g. ME *fisik*, later altered to *physic*). With the revival of classical scholarship in the 16th century, most of these had their Y restored to match the Gr more closely (and an unetymological pseudo-Gr Y is not unknown), but in a few instances usage still fluctuates. Thus ME *pigmey* (via Lat < Gr *pugmaios*) was altered to *pygmy*, today the commoner form, although *pigmy* is occasionally still used; similarly, the Y of Graeco-Lat *Egypt* (< Gr *Aiguptos*), which is the ultimate source of *gypsy*, has not prevented an I-form *gipsy* being used, though less frequently than the Y-form.
- The spelling *giro* with I, as against *gyrate* with Y, originated as an Italian banking term, and, like *timpani* (< Gr *tumpanon*) reflects the general Ital respelling of Gr Y as I.
- The Y in *syphon* (via Lat < Gr *siphōn*) as an alternative to *siphon* is not justified by reference to any other language: Gr, Lat and Fr all use I.

## The Fourth Wave: New Gr Spellings

Gr-derived words, as we have seen, entered Eng in waves, each wave tending to be spelt according to different criteria. The first wave (*bishop*, *church*, etc.) was fully anglicized, while the third wave, which has been the chief subject of this chapter, was generally spelt according to Graeco-Lat patterns of transliteration, though with a wide variety of distortions to the spelling of individual words. The words of the second wave occupy a mid-position, being first anglicized then respelt according to Graeco-Lat orthographic rules: *phusikos* > *fisik* > *physic*.

By the time of the fourth wave, which was dominated by the mass of specialized terminology needed for the advance of science especially from the 19th century onwards, Gr was better understood by the educated classes (thanks to the Victorian 'classical education'), and there was a tendency for words to be transliterated directly into Eng from Gr (or via other modern languages, e.g. *plankton* from German) rather than mediated by Graeco-Lat conventions.

The effect of this on Eng spelling can be demonstrated by certain words beginning with C and K. While Gr-derived words that have come to Eng via Lat tend to be spelt with C, pronounced /s/ or /k/ depending on the

following sound, more recent introductions in this 'fourth wave' generally use κ, pronounced /k/: compare *katabatic* 'blowing downwards' and
*catastrophe* (< Gr κατα- 'down'; the spelling *catabatic* is attested only once
in the *Oxford English Dictionary*, from the late 19th century in a medical
context = 'gradually abating'), *kleptomaniac* and *clepsydra* 'water clock'
(< Gr *kleptēs* 'thief'), and also *kinetic* and *cinema* (< Gr *kinētikos* 'moving',
*kinēma* 'movement'; *cinema* via Fr; an Eng form *kinema* is attested, though
rarely, throughout much of the 20th century). Another example is
*kaleidoscope*, in which the combining form κal- (< Gr *kalos* 'beautiful')
parallels Graeco-Lat cal- in *ca(l)listhenics* (< Gr *kalos* 'beautiful', *kallos*
'beauty'). Beside the late-19th-century borrowing *kudos* (< Gr *kudos*
'praise'), Eng has earlier borrowings such as *cynic* and *cyst* (< Gr
*kunikos*, *kustis*). As noted above under 'Gr οι transliterated as œ/οe
or ε', *koine* and the coeno- of *coenobite* represent the same Greek stem.

Some of the new spellings arose in competition with the traditional
Graeco-Lat forms, such as *cainozoic*, though not *\*kainozoic* (< Gr *kainos*
'recent') beside *caenozoic*. Pronunciation, we have already noted above,
varies with the spelling: *cainozoic* is pronounced /kaɪn-/ or /keɪn-/),
*caenozoic* /siːn-/); *caenozoic* in turn is sometimes reduced, especially in
AmE spelling, to *cenozoic* which may be pronounced /siːn-/ or /sɛn-/).[10]

The normal Graeco-Lat transliteration *\*ancylosis* (< Gr *ankulōsis*
'stiffening of the joints') would wrongly suggest that the c would be
pronounced /s/ before y. To avoid this, two alternative devices have been
used; a 'modern' transliteration with κ as in *ankylosis*, and the insertion
of an η to give *anchylosis* (which wrongly suggests ch transliterating
Gr *chi*).

# The Fifth Wave: The Transliteration of Modern Gr

The 'fifth wave' of Gr, that of ModGr loanwords in ModE, has
introduced only a small number of words, mainly in the field of food
and drink.

Both the spoken and the written forms of ModGr show significant
differences from classical Gr. There are, for example, fewer vowel sounds,
no distinctions of vowel length, and no aspirations. In writing, all
diacritics (such as those indicating aspiration), other than an acute accent
(as in *Lésvos*) to show stressed vowels, were abolished in 1982. Since
all the letters and digraphs of classical Gr have been retained in ModGr

despite the many differences in pronunciation, the sound–spelling correspondences are obviously different from those of classical Gr – for example, among the consonants the letter B now represents /v/ rather than /b/, and /b/ is now written MΠ, as in Gr *mpouzouki* 'bouzouki (a musical instrument)' and *rempetika* 'rebetika (a genre of song)'; among vowels, certain sound values are now represented by several symbols (e.g. /i/ is now represented by five separate graphemes, H, I, Y, EI and OI, which had five different sound values in classical Gr); and in some cases former vowels now represent consonants (the Y of AY and EY now represents a consonant /v/ (or /f/, depending on the following sound).

The official transliteration of today's Gr language into the Roman alphabet reflects such sound-changes and thus avoids many of the disadvantages both of the old Graeco-Lat transliteration and of ModGr spelling. This can be seen, for example, in the modern transliterations of place-names, such as *Lésvos* for Graeco-Lat and traditional Eng *Lesbos*, *Évia* for *Euboea*, *Epídavros* for *Epidaurus*, *Fílipi* for *Philippi*, *Ródos* for Eng *Rhodes*, etc.

These changes are reflected equally in the spelling of ModGr loanwords in Eng: *avgolimono* 'egg-lemon soup', *evzone* 'Gr infantryman' (with ModGr *ev-* rather than Graeco-Lat EU- as in *euphemism*), *feta* 'cheese' and *filo* 'pastry' (with F where Graeco-Lat would have had PH, as in *physics*, though a spelling *phyllo*, reflecting the Gr ΦΥΛΛΟ, is also found in Eng), *meze* 'snack' (< Gr *mezes*), *moussaka* (< Gr *mousakas*, with OU where Graeco-Lat would have had U for Gr OY, as in ModE *music*), *ouzo* 'alcoholic drink', *retsina* 'wine', *souvlaki* 'kebab' (a Graeco-Lat transliteration of the first syllable would have been *SUB-), *taramosalata* 'roe salad', *tzatziki* 'yoghurt dish' (< Gr *tsatsiki*).

## Notes

1 Calculated by sampling the first edition of the *Oxford English Dictionary*. A list of the last headword given on each 40th page showed 42 Greek derivatives out of a total of 387 words.

2 As in the other analytical sections in this book, the most frequent language names in this section will be abbreviated.

3 In the Greek transliterations, *eta* and *omega* will be distinguished from *epsilon* and *omicron* by the use of a macron: thus *eta* will be transliterated $\bar{e}$ as opposed to *e* for *epsilon*. Length in other vowels will be ignored as it is not reflected in Greek spelling.

4   Greek letters will be written in their capital-letter forms. These must in some cases be distinguished from the letters of the Roman alphabet, which are written in small capitals. Thus B = Greek *beta*, while B represents the second letter of the Roman alphabet.

5   As is common practice, the Greek letter X will in this book be transliterated as CH rather than as KH, although Greek K will be transliterated as K: thus *episkopos, schisma, konchē, charaktēr*.

6   Wingate (1988).

7   Baldick (1990).

8   Combining forms are word-forming elements such as BIO-, HYDRO-, MICRO-, PHOTO-, -CRACY, -GRAPHY, -LOGY, which, like prefixes and suffixes, may be added to already existing words to form new words (e.g. *micro-oven, photosensitive, bureaucracy* and, with a linking -O- which need not concern us here, *oceanology*), but which may also themselves combine to form words (e.g. *hydrology, photography*). Words of this latter type are often referred to as 'neo-classical compounds', that is compound words in English (and other languages) which, although consisting of Greek- or Latin-derived elements, are not based on actual Greek or Latin words (for example, the Modern English word *hydrolysis* is formed from Greek-derived elements HYDRO- and -LYSIS, but there was no word *hudrolusis* in classical Greek; the same applies to such 19th-century creations as *biology* and *megalith*). From the point of view of spelling, however, it makes no difference whether a Modern English word is a neo-classical compound (e.g. *photography* < PHOTO- + -GRAPHY) or is derived from an attested classical Greek word (e.g. *calligraphy* < Gr *kalligraphia*).

9   The entry for *aneurysm* in the *Oxford English Dictionary* suggests that the -ISM form is more common than the etymologically correct -YSM. A Google search on the Internet suggests otherwise, with far more hits for *aneurysm* than for *aneurism*.

10   In the entry **kainosite**, the *Oxford English Dictionary* cites a 1925 article from the *Mineralogical Magazine* in which the writer deplores the change of the name of the mineral from *kainosite* to *cenosite*.

  With the tendency for Graeco-Latin AE and OE to be reduced to E in Modern English, especially in American English spelling, the combining forms CAENO- and COENO- merge as CENO-, which also exists as a derivative of Greek *kenos*, meaning 'empty', as in *cenotaph*.

# 8

# The Exotic Input

Having analysed the elements of present-day English spelling which originate in Old English (and the Old Norse of the Viking invaders), French, Latin and Greek – the 'core' languages underlying Modern English vocabulary and spelling – we must now turn our attention to what we will refer to as the 'exotic' languages; that is to say, all the other European languages and the non-European languages which have contributed in any way to English vocabulary and spelling.[1] The only defining feature uniting this group is precisely that it includes any language other than those of the 'core' group: thus, Germanic languages related to English and Old Norse, such as Danish, Dutch and German; Romance languages derived, like French, from Latin, such as Italian and Spanish; other languages of the Indo-European family and therefore related to some extent to all the foregoing, such as Gaelic, Welsh, Russian, Czech, Sanskrit, Urdu and Farsi (Persian); and languages belonging to unrelated language families, some of which are often thought of – by speakers of English, at least – as truly exotic, such as Arabic, Hebrew, Chinese, Japanese, Thai, Tamil, Zulu, Sioux, Hawaiian, and some of which readers may never have come across before.[2]

We will not simply be considering the number and nature of the *new* complexities that borrowings from the 'exotic' languages have introduced into the English spelling system – complexities, that is, not already met with in previous chapters – but will be looking more widely at the overall contribution of these languages to English spelling. It would be

*The History of English Spelling*, First Edition. Christopher Upward and George Davidson.

wrong to focus solely, or even mainly, on the difficulties and irregularities that derive specifically from borrowings from the 'exotic' language group when, as we will see, a great many words of exotic origin create no new or unique sound–spelling correspondences at all with regard to the sound–symbol correspondences of English spelling: to take one very simple set of examples, compare *ben* (< Scottish Gaelic), *yen* (< Chinese), *zen* (< Japanese) with *den, men, ten* (< Old English). And while *sauerkraut* (< German), in which AU = /aʊ/, does add a new complexity to English spelling (compare *caught, taut, haughty* on the one hand and *out, hour, brown* on the other), *kowtow* (< Chinese *k'o-t'ou*) has the same spelling for its vowels as *cow, town* (< Old English) and *powder* (< French), and so creates no special problems; but both equally illustrate the contribution of an 'exotic' language to Modern English spelling.

We have already raised in the Introduction (see pp. 9–10) the question of whether it is possible to draw a line between genuinely English words of foreign origin and foreign words not truly integrated into English vocabulary. The reader is reminded that our conclusion, and that of others who have asked the same question, is that no such line can be drawn. In the lists provided in this chapter, we have concentrated on words whose Englishness is for the most part unquestionable, but in order to illustrate some particular spelling or sound–spelling correspondence we have not hesitated to include words whose status in English vocabulary is less certain.

Little need be said about the ways in which words have entered English from the 'exotic' language group. England may be part of an island but it has never been isolated. On its own doorstep, it came into contact with the Celtic languages. Just across a narrow stretch of water lies continental Europe, with the countries of which we have both fought and traded for centuries. The Bible made (at least some) English speakers familiar with Hebrew, the Crusades brought English speakers into contact with Arabic. As English, and later British, explorers and traders spread out across the world, and the British Empire grew, English came into contact with an ever-greater range of languages and cultures. And borrowings from other languages and cultures, such as those of Central and South America, have also entered English via the languages of other European empires, such as French, Spanish and Portuguese (in which case it is usually the form of the word in the 'carrier language', such as Spanish or Portuguese, rather than the form of the word in the 'source language', e.g. Tupi or Quechua, that underlies the English word, as can be seen, for example, in *condor* < Spanish *cóndor* < Quechua *kuntur* and *cougar* < French *couguar*, ult. < Tupi *siwasuarana*).

## The Writing Systems of the Exotic Languages

The writing systems in use among the 'exotic' languages are very varied in form:[3]

- Some languages, such as those of western Europe but also some from further afield such as Turkish, Malay and languages of Africa and Australasia, are written with the Roman alphabet.
  - The letters of the alphabet may be supplemented by one or more accents and diacritics, as in Romanian Ţ (= [ts]), Turkish ş (= [ʃ]), Czech č (= [tʃ]), Swedish å (= [ɔ]). Accents and diacritics may or may not be retained in the English spellings: e.g. compare *façade* and *facade* < French *façade*, *smorgasbord* < Swedish *smörgåsbord*. In other cases an exotic grapheme with a diacritic may be replaced by an English grapheme representing the same sound: Portuguese *melaço, monção, sargaço* > English *molasses, monsoon, sargasso*.
  - Borrowings from languages which use the Roman alphabet may add complications to the system (or systems) of sound–symbol correspondences in English by introducing spellings which reflect the sound–symbol correspondences of the source languages: e.g. the GH = [g] of Italian *spaghetti*, the W = [ʊ] of Welsh *cwm*.
  - Sound–symbol correspondences in borrowings may not always be consistent: e.g. *macho* with English /tʃ/ but *machismo* with English /tʃ/ or more often /k/ (but both with [tʃ] in Spanish).
  - Sound–symbol correspondences may change through time to match those of English more closely: for example, the formerly recommended pronunciation /ʃiː/ for *ski* is now obsolete.
- Some languages are written in alphabets of letters of a different form, such as the Cyrillic alphabet of Russian and some other Slavic languages. For these, there is often an established system, and sometimes more than one system, of transliteration into the Roman alphabet, just as we have seen in the case of Greek.
  - Because there may be more than one accepted transliteration system into English, there may be more than one accepted English spelling for many of these borrowings: e.g. *burka/burqa/ burkha/boorka*, etc. or *chapatti/chapati/chupati*, etc.
- Some languages have writing systems which are alphabet-like but not strictly alphabetic. For example, the Hebrew 'alphabet' in fact only records consonants, though there exists a supplementary system of symbols to indicate vowels (as is done, for example, in children's

books). Here again, there may be one or more than one recognized system of transliteration into the Roman alphabet.

- Some languages use symbols that record whole syllables rather than consonants and vowels separately. In some, such as the katakana and hiragana of Japanese writing, there is a clear one-to-one relationship between the symbols and the sounds represented; for example, in hiragana の = [no]. In others, such as Chinese characters, there is no such relationship between the symbol and the sound: for example, both 木 and 目 are (in the Chinese of Beijing) pronounced [mu], but there is nothing in the forms of the characters themselves to indicate their pronunciation.

  ○ With the languages of this type, there is again generally one, but sometimes more than one, recognized system of transliteration into the Roman alphabet.

    • There are, for example, three main systems of Romanization systems for Mandarin Chinese, one now used only in place-names, as illustrated by the name of the capital city variously written in English as *Peking* or *Beijing* or, though less frequently, *Pei-ching*. The full name of Chairman Mao, the former Chinese communist leader, can be written *Mao Tse-tung* or *Mao Zedong* (both forms representing the same pronunciation in Chinese, the former using the Wade–Giles[4] transcription developed in the 19th century, the latter the Pinyin system developed in the mid-20th); and similarly *t'ai chi ch'uan*, the Wade–Giles spelling of the name given to a system of physical exercise, is written *taijiquan* in Pinyin. The ' symbol, which indicates aspiration in the Wade–Giles system, is frequently omitted or misplaced in English: *chi* is perhaps more common in English than the strictly correct Wade–Giles *ch'i* (*qi* in Pinyin) for the name of a posited life-force or energy that flows through the body.

    • Which Romanization forms the basis of the English spelling of a word may depend to a great extent on the preferred system when or where the word is first introduced or becomes well known in English-speaking circles. For example, the *kung* of *kung fu* and the *gong* of *qigong* are the same Chinese word in Wade–Giles and Pinyin respectively.

    • The sound–symbol correspondences may reflect English sound–symbol correspondences or pronunciations closer or not so close to the Chinese: for example, *kung* may be pronounced

231

/kʌŋ/ or /kʊŋ/, *gong* /gɒŋ/ or /gʊŋ/ or /kʊŋ/ by English-speakers; /gʊŋ/ and /kʊŋ/ come closest to the Chinese pronunciation. See also *feng shui* under 'ᴇ' below (p. 246).

- Some languages have, or had at the time of first contact with English and perhaps still until recently, no written form at all.

  ○ In such cases English spellings of borrowings will be based on the spoken form of the word in the source language and will generally reflect attempts to spell the sounds of the source languages using the letters and sound–symbol correspondences of English, thus introducing no new problems. This is, for example, the case with borrowings from Native American, African and Australian languages.

    ▪ As a word becomes better known and in more widespread use, there may over time be some simplification of the spelling. Compare, for example, the earliest spellings of *raccoon* – *arocoun, aroughcoune, aroughcun, arroughcan, rahaugcum, rahaughcum, rarowcun, raugroughcum* – which more closely resemble the Algonquian form of the animal's name.

    ▪ On the other hand, the accepted modern spelling may be more complex and more 'foreign' than an earlier one: e.g. *kgotla* 'assembly of tribal elders in Botswana', for which 19th-century English spellings *cotla* and *kotla* are attested.

    ▪ It is also the case that fashions in spelling change: for example, some words formerly spelt with oo are now spelt with ᴜ: e.g. *gnu, guru, Hindu, sadhu* (with obsolete spellings *gnoo, gooroo, Hindoo, sadhoo*); but compare *bamboo, shampoo* still with final oo.

## The Effect of 'Exotic' Vocabulary on English Spelling

We may summarize the effect of 'exotic' vocabulary on English spelling as follows:

- Some words introduce nothing new to the system. We have already noted examples such as *ben, yen* and *zen*. Simplification at the time of borrowing or later may remove potential problems: e.g. *raccoon, ski* as discussed above, *shamrock* (< Irish Gaelic *seamróg*).
- Some words may have graphemes with familiar sound–spelling correspondences but in unexpected positions: e.g. initial /ŋ-/ in the

currencies *ngultrum* and *ngwee*; final -K (as opposed to -CK) in *amok*, *anorak*, *flak*, *sputnik*, *trek*, *yak*, etc.

- ○ In some such cases, the sound–spelling correspondences may be altered to make the word fit better with the English sound system: e.g. *ngaio* 'New Zealand tree' < Maori, pronounced /ˈnaɪəʊ/, not /ˈŋaɪ-/, which produces the unexpected correspondence NG = /n/.
- Some borrowings may introduce new sound–spelling correspondences: e.g. final -TZ = /ts/ in *chintz*, *kibbutz*, *quartz*, *schmaltz*; initial CI- = /tʃ/ in *ciao*, *ciabatta* (as opposed to the pronunciation of CI- in *cider*, *circle*, etc.).
- The sound–spelling correspondences introduced with 'exotic' vocabulary may be inconsistent: e.g. *macho* and *machismo* as discussed above (p. 230).

# The Treatment of Recent Borrowings into English

One reason why exotic vocabulary has made such an impact on English spelling is that, at least in recent centuries, English has not, unlike many other languages, naturalized the spellings of its borrowings. Compare *shamrock* (< Irish Gaelic *seamróg*), borrowed in the late 16th century, with *taoiseach* (which retains the Irish Gaelic spelling), borrowed in the 20th.

- In this regard, we may compare the name of the English newspaper *The Telegraph* (retaining the PH of Greek origin) with the Dutch newspaper *De Telegraaf* (in which the Greek PH has been replaced by a Dutch F). Compare further:
  - ○ English *photography*, French *photographie* but Dutch *fotografie*, German *Fotografie* (but most such German words have PH-), Italian *fotografia*, Spanish *fotografía*, Portuguese *fotografia*, Swedish *fotografi*.
  - ○ English *phoneme*, French *phonème*, German *Phonem* but Dutch *foneem*, Italian *fonema*, Spanish *fonema*, Portuguese *fonema*, Swedish *fonem*.
- In borrowing Italian *ciao*, English has retained the 'exotic' Italian spelling, whereas Spanish, for example, has respelt the word as *chau*, Portuguese as *tchau*, German as *tschau* and Romanian as *ceau*, all these latter spellings having predictable sound–spelling correspondences in the languages concerned.

# Analysis of the 'Exotic' Input

Only a representative selection of example words and languages has been included in the entries below.

- Although the examples are divided into instances of initial, medial and final letters according to the position of the letter in question, there are of course many words in which a given letter appears in more than one position.
- The same word may be used as illustrative of more than one spelling.
- Rare words are generally excluded, but some have been included when needed to show a particular source language or an interesting spelling or sound–spelling correspondence.
- Pronunciations and brief indications of meaning are frequently provided for less familiar words.
- In some cases, both the source language and the carrier language(s) have been noted.
- The origins of some English words in this exotic category are uncertain or disputed. Many potentially interesting examples were omitted for this reason.
- Where no source word is given, the word is the same in the source or carrier language as it is in English.
- Source and carrier languages are not in this chapter given the labels 'Old', 'Middle' or 'Modern'. Thus, for example, Middle Dutch and Modern Dutch words are simply labelled 'Dutch'. Somewhat vaguer terms such as 'early' and 'obsolete' are occasionally used.

## A

In general, an A in English reflects an A or an [a] or [ɑː] in the source or carrier language, and in most cases represents /æ/, /ɑː/ or, when unstressed, /ə/ in Modern English.

- In initial position: *abalone* 'shellfish' (< Spanish *abulón*); *abseil, angst* (< German); *allegro* (< Italian); *anime* (< Japanese); *anorak* (< Inuit *anoraq*); *atoll* (< Dhivehi *atolu*); *ayah* 'nurse' (< Hindi *aya* < Portuguese); *ayatollah* 'Muslim cleric' (< Persian < Arabic).
  - In several words (*albatross, alchemy, alcohol, alcove, alfalfa, algebra, algorithm, alkali*) the initial AL- derives from the Arabic definite

article (= 'the'), but these words all reached English via one of the Romance languages, and not directly from Arabic.

○ *Afrit/afreet* 'demon' (< Arabic *'ifrit*); *ankh* 'emblem of life' (< Egyptian *'nh*): note that both Arabic *'ifrit* and Egyptian *'nh* begin with a consonant sound, a voiced sound (called *'ayn* in Arabic) formed at the back of the mouth, that is ignored in the English pronunciation and spelling.

○ *Amen* (ult. < Hebrew) may be pronounced with initial /ɑː/ or /eɪ/.

• In medial position:

○ Pronounced /æ/, /ɑː/ or, if unstressed, /ə/: *bamboo* (< Malay *bambu*); *brandy* (< Dutch *brandewijn*); *bwana* (< Swahili); *giraffe* (< Italian *giraffa* < Arabic); *hamster* (< German); *iguana* (< Spanish < Arawak *iwana*); *kebab* (formerly *cabob*; < Persian, Urdu and Arabic *kabab*); *pal* (< Romany *phal*); *parka* (< Aleut < Russian, ult. < Nenets); *safari* (< Swahili); *samovar* (< Russian); *sampan* 'boat' (< Cantonese Chinese *saambaan*); *sangria* (< Spanish); *sonata* (< Italian); *sake* (< Japanese); *sari* (< Hindi); *tomato* (pronounced /eɪ/ in American English; prob. via Spanish < Nahuatl *tomatl*).

○ Pronounced /eɪ/: *bagel* (< Yiddish *beygel*); *baobab* (orig. *bahobab*; < an African language); *kaolin* (via French < Chinese place-name *Kao-ling*); *kapok* (< Malay *kapoq*); *potato* (< Spanish *patata*); *sago* (< Malay *sagu*); *zany* (poss. via French < Italian *zani, zanni*).

○ Pronounced /ɔː/ or /ɒ/: *balsa* (< Spanish); *balti* (also /æ/; < Urdu); *schmaltz* (< Yiddish < German *Schmalz*); *waltz* (< German *Walzer*); *yacht* (< early Dutch *jaght*).

○ Pronounced /eɪ/ before silent E: *hurricane* (< Spanish *huracán* < Taino); *marmalade* (< Portuguese *marmelada*).

○ Pronounced /ə/ or /ɪ/ in the second syllable of *karaoke* (< Japanese), A = /ɪ/ being a quite unpredictable sound–spelling correspondence for English.

• In final position: *aloha* (< Hawaiian); *alpaca* (< Spanish < Aymara *allpaca*); *bandan(n)a* (< Hindustani *bandhnu*); *cantata, vendetta* (< Italian); *chukka* 'period of play in polo' (formerly also *chucker* and still in US *chukker*; < Hindi *cakkar*); *geisha* (< Japanese); *karma, yoga* (< Sanskrit); *koala* (< Dharuk); *lama* (< Tibetan *blama*); *llama* (< Spanish < Quechua); *mazurka* 'dance' (< Polish); *okra* (prob. < Igbo *okuru*); *pagoda* (< Portuguese *pagode*); *paprika* (< Hungarian); *polka* (< Czech); *samba* (< Portuguese); *samosa* 'Indian pastry' (< Hindi, Urdu and Persian); *sauna* (< Finnish); *vodka* (< Russian).

○ *Yarbu‛*, the Arabic source of *jerboa*, has a final consonant that is ignored in the English pronunciation and spelling. Similarly with *henna* (< Arabic *hinna‛*). Compare *afrit* and *ankh* above.

• The German Ä is simplified to A in e.g. *lammergeier* 'vulture' (< *Lämmergeier*), and this is reflected in the English pronunciation /ˈlæm-/ (German /ˈlɛm-/). In English, *doppelgänger* 'ghostly double' may retain or drop the German diacritic, and the pronunciation of the A-vowel may equally vary between /æ/ and /ɛ/.

## AA

Many words that are spelt with AA in English are of South African (Afrikaans) origin and are not well known outside South Africa. Others have entered English from the cookery terminology of the Indian sub-continent (*chaat, naan, saag*, etc.); these are often spelt with a single A. The AA generally reflects a long A in the source language.

• In initial position: *aardvark, aardwolf* (< Afrikaans).
• In medial position: *advocaat* 'alcoholic drink' (< Dutch); *baas, braai, kraal, laager* (< Afrikaans); *bazaar* (< Persian *bazar*, prob. via Italian; an -AA- spelling *bazaard* first appeared in the 18th century, the current spelling in the 19th); *salaam* (< Arabic).

## AE

AE in Modern English words is normally an indicator of Latin or Greek origin: *algae, Caesar, aesthetic, aerodrome*. There are few examples of AE in Modern English words originating in other languages, and of those even fewer are in common use.

• In medial position:
  ○ Pronounced /eɪ/: *maelstrom* (< obsolete Dutch *maelstroom*);
  ○ Pronounced /aɪ/: *maestoso* 'musical instruction', *maestro* (< Italian); *paella* (/paɪˈɛlə/; < Spanish).
• In final position:
  ○ Pronounced /eɪ/: *reggae* (of uncertain origin);
  ○ Pronounced /aɪ/ or /eɪ/: *tae kwon do* (< Korean).

## AH

The spelling AH generally represents /ɑː/ in Modern English.

- In medial position: *autobahn* (< German); *baht* 'unit of currency' (< Thai); *Brahmin* (< Sanskrit *Brahmana*); *Fahrenheit* (usually /æ/; < German surname); *mah-jong* 'game' (< Chinese *majiang* or related forms in other dialects).
  - *Dahlia* (/eɪ/; < Swedish surname *Dahl*) is an unpredictable exception to the general sound–spelling correspondence. With *mahlstick* 'artist's tool' (< Dutch *maalstok*, partly anglicized) the pronunciation /ɔː/ is better matched by the alternative spelling *maulstick*.
- In final position, the AH spelling is generally found in words borrowed from languages of the Middle East and the Indian subcontinent. The H may correspond to a letter in the source language or may simply indicate a long vowel: *ayah* 'nurse' (< Hindi *aya* < Portuguese); *ayatollah* 'Muslim cleric' (< Persian < Arabic); *cheetah* (< Hindi *cita*); *coolibah* 'Australian tree' (< Yuwaaliyaay *gulabaa*); *hallelujah* (< Hebrew *halelujah*); *howdah* 'seat on elephant' (< Urdu and Persian *haudah*); *loofah* (< Arabic *lufa*); *messiah* (via Latin and Greek < Aramaic *meshikha*, Hebrew *mashiakh*); *mitzvah* (< Hebrew); *pariah* (< Tamil); *shah* (< Persian).
  - There may be alternative forms without H: *halvah/halva* (< Yiddish, ult. < Arabic); *hookah/hooka* (< Arabic *huqqah*); *mynah/myna/mina* 'Indian bird' (< Hindi *maina*); *verandah/veranda* (< Hindi *varanda* < Portuguese).

### AI

- In initial position: *aikido* 'martial art' (/aɪ/; < Japanese).
- In medial position:
  - Pronounced /aɪ/: *balalaika* (< Russian); *braai* (see under 'AA'); *daikon* 'vegetable', *haiku* 'form of poetry' (< Japanese); *daiquiri* (also /ˈdæ-/; < Cuban place-name); *kaiser* (< German); *krait* 'snake' (< Hindi *karait*); *t'ai chi* (or *taiji*) 'exercise' (< Chinese).
  - Pronounced /æ/: *plaid* (of uncertain origin; pronounced /eɪ/ in Scotland).
  - Pronounced /eɪ/, /ɛə/: *cairn* (< Scottish Gaelic); *cocaine* (< Spanish *coca* + suffix -INE); *maize* (< former Spanish *mahiz*, now *maiz* < Taino *mahiz*).
  - Note also *Dail* 'Irish parliament' in which AI is generally pronounced /aɪ/ or /ɔɪ/.
- In final position, pronounced /aɪ/: *assegai* (< Portuguese *azagaia* < Arabic, ult. < Berber); *bonsai*, *samurai* (< Japanese); *shanghai* (< Chinese place-name).

- Note *taffrail* 'rail round stern of ship' (formerly spelt *tafferel* < Dutch *tafereel*; altered under the influence of English *rail*); *mohair* (< Italian *mocaiarro*; altered under the influence of English *hair*).

AO

In general vocabulary, only in final position: = /aʊ/ in *cacao* (< Spanish < Nahuatl *cacahuatl*); *ciao* (< Italian).

- ○ Also followed by silent H: *pharaoh* (/-əʊ/; via French and Latin < Greek *pharao* < Hebrew *par'oh* < Egyptian).
- ○ In medial position, only in *Maori* (= /aʊ/).

AOI

In medial position: AOI (= /iː/) in *taoiseach* 'Irish prime minister'.

AU

- In initial position, with pronunciation varying between English /ɔː/ and source language [aʊ]: *autobahn*, *autostrada* (respectively < German and Italian); *auto-da-fé* (< Portuguese).
- In medial position:
  - ○ Pronounced /aʊ/: *gaucho* (< Spanish); *meerschaum* 'mineral' (also /ə/), *sauerkraut*, *Weltanschauung* 'world-view' (< German).
  - ○ Pronounced /ɔː/: *caucus* (poss. < Algonquian); *flautist* (< Italian); *juggernaut* (< Hindi *Jagannath* 'title of Hindu god Vishnu'); *keelhaul* (partly anglicized < Dutch *kielhalen*); *launch* 'boat' (< Spanish *lancha*); *leprechaun* 'elf' (< Irish Gaelic *leipreachán*); *maulstick* 'artist's tool' (< Dutch *maalstok*, partly anglicized); *onslaught* (< Dutch *aanslag*, modified by English *slaught* 'slaughter').
  - ○ As with certain words of Greek origin (e.g. *glaucoma*, *trauma*), English pronunciation of some AU words in the exotic category may vary between /aʊ/, the phonetic value of the vowel in the source language, and /ɔː/, the usual Modern English value of AU: *caudillo* 'dictator' (< Spanish), *sauna* (< Finnish).
- In final position:
  - ○ Pronounced /aʊ/: *luau* 'feast' (< Hawaiian *lu'au*); *pilau* 'rice' (also *pilaf/pilaff*; < Persian *pulaw*; poss. also via French *pilau*).
  - ○ Pronounced (/aʊ/ or /ɔː/: *landau* 'carriage' (< German place-name).

*AW*

- In medial position: *mulligatawny* 'soup' (< Tamil *milakutanni*); *shawl* (< Urdu and Persian *shal*); *tomahawk* (orig. written *tomahack*; < Renape *tamahak*); *yawl* (< Low German *jolle* or Dutch *jol*).
- In final position: *coleslaw* (< Dutch *koolsla*); *macaw* (< archaic Portuguese *macau*); *pawpaw* (variant of *papaya*; < Spanish, prob. < Taino); *rickshaw* (also *ricksha*; < Japanese *jinrikisha*); *squaw* (< Massachusett *squa* or similar forms in related languages).

*AY*

- In initial position – see under 'A'.
- In medial position, pronounced /eɪ/: *cayman* (also *caiman*; < Spanish *caimán*, perh. < Carib, perh. < an African language); *claymore* 'large sword' (< Scottish Gaelic *claidheamh mòr*).
- In final position, generally pronounced /eɪ/: *cay* 'island' (also pronounced /kiː/; < Spanish *cayo*, Old French *cay/caye*); *satay* 'grilled meat' (< Malay *satai/sate*, Indonesian *sate*).

**B**

Modern English B normally corresponds to B or [b] in the source or carrier language.

- In initial position: *bambino* (< Italian); *bamboo* (< Malay *bambu*); *basenji* 'dog breed' (< a Bantu language); *bazaar* (< Persian, prob. via Italian); *ben* 'mountain' (< Scottish Gaelic *beinn*); *blitz* (< German); *bodhisattva* (< Sanskrit); *bonanza* (< Spanish); *bonsai* (< Japanese); *bungalow* (< Hindustani *bangla*); *bwana* (< Swahili).
  - An example of Modern English B not from [b] in the source language: *bandicoot* 'Australian animal' (< Telugu *pandi-kokku*).
- In medial position: *adobe, embargo* (< Spanish); *barbecue* (< Spanish *barbacoa*, prob. < Taino); *cannibal* (< Spanish *Canibales* 'name of West Indian tribe'); *cobalt* (< German *Kobalt*); *cobra, samba* (< Portuguese); *jerboa* (< Arabic *yarbuʿ*); *ombudsman* (< Swedish); *rouble* (< Russian *rublʲ*); *springbok* 'antelope' (< Afrikaans); *taboo* (< Tongan *tabu*); *wildebeest* (< Afrikaans *wildebees*); *wombat* 'Australian animal' (< Dharuk *wambat*).
- In final position: *hijab* 'covering for head' (< Arabic); *sahib* (< Urdu).

### BB

- In medial position, = /b/: *kibbutz, rabbi, Sabbath, shibboleth* (directly or ult. < Hebrew); *gabbro* 'rock', *obbligato* (< Italian).

### BH

All words with initial or medial BH are from languages of the Indian subcontinent: the BH represents an aspirated [b] (approximately [b + h]) in these languages but in English is simply /b/.

- In initial position: *bhaji* 'fried vegetables' (< Hindi); *bhakti* 'religious devotion' (< Sanskrit); *bhangra* 'style of music' (< Punjabi); *bhikku* 'Buddhist mendicant' (< Pali); *bhindi* 'vegetable' (< Hindi); *bhuna* 'Indian dish' (< Hindi and Urdu).
- In medial position: *sabha* 'assembly' (< Hindustani).

### C

C generally corresponds to C in the source or carrier language, but sometimes to K. Some languages have a [k]-like sound formed further back in the mouth, written or transcribed as Q, and this sound or letter may also be represented by C in English, though more often by K. In a few cases, there are alternative English spellings with K and Q. C has a number of possible pronunciations, generally depending on the pronunciation of C in the source language.

- In initial position:
  - Pronounced /k/: *cameo, cantata* (< Italian); *cargo* (< Spanish); *catamaran* (< Tamil *kattumaram*); *cockatoo* (< Dutch *kakatoe* < Malay); *cockroach* (< Spanish *cucaracha*); *coffee* (prob. < Italian *caffè* < Turkish *kahveh* < Arabic); *corgi, cwm* (< Welsh); *cot* 'bed' (< Hindi *khat*); *cruise* (< Dutch *kruisen*);
    - An example of a word with alternative forms in C, K and Q is *cadi/kadi/qadi* (< Arabic *qadi*).
    - *Commandeer, commando* and *commodore* (originally spelt *commandore*) entered English from Afrikaans (*kommandeer, kommando*) and Dutch (*komandeur*), but their ultimate roots are in the Romance languages (e.g. Portuguese *commando*, French *commander*) and English has reverted to the Latinate C-spellings.

- *Ceilidh* 'social gathering' (< Scottish Gaelic *cèilidh*) has initial c pronounced /k/ as in Gaelic where /s/ might be expected in English due to the following front vowel.
  - Pronounced /tʃ-/ or /s-/: *cello, vermicelli* (all /tʃ-/; < Italian); *cedilla* (/s-/; < Spanish). See also under 'CI' below.
- In medial position:
  - Pronounced /k/: *avocado* (< Spanish, formerly *avocado*, now written *abogado*; ult. < Nahuatl *ahuacatl*); *bandicoot* 'Australian animal' (< Telugu *pandi-kokku*); *delicatessen* (< German *Delikatessen*); *fiasco, replica* (< Italian); *hurricane* (< Spanish *huracán* < Taino); *macaroni* (< Italian); *scow* 'boat' (< Dutch *schouw*); *tapioca* (< Spanish and Portuguese < Tupi); *tycoon* (< Japanese *taikun*).
  - Pronounced /tʃ/: *duce, trecento* (< Italian).
  - Pronounced /s/: *nuncio* (< Italian *nunzio*).
  - Pronounced /ʃ/ or /s/: *aficionado* (< Spanish, in which language c = [s] in Latin America and [θ] in Europe).
- In final position: *frolic* (< Dutch *vroolijk*); *lac* 'resin' (< Persian *lak*, Hindi *lakh*); *roc* 'mythical bird' (< Arabic *rokh*, Persian *rukh*).
  - Some words ending in -c entered English via French, from various sources: e.g. *lilac* (< Arabic and Persian *lilak* < Sanskrit); *talc* (< Arabic *talq* or Persian *talk*); *traffic* (< Italian *traffico*).
  - *Zinc* (< German *Zink*) first entered English in the 17th century with the German spelling *zink* (compare *ink, sink*, etc.), but was later given the French form *zinc*.

### Ç

In words of French origin, it is now common practice in English to omit the cedilla from under the c: thus *façade* or *facade*. A cedilla may still be seen in words from other sources, e.g. *açaí* 'type of fruit' (also *assai*; < Portuguese < Tupí).

### CC

- In medial position:
  - Pronounced /k/: *broccoli, piccolo, staccato, stucco* (< Italian); *felucca* 'Mediterranean boat' (< Italian *feluca/felucca*); *moccasin* (< Algonquian, e.g. Massachusett *mohkisson*, Narragansett *mokussin*); *raccoon* (also *racoon*; < Algonquian *aroughcun*).

- The single c of Spanish *pecadillo*, *tobaco*, *yuca* is doubled in English *peccadillo*, *tobacco*, *yucca*.
○ Pronounced /tʃ/ before a front vowel: *capriccio*, *cappuccino*, *focaccia* (< Italian). See also under 'cɪ' below.

CCH

From Italian, pronounced /k/: *gnocchi*, *zucchini*.

CH

See also under 'TCH'.

- In initial position:
  ○ Pronounced /tʃ/: *chador*, *cheetah*, *chutney* (< Hindi *caddar*, *cita*, *catni*); *cherub* (via Greek, Latin and French < Hebrew *kerubh*); *chimpanzee* (via French < Kikongo *chimpenzi*); *chilli*, *chocolate* (< Spanish < Nahuatl); *chinchilla* (< Spanish); *chipmunk* (< Algonquian, poss. Ojibwa *achitamon*); *chow mein* (< Chinese *chao mian*, Cantonese Chinese *chaau mihn*).
  ○ Pronounced /k/: *chianti* (< Italian).
  ○ Pronounced /ʃ/: *cheroot* (< Tamil *curuttu*).
  ○ Pronounced /h/ or /x/: *Chanukah* 'Jewish festival' (also *Hanukkah*; < Hebrew); *chutzpah* (< Yiddish *khutspe* < Hebrew).
- In medial position:
  ○ Pronounced /tʃ/: *alcheringa* 'Aboriginal dreamtime' (< an Aboriginal language); *anchovy* (< Spanish and Portuguese *anchova*); *artichoke* (< Italian dialect *articiocco*); *gutta-percha* (< Malay *getah-percha*); *honcho* (< Japanese *hancho*); *poncho* (< Spanish); *souchong* 'tea variety' (also pronounced /ʃ/; < Chinese *siao chung*, Cantonese Chinese *siu chung*);
    ▪ *Macho* (< Spanish) is pronounced in English with a /tʃ/, but the corresponding noun *machismo* may be pronounced with /tʃ/ or /k/, the latter pronunciation perhaps due to the influence of English words in which CH = /k/ or simply due to an incorrect idea of Spanish pronunciation.
    ▪ Some words have variant forms with T: e.g. *dacha/datcha* 'cottage' (< Russian *dacha*); *lychee/lichee/litchi* (< Chinese *li-chi*).
  ○ Pronounced /ʃ/: *machete* (< Spanish; note, not /tʃ/ as in *macho*); *pistachio* (< regional Italian *pistacio*).

242

- ○ Pronounced /k/: *masochism* (< the name of the writer Leopold von Sacher-Masoch); *mocha* (< place-name in Yemen).
- ○ Pronounced /k/ or /x/: *leprechaun* 'elf' (< Irish Gaelic *leipreachán*).
- ○ Silent: *yacht* (< early Dutch *jaght*).
- ○ Note also the unpredictable sound–symbol correspondences in *dachshund* (pronounced /'dæksənd/ or /'dæʃənd/) and *fuchsia* (/'fjuːʃə/) (both < German). The related chemical name *fuchsine* is, however, pronounced /'fuːksiːn/.
- In final position:
  - ○ Pronounced /tʃ/: *cockroach* (< Spanish *cucaracha*); *hooch* 'alcoholic drink' (also *hootch*; < *Hoochinoo*, name of Native American people); *larch* (< German *Lärche*); *launch* 'boat' (< Spanish *lancha*); *punch* 'drink' (prob. < Sanskrit *panca*); *ranch* (< Spanish *rancho*).
  - ○ Pronounced /k/ or /x/: *loch* (< Scottish Gaelic); *taoiseach* 'Irish prime minister' (< Irish Gaelic).
    - ▪ *Pibroch* 'bagpipe music' (< Scottish Gaelic *pìobaireachd*) shows simplification of the final Gaelic consonant cluster [xk] to English /x/ or /k/.

### CI

In words of Italian origin, = /tʃ/: *ciabatta*, *ciao*, *cappuccino*, *focaccia*, etc.

### CK

Always pronounced /k/. Modern English CK corresponds to a number of spellings in the source or carrier languages.

- In medial position: *cockatoo* (< Dutch *kakatoe* < Malay); *cockroach* (< Spanish *cucaracha*); *gecko* 'lizard' (< Malay *gekoq*); *glockenspiel* (< German); *hickory* (earlier *pohickory*; < Algonquian *pawcohiccora*); *jackal* (< Turkish *çakal*); *nickel* (< Swedish < German *Kupfernickel*); *rickshaw* (< Japanese *jinrikisha*); *seersucker* 'fabric' (< Hindi *sirsakar*, Persian *shir o shakkar*).
- In final position: *deck* (< early Dutch *dec*); *dock* (< early Dutch *docke*); *shamrock* (< Irish Gaelic *seamróg*); *smack* 'boat' (< Dutch *smak*, Low German *smack*).
  - ○ Some words have variants without c, e.g. *amuck/amok* (< Malay *amoq*), *arrack/arak* 'alcoholic spirit' (< Arabic *'araq*).

○ *Hammock* is first attested in English in the 16th century with the Spanish form *hamaca*. Another early (17th-century) loan was *hock* 'white wine', from German *Hochheimer*.

CZ

- In initial position:
  ○ Pronounced /z/: *czar* (= *tsar*; the word was spelt CZ- when first introduced into English in the 16th century; Milton uses the spelling *ksar* in *Paradise Lost*).
  ○ Pronounced /tʃ/: *Czech* (< Polish).

**D**

D generally corresponds to D or [d] in the source or carrier language.

- In initial position: *decoy* (< Dutch *de kooi*); *dekko* (< Hindi *dekho*); *delicatessen*, *diktat* (< German); *dilettante*, *ditto* (< Italian); *dim sum* 'Chinese pastry' (< Cantonese Chinese *dim sam*); *dinghy* (< Hindi and Bengali *dingi*); *divan* (< Turkish); *durian* 'fruit' (< Malay).
- In medial position: *crescendo*, *gondola* (< Italian); *godown* 'warehouse' (< Malay *gudang*); *pagoda* (< Portuguese *pagode*); *poodle* (< German *Pudel*); *pundit* (< Hindi *pandit* < Sanskrit *pandita*); *rodeo* (< Spanish); *vodka* (< Russian).
  ○ *Aduki* 'bean' (< Japanese) has variant forms *adzuki, azuki, adsuki*.
- In final position: *apartheid* (/-t/ or /-d/; < Afrikaans); *bard* (< Scottish and Irish Gaelic); *compound* 'enclosed space' (< Malay *kampong, -pung*); *cummerbund* (< Urdu and Persian *kamar-band*); *dachshund, lieder* (< German); *eland* 'African animal' (< Afrikaans); *fjord* (< Norwegian); *jihad* (< Arabic); *tamarind* 'fruit' (< Spanish and Portuguese < Arabic).
  ○ *veld* (< Dutch *veldt*) is also spelt *veldt* and pronounced /vɛlt/ or /fɛlt/.
  ○ Of Persian origin, *turban* was formerly sometimes written with a final D (compare Persian *dulband*).

DD

- In medial position, pronounced /d/: *caddy* (< Malay *kati*); *eisteddfod* 'Welsh festival' (< Welsh; DD may also be pronounced /ð/ as in Welsh).

## DH/DDH

DH represents a sound in Indian languages that is not part of the English sound-system, very approximately [d] + [h]. Early borrowings were generally spelt with a simple D; when the DH spelling came into use in English, it was sometimes applied to words in which it was etymologically incorrect, e.g. *dhal, dhow*. DH is pronounced /d/ in Modern English.

- In initial position: *dhal* 'pea' (also *dal*; < Hindi *dal*); *dhansak* 'Indian dish' (< Gujarati); *dharma* 'law' (< Sanskrit); *dhoti* 'loincloth' (< Hindi); *dhow* 'boat' (< Arabic *dawa*).
- In medial position: *Buddha, sadhu/saddhu* 'ascetic', *samadhi* 'meditative awareness' (< Sanskrit); *jodhpurs* (< place-name in India).
- Two DH words of Celtic origin are *skene-dhu* 'type of knife' (< Scottish Gaelic *sgian dhubh*) in which the DH is pronounced /d/ and *ceilidh* 'social gathering' (< Scottish Gaelic *cèilidh*) in which the DH is silent.

## DJ

DJ, pronounced /dʒ/, is an occasional variant of J, as in *djellaba/jellaba* 'Arab cloak' (< Arabic *jallaba*), *hadj/hajj* 'Muslim pilgrimage' (< Arabic *hajj*).

## DZ

- In initial position (in names of animals not well known in Britain): *dzeren* 'species of antelope' (< Mongolian); *dziggetai* 'species of horse' (< Mongolian *dschiggetei, tchikhitei*); *dzo* 'Tibetan ox' (same as *zho*; < Tibetan *mdso*).
- In medial position: *adzuki* 'bean' (also *adsuki, aduki*, etc.; < Japanese); *podzol* 'type of soil' (< Russian).

## E

In general, an E in English reflects an E, usually = [ɛ] or [e], in the source or carrier languages, and in most cases represents /ɛ/, /eɪ/ or /iː/ in Modern English. It may replace an I = /iː/ in the source or carrier language. It may also be silent.

- In initial position:
  - Pronounced /ɛ/: *effendi* 'title of respect' (< Turkish *efendi*); *embargo*, *esparto* (< Spanish); *emir* (also *ameer/amir*; < Arabic *amir*); *espresso* (< Italian).
  - Pronounced /eɪ/: *edelweiss* (< German).
  - Pronounced /iː/: *eland* 'African animal' (< Afrikaans); *emu* (prob. < Portuguese *ema*).
- In medial position:
  - Pronounced /ɛ/: *ben* 'mountain', *glen* 'valley' (< Scottish Gaelic *beinn*, *gleann*); *delicatessen*, *pretzel* (< German); *flamenco* (< Spanish); *ghetto*, *tempo* (< Italian); *henna* (< Arabic *hinnaʿ*); *ketchup* (< Malay *kechap* and/or Amoy Chinese *ke-tsiap*); *steppe* (< Russian *stepʲ*); *trek* (< Afrikaans *trekken*); *zebra* (also /iː/; < Italian or Portuguese); *zen* (< Japanese).
    - Chinese *feng shui* 'rules for arrangement of room, building, etc.' may be pronounced /fɛŋ ˈʃuːɪ/, an anglicized pronunciation that follows the spelling, or /fʌŋ ˈʃweɪ/, a pronunciation that more closely resembles the Chinese.
  - Pronounced /eɪ/: *lederhosen* 'trousers' (< German); *rodeo* (< Spanish).
  - Pronounced /iː/: *sepoy* 'Indian soldier' (poss. via Portuguese < Urdu and Persian *sipahi*); *stampede*, *stevedore* (< Spanish *estampida*, *estivador*); *supremo* (< Spanish).
  - With modification of pronunciation before R: *dervish* (< Turkish < Persian *darvish*); *scherzo* (< Italian); *sherpa* (< Tibetan *sharpa*).
  - Unstressed, pronounced /ɜː/, /ə/, /ɪ/ or with a syllabic consonant: *jerboa* (< Arabic *yarbuʿ*); *mujahedin* (< Arabic); *pumpernickel* (< German); *snorkel* (< German *Schnorchel*); *soviet* (< Russian); *tungsten* (< Swedish).
- In final position:
  - Pronounced /ɪ/: Many of the words in this group come from Spanish, Italian and Japanese. In pronouncing the final E, they resemble words of Greek and Latin origin such as *hyperbole*, *epitome*, *posse* and *aborigine*): *abalone* /æbəˈləʊnɪ/ 'shellfish' (< Spanish *abulón*); *adobe* 'brick' (< Spanish); *anime* (< Japanese); *coyote* (< Spanish < Nahuatl *coyotl*); *curare* (also *curari*; < Spanish and Portuguese < Carib *kurari*); *dilettante*, *finale*, *forte*, *minestrone* (< Italian); *kamikaze*, *karaoke*, *karate* (< Japanese); *peyote* 'drug' (< Spanish < Nahuatl *peyotl*); *sake* 'rice wine' (< Japanese); *tsetse* 'fly' (via Afrikaans < Tswana); *ukulele* (< Hawaiian).

○ Silent: *artichoke* (< Italian dialect *articiocco*); *bangle* (< Hindi *bangri*); *caste* (< Spanish and Portuguese *casta*); *galore* (< Irish Gaelic *go leor*); *jungle* (< Hindi and Marathi *jangal*); *noodle, poodle* (< German *Nudel, Pudel*); *rouble* (< Russian *rublʲ*); *vamoose* (< Spanish *vamos*); *vole* (< Norwegian *vollmus*).

▪ Although *chocolate*, like *coyote* and *peyote*, is ultimately derived from Nahuatl and has Spanish as its carrier language, the final E is not pronounced. See also entries under 'T' at 'In final position'.

### EA

The grapheme EA is not frequently found in 'exotic' words. In the following examples it is pronounced /iː/, except in *taoiseach*, where it is unstressed and pronounced /ə/.

• In initial position: *easel* (< Dutch *ezel*, German *Esel*).
• In medial position: *beleaguer* (< Dutch *belegeren*); *mealie* 'ear of maize' (< Afrikaans *mielie*); *taoiseach* 'Irish prime minister' (< Irish Gaelic); *teak* (< Portuguese *teca* < Malayalam).
• In final position: *tea* (< Amoy Chinese *t'e*).

### EE

EE, pronounced /iː/ in English, has a number of sources, as the examples below show. It sometimes represents the spelling of the source word, but more often the pronunciation.

• In medial position: *cheetah* (< Hindi *cita*); *colleen* 'girl' (< Irish Gaelic *cailín*); *keelhaul* (< Dutch *kielhalen*); *meerkat* 'animal' (< Afrikaans); *meerschaum* 'mineral' (< German); *parakeet* (< Spanish *periquito*, Italian *parrochetto*, French *perroquet*); *reef* 'underwater rocks' (< Dutch *rif*); *seersucker* 'fabric' (< Hindi *sirsakar*, Persian *shir o shakkar*); *wildebeest* (< Afrikaans *wildebees*).
• In final position: *banshee* 'wailing fairy' (< Irish Gaelic *bean sidhe*); *chimpanzee* (via French < Kikongo *chimpenzi*); *coffee* (prob. < Italian *caffè* < Turkish *kahveh* < Arabic); *corroboree* 'Australian Aboriginal dance' (< Dharuk *garaabara*); *dungaree, kedgeree, ghee* 'clarified butter' (< Hindi *dungri, khichri, ghi*); *manatee* 'aquatic mammal' (< Spanish *manatí* < Carib); *rupee* (< Hindi *rupaiya*).

- In some borrowings, the EE spelling alternates with an I spelling in English, the EE reflecting the pronunciation while the I reflects the spelling or transliteration of the source word: *afrit/afreet* 'demon' (< Arabic *'ifrit*); *amir/ameer* 'Muslim leader' (< Arabic *amir*); *harem/harim/hareem* (< Arabic *harim*); *litchi/lychee/lichee* (< Chinese *li-chi*); *rani/ranee* 'Hindu queen' (< Hindi *rani*); *tepee/teepee/tipi* 'Native American tent' (< Dakota *tipi*).

EI

- In initial position, pronounced /aɪ/: *eisteddfod* 'Welsh festival' (< Welsh); *eider* 'duck' (< Swedish < Icelandic).
- In medial position:
  ○ Pronounced /aɪ/, mostly in borrowings from German: *apartheid* (< Afrikaans); *edelweiss* 'flower', *Fahrenheit* 'temperature scale', *leitmotiv/leitmotif*, *poltergeist* (< German); also dog breeds such as *Rottweiler* and *Weimaraner*.
  ○ Pronounced /eɪ/: *abseil* (also /-saɪl/ as in German; < German); *capoeira* 'martial art' (< Portuguese); *ceilidh* 'social gathering' (< Scottish Gaelic *cèilidh*); *chow mein* (< Chinese *chao mian*, Cantonese Chinese *chaau mihn*); *freight* (< Dutch or Low German *vrecht*); *geisha* (< Japanese); *sheikh* (also /ʃiːk/; < Arabic *shaikh*); *sleigh* (< Dutch *slee*).
  ○ Pronounced /ɪə/: *Madeira* 'wine' (< Portuguese; < place-name).
- In final position, pronounced /eɪ/: *lei* 'flower necklace' (< Hawaiian).

EW

In medial and final positions: *cashew* (< Portuguese *acajú/cajú* < Tupi); *slew* 'quantity' (< Irish Gaelic *sluagh*); *trews* 'tartan trousers' (< Scottish Gaelic *triubhas*).

- Only *slew* has an alternative UE spelling.

EY

In medial and final positions:

  ○ Pronounced /iː/ *geyser* (< Icelandic place-name *Geysir*); *key* 'island' (< Spanish *cayo*; the spelling and pronunciation were

248

influenced by *key* 'tool for locking doors' and *key* 'quay', the /iː/ pronunciation of which is apparently of northern English or Scottish origin).

○ Pronounced /eɪ/: *peyote* 'drug' (< Spanish < Nahuatl).
○ Pronounced /ɪ/: *chop suey* (< Cantonese Chinese *jaahp seui*); *chutney* (< Hindi *catni*).


## F

F in English generally corresponds to F in the source or carrier languages, and usually to [f] but also to [v], as in Welsh, and to [ɸ] (an [f]-like sound made by passing air between the lips), as in Japanese *Fuji*.

* In initial position: *falsetto, fiasco, fresco* (< Italian); *fatwa* 'religious decree' (< Arabic); *fjord* (< Norwegian); *flak* (< German); *flamingo* (< Portuguese *flamengo*); *flotilla* (< Spanish); *frolic, furlough* (< Dutch *vroolijk, verlof*); *futon* 'bed' (< Japanese).
  ○ An interesting sound and spelling change can be seen in the, rather rare, English words *fluellin* 'plant' and *flummery* 'oatmeal dish' (< Welsh *Llywelyn, llymri*), where English FL /fl-/ has replaced the Welsh LL = [ɬ] (an [l]-like sound but with audible friction).
* In medial position: *eisteddfod* 'Welsh festival' (< Welsh; F also pronounced /v/ as in Welsh); *kaftan* (< Russian < Turkish); *confetti, manifesto* (< Italian); *kraft* 'strong paper' (< Swedish or German); *portfolio* (< Italian *portafoglio*); *safari* (< Swahili); *shofar* 'ram's horn trumpet' (< Hebrew *shophar*); *shufti* 'look', *sufi* (< Arabic); *tofu* (< Japanese).
* In final position (there are few common words of exotic origin ending in a single F in English; see under 'FF' below): *pilaf* (also *pilaff*; < Turkish and Persian *pilav*).
  ○ Phonologically final before a silent E: *strafe* (< German).


### FF

* In medial position: *buffalo* (< Italian *bufalo*, Spanish *búfalo*); *coffee* (prob. < Italian *caffè* < Turkish *kahveh* < Arabic); *daffodil* (< Dutch); *duffel/ duffle* 'fabric' (< Dutch, from place-name *Duffel*); *effendi* 'title of respect' (< Turkish); *graffiti* (< Italian); *paraffin* (< German *Paraffin* < Latin); *taffrail* (see history of word under 'AI'); *waffle* (< early Dutch *wafel*).

- In final position: *muff* 'wrap for hands' (< Dutch *mof*); *pilaff* (see *pilaf* above); *stroganoff* (< Russian personal name); *tariff* (< Italian *tariffa*).
  - Phonologically final before a silent E: *giraffe* (< Italian *giraffa* < Arabic).


## G


There are sound–spelling correspondence problems with G in English, in that without (and often even with) a knowledge of the source or carrier language, it is impossible to predict whether G before a front vowel will be pronounced /dʒ/ (as in *ginseng*) or /g/ (as in *gingham*).

- In initial position:
  - Pronounced /g/: *gala*, *gondola* (< Italian); *galleon* (< early Spanish *galeón*); *galore* (< Irish Gaelic *go leor*); *gecko* 'lizard' (< Malay *gekoq*); *geisha* (< Japanese); *geyser* (< Icelandic place-name *Geysir*); *gingham* (prob. < Dutch *gingang* < Malay *genggang*); *glasnost* 'openness' (< Russian); *glitzy* (prob. < German *glitzern*); *glockenspiel* (< German); *gong* (< Malay and Javanese); *goulash* (< Hungarian *gulyás*); *guru* (< Hindi); *gusto* (< Spanish).
  - Pronounced /dʒ/: *ginseng* (< Chinese *jen-shen*); *giraffe* (< Italian *giraffa* < Arabic); *gymkhana* (< Urdu *gend-khana*, altered by association with *gymnastics*).
- In medial position:
  - Pronounced /g/: *assegai* (< Portuguese *azagaia* < Arabic, ult. < Berber); *cigar* (< Spanish *cigarro*); *dugong* (< Malay *duyong*); *embargo* (< Spanish); *igloo* (< Inuit *iglu*); *indigo* (< Italian dialect); *lager* (< German); *legato*, *regatta* (< Italian); *mogul* (< Urdu *mugal* < Persian *mughul* < Mongolian); *sago* (< Malay *sagu*); *slogan* (< Scottish Gaelic *sluagh-ghairm*); *wigwam* (< Algonquian, such as Ojibwa *wigwaum*); *yoga* (< Sanskrit).
    - The spelling of *wagon* (< Dutch *wagen*) has varied with *waggon* since its introduction in the 16th century.
  - Pronounced /dʒ/: *adagio* (< Italian); *intelligentsia* (< Russian); *magenta* (< Italian place-name).
- In final position: *bog* (< Scottish and Irish Gaelic *bogach*); *gulag* (< Russian); *iceberg* (prob. < Dutch *ijsberg*); *saag* 'Indian dish', *thug* (< Hindi *sag*, *thag*); *slag* (< Low German *slagge*).

## GG

- In medial position:
  - ○ Pronounced /g/: *juggernaut* (< Hindi *Jagannath* 'title of god Vishnu'); *smuggle* (< Low German *smuggeln*).
    - ▪ *Toboggan* is ultimately from an Algonquian language (e.g. Micmac *tabâkun*, Abenaki *udabagan*) but came into English via Canadian French *tabagane*.
  - ○ Pronounced /dʒ/: *arpeggio, loggia* (< Italian).

## GH

- In initial position, pronounced /g/: *gharial* 'Indian crocodile', *ghat* 'mountain pass', *ghi* 'clarified butter' (< Hindi); *ghetto* (< Italian); *ghoul* (< Arabic *ghul*).
  - ○ The word *gherkin* is a Dutch loan (prob. < an early Dutch form *⋆aggurkijn*), but its spelling with H is not; the H appears rather to serve as an indicator of the correspondence G = /g/ before a front vowel, as in Italian *ghetto* (compare the 16th-century English forms such as *gheerle* for *girl*, *ghes* for *geese*, etc.; see p. 45). Other examples of unexpected GH are seen in *gharry* 'small carriage' (< Hindi *gari*) and *ghillie* (usu. *gillie*; < Scottish Gaelic *gille* 'boy, servant', though in accordance with the rules of Gaelic grammar a GH spelling is also found, e.g. *leis a' ghille* 'with the boy', and may have influenced the English spelling).
- In medial position:
  - ○ Pronounced /g/: *dinghy* (< Hindi and Bengali *dingi*); *spaghetti* (< Italian).
    - ▪ *Yoghurt* (< Turkish *yogurt*) is now commonly spelt without the H in English.
  - ○ Silent: *freight* (< Dutch or Low German *vrecht*); *onslaught* (< Dutch *aanslag*; modified by *slaught* 'slaughter').
    - ▪ *Blighty* 'soldiers' slang for Britain' (< Hindi *bilayati*).
- In final position, silent: *furlough* (< Dutch *verlof*); *shillelagh* 'club' (< Irish place-name); *sleigh* (< Dutch *slee*).

## GL

GL is pronounced /lj/ in some words of Italian origin: *conchiglie* 'shell-shaped pasta', *imbroglio* 'tricky dramatic situation', *intaglio* 'incised design' and *seraglio* 'harem'.

GN

- In initial position pronounced /n/: *gneiss* 'rock' (< German); *gnocchi* 'potato balls' (also pronounced /nj/; < Italian); *gnu* 'African animal' (also pronounced /nj-/; < Khoikhoi *t'gnu*).
  ○ The pronunciation of *gnu* as 'g-noo' is facetious.
- In medial position, usually pronounced /nj/: *cognoscente* 'connoisseur', *lasagne*, *signor* (< Italian); but the GN is pronounced /gn/ in Italian-derived *incognito*.

GU

- In initial position:
  ○ Pronounced /g/: *guelder rose* (< Dutch *Gelderse roos*); *guerrilla* (< Spanish); *guilder* (< Dutch *gulden*).
  ○ Pronounced /gw/, most often in words of Spanish origin before A: *guacamole*, *guano*, and *guava* (< Spanish *guayaba*).
- In medial position:
  ○ Pronounced /g/: *beleaguer* (< Dutch *belegeren*).
  ○ Pronounced /gw/: *iguana* (< Spanish < Arawak *iwana*); *linguini* 'pasta in strands', *segue* 'play music without pause' (< Italian).
- In final position:
  ○ Phonologically final before silent E: *brogue* 'shoe' (< Irish Gaelic *bróg*, Scottish Gaelic *bròg*).

**H**

H generally corresponds to H or [h] in the source or carrier language.

- In initial position: *hacienda* (< Spanish, in which language H is now silent); *halal*, *hashish*, *henna* (< Arabic *hinna'*); *hara-kiri* (< Japanese); *hartebeest* 'antelope' (< obsolete Afrikaans); *hinterland* (< German); *howdah* 'seat on elephant' (< Persian and Urdu *haudah*); *hula* (< Hawaiian); *hummus* (< Turkish *humus*); *hurricane* (< Spanish *huracán* < Taino); *hussar* (< Hungarian *huszár*).
  ○ It is to the general Italian deletion of initial H that Modern English owes *oboe*, adapted by Italian from French *hautbois*. Similarly, Italian *arpeggio* is based on the same root as English *harp*.
- In medial position:

- ○ *ahimsa* 'doctrine of non-violence', *maharaja* (< Sanskrit); *apartheid* (< Afrikaans; -HEID = English -HOOD, -HEAD); *jihad, tahini* 'sesame paste' (< Arabic); *sahib* (< Urdu); *tomahawk* (< Renape *tamahak*).
- ○ For *dachshund*, see under 'CH'; for *mohair*, see under 'AI'.
- See also under 'AH', 'OH', etc.

## I

In general, an I in English reflects an I and/or the sounds [i] or [ɪ] in the source or carrier languages, and in most cases represents /ɪ/, /iː/ or /aɪ/ in English.

- In initial position:
  - ○ Pronounced /ɪ/: *igloo* (< Inuit *iglu*); *iguana* (< Spanish < Arawak *iwana*); *ikebana* 'flower-arranging' (< Japanese); *imam* (< Arabic); *impala* 'animal' (< Zulu); *inferno, influenza* (< Italian).
  - ○ Pronounced /aɪ/: *isinglass* 'fish gelatine' (prob. < obsolete Dutch *huisenblas*).
- In medial position:
  - ○ Pronounced /iː/: *aikido* 'martial art', *akita* 'breed of dog' (< Japanese); *amigo, mosquito* (< Spanish); *incognito, pizza* (< Italian); *kiwi* (< Maori).
  - ○ Pronounced /aɪ/ or /iː/: *pika* 'small animal' (< Evenki *piika*).
  - ○ Pronounced /ɪ/: *diktat, kindergarten, kitsch* (< German); *flamingo* (< Portuguese *flamengo*); *frolic* (< Dutch *vroolijk*); *hashish* (also /-iːʃ/; < Arabic); *indigo* (< Italian dialect); *kibbutz* (< Hebrew *qibbuts*); *kimono, sashimi* (< Japanese); *madrigal* (< Italian *madrigale*); *paprika* (also /-ˈpriː-/; < Hungarian); *pundit* (< Hindi *pandit* < Sanskrit *pandita*); *soviet* (< Russian *sovʲet*); *swastika* (< Sanskrit *svastika*).
    - Before a final A or O, mainly in words from Italian: *aria, impresario, malaria, portfolio, scenario, studio* stressed on the syllable before I but the more recent borrowing *pizzeria* stressed on the I of the ending; also *intelligentsia* (< Russian); *patio, sangria* (< Spanish); *sharia* (< Arabic).
    - Two I's occur juxtaposed and pronounced as two syllables in *shiitake* 'species of mushroom' (< Japanese).
- In final position:
  - ○ Pronounced /iː/ or /ɪ/: *corgi* (< Welsh); *gourami* 'species of fish' (< Malay *gurami*); *khaki, sari* (< Hindi); *muesli* (< Swiss German);

253

*origami, sushi, tsunami* (< Japanese); *safari* (< Swahili); *tahini* 'sesame paste' (< Arabic).

- In words of one syllable, always /iː/: *ch'i/qi* (< Chinese); *ski* (< Norwegian).
- Italian-derived plurals in -I, such as *confetti, graffiti, literati* (< obsolete Italian *litterati*), *macaroni, paparazzi, spaghetti, timpani*, are pronounced with a final /iː/, whereas Latin plurals in -I, such as *alumni, bacilli, stimuli*, are pronounced with a final /aɪ/.
  ○ Pronounced /aɪ/: *rabbi* (< Hebrew).
- In some borrowings, I alternates with EE in Modern English: e.g. *afrit/afreet* 'demon' (< Arabic *'ifrit*); see further examples under 'EE'.

IE

- In medial position, pronounced /iː/: *blitzkrieg, glockenspiel, lieder* 'songs' (all < German).
- In final position: *cookie* (< Dutch *koekje*); *coolie* (< Hindi and Telugu *kuli*); *corrie* (< Scottish Gaelic *coire*); *cowrie* 'shell' (< Hindi and Urdu *kauri*); *gillie* 'hunter's assistant' (< Scottish Gaelic *gille*); *mealie* 'ear of maize' (< Afrikaans *mielie*); *zombie* (< a West African language, poss. Kikongo *nzambi, zumbi*).
  ○ Note that in most of these words, the final E has no basis in the source word but gives the English word a less foreign look (compare English *grannie, groupie, lassie*, etc. and the more 'exotic-looking' forms ending in I given in the section above).

**IH**

In medial position: *shih-tzu* 'breed of dog' (< Chinese).

**J**

J has a variety of sources and pronunciations, depending on the source or carrier language. It most often = /dʒ/ in English.

- In initial position:
  ○ Pronounced /dʒ/: *jackal* (< Turkish *çakal*); *jaguar* (< Portuguese < Tupi-Guarani *jaguara/yaguara*); *jerboa* (< Arabic *yarbu'*); *jerky* 'dried meat' (< Spanish *charqui* < Quechua); *jinn* 'demon' (< Arabic

254

*jinni*); *jodhpurs* (< place-name in India); *judo* (< Japanese); *juggernaut* (< Hindi *Jagannath* 'title of Hindu god Vishnu'); *jungle* (< Hindi and Marathi *jangal*); *junk* 'boat' (< Portuguese *junco* < Javanese *djong*); *jute* (< Hindi and Bengali *jut*).

- J is found before a consonant in *jnana* 'spiritual knowledge' (pronounced /dʒəˈnɑːnə/; < Sanskrit).

○ Pronounced /h/, imitating Spanish [x]: *jalapeño* 'green chilli', *jojoba* 'plant or wax'.

  - The first syllable of *junta* is commonly anglicized to /dʒ/, though conscious imitation of the Spanish may give J the value /h/ and U the value of U in *put*.

- In medial position:

○ Pronounced /dʒ/: *bhaji* 'fried vegetables', *ganja* 'cannabis', *raja* (< Hindi); *hijab* 'head covering' (< Arabic); *mah-jong* 'game' (< Chinese *majiang* or similar forms in other dialects); *ninja* (< Japanese); *pyjamas* (< Urdu *pay-jama/pa-jama*).

○ Pronounced /h/: *fajita* 'strip of meat' (< Spanish).

  - In *marijuana*, the JU is usually pronounced /w/ or /hw/, though a pronunciation /-juˈɑːnə/ is also heard.

○ Pronounced /j/: *hallelujah* (< Hebrew *halelujah*).

  - In *fjord* (also *fiord*; < Norwegian) the J may be pronounced /j/, but is more often pronounced as a full stressed vowel /iː/.

- In final position: *Raj* 'British rule in India' (< Hindi); *haj/hajj/hadj* 'Muslim pilgrimage' (< Arabic).


## K

In many languages, there is a distinction between two kinds of K-sound, with a [k]-like sound formed further back in the mouth often written or transliterated as Q. Since this sound distinction does not exist in English, words that have it in the source language are generally written with K in English (*anorak*, *amok*), but there may be alternative spellings with Q (*Koran/Qur'an*, *burka/burqa*) and also with C (*kadi/qadi/cadi*). K, Q, C all = /k/ in English.

- In initial position: *karate*, *kimono* (< Japanese); *karma* (< Sanskrit); *kachina* 'ancestral spirit' (< Hopi *qacina*); *kindergarten*, *kitsch* (< German); *Koran* (< Arabic *qur'an*); *korma* 'Indian dish' (< Urdu); *kosher* (< Yiddish < Hebrew); *kraal* 'village' (< Afrikaans); *kremlin*

(< Russian *kreml*ʲ); *krill* 'small sea creatures' (< Norwegian *kril*); *kulfi* 'Indian ice-cream' (< Hindi); *kung fu* (< Chinese); *kyle* 'strait' (< Scottish Gaelic *caol*).

○ With a silent initial κ are *knapsack* (< Low German *knapsack* or Dutch *knapzak*) and *knout* 'whip' (< Russian *knut*).

○ Initial clusters that are foreign to the English core systems in either pronunciation or spelling are seen in *kgotla* 'tribal assembly in Botswana' (< Tswana; 19th-century spellings were *cotla* and *kotla*); *Knesset* 'Israeli parliament' (/kn-/; < Hebrew); *knish* 'filled dough ball' (/kn-/; < Yiddish); *kshatriya* 'member of Hindu caste' (< Sanskrit); *kvass/kvas* 'rye beer' (< Russian *kvas*); *kvetch* 'complain' (< Yiddish); *Kwanzaa* 'African-American festival' (< Swahili); *tae kwon do* (< Korean).

• In medial position: *aikido* 'martial art', *sudoku* 'number puzzle' (< Japanese); *baksheesh* 'tip or bribe' (also *bakhshish*, etc.; < Persian *bakhshish*); *diktat*, *sauerkraut* (< German); *pakora* 'Indian snack' (< Hindi); *Eskimo* (< French plural *esquimaux*, Spanish *esquimao* < Algonquian; *eskimo* is a Danish spelling first attested in English in the 19th century); *hooka(h)* (< Arabic *huqqah*); *kookaburra* 'Australian bird' (< Wiradhuri *kukuburra*); *paprika* (< Hungarian); *parka* (< Aleut < Russian, ult. < Nenets); *shekel* 'coin' (< Hebrew *sheqel*); *ukulele* (< Hawaiian); *vodka* (< Russian).

○ A modern example of anglicization is seen in *snorkel*, from German *Schnorchel*. Up into the 1950s, this was often semi-anglicized as *schnorkel*, until gradually the fully anglicized form *snorkel* became normal in the 1960s.

• In final position: In the core systems of English spelling, a single final κ is not found following a single vowel-letter representing a short vowel; there English uses CK (e.g. *black*, *sock*, *thick*, etc. κ is normal after or within a vowel written as a digraph or after a consonant (e.g. *bleak*, *dark*, *hawk*, *snake*, *think*, etc.). This rule is not adhered to in many exotic borrowings: *aardvark* (< Afrikaans); *amok* (also *amuck*; < Malay *amoq*); *anorak* (< Inuit *anoraq*); *apparatchik* 'party official' (< Russian); *flak* (occasionally spelt *flack*; < German); *kapok* (< Malay *kapoq*); *kayak* (< Inuit *qayaq*); *skunk* (< Abenaki *segankw*); *springbok* 'antelope' (< Afrikaans); *sputnik* (< Russian; and in -NIK in English compounds such as *beatnik*, *peacenik*, *refusenik*); *trek* (< Afrikaans *trekken*); *wok* 'cooking pan' (< Cantonese Chinese); *yak* (< Tibetan *gyag*).

○ Phonologically final before a silent E, the κ in *artichoke* replaces CC in Italian dialect *articiocco*.

## KH

The KH spelling reflects an aspirated consonant (somewhat like [k] + [h]) or a fricative (like [x] as in Scottish *loch*) in the source or carrier languages, all from the Middle East or Indian subcontinent. In English, there is no difference in pronunciation between KH and K.

- In initial position: *khaki* (< Hindi); *khamsin* 'hot wind' (< Arabic); *khan* (spelt *caan* when first borrowed in the 15th century; < a Turkic language).
  ○ *Khazi*, a slang word for 'toilet' dating from the 19th century, is not, despite its spelling, of eastern origin, but probably derives from Italian or Spanish *casa* 'house'. It has various spellings in English (*kazi*, *kharzie*, *karsey*, etc.).
- In medial position: *astrakhan* 'fabric' (< Russian place-name); *bakhshish* 'tip or bribe' (a spelling of *baksheesh* – see under 'K'); *burkha* (a spelling of *burka/burqa* – see under 'K'); *gymkhana* (< Urdu *gend-khana*, altered by influence of *gymnastics*); *kolkhoz* 'collective farm in USSR' (< Russian).
- In final position: *ankh* 'emblem of life' (< Egyptian *'nh*); *lakh* '100,000' (also *lac*; < Hindi and Hindustani); *rukh* 'mythical bird' (another spelling of *roc*, which is the more common spelling in English; < Arabic *rokh, rukhkh*, Persian *rukh*); *sheikh* (< Arabic *shaikh*).

## KK

- In medial position, = /k/: *chukka* 'period of play in polo' (formerly also *chucker*; < Hindi *cakkar*); *dekko* (< Hindi *dekho*); *Hanukkah* 'Jewish festival' (also *Chanukah*; < Hebrew *chanukkah*); *hokku* 'verse form' (< Japanese); *lekker* 'pleasant' (< Afrikaans); *pukka* (also *pucka*; < Hindi and Punjabi *pakka*); *quokka* 'species of wallaby' (< Nyungar *kwaka*).

## L

L corresponds to L or [l] in the source or carrier language.

- In initial position: *laager* (< Afrikaans); *lager, leitmotiv* (< German); *lama* (< Tibetan *blama*); *lambada* 'dance' (< Portuguese); *lido* (< Italian place-name); *lariat* (< Spanish *la reata*); *lasso* (< Spanish *lazo*); *latke* 'potato pancake' (< Yiddish); *lemming* 'small animal' (< Norwegian); *limerick* (< Irish place-name); *loch* (< Scottish Gaelic); *loquat* 'fruit'

(< Cantonese Chinese *lauh gwat*); *luau* (< Hawaiian *lu'au*); *loot* (< Hindi *lut*); *lory* 'species of bird' (< Malay *luri*); *lox* 'smoked salmon' (< Yiddish *laks*); *litchi/lychee/lichee* (< Chinese *li-chi*).

- In medial position: *baklava* 'sweet dessert' (< Turkish); *blitz* (< German); *broccoli* (< Italian); *buffalo* (< Italian *bufalo*, Spanish *búfalo*); *bulwark* (< early Dutch *bolwerc*); *bungalow* (< Hindustani *bangla*); *galore* (< Irish Gaelic *go leor*); *glen* 'valley' (< Scottish Gaelic *gleann*); *kaolin* (via French < Chinese place-name *Kao-ling*); *klutz* 'fool' (< Yiddish); *molasses, palaver* (< Portuguese *melaço, palavra*); *plaza, silo* (< Spanish); *plunder* (< German); *polo* (< Balti); *shibboleth* (< Hebrew); *slim* (< Dutch); *ukulele* (< Hawaiian); *violin* (< Italian *violino*).

- In final position: *bagel* (< Yiddish *beygel*); *ghoul* (< Arabic *ghul*); *kraal* 'village' (< Afrikaans); *madrigal* (< Italian *madrigale*); *mogul* (< Urdu *mugal* < Persian *mughul* < Mongolian); *shawl* (< Urdu and Persian *shal*); *yodel* (< German *jodeln*).

  ○ Phonologically final before a silent E: *bangle* (< Hindi *bangri*); *coracle* 'small boat' (< Welsh *corwgl*); *duffle* (or *duffel*; < Dutch < Belgian place-name); *rouble* (< Russian *rubl'*); *stipple* (< Dutch *stippelen*).

  ○ *Axolotl* 'salamander' (< Nahuatl) and *dirndl* 'dress' (< German) are notable in that in each case the L follows a consonant but is not followed by E contrary to the normal rules of English spelling (compare *bottle, middle*).

  ○ *Noodle, poodle* (< German *Nudel, Pudel*) date from the early 19th century or before and are anglicized in spelling, whereas the late-19th-century borrowing *strudel* has not been anglicized as *\*stroodle*. Similarly, *nickel* (18th century; < Swedish < German) has retained the -EL spelling (compare *fickle* < OE *ficol*, ME *fykel* and *pickle* < Dutch *pekel*); *nickle* is an accepted alternative spelling in America. See also under 'OO'.

## LL

LL is generally pronounced /l/ in English, except in a few words of Spanish origin in which a /lj/ or /j/ pronunciation closer to Spanish may be preserved, at least as an alternative pronunciation, e.g. *caudillo* 'Spanish dictator' (usu. /-'diːljəʊ/ but also /-'dɪləʊ/), *tortilla* (/-'tɪlə/ or /-'tiːjə/. American English preserves Spanish or Spanish-like pronunciations not usually heard in British English, e.g. *mantilla* (British English /-'tɪlə/, American usually /-'tiːjə/).

- In initial position: *llama* (< Spanish < Quechua); *llano* 'plain' (sometimes /lj-/; < Spanish).
- In medial position: *armadillo, chinchilla, flotilla, guerrilla* (< Spanish); *ballot* (< Italian dialect *ballotto*); *billabong* (< Wiradhuri *bilabang*); *cello* (< Italian *violoncello*); *colleen* 'girl' (< Irish Gaelic *cailín*); *djellaba/jellaba* 'Arab cloak' (< Arabic *jallaba*); *dollar* (< Dutch *daler*); *doolally* 'crazy' (< Indian place-name *Deolali*); *hallelujah* (< Hebrew *halelujah*); *intelligentsia* (< Russian); *mortadella* 'sausage' (< Italian); *mullah* 'Muslim cleric' (< Persian and Urdu *mulla*, Turkish *molla* < Arabic); *paella* (< Spanish); *peccadillo* (< Spanish *pecadillo*, Italian *peccadiglio*); *vanilla* (< Spanish *vaynilla*, now spelt *vainilla*).
  - In *alligator* (< Spanish *el lagarto* 'the lizard', the Spanish definite article has been incorporated into the noun in its English form.
  - The L is pronounced in *polka* (< Czech), unlike the L of Old-English-derived *folk* and *yolk*.
- In final position: *atoll* (< Dhivehi *atolu*); *drill* 'make holes' (< Dutch *drillen*); *krill* 'sea creature' (< Norwegian *kril*); *quoll* 'Australian animal' (< Guugu Yimidhirr *dhigul*); *troll* 'mythical being' (< Swedish *troll*, Danish *trold*).

# M

Modern English M normally corresponds to M or [m] in the source or carrier language.

- In initial position: *macho, mambo* (< Spanish); *manifesto, motto* (< Italian); *manga* 'comic book' (< Japanese); *mangel-wurzel* 'vegetable' (< German *Mangold-wurzel*); *mango* (< Portuguese *manga*, prob. < Malayalam); *meerkat* 'animal' (< Afrikaans); *meerschaum* 'mineral' (< German); *menorah* 'Jewish candelabrum' (< Hebrew); *moa* 'extinct bird' (< Maori); *moccasin* (< Algonquian; e.g. Massachusett *mohkisson*, Narragansett *mokussin*); *mogul* (< Urdu *mugal* < Persian *Mughul* < Mongolian); *mosquito, mustang* (< Spanish); *mufti, mujahidin* (< Arabic); *mynah/myna/mina* 'bird' (< Hindi *maina*).
  - An initial vowel has been lost in *mamba* 'snake' (< Zulu *imamba*).
- In medial position: *amen* (< Hebrew); *amigo, armada* (< Spanish); *amir* 'Muslim leader' (also *ameer*; < Arabic); *amok* (also *amuck*; < Malay *amoq*); *cameo, tombola* (< Italian); *catamaran* (< Tamil *kattumaram*); *chimpanzee* (via French < Kikongo *chimpenzi*); *impala* 'animal' (< Zulu);

*kimono, sashimi* 'sliced raw fish' (< Japanese); *samosa* 'Indian pastry' (< Hindi, Urdu and Persian); *sampan* 'boat' (< Cantonese Chinese *saambaan*); *shaman* (< Russian < Tungus); *shampoo* (< Hindi *campo*); *shamrock* (< Irish Gaelic *seamróg*); *swami* 'religious teacher' (< Hindi *svami*); *scampi* (< Italian); *smack* 'boat' (< Dutch *smak*, Low German *smack*); *wombat* 'Australian animal' (< Dharuk *wambat*).

- ○ *Gymkhana* is a distortion of Urdu *gend-khana*, altered by association with *gymnastics*, which is of Greek origin.
- • In final position: *boom* 'spar', *slim* (< Dutch); *cwm* 'hollow' (< Welsh); *dim sum* 'Chinese pastry' (< Cantonese Chinese *dim sam*); *dirham* 'currency', *imam* (< Arabic); *kilim* 'rug' (< Turkish); *pogrom* (via Yiddish < Russian); *shalom* (< Hebrew); *slalom* (< Norwegian); *wigwam* (< Algonquian, such as Ojibwa *wigwaum*).
  - ○ Phonologically final before a silent E: *grime* (< Flemish *grijm*).
  - ○ A final vowel has been lost in *ashram* (< Sanskrit *ashrama*); similarly with *yam* (< Portuguese *inhame*, archaic Spanish *iñame*). A whole syllable has been lost from the end of *totem* (< Ojibwa *ototeman*).
  - ○ *Gingham* is probably from Dutch *gingang* (< Malay *genggang*).

MB

Almost all examples of MB are split across two syllables, e.g. *bamboo, wombat*. However, MB does occur word-initially in *mbira*, the name of an African musical instrument (< Shona).

MM

Only found in medial position: *cummerbund* (< Urdu and Persian *kamar-band*); *hammock* (< Spanish *hamaca*); *hummus* (< Turkish *humus*); *lammergeier* 'vulture' (< German *Lämmergeier*); *lemming* 'small animal' (< Norwegian); *mammoth* (< Russian *mamont*, formerly *mamant*); *pemmican* 'dried meat paste' (also *pemican*; < Cree *pimihkan*); *persimmon* 'fruit' (< Algonquian *pessimmins*); *umma* 'Muslim community' (< Arabic).

- ○ The Latinate MM of COMM- is simplified in Spanish, and *incommunicado*, from Spanish *incomunicado*, is first attested in English in the 19th century spelt with a single M; but in the 20th century it became generally aligned with English forms with MM such as *communicate*.
- ○ For *commandeer, commando* and *commodore*, see under 'c'.

# N

Modern English N normally corresponds to N or [n] in the source or carrier language.

- In initial position: *nan/naan* 'bread' (< Urdu and Persian *nan*); *nabob* 'man of wealth' (< Spanish *nabab*, Portuguese *nababo* < Urdu); *nacho* 'Mexican savoury' (< Spanish); *netsuke* 'fastening', *ninja* (< Japanese); *nickel* (< Swedish < German); *nirvana* (< Sanskrit); *niqab* 'Muslim woman's veil' (< Arabic); *nix* (< German *nichts*); *noodle* (< German *Nudel*); *nosh* 'food' (< Yiddish *nashn*); *nuncio* (< Italian *nunzio*).
- In medial position: *anorak* (< Inuit *anoraq*); *balcony* (< Italian *balcone*); *banana* (< Spanish or Portuguese, ult. < an African language); *bonsai*, *ikebana* 'flower-arranging' (< Japanese); *bwana* (< Swahili); *casino*, *influenza* (< Italian); *domineer* (< Dutch *domineren*); *flense* 'strip whale' (< Dutch *flensen*, Danish and Norwegian *flense*); *panatella* 'cigar' (< Spanish *panatela*); *pimento* (< Spanish *pimiento*); *plunder* (< German *plundern*); *pundit* (< Hindi *pandit* < Sanskrit *pandita*); *shantung* (< Chinese place-name, now usually *Shandong*); *tundra* (< Russian).
  - In some cases, an English N before a consonant represents vowel nasalization in the source language: *bandan(n)a* (< Hindustani), *chintz* (< Hindi).
- In final position: *banyan* 'tree' (< Portuguese *banian* < Arabic); *caravan* (ult. < Persian *karwan*; perhaps influenced by French *caravane*, Italian *caravana*); *clan* (< Scottish Gaelic); *divan* (< Turkish); *futon* 'bed', *zen* (< Japanese); *kaftan* (< Russian < Turkish); *manikin* (also *mannikin*; < Dutch *mannekijn*); *mandolin* (also *mandoline*; < Italian *mandolino*); *monsoon* (replacing a nasalized vowel in the immediate source word; < Portuguese *monção* < Arabic); *sampan* 'boat' (< Cantonese Chinese *saambaan*); *squadron* (< Italian *squadrone*); *terrapin* (< Algonquian, e.g. Abenaki *turepé*); *wagon* (< Dutch *wagen*); *yen* 'desire' (prob. < Cantonese Chinese *yahn*).
  - Phonologically final after a silent E: *hurricane* (< Spanish *huracán* < Taino); *marline* 'thin rope on boat' (< Dutch *marlijn*).
  - From the time of its entry into English in the 17th century, *orangutan* (< Malay *orang (h)utan*) has had an alternative assimilated form *orang-utang*.

## Ñ

Ñ occurs in English in some words of Spanish origin (*jalapeño* 'pepper', *mañana* 'tomorrow'). *Cañon* is more often spelt *canyon*. *Castanet* (< Spanish *castañeta*) has lost the ñ altogether in English. *Vicuña* 'llama-like animal' may also be spelt *vicuna* and the pronunciation of the latter form may or may not reflect the spelling: /vɪˈkjuːnə/ or /vɪˈkuːnjə/.

- *Piraña* is sometimes seen as an alternative spelling for *piranha* (< Portuguese), Spanish ñ and Portuguese NH both being pronounced /ɲ/. English pronunciation varies between /pɪˈrɑːnə/ and /pɪˈrɑːnjə/.

## NG

- NG is found in initial position in English only in words from other languages designating flora and fauna, currencies and other culture-specific items. As /ŋ/ is not normally found in initial position, it may be preceded by a /ə/, so making it non-initial, or may be replaced by /n/ in English pronunciation: *ngaio* 'New Zealand shrub' (< Maori); *ngaka* 'traditional African healer' (< Tswana); *ngapi* 'fish sauce' (< Burmese); *ngultrum* 'Bhutanese currency' (< Dzongkha); *ngwee* 'Zambian currency' (< Chichewa).
- In medial position, as /ŋ/ or /ŋg/ as in English: *angst* (< German); *bangle* (< Hindi *bangri*); *bungalow* (< Hindustani *bangla*); *dingo* (< Gamilaraay *jungho*); *dinghy* (usu. /ˈdɪŋɪ/; < Hindi and Bengali *dingi*); *donga* 'gully' (< Afrikaans < Zulu); *dungaree* (< Hindi *dungri*); *flamingo* (< Portuguese *flamengo*); *isinglass* 'fish gelatine' (/ˈaɪzɪŋglɑːs/; prob. < obsolete Dutch *huisenblas*); *jungle* (< Hindi and Marathi *jangal*); *linguini* 'pasta' (< Italian); *manga* 'comic book' (< Japanese); *mango* (< Portuguese *manga*, prob. < Malayalam); *pangolin* 'species of animal' (< Malay *pengguling*); *sangria* (< Spanish); *springbok* 'animal' (< Afrikaans); *tanga* 'bikini' (< Portuguese < Kimbundu *ntango*); *tango* (< Spanish); *tungsten* (< Swedish).
  - In *gingili* 'sesame' (/ˈdʒɪndʒɪlɪ/; < Hindi and Marathi *jinjali*) the N and G are split between syllables.
- In final position: *billabong* 'backwater' (< Wiradhuri *bilabang*); *biltong* 'dried meat' (< Afrikaans); *dugong* (< Malay *duyong*); *ginseng* (< Chinese *jen-shen*); *gong* (< Malay and Javanese); *lemming* 'small animal' (< Norwegian); *mustang* (< Spanish *mestengo*); *oolong* 'variety of tea' (< Chinese *wu-lung*); *sarong* (< Malay *sarung*); *souchong*

'variety of tea' (< Chinese *siao chung*, Cantonese Chinese *siu chung*); *tong* 'secret society' (< Cantonese Chinese *tohng*).


## NH

NH usually crosses a syllable boundary in English and is pronounced /n/ + /h/, as in, for example, *Fahrenheit* 'temperature scale' and *anhinga* 'species of bird'. The only common examples of NH with a different phonetic realization are *piranha* 'South American fish' (< Portuguese < Tupi) in which NH = /n/ or /nj/ in English, and *senhor* 'Mr' (< Portuguese) in which NH = /nj/.

- ○ *Menhir* 'standing stone' is from Breton, and here again the NH is pronounced /n/ + /h/.


## NN

The double NN in English may indicate that the preceding vowel is short, and correspond to a single N in the source or carrier language.

- In medial position: *belladonna* 'drug', *cannelloni* 'pasta', *Madonna*, *pannacotta* 'sweet dessert' (< Italian); *gunny* 'sacking' (< Hindi *gani*); *henna* (< Arabic *hinnaʿ*); *pickanniny* 'child' (prob. < Portuguese *pequenino*).
  - ○ Some words vary between NN and N, e.g. *bandanna/bandana* (< Hindustani *bandhnu*, in which the AN represents a nasalized vowel). *Cannibal* and *savanna(h)* (both < Spanish) also varied between single and double N in former centuries; the modern preference for NN may have been encouraged by the preceding stressed short vowel.
- In final position: *jinn* 'demon' (< Arabic *jinni*).


## O

O in English generally reflects an O or an [ɒ] or [o] in the source or carrier languages, and in most cases represents /ɒ/, /əʊ/ or, when unstressed, /ə/ in English.

- In initial position, pronounced /ɒ/, /əʊ/ or, when unstressed, /ə/: *obbligato*, *opera*, *oratorio* (< Italian); *oblast* 'administrative district'

(< Russian); *oboe* (< Italian; see note under 'H'); *okapi* 'African animal' (< Mbuba); *okra* (prob. < Igbo *okuru*); *olio* 'Spanish stew' (< Spanish *olla*); *om* 'sacred syllable' (< Sanskrit); *ombudsman* (< Swedish); *onslaught* (< Dutch *aanslag*); *opossum* 'American animal' (< Algonquian *opassom, aposum*); *orang-utan* (< Malay); *origami* (< Japanese).

- In medial position, as /ɒ/, /əʊ/, /ɔː/ or /ə/: *amok, kapok* (< Malay *amoq, kapoq*); *boss* (< Dutch *baas*); *broccoli, gondola* (< Italian); *condor* (< Spanish *cóndor* < Quechua *kuntur*); *copra* (< Portuguese and Spanish < Malayalam *koppara*); *corgi* (< Welsh); *corridor* (< Italian *corridore*); *cot* 'bed' (< Hindi *khat*); *dollar* (< Dutch *daler*); *korma* 'Indian dish' (< Urdu); *kosher* (< Yiddish < Hebrew); *pagoda* (< Portuguese *pagode*); *robot* (< Czech *robota*); *shogun, sudoku* (< Japanese); *vodka* (< Russian).
  - With a silent word- or syllable-final E indicating the pronunciation /əʊ/: *coleslaw* (< Dutch *koolsla*); *dope* (< Dutch *doop*); *vole* (< Norwegian *vollmus*).
  - Spanish *cucaracha* has become English *cockroach* by assimilation to *cock* and *roach*.
  - Note the possible pronunciations of *coyote*, /kɔɪˈəʊtɪ/, /ˈkɔɪəʊt/ or, especially in America, /kaɪˈəʊtɪ/. The last of these makes for a very unexpected sound–spelling correspondence OY = /aɪ/.
- In final position, very commonly in words from Italian, Spanish and Portuguese, and also from Japanese: *concerto, ditto, ghetto, motto, piano, piccolo, portico, risotto, staccato, stiletto, stucco, studio, torso* (< Italian); *bolero, bongo* 'drum', *flamenco, gusto, oloroso* 'sherry', *rodeo, sombrero* (< Spanish); *flamingo* (< Portuguese *flamengo*); *bushido, honcho* (< Japanese *hancho*), *judo, kendo, kimono, sumo* (< Japanese); and in addition *calico* (< *Calicut*, town in India); *gecko* 'lizard' (< Malay *gekoq*); *Gestapo* (< German); *matzo* 'biscuit' (also *matzoh*; < Yiddish *matse* < Hebrew); *politburo* (< Russian).
  - Some of the Spanish-derived words originate in languages of South and Central America and the Caribbean: *avocado* (< Nahuatl *ahuacatl*); *guano* (< Quechua *huano*); *tobacco* (Spanish *tabaco* < Haitian Carib; *tabaco/tabacco* in English until the 18th century, when it was ousted by *tobacco*); *tomato* (prob. via Spanish *tomate* < Nahuatl *tomatl*; *tomate* in 17th-century English; the modern form is possibly influenced by *potato*, or else is a pseudo-Spanish form). Unlike *tomato*, *chocolate* (< Spanish *chocolate* < Nahuatl *chocolatl*) has not taken on an -o ending, perhaps through the influence of French *chocolat*.

○ There is a change from -A to -O in the ending of some English words derived from Italian, Spanish and Portuguese: e.g. *salvo* (originally *salva*; < Italian *salva*; *potato* (< Spanish *patata*).

OA

There are few examples of OA as a single grapheme in 'exotic' vocabulary, most cases of OA being split over two syllables, as in *koala*, *jerboa* 'small animal', *quinoa* 'South American cereal'.

- In medial position: *groat* 'old English coin' (< Dutch *groot*); *uproar* (< Dutch *oproer*).
- In final position: *cocoa* (an alteration of *cacao*; in the 16th to 18th centuries, also written *cacoa*, and sometimes in the 18th century *cocao*; < Spanish *cacao* < Nahuatl *cacauatl*).
  ○ For *cockroach*, see above under 'o'.
  ○ *Coach* ultimately derives from Hungarian *kocsi*, but came into English through French *coche*, a spelling which was also found in English in the 16th and 17th centuries.

OE

Most exotic English words spelt with OE are of Afrikaans origin, and most are not well known outside southern Africa: e.g. *boerewors* 'type of sausage', *snoek* 'type of fish', *stoep* 'veranda', *veldskoen* 'rawhide boot'. In such words OE is pronounced /ʊ/ or /uː/. See also *Boer* below.

- In initial position: In *Oersted* 'unit of magnetic field strength' (< Danish personal name *Oersted* or *Ørsted*), OER- is pronounced /ɜː/.
- In medial position:
  ○ *Boer* (< Dutch) has several possible pronunciations, such as /bɔː/, /ˈbəʊə/ and /bʊə/.
  ○ *Foehn* is an alternative spelling of *föhn* 'alpine wind' (/fɜːn/; < German *Föhn*).
  ○ The OE of the geological term *loess* is, like the OE of *foehn*, an alternative spelling of the ö of German *Löss*; however, in this case, the English pronunciation unpredictably varies between a disyllabic /ˈləʊɛs/ and monosyllabic /lɜːs/, an approximation of the German pronunciation.
- In final position, pronounced /əʊ/: *chigoe* 'flea' (West Indian name of uncertain origin, possibly a Carib word *chico*); *floe* (prob. <

Norwegian *flo*); *pekoe* 'variety of tea' (< Min Chinese *pekho*). When introduced in the 18th century, *pekoe* was also written as *peckho, pecko, peco* and *peko*, and *chigoe* has also been written in the past as *chego* and *chigo*. Given the number of exotic words ending in -o in English (see above), it is not clear why these three have gained the additional E (thus matching *foe, throe, toe*, etc. of Old English origin).

○ The sound–spelling relationship OE = /uː/ in *canoe* is exceptional. *Canoe* was introduced into English in the mid-16th century as *canoa* (< Spanish *canoa* < Arawak < Carib), and between the 16th and 18th centuries existed in other forms such as *canow, cano, canou, canoo, cannoe* before settling as *canoe*.

## OH

• In initial position: *ohm* 'unit of electrical resistance) (/əʊm/; < German personal name).
• In medial position: *kohl* 'cosmetic' (< Arabic *kuhl*); *kohlrabi* 'vegetable' (< German).
    ○ *Fohn* is an alternative spelling of *foehn/föhn* (see under 'OE' above).
• In final position: *noh* 'Japanese theatre' (also *no*; < Japanese); *pharaoh* (ult. < Egyptian *pr-ʿo*, via Hebrew, Greek, Latin and French; the English form most resembles Greek and Latin *pharao*, but the H comes from the Hebrew form *parʿoh*).

## OI

• In medial position: *coir* 'fibre' (< Malayalam *kayar*); *dacoit* 'robber' (< Hindi *dakait*); *foist* (prob. < Dutch dialect *vuisten*); *loiter* (< Dutch *loteren*); *moidore* 'gold coin' (< Portuguese *moeda de ouro*); *troika* 'sleigh' (< Russian).
    ○ OOI (= /ɔɪ/) in words of South African origin, from Afrikaans: *rooibos, rooinek*, etc.
• In final position, having I where English spelling generally has Y (e.g. *boy, coy, employ*): *borzoi* 'dog breed' (< Russian); *koi* 'fish' (< Japanese); *pak choi* 'Chinese cabbage' (also *bok choy* and other spellings; < Cantonese Chinese *baahk choi*).

## OO

Generally pronounced /uː/.

- In initial position: *oolong* 'tea' (< Chinese *wu-lung*).
- In medial position: *bandicoot* 'Australian animal' (< Telugu *pandi-kokku*); *boondocks* 'remote area' (< Tagalog *bundok*); *hooch* 'alcoholic drink' (also *hootch*; < *Hoochinoo*, name of Native American people); *hookah/hooka* (< Arabic *huqqah*); *monsoon* (-OON representing a nasalized vowel in the source word; < Portuguese *monção* < Arabic); *tycoon* (< Japanese *taikun*).
- In final position: *bamboo* (< Malay *bambu*); *igloo* (< Inuit *iglu*); *taboo* (also *tabu*; < Tongan *tabu*); *tattoo* 'design' (< Tahitian *tatau*); *voodoo* (via Creole French < Ewe *vodu*).
  ○ Where there is no already existing written form of the source word, the spelling is usually OO: e.g. from Australian Aboriginal languages *boomerang, didgeridoo, kangaroo, kookaburra, woomera*, and from North American Native American languages *moose, papoose, raccoon*. Folk etymology may play a part in altering the form of the word: *woodchuck* 'American marmot' (< Algonquian, such as Cree *otcheck*, Narragansett *ockqutchaun*, influenced by English *wood*).
  ○ A notable number of words in the OO group come from Dutch or Afrikaans. All are pronounced /uː/ in English or, before R, /ʊə/. See also under 'Oʀ' above. In Dutch and Afrikaans, OE is pronounced /uː/, and OO /oː/:
    ▪ *boor* (< Dutch *boer*); *cookie* (< Dutch *koekje*); *groove* (< Dutch *groeve*); *sloop* (< Dutch *sloep*); *snoop* (< Dutch *snoepen*); *stoop* 'porch' (< Dutch *stoep*); *tattoo* 'military display' (< Dutch *taptoe*);
    ▪ *boom* 'spar on mast' (< Dutch *boom*); *spook* < Dutch *spook*); *spoor* (< Afrikaans *spoor*);
    ▪ *caboose* 'train wagon' (prob. < Dutch *kabuis*); *freebooter* (< Dutch *vrijbuiter*);
    ▪ *booze* (< Dutch *busen*).
  ○ A number of words, mainly ones derived from Hindi or some other of the languages of the Indian subcontinent, have English OO for /uː/: *cheroot* (< Tamil *curuttu*); *coolie* (< Hindi and Telugu *kuli*); *loot* (< Hindi *lut*); *mooli* 'vegetable' (< Hindi *muli*); *shahtoosh* 'shawl' (< Punjabi *shatush*); *shampoo* (< Hindi *campo*). Some words formerly spelt with a final OO are now usually spelt with a final U: *gooroo/guru, Hindoo/Hindu*. (See more under 'U' at 'In final position'.)
    ▪ Notice also *doolally* 'crazy' (< Indian place-name *Deolali*).

- A number of words derived from American Spanish have Modern English oo for Spanish o: *buckaroo* 'cowboy' (< *vaquero*), *calaboose* 'jail' (< *calabozo*), *vamoose* (< *vamos*).
  - Note also the usual /uː/ pronunciation of the final o of *lasso* (< *lazo*), which gives an unpredictable sound–spelling correspondence (though /əʊ/ is also considered correct).
- In keeping with the general rule that recent borrowings into English tend to keep the spelling of the source language while earlier borrowings tend to be anglicized, compare the late-18th-century borrowings *noodle* and *poodle* (< German *Nudel, Pudel*) and the late-19th-century borrowing *strudel* (German *Strudel*). Similarly *doodle* is probably from Low German *dudeltopf*. See also under 'L' at 'In final position'.
- For Modern English *typhoon*, see the note under 'PH'.

*OU*

- There are very few English words with OU in initial position. Three are from Afrikaans: *ouma* 'elderly woman' and *oupa* 'elderly man', in which OU is pronounced /əʊ/ and *outspan* 'campsite' which has English OUT- for Afrikaans UIT-.
- In medial position:
  - Pronounced /uː/: *ghoul* (< Arabic *ghul*); *goulash* (< Hungarian *gulyás*); *gourami* 'fish' (< Malay *gurami*); *patchouli* 'plant and oil from it' (< Tamil *pacculi*); *rouble* (< Russian *rublʲ*); *souchong* 'tea variety' (< Chinese *siao chung*, Cantonese Chinese *siu chung*); *souk* 'Arab market' (also written *sooq, suk, sukh, suq*, etc.; < Arabic *suq*).
    - The following animal and bird names have entered English via French: *agouti* (ult. < Tupí *aguti, acuti*), *cougar* (< French *couguar*, ult. < Tupi *siwasuarana*) and *toucan* (ult. < Tupi *tucana*).
  - Pronounced /aʊ/: *compound* 'enclosed place' (< Malay *kampong, kampung*); *houdah* 'seat on elephant' (an alternative spelling of *howdah*; < Urdu and Persian *haudah*); *knout* 'whip' (< Russian *knut*); *mountebank* (< Italian *montambanco/montimbanco*); *trousers* (via earlier *trouse* < Irish and Scottish Gaelic *triubhas*).
  - With other pronunciations: *furlough* (< Dutch *verlof*).
- In final position: Words with a final OU have generally entered English via French, whatever the ultimate source language; the sound–spelling

correspondence OU = /uː/ is standard in French: *bayou* (< Choctaw *bayuk*), *caribou* (< Algonquian), *kinkajou* (< French *quincajou* < Algonquian), *manitou* 'deity, spirit' (< Ojibwa *manito*).

*OW*

As with words derived from the core language sources (compare *grow*, *growl*), ow in exotic words is in some cases pronounced /əʊ/ and in other cases /aʊ/.

- In medial position:
  ○ Pronounced /əʊ/: *bowsprit* 'spar on bow of ship' (prob. < Dutch *boegspriet* or Low German *bogspret*).
  ○ Pronounced /aʊ/: *chow mein* (< Chinese *chao mian*, Cantonese Chinese *chaau mihn*); *cowrie* 'shell' (< Hindi and Urdu *kauri*); *dhow* 'boat' (< Arabic *dawa*); *godown* 'warehouse' (< Malay *gudang*); *howdah* 'seat on elephant' (< Persian and Urdu *haudah*).
    ▪ *Howitzer* (Modern German *Haubitze*), though Czech in origin, appears to have reached English via German or Dutch, with various early spellings attested such as *haubitz*, *hauwitz*.
- In final position:
  ○ Pronounced /əʊ/: *bungalow* (< Hindustani *bangla*); *serow* 'Asian goat' (< Lepcha *sa-ro*).
  ○ Pronounced /aʊ/: *hoosegow* 'jail' (< American Spanish *juzgado*); *how* 'Native American greeting' (< Siouan; compare Sioux *hao*, Omaha *hau*); *kowtow* (< Chinese *k'o-t'ou*); *powwow* (Algonquian, e.g. < Narragansett *powwaw*, Massachusett *pauwau*); *scow* 'boat' (< Dutch *schouw*).

*OY*

- In medial position: *coypu* 'South American animal' (< Spanish *coipú* < Araucanian); *soya* (< Dutch *soja/soya* < Japanese *shoyu*; see also *soy* below).
- In final position: *bok choy* 'Chinese cabbage' (also *pak choi* and other spellings; < Cantonese Chinese *baahk choi*); *carboy* 'bottle' (< Persian *qaraba*); *decoy* (< Dutch *de kooi*); *goy* 'non-Jew' (via Yiddish < Hebrew); *sepoy* 'Indian soldier' (poss. via Portuguese < Urdu and Persian *sipahi*); *soy* (< Japanese *soy/shoy/shoyu*).

# P

Modern English P normally corresponds to P or [p] in the source or carrier languages.

- In initial position: *paella* (< Spanish); *pagoda* (< Portuguese *pagode*); *pakora*, *puri* 'wheat cake' (< Hindi); *panatella* 'cigar' (< Spanish *panatela*); *pampas*, *puma* (< Spanish < Quechua); *panga* 'large knife' (< Swahili); *pashmina* 'shawl' (< Persian); *pastrami* (< Yiddish < Romanian); *pergola*, *presto* (< Italian); *pibroch* 'bagpipe music' (< Scottish Gaelic *piobaireachd*); *polka* (< Czech); *poltergeist* (< German); *potato* (< Spanish *patata*); *powwow* (< Algonquian, e.g. Narragansett *powwaw*, Massachusett *pauwau*); *pundit* (< Hindi *pandit* < Sanskrit *pandita*); *pyjamas* (< Urdu *pay-jama/pa-jama*).
- In medial position: *chaparral* 'dense shrubs', *esparto* 'grass', *tapas* (< Spanish); *chapatti* (< Hindi *capati*); *chipmunk* (earlier *chitmunk*; < Algonquian, poss. Ojibwa *achitamon*); *copra* (< Portuguese and Spanish < Malayalam *koppara*); *coypu* 'South American animal' (< Spanish *coipú* < Araucanian); *cupola*, *replica*, *scampi*, *soprano* (< Italian); *kapok* (< Malay *kapoq*); *kopek* 'Russian coin' (< Russian *kopeika*); *marzipan*, *spanner* (< German); *sampan* 'boat' (< Cantonese Chinese *saambaan*); *split* (< Dutch *splitten*); *sputnik* (< Russian); *tapioca* (< Spanish and Portuguese < Tupi); *tempura* 'Japanese dish' (< Japanese); *terrapin* (< Algonquian, e.g. Abenaki *turepé*); *vampire* (via French < Hungarian *vampir*); *wampum* 'money beads' (< Algonquian, e.g. Massachusett *wampompeag*); *wapiti* 'American deer' (< Algonquian, e.g. Cree *wapitik*, Shawnee *wahpetee*).
- In final position: *hop* (< Dutch *hoppe*); *ketchup* (< Malay *kechap* and/or Amoy Chinese *ke-tsiap*); *rollmop* 'rolled herring' (< German *Rollmops*); *sloop* (< Dutch *sloep*); *snoop* (< Dutch *snoepen*); *stoop* 'porch' (< Dutch *stoep*); *wickiup* 'Native American hut' (< Algonquian, e.g. Fox *wikiyapi*).
  - Phonologically final before a silent E: *dope* (< Dutch *doop*); *landscape* (< Dutch *landschap*).
  - It is interesting to note how many of the words in the word-final P category derive from Dutch. To the ones listed here could be added some from Afrikaans, such as *dop* 'brandy' and *dorp* 'village'.

270

The only common English word with PF is *pfennig* 'former German currency', in English pronounced with initial /f/ or /pf/. If the P is pronounced, then we have a predictable spelling of an exotic initial consonant group /pf/; if the P is not pronounced, then we have an unpredictable sound–spelling correspondence PF = /f/.

Most words spelt with PH in English are of Greek origin. Only a few are from other source languages, and some of them have passed through Greek (and Latin and/or French) before entering English.

- In initial position: *pharaoh* (/-əʊ/; via French and Latin < Greek *pharao* < Hebrew *par'oh* < Egyptian); *Pharisee* (via Latin < Greek *pharisaios* < Aramaic *perishayya*).
- In medial position: Modern English *typhoon* derives from more than one source; Portuguese *tufão* < Arabic, probably influenced by both Greek *typhon* 'whirlwind' and Chinese *t'ai feng* 'great wind'.
  - *Camphor* (< Sanskrit via Malay *kapur*, Arabic *kafur* and French) derives its PH spelling from medieval Latin *camphora* and Greek *kaphoura*. *Cipher* (ult. < Arabic *sifr*) probably also derives its PH from medieval Latin *ciphra*.
- In final position: *aleph*, *qoph* 'letters of Hebrew alphabet' (< Hebrew); *caliph* (also *calif*; via Latin and French < Arabic *khalifah*); *seraph* (formed on basis of plural *seraphim*; via Latin < Hebrew *seraphim*).

In medial position, always = /p/: *apparatchik* 'party official' (< Russian); *cappuccino* 'coffee', *grappa* 'alcoholic drink' (< Italian); *ippon* 'point awarded in judo, etc.', *seppuku* 'hara-kiri' (< Japanese); *koppie* 'small hill' (also *kopje*; < Afrikaans); *pepperoni* (also *peperoni*; < Italian *peperoni*); *steppe* (< Russian *step*ʲ); *skipper* (< Dutch or Low German *schipper*); *stipple* (< Dutch *stippelen*); *zeppelin* 'airship' (< German personal name).

- English *schnapps* reflects the German spelling of the time when the word was borrowed; the Modern German form is *Schnaps*.

271

## PT

Most words spelt with initial PT- in English are of Greek origin (e.g. *pterodactyl*). In all, the initial P is silent. *Ptomaine* is from Italian *ptomaina* but its ultimate source is Greek. *Ptarmigan* 'species of grouse' is from Scottish Gaelic *tàrmachan*; the P was first added in the 18th century, presumably by analogy with Greek words with initial PT-.

## Q

In the core spelling system(s) of English, Q is always followed by U (e.g. *queen, quick, quorum*). As noted already under 'c' and 'k', many languages have more than one K-like sound, the one formed further back in the mouth often written or transliterated as Q. Since this K/Q distinction does not exist in English pronunciation, the words are generally written with K or C in English. A few words, however, are or may be spelt with Q, without a following U.

- In initial position, without a following U:
  - Pronounced /k/; most words quite rare in English: *qadi* 'Muslim judge' (also *cadi* and *kadi*; < Arabic); *qintar* 'monetary unit in Albania' (< Albanian); *qiviut* 'musk ox wool' (< Inuit); *qoph* 'letter of Hebrew alphabet' (< Hebrew); *Qur'an* (also *Koran*; < Arabic); *qursh* 'monetary unit in Saudi Arabia' (< Arabic *qursh, qirsh*).
  - Pronounced /tʃ/: *qi* 'life force' (also *ch'i*; < Chinese); *qigong* 'form of exercise' (also *ch'i-kung*; < Chinese). (See p. 231 for remarks on the transliteration of Chinese.)
- In initial position, with a following U:
  - QU pronounced /k/ or /kw/: *quetzal* 'South American bird' (< Spanish < Nahuatl); *quinoa* 'cereal' (< Spanish *quinua*, formerly also *quínoa* < Quechua *kinua/kinoa*).
  - QU pronounced /kw/: *quagga* 'African animal' (< obsolete Afrikaans < Khoikhoi *quacha*); *quahog* 'American clam' (< Narragansett *poquaûhock*); *quaich* 'shallow cup' (< Scottish Gaelic *cuach*); *quark* 'type of cheese', *quartz* (< German); *quinine* (< Spanish *quina* < Quechua *kina*); *quisling* 'traitor' (< Norwegian personal name); *quokka* 'Australian animal' (< Nyungar *kwaka*); *quoll* 'Australian animal' (< Guugu Yimidhirr *dhigul*).
  - Notice that even a knowledge of the source language is no sure indicator of pronunciation in the above group: *quetzal* and *quinoa*

may retain the initial [k] of Spanish, but *quinine* has been fully anglicized with an initial /kw/.

- In medial position:
  - QU pronounced /kw/: *kumquat* 'fruit' (< Cantonese Chinese *gam gwat*); *loquat* 'fruit' (< Cantonese Chinese *lauh gwat*); *squacco* 'species of heron' (< Italian dialect *sguacco*); *squadron* (< Italian *squadrone*); *squash* 'vegetable' (< Narragansett *askutasquash*); *squaw* (< Algonquian, e.g. Massachusett *squa*, Narragansett *squaws*).
  - QU pronounced /k/: *daiquiri* 'cocktail' (< place-name in Cuba); *mosquito* (< Spanish); *palanquin* (also *palankeen*; < Portuguese < Javanese); *tequila* 'alcoholic drink' (< place-name in Mexico).
    - The QU in *conquistador* (< Spanish) is usually pronounced /kw/ in British English and /k/ in American English.
- In final position: There are few words in English written with a final Q, generally technical words from Hebrew, Arabic or Persian with alternative forms written with K: e.g. *nastaliq/nastalik* 'Persian script' (< Persian), *tsaddik/zaddik* 'pious person' (< Hebrew).

### R

In most cases, R in English corresponds to R or some [r]-like sound in the source or carrier languages. In a few examples, the R replaces another sound or letter or has been added into the word at some point in its development. Word-finally and before a consonant, R is no longer pronounced in Standard British English.

- In initial position: *rabbi* (< Hebrew); *raccoon* (< Algonquian *aroughcun*); *raja*, *roti* 'bread' (< Hindi); *raku* 'pottery', *reiki* 'therapy' (< Japanese); *Ramadan* 'Muslim month of fasting' (< Arabic); *ravioli*, *rondo* (< Italian); *rickshaw* (< Japanese *jinrikisha*); *ringgit* 'monetary unit of Malaysia' (< Malay); *robot* (< Czech *robota*); *rodeo* (< Spanish); *rondavel* 'circular hut' (< Afrikaans); *roster* (< Dutch *rooster*); *Rottweiler* 'breed of dog' (< German); *rouble* (< Russian *rublʲ*); *rumba* (< Spanish).
- In medial position: *aardvark* (< Afrikaans); *alfresco*, *opera*, *soprano* (< Italian); *anorak* (< Inuit *anoraq*); *burka* 'Muslim woman's cloak' (also *burqa/burkha/boorka*; < Urdu or Persian); *cherub* (via Greek, Latin and French < Hebrew *kerubh*); *corundum* (< Tamil *kuruntam*); *curare* 'poison, muscle relaxant' (< Spanish and Portuguese, prob. < Carib *kurari*); *durian* 'fruit' (< Malay); *ersatz*, *marzipan*, *sauerkraut*

(< German); *hickory* 'nut, tree' (earlier *pohickory*; < Algonquian *pawcohiccora*); *karate*, *samurai* (< Japanese); *karma* (< Sanskrit); *marimba* 'African xylophone' (< Kimbundu); *marina* (< Italian and Spanish); *sari* (< Hindi); *sarong* (< Malay *sarung*); *tundra* (< Russian); *yurt* 'domed skin tent' (< Russian *yurta*).

- English ER for source language A: *juggernaut* (< Hindi *Jagannath* 'title of god Vishnu') has had the additional R since at least the 17th century.
- English R for source language L: *turban* is ultimately from Persian *dulband*. Forms with both R and L are found in early English borrowings, e.g. *tulipant*, *turbant* in the 17th century.

- In final position: *alligator* (< Spanish *el lagarto* 'the lizard'; for the origin of the final R, comparison with *tater* for *potato* has been suggested); *bazaar* (< Persian *bazar*, prob. via Italian); *caber* 'tree trunk tossed in sport' (< Scottish Gaelic *cabar*); *caviar* (also *caviare*; < obsolete Italian *caviaro*, < Greek or Turkish); *chador* 'woman's head covering' (< Hindi *caddar* < Persian); *hussar* (< Hungarian *huszár*); *kosher* (< Yiddish < Hebrew); *matador*, *toreador* (< Spanish); *shofar* 'ram's horn trumpet' (< Hebrew *shophar*); *zither* (< German).
  - Before a silent E: *claymore* 'large sword' (< Scottish Gaelic *claidheamh mòr*); *commodore* (< Dutch *komandeur*); *crore* '10 million rupees' (< Hindi *karor*); *galore* (< Irish Gaelic *go leor*); *sagamore* 'Native American chief' (< Abenaki *sakema*, *sagamo*); *stevedore* (< Spanish *estivador*); *tussore* 'coarse silk' (< Hindi *tasar*).

## RH

Words spelt with RH in English are mostly derived from Greek (e.g. *rhetoric*, *rhinoceros*). A few words from other sources have gained an H where none is justified etymologically. *Rumba*, the dance (< Spanish *rumba*), is occasionally spelt with an initial RH. *Rhatany* 'astringent substance' is derived from Spanish *ratania* and Portuguese *ratânhia*, from Quechua *ratánya*). The name of the South African antelope, the *rhebok*, derives from Dutch *reebok*, and can be written *reebok*.

## RR

A double R in English may or may not be a reflection of a double R in the source or carrier language; in some cases, a double R in English may be taken as indicating a preceding short vowel.

- In medial position: *arrack* 'alcoholic spirit' (also *arak*; < Arabic *'araq*); *barracuda* 'fish', *corral, guerrilla, sierra* (< Spanish); *curry* (< Tamil and Malayalam *kari*); *gharry* 'small carriage' (< Hindi *gari*); *hurricane* (< Spanish *huracán* < Taino); *knobkerrie* 'club' (< Afrikaans *knopkierie*); *kookaburra* 'Australian bird' (< Wiradhuri *kukubarra*); *sherry* (< Spanish place-name *Xeres*, now *Jerez*); *sporran* 'purse worn with kilt' (< Scottish Gaelic *sporan*); *terracotta* (< Italian); *terrapin* (< Algonquian, e.g. Abenaki *turepé*).

## S

s in English usually corresponds to s or an s-like sound in the source or carrier language, but, as seen below, there are in some cases other underlying sounds.

- In initial position: *sadhu/saddhu* 'holy man' (< Sanskrit); *safari* (< Swahili); *sago* (< Malay *sagu*); *samba* (< Portuguese); *samosa* 'Indian pastry' (< Hindi, Urdu and Persian); *samovar* 'kettle' (< Russian); *sampan* 'boat' (< Cantonese Chinese *saambaan*); *samurai, sushi* (< Japanese); *sangria, sombrero* (< Spanish); *sarsaparilla* 'plant, drink' (< Spanish *zarzaparrilla*); *sash* (originally *shash*; < Arabic *shash*); *sepoy* 'Indian soldier' (poss. via Portuguese < Urdu and Persian *sipahi*); *seraph* (via Latin < Hebrew); *sika* 'deer' (< Japanese *shika*); *ski* (< Norwegian); *skipper* (< Dutch *schipper*); *skunk* (< Abenaki *segankw*); *slogan* (< Scottish Gaelic *sluagh-ghairm*); *smuggle* (< Low German *smuggeln*); *snorkel* (formerly *schnorkel*; < German *Schnorchel*); *sofa* (< Arabic *suffah*); *solo, stanza* (< Italian); *springbok* 'antelope' (< Afrikaans); *steppe* (< Russian *step$^j$*); *strath* 'valley' (< Scottish Gaelic *srath*); *strudel* (< German; sometimes pronounced with initial /ʃ/ as in German); *swindler* (< German *Schwindler*).
  ○ *Sfumato*, a term used in art, and *sforzando*, a term used in music, both from Italian, have an unpredictable sound–spelling correspondence in that initial /sf/ in English is more likely to be associated with Graeco-Latin SPH, as in *sphere, sphincter, sphinx*.
  ○ *Sgraffito*, a term used in art, also from Italian, has an initial consonant cluster that is unusual for English but which has nevertheless a predictable sound–spelling correspondence SGR = /sgr/.
  ○ *Sferics*, from *atmospherics*, is a more common spelling than *spherics*.

275

- ○ *Sgian-dubh* 'Scottish ornamental knife' is pronounced with initial /sk/, as shown by the anglicized spelling *skene-dhu*, thus giving both an unusual initial cluster SG in English and an unexpected sound–spelling correspondence SG = /sk/.
- ○ SV is found in initial position in *svelte* (via French < Italian *svelto*), and in rarer words, or less common forms of words, e.g. *svastika* 'swastika' (< Sanskrit), *sverdrup* 'unit of flow of ocean water' (< Norwegian personal name) and *Svengali* 'controlling person' (< name of character in book).

- In medial position: *castanet* (< Spanish *castañeta*); *easel* (< Dutch *ezel*, German *Esel*); *fiasco* (< Italian); *geyser* (< Icelandic place-name *Geysir*); *ginseng* (< Chinese *jen-shen*); *glasnost* 'openness' (< Russian); *hamster*, *poltergeist* (< German); *kismet* (< Turkish *qismet*); *maestro* (< Italian); *moccasin* (< Algonquian; e.g. Massachusett *mohkisson*, Narragansett *mokussin*); *monsoon* (< Portuguese *monção* < Arabic); *muesli* (< Swiss German); *ombudsman*, *tungsten* (< Swedish); *perestroika* 'reform' (< Russian); *wildebeest* (< Afrikaans *wildebees*).
- ○ *Lasagna* (< Italian) is more often pronounced with a /z/ than an /s/.
- In final position: *adios* (< Spanish); *hummus* (< Turkish *humus*); *kris* 'knife' (< Malay *keris*); *molasses* (< Portuguese *melaço*); *pampas* (taken as singular with final /s/ or as plural with final /z/; < Spanish < Quechua); *sassafras* 'tree, bark and infusion' (< Spanish *sasafrás*); *walrus* (< Dutch).
  - ○ Before a final silent E:
    - Pronounced /s/: *caboose* 'wagon' (prob. < Dutch *kabuis*); *mongoose* (< Marathi *mangus*); *moose* (< Algonquian, e.g. Abenaki *mos*, Narragansett *moos*); *papoose* 'Native American child' (< Algonquian, e.g. Narragansett *papoos*); *vamoose* (< Spanish *vamos*).
    - Pronounced /z/: *cruise* (< Dutch *kruisen*); *flense* 'strip whale meat' (< Dutch *flensen*, Danish and Norwegian *flense*); *fuse* (< Italian *fuso*).

SC

- In initial position:
  - ○ SC pronounced /s/: *scenario* (< Italian); *scimitar* (< Italian *scimitarra*).
  - ○ SC pronounced /sk/: *scampi* (< Italian); *scarp* 'steep slope' (< Italian *scarpa*); *scoop* (< Dutch *schope*); *scope* (< Italian *scopo*); *scow* 'boat' (< Dutch *schouw*); *scum* (< Dutch *schum*).

- In medial position:
  - ○ In Italian loans, SC before front vowels is pronounced /ʃ/ as in Modern Italian: *cognoscenti, crescendo, fascist*.
  - ○ In other words, SC is pronounced /sk/, e.g. *landscape* (< Dutch *landschap*); similarly across a syllable boundary, as in *fresco, fiasco* (< Italian).

### SCH

- In initial position:
  - ○ Pronounced /ʃ/: *schadenfreude, schnauzer* 'breed of dog', *schnitzel* (< German); *schipperke* 'breed of dog' (also /sk/; < Flemish); *schmaltz* (< Yiddish < German *Schmalz*); *schnozzle* 'nose' (prob. < Yiddish *shnoitsl*); *schnapps* (< German *Schnaps*); *schwa* 'the sound [ə]' (< German < Hebrew).
  - ○ Pronounced /sk/: *scherzo* (< Italian); *school* 'fish' (< early Dutch *schole*).
- In medial position:
  - ○ Pronounced /ʃ/ in loans from German: *meerschaum* 'mineral', *pinscher* 'breed of dog', *schottische* 'dance', *Weltanschauung* 'world-view'.
  - ○ Pronounced /ʃ/ or /sk/ in loans from Italian: *bruschetta, maraschino*.
- In final position: *borsch* 'beetroot soup' (< Russian *borshch*); *kirsch* 'alcoholic drink', *kitsch* 'something of low quality or taste', *putsch* 'uprising' (< German).

### SH

- In initial position: *shah* (< Persian); *shako* (< Hungarian *csákó*; perhaps via French); *shampoo* (< Hindi *cāmpo*, where C = [tʃ] and AM represents a nasalized vowel); *shamrock* (< Irish Gaelic *seamróg*); *shanghai* (< Chinese place-name); *shawl* (< Urdu < Persian *shal*); *shekel* (< Hebrew *sheqel*); *sheikh* (< Arabic *shaikh*); *sherpa* (< Tibetan *sharpa*); *sherry* (< Spanish; name of town of *Xeres*, now Jerez, the Spanish x formerly being pronounced [ʃ] and the word being introduced into English as *sherries*, then interpreted as a plural); *shillelagh* 'club' (< Irish place-name); *shogun* 'military leader' (< Japanese); *shufti* 'quick look' (< Arabic); *shul* 'synagogue' (< Yiddish; also *schul*).
  - ○ *Shchi* 'cabbage soup' (/ʃtʃiː/; also written *shtchi*, etc.; < Russian) has a particularly 'exotic' initial consonant group.
- In medial position: *ashram* (< Sanskrit *ashrama*); *banshee* 'wailing fairy' (< Irish Gaelic *bean sídhe*); *bolshevik* (< Russian); *bushido* 'samurai code',

277

*geisha* (< Japanese); *cushy* (< Hindi *khush, khushi*); *kosher* (< Yiddish < Hebrew); *pasha* 'title of nobility' (< Turkish); *rishi* 'sage' (< Sanskrit); *shashlik* 'lamb kebab' (< Russian); *yashmak* 'veil' (< Arabic *yashmaq*).

○ *Dachshund* is strictly speaking not an example of medial sh, deriving as it does from German *Dachs+hund* 'badger-dog', but is often in English pronounced with a medial /ʃ/.

• In final position: *baksheesh* 'gift; tip' (also *bakhshish*; etc.; < Persian *bakhshish*); *dervish* (< Turkish < Persian *darvish*); *goulash* (< Hungarian *gulyás*); *hashish* (< Arabic); *nosh* 'food' (< Yiddish *nashn*); *shahtoosh* 'shawl' (< Punjabi *shatush*); *squash* 'vegetable' (< Narragansett *askutasquash*); *tush* 'buttocks' (< Yiddish *tokhes*).

## SJ

• In initial position, pronounced /ʃ/: *sjambok* 'whip' (< Afrikaans < Malay < Urdu).

## SS

• In medial position: *assegai* (< Portuguese *azagaia* < Arabic, ult. < Berber); *bossa nova* 'dance' (< Portuguese); *cassava* 'plant' (< Spanish *cazabe* < Taino; poss. influenced by French *cassave*); *cassowary* 'bird' (< Malay *kesuari*); *Cossack* (< Russian *kazak*, Ukrainian *kozak* < Turkic); *delicatessen* (< German *Delikatessen*); *espresso, generalissimo* (< Italian); *messiah* (via Latin and Greek < Aramaic *meshikha*, Hebrew *mashiakh*); *molasses* (< Portuguese *melaço*; spelling poss. influenced by French *mélasse*); *passacaglia* (< Italian < Spanish *pasacalle*); *sargasso* (< Portuguese *sargaço*).

○ *Hussar* (< Hungarian *huszár*) has the same sound–symbol correspondence ss = /z/ as in *possess*.

• In final position: *blunderbuss* 'gun' (< Dutch *donderbus*); *boss* (< Dutch *baas*); *edelweiss* 'flower', *gneiss* 'rock', *loess* 'soil' (< German); *isinglass* 'fish gelatine' (prob. < obsolete Dutch *huisenblas*); *kvass* 'rye beer' (also with single s; < Russian *kvas*); *morass* (< Dutch *morasch* (later *moeras*) or Low German *moras*).

## T

In general, t reflects a t or [t] in the source or carrier language.

- In initial position: *taboo* (< Tongan *tabu*); *taco, tortilla* 'Mexican food' (< Spanish)' *tahini* 'sesame paste' (via Greek < Arabic); *taiga* 'forest' (< Russian); *tamarind* 'fruit' (< Spanish and Portuguese < Arabic); *tandoori* 'Indian cooking style' (< Urdu and Punjabi *tandur*); *taoiseach* 'Irish prime minister' (< Irish Gaelic); *tattoo* 'design' (< Tahitian *tatau*); *tepee/teepee/tipi* 'Native American tent' (< Dakota *tipi*); *tofu* (< Japanese); *tomahawk* (< Renape *tamahak*); *torso* (< Italian); *tornado* (< Spanish *tronado*); *torte* 'flat tart' (< German); *trap* 'rock' (< Swedish *trapp*); *trek* (< Afrikaans *trekken*); *trews* 'tartan trousers' (< Scottish Gaelic *triubhas*); *tush* 'buttocks' (< Yiddish *tokhes*); *tycoon* (< Japanese *taikun*).
  - For *t'ai chi/taiji* 'Chinese physical exercise', see the note on Chinese transcription, p. 231.
- In medial position: *batik* (< Malay < Javanese); *catamaran* (< Tamil *kattumaram*); *cheetah, chutney* (< Hindi *cita, catni*); *cockatoo* (< Dutch *kakatoe* < Malay); *concerto, oratorio, stanza* (< Italian); *futon* 'bed' (< Japanese); *hinterland, leitmotiv* (< German); *mahatma* 'title of honour' (< Sanskrit *mahatman*); *margarita* 'cocktail', *siesta, tortilla* (< Spanish); *shantung* 'fabric' (< Chinese place-name, now usually *Shandong*); *perestroika* 'reform', *sputnik, steppe* (< Russian); *yeti* 'Himalayan creature' (< Tibetan *yeh-teh*).
- In final position: *angst, diktat* (< German); *bandit* (< Italian *bandito*); *castanet* (< Spanish *castañeta*); *cot* 'bed' (< Hindi *khat*); *duet, fascist* (< Italian); *juggernaut* (< Hindi *Jagannath* 'title of god Vishnu'); *kaput* (< German *kaputt*); *kumquat* 'fruit' (< Cantonese Chinese *gam gwat*); *mart* 'market' (< Dutch *marct/mart*); *pundit* (< Hindi *pandit* < Sanskrit *pandita*); *rant* (< Dutch *randen, ranten*); *robot* (< Czech *robota*); *sherbet, yogurt* (< Turkish); *snout* (< Dutch or Low German *snut*); *glasnost* 'openness', *soviet* (< Russian); *wombat* 'Australian animal' (< Dharuk *wambat*).
  - *Gauntlet* as in 'run the gauntlet' is an altered form of Swedish *gatlopp* under the influence of *gauntlet* 'glove' (< French).
  - Phonologically final before a silent E: *caste* (< Spanish and Portuguese *casta*); *chocolate, mesquite* 'spiny tree' (< Spanish < Nahuatl; see note on Spanish-derived final E on p. 247); *granite* (< Italian *granito*); *jute* (< Hindi and Bengali *jut*); *malamute* 'breed of dog' (< Inuit *malemiut*); *skate* (< Dutch *schaats*, taken to be a plural form in English; compare *sherry* < *sherries*).

## TCH

See also under 'CH'.

- In medial position: *apparatchik* 'bureaucrat' (< Russian); *ketchup* (< Malay *kechap* and/or Amoy Chinese *ke-tsiap*); *litchi* (also *lychee/lichee*; < Chinese *li-chi*); *patchouli* 'plant, perfume' (< Tamil *pacculi*).
  - *Datcha* is a less common spelling of *dacha* 'cottage' (< Russian *dacha*).
- In final position: *etch* (< Dutch *etsen*); *kvetch* 'complain' (< Yiddish); *potlatch* 'Native American ceremony' (< Chinook Jargon *patlach*); *nautch* 'Indian dance' (< Hindi *nac*, where c = [tʃ]); *sketch* (< Dutch *schets*).

## TH

- In initial position:
  - Pronounced /θ/: *thug* (< Hindi *thag*, in which TH = [t - h]).
  - Pronounced /t/: *thar* 'Himalayan goat' (< Nepali). Similarly for *Thai*.
- In medial position, pronounced /ð/: *smithereens* (poss. < Irish Gaelic *smidirín*); *zither* (< German).
  - A word such as *apartheid* is not an example of medial TH as the TH occurs across a word-break: *apartheid* = *apart-heid* 'apart-hood'.
  - The form *Neanderthal*, in which TH = /t/, is attested in English from 1861, when *Thal* was the spelling for the German word for 'valley'; but since 1902 German has written the word as *Tal*, and the modern form *Neandertal* is today also found in English.
  - *Algorithm* derives from Arabic via French; its modern form has been influenced by Greek *arithmos* 'number'.
- In final position: *mammoth* (< Russian *mamont*, formerly *mamant*; the TH may have entered English via Dutch and German); *Sabbath*, *shibboleth* (directly or ult. < Hebrew); *strath* 'valley' (< Scottish Gaelic *srath*).
  - *Behemoth* and *leviathan* are two monstrous animals mentioned in the Bible. *Behemoth* represents Hebrew *behemoth*; *leviathan* comes to us via Latin from Hebrew *livyathan*.

## TS

- In initial position: *tsaddik* 'righteous person' (also *zaddik*, *tzaddik*, etc.; < Hebrew); *tsar* (also *tzar*, *czar*; < Russian); *tsunami* 'huge wave' (< Japanese).

○ The initial consonant cluster of *tsetse* 'fly' (via Afrikaans < Tswana) is often simplified from /ts/ to /t/. The corresponding spelling *tetse* is at best non-standard, but usually simply a spelling error.

• In medial position: *intelligentsia* (< Russian); *ju-jitsu* (< Japanese *jujutsu*); *netsuke* 'clothing ornament', *shiatsu* (< Japanese).

TT

• In medial position, generally following a stressed short vowel; = /t/: *annatto* 'dye' (< Carib); *attar* 'fragrant oil' (also *ottar*, *otto*; < Persian *'atir* < Arabic); ATTO- 'to the power of minus 18' (< Danish and Norwegian *atten*); *chapatti* (< Hindi *capati*); *gutta-percha* (< Malay *getah-percha*); *harmattan* 'West African wind' (< Twi *haramata*); *mulatto, palmetto* palm tree' (< Spanish *mulato, palmito*); *potto* 'African animal' (< an African language, e.g. Wolof *pata*); *rattan* 'cane' (< Malay *rotan*); *schottische* 'dance' (< German); *suttee* 'burning of widow on husband's funeral pyre' (also *sati*; < Sanskrit *sati*); *tattoo* 'design' (< Tahitian *tatau*); *tattoo* 'military display' (< Dutch *taptoe*).

○ Many English words ending in TT plus a simple vowel derive from Italian: among these are *amaretto* 'liqueur', *confetti, dilettante, ditto, falsetto, ghetto, grotto* (< Italian *grotta*), *latte, libretto, motto, regatta, risotto, spaghetti, stiletto, vendetta*.

TZ

Most of the words in this category derive from German, Yiddish or Hebrew.

• In initial position: *tzaddik* 'sage' (see other spellings at *zaddik*; < Hebrew); *tzar* (also *tsar, czar*; < Russian); *tzimmes* 'vegetable stew' (also *tsimmes*; < Yiddish *tsimes*).

• In medial position: *bar mitzvah* (< Hebrew); *chutzpah* (< Yiddish *khutspe* < Hebrew); *glitzy* (prob. < German *glitzern*); *matzo* (also *matzoh*; < Yiddish *matse* < Hebrew); *pretzel* (< German *Brezel/Bretzel*); *schnitzel* (< German); *seltzer* (< German *Selterser*; from the place-name Nieder-Selters); *shih-tzu* 'breed of dog' (< Chinese); *spritzer* 'alcoholic drink' (< German).

○ For *howitzer*, see under 'ow'.

• In final position: *blitz* (< German); *chintz* 'fabric' (< Hindi *chint*; as the plural of *chint*, originally written *chints*; first written *chintz* in the late 18th century; perhaps by analogy with *quartz*, etc.); *ersatz*

281

(< German); *glitz* (from *glitzy*); *hertz* (< German personal name); *kibbutz* (< Hebrew *qibbuts*); *schmaltz* (< Yiddish < German *Schmalz*); *spitz* 'breed of dog' (< German).

○  *Quartz* and *waltz* reflect the German spelling at the times of borrowing (17th and 18th centuries respectively); German today writes *Quarz, Walzer.*

# U

U generally corresponds to a U or [u] in the source or carrier languages.

- In initial position:
  ○ Pronounced /uː/ or /ʊ/: *umiak* 'Eskimo boat' (< Inuit *umiaq*); *umlaut* 'mark indicating sound change' (< German).
    ▪ In *ulema* 'Muslim theologians' (< Arabic, Turkish and Persian *'ulema*) and *umma* 'Muslim community' (< Arabic *'umma*), the initial consonant letter of Arabic *'ulema* and *'umma* has been lost in the English spelling of the word. (Compare the comment on *afrit* and *ankh* under 'A' at 'In initial position'.)
  ○ Pronounced /juː/: *ukulele* (< Hawaiian).
  ○ Pronounced /ʌ/: *umbrella* (< Italian *ombrella*).
- In medial position:
  ○ Pronounced /uː/ or /ʊ/: *bulwark* (< early Dutch *bolwerc*); *chutzpah* (< Yiddish *khutspe* < Hebrew); *hula* (< Hawaiian); *hussar* (also /hə-/; < Hungarian *huszár*); *influenza* (< Italian); *judo, sushi* (< Japanese); *jute* (< Hindi and Bengali *jut*); *kaput* (< German *kaputt*); *kibbutz* (< Hebrew *qibbuts*); *ombudsman* (< Swedish); *samurai* (also /jʊ/; < Japanese); *supremo* (also /juː/; < Spanish); *sputnik* (also /ʌ/; < Russian).
  ○ Pronounced /juː/: *barracuda, tuna* (both usually /juː/ but also /uː/; < Spanish); *studio* (< Italian).
  ○ Pronounced /ʌ/, or /ə/ when unstressed: *buffalo* (< Italian *bufalo*, Spanish *búfalo*); *chipmunk* (< Algonquian, poss. Ojibwa *achitamon*); *corundum* (< Tamil *kuruntam*); *felucca* 'boat' (< Italian *feluc(c)a*); *junk* 'boat' (< Portuguese *junco* < Javanese *djong*); *luck* (< early Dutch *luc/luk*, Low German *lucke*); *mullah* 'Muslim cleric' (also /mʊ-/; < Persian and Urdu *mulla*, Turkish *molla* < Arabic); *mumbo-jumbo* (prob. < a West African language, e.g. Mandingo *mama dyumbo*);

*mustang* (< Spanish *mestengo*); *smuggle* (< Low German *smuggeln*); *tungsten* (< Swedish); *walrus* (< Dutch).

○ With a following R before another consonant, pronounced /ɜː/ or /ə/: *burka/burqa/burkha/boorka* 'Muslim woman's cloak' (< Urdu or Persian); *furlough* (< Dutch *verlof*); *jodhpurs* (< place-name in India); *mazurka* 'dance' (< Polish); *yoghurt/yogurt* (< Turkish *yogurt*). For *turban*, see the note under 'R', p. 274.

▪ In words from Arabic beginning with MU-, the pronunciation varies: *muezzin* (/muː-/ or /mjuː-/), *mujahedin* (/muː-/), *muslim* (/mʊ-/ or /mʌ-/).

▪ The pronunciation of *rucksack* varies, the RUCK- being sometimes given a German value like English *rook*, but sometimes anglicized to rhyme with *luck*. Similarly with the *Bunsen burner*, named after its German inventor Robert Bunsen, which may be pronounced in the German manner /ˈbʊnzn/ or, more often, anglicized as /ˈbʌnsn/.

▪ One particular feature of borrowings from the languages of the Indian subcontinent is the use of English U = /ʌ/ for short A in the source language: *bungalow* (< Hindustani *bangla*), *chutney* (< Hindi *catni*), *curry* (< Tamil and Malayalam *kari*), *juggernaut* (< Hindi *Jagannath* 'title of god Vishnu'), *jungle* (< Hindi and Marathi *jangal*), and similarly *chukka, cummerbund, dungaree, pukka, punch, pundit, thug*. *Mung* 'bean' (< Hindi) may be pronounced /mʌŋ/ or /muːŋ/ and with the latter pronunciation may also be written *moong*.

▪ A similar U < A derivation is seen in some words from other sources: e.g. *ketchup* (< Malay *kechap* and/or Amoy Chinese *ke-tsiap*); *skunk* (< Abenaki *segankw*).

▪ Spanish-derived *junta* may be said with an anglicized pronunciation /ˈdʒʌntə/, a more Spanish-like pronunciation /ˈhʊntə/, or something between the two /ˈdʒʊntə/.

▪ For *feng shui*, see under 'E' at 'In medial position'.

• In final position: Word-final U does not occur in long-established English words, but is encountered in loans from various languages: e.g. *impromptu, menu* from French, *flu* as an abbreviation of Italian *influenza, in situ* from Latin. In this position U is always pronounced long, usually with a preceding /j/.

○ Pronounced /uː/: *babu* 'respectful title for man in India' (< Hindi); *haiku, sudoku, tofu* (< Japanese); *ju-jitsu, kung fu* (< Chinese); *sadhu*

283

'holy man' (also *saddhu*; < Sanskrit *sadhu*); *shih-tzu* 'breed of dog' (< Chinese); *uhuru* 'freedom' (< Swahili).

- A number of words with final U can be, or have in the past been, written with oo: *gnu* 'African antelope' (< Khoikhoi *t'gnu*), spelt *gnoo* in one 18th-century source; *guru*/(formerly) *gooroo* (< Hindi); *Hindu*/(formerly) *Hindoo*; *igloo*/(rarely) *iglu* (< Inuit *iglu*); *kudus*/(less commonly) *koodoo* 'African antelope' (< Afrikaans *koedoe*); *taboo*/(less commonly) *tabu* (< Tongan *tabu*).
  ○ Pronounced /juː/: *coypu* 'South American animal' (/uː/ or /juː/; < Spanish *coipú* < Araucanian); *emu* (prob. < Portuguese *ema*).

### UE

See also 'GU', 'QU' and 'UH and ÜH'.

- In medial position: *muesli* is from Swiss German *Müesli* (also *Muesli*, *Müsli*); the UE is pronounced /juː/ or /uː/. In *pueblo* (< Spanish), the UE is usually pronounced /wɛ/ but may be pronounced as two syllables.
- In final position: *barbecue* (also written *barbeque*) is of Caribbean origin, reaching English via Spanish, and in the 17th century was spelt without E.

### UH and ÜH

Only one of the following words is at all common, but they serve to illustrate two spellings that English has inherited from German, UH and ÜH. The capital letters at *Glühwein* and *Sprachgefühl* (normal in German nouns, and once standard in English as well) suggest that these words have not yet been fully naturalized in English:

- UH: *gluhwein* 'mulled wine' (in which UH = /uː/; also *Glühwein*, in which ÜH = /yː/ as in the German pronunciation of the word); *kieselguhr* 'mineral' (also *kieselgur*); *uhlan* 'cavalryman'.
- ÜH: *führer* 'Nazi leader' (also written *fuehrer*, and often with a capital F; ÜH = /yː/ as in German or anglicized as /jʊə/); *Sprachgefühl* 'feeling for a language'.

### UI

Most examples of UI in the exotic category are in words from Dutch or Afrikaans, with various pronunciations: *cruise* (< Dutch *kruisen*);

*duiker* 'antelope' (< Afrikaans; UI = /aɪ/); *guilder* 'coin' (< Dutch *gulden*; UI = /ɪ/).

- *Uillean pipes* 'Irish bagpipes' (*uillean* pronounced /'ɪljɪn/ or /'uːlɪən/; < Irish Gaelic *píob uilleann* 'elbow pipe').

### UU

To find examples of UU in English, one is forced to hunt well beyond the bounds of everyday English vocabulary, but the following three words are found in English dictionaries: the *busuuti* (/buː'suːtɪ/; < Luganda) is a type of Ugandan dress; *muumuu*, the name of a Hawaiian dress, is pronounced as four syllables (*mu-u-mu-u*) in Hawaiian but is a two-syllable word in English, /'muːmuː/; a *puukko*, pronounced /'puːkəʊ/, is a Finnish knife.

- *Weltanschauung* 'world-view' is from German; the two U's are split across a syllable boundary: *-schau-ung* (as in the related English word *show-ing*).

### V

v in English generally corresponds to v or [v] in the source or carrier languages, but may have other origins.

- In initial position: *vamoose* (< Spanish *vamos*); *vampire* (via French < Hungarian *vampir*); *vanilla* (< Spanish *vaynilla*; now spelt *vainilla*); *veld* (< Afrikaans); *vendetta*, *volcano* (< Italian); *verandah/veranda* (< Hindi *varanda* < Portuguese); *vigilante* (< Spanish); *viscacha* (< Spanish *vizcacha* < Quechua); *vodka* (< Russian); *vole* (< Norwegian *vollmus*).
  - *Veneer*, first found at the beginning of the 18th century in the form *fineer*, shows considerable distortion from German *Furnier*, itself derived from French *fournir*.
  - In many words from German and Afrikaans, an initial v may be pronounced /f/ rather than /v/: *verboten* 'forbidden' (< German); *volk* 'people', *vrou* 'woman' (< Afrikaans).
- In medial position: *avocado* (< Spanish, formerly *avocado*, now written *abogado*; ult. < Nahuatl *ahuacatl*); *anchovy* (< Spanish and Portuguese *anchova*); *avatar* (< Sanskrit *avatara*); *bravo*, *lava* (< Italian); *caravan* (in 16th-century *karouan*; ult. < Persian *karwan*; perhaps influenced

by French *caravane*, Italian *caravana*); *dervish* (< Turkish < Persian *darvish*); *divan* (< Turkish < Persian *diwan*); *guava* (< Spanish *guayaba*); *maven* 'expert' (< Yiddish *meyvn* < Hebrew); *palaver* (< Portuguese *palavra*); *soviet* (< Russian); *stevedore* (< Spanish *estivador*).

- ◦ See also 'KV'.
- In final position: There are few words with final v in English. The commonest one is probably *Slav*. Some are of uncertain origin: *chiv/shiv* 'knife' may or may not derive from Romany *chiv*. *Mazeltov* 'congratulations' is from Yiddish *mazltov*, from Hebrew.
  - ◦ The final v is generally pronounced /v/ in the Russian names *Kalashnikov* 'rifle' and *Molotov* (as in *Molotov cocktail* 'hand-thrown bomb') and in *leitmotiv* (< German; also spelt *leitmotif*).
  - ◦ Phonologically final before a silent E: *groove* (< Dutch *groeve*); *mangrove* (< Spanish or Portuguese; prob. < a Caribbean language); *margrave* 'title of nobility' (< Dutch *marcgrave*); *recitative* (< Italian *recitativo*).

# W

w in English generally corresponds to w or a w-like sound in the source or carrier languages.

- In initial position: *wadi* 'valley' (< Arabic); *wagon* (< Dutch *wagen*); *wallah* 'person' (< Hindi *-wala*); *wallaroo* 'large kangaroo' (< Dharuk *wolaru*); *waltz* (< German *Walzer*); *wasabi* 'root used in cookery' (< Japanese); *wentletrap* 'marine snail' (< Dutch *wenteltrap*); *wiki* 'Internet system' (< Hawaiian *wikiwiki*); *wickiup* 'Native American hut' (< Algonquian, e.g. Fox *wikiyapi*); *wildebeest* (< Afrikaans *wildebees*); *wok* 'cooking pan' (< Cantonese Chinese); *wombat* 'Australian animal' (< Dharuk *wambat*); *woodchuck* 'American marmot' (< Algonquian, such as Cree *otcheck*, Narragansett *ockqutchaun*, the initial syllable becoming 'wood-' by folk etymology).
  - ◦ Silent before R: *wrasse* 'fish' (prob. < Cornish *wrach*).
- In medial position: *bulwark* (< early Dutch *bolwerc*); *bwana* (< Swahili); *cassowary* 'bird' (< Malay *kesuari*); *fatwa* 'religious decree' (< Arabic); *gurdwara* 'Sikh place of worship' (< Punjabi *gurduara*); *kiwi* (< Maori); *kwashiorkor* 'malnutrition in children' (< Ga *kwashioko*); *mugwump* 'important person' (< Massachusett *mugquomp*); *ngwee* 'Zambian currency' (< Chichewa); *salwar* or *shalwar* 'trousers' (< Hindi *salwar*,

Urdu *shalwar*); *swami* 'religious teacher' (< Hindi *svami*); *swastika* (< Sanskrit *svastika*); *wigwam* (< Algonquian, e.g. Ojibwa *wigwaum*)

○ See also under 'AW', 'EW', 'OW'.

○ In words of Welsh origin which retain the Welsh spelling, w may function as a vowel or a consonant: *cwm* /kʊm/ or /kuːm/ 'mountain hollow', *gwyniad* /ˈgwɪnɪæd/ 'species of fish' and *hwyl* /ˈhuːɪl/ 'emotional fervour'.

• In final position: see under 'AW', 'EW', 'OW'.

• Nouns from German vary between /w/ and /v/ for w. For example, the w of *wiener* 'sausage' is pronounced /w/, but more often as /v/ in *Wiener schnitzel*. *Wurst* 'sausage' may have initial /w/ or /v/. *Edelweiss* 'flower' has /v/. *Wolfram* 'tungsten' is fully anglicized with initial /w/, as is *wanderlust*, but *wunderkind* more often has the /v/ of German than the /w/ of English. *Weltanschauung* 'world-view' has /v/. *Weimaraner* and *Rottweiler* 'breeds of dog' can be pronounced with /w/ or /v/, but /v/ is more usual. *Wehrmacht* 'German army' has initial /v/, but *Luftwaffe* 'German air force' has /v/ or /w/. See also *gluhwein* under 'UH'. For *howitzer* see under 'OW'.

## WH

The source words underlying WH have a variety of spellings.

• In initial position: *whangee* 'bamboo' (< Chinese *huang* or *huang-li*); *whiskey/whisky* (< Irish Gaelic *uisce beatha(dh)*, Scottish Gaelic *uisge beatha*); *whiting* 'fish' (< Dutch *wijting*).

○ *Whydah* 'species of bird' is from English *widow* with spelling influenced by the name of the town in Benin now spelt Ouidah.

• In medial position: *kowhai* 'shrub' (< Maori); *narwhal* (also *narwal*; < Norwegian and Danish *narhval*, Swedish *narval*, Dutch *narwal*).

## WW

In *qawwali* 'Muslim religious music' (< Urdu, Persian and Arabic), the ww may be pronounced as either /v/ or /w/.

## X

• In initial position, x is mostly associated with words of Greek origin formed with elements such as XENO-, XERO-, XYLO-. *Xebec* (also written *zebec*), the name of a type of boat, comes ultimately from Arabic *shabbak*, but the form of the word in English has been influenced by French and Spanish.

- In medial position: *axolotl* 'salamander' (< Nahuatl); *dixie* 'container' (< Hindi *degci*).
- In final position: *lox* 'smoked salmon' (< Yiddish *laks*); *nix* (< German *nichts*).

## Y

- As a consonant, y in English generally corresponds to y or [j] in the source or carrier languages, but may have other origins:
  - In initial position: *yacht* (< early Dutch *jaght*); *yak* (< Tibetan *gyag*); *yakuza* 'criminal' (< Japanese); *yam* (< Portuguese *inhame*, archaic Spanish *iñame*); *yarmulka* 'skullcap' (< Yiddish < Polish); *yashmak* 'veil' (< Arabic *yashmaq*); *yen* 'desire' (prob. < Cantonese Chinese *yahn*); *yeti* 'Himalayan creature' (< Tibetan *yeh-teh*); *yodel* (< German *jodeln*; German J = /j/); *yoga* (< Sanskrit); *yogurt/yoghurt/yoghourt* (< Turkish *yogurt*); *yucca* (< Spanish *yuca* < Taino); *yurt* 'domed skin tent' (< Russian *yurta*).
  - In medial position: *ayah* 'nurse' (< Hindi *aya* < Portuguese); *ayatollah* 'Muslim cleric' (< Persian < Arabic); *banyan* 'tree' (< Portuguese *banian* < Arabic); *canyon* (< Spanish *cañon*); *keffiyeh* 'Arab head-dress' (< Arabic *keffiya*, *kuffiya*); *kyu* 'grade in judo' (< Japanese); *sukiyaki*, *teriyaki* 'Japanese food' (< Japanese); see also 'AY', 'EY', 'OY'.
  - In final position: see under 'AY', 'EY', 'OY'.
- As a vowel, y in English generally corresponds to a written y or a spoken /j/, /iː/, /ɪ/ or /aɪ/ in the source or carrier languages, but may have other origins:
  - In initial position: *ylang-ylang* (y = /iː/; also *ilang-ilang*; < Tagalog); *yttrium* and *ytterbium* 'chemical elements' (y = /ɪ/; < *Ytterby*, Swedish place-name).
  - In medial position:
    - Pronounced /ɪ/: *biryani* (also *biriyani*, *biriani*; y = /ɪ/ or /j/; < Hindi); *gymkhana* (< Urdu *gend-khana*; with the first syllable refashioned by association with Greek GYM- as in *gymnastics*); *gwyniad* /'gwɪnɪæd/ 'species of fish', *hwyl* /'huːɪl/ 'emotional fervour' (< Welsh); *pyjamas* (< Urdu *pay-jama*/

288

*pa-jama*); *tympani*, an alternative spelling of *timpani* 'kettledrums' (< Italian, plural of *timpano*), presumably influenced by the Latin source word *tympanum*.

- Pronounced /aɪ/: *lychee* (also *litchi*/*lichee*; also /ˈlɪ-/; < Chinese *li-chi*); *mynah*/*myna* 'Indian bird' (also *mina*; < Hindi *maina*); *tycoon* (< Japanese *taikun*); *typhoon* (see note under 'PH').
  - In final position: *anchovy* (< Spanish and Portuguese *anchova*); *balcony* (< Italian *balcone*); *brandy* (< Dutch *brandewijn*); *caddy*, *lory* 'parrot' (< Malay *kati*, *luri*); *curry* (< Tamil and Malayalam *kari*); *cushy* (< Hindi *khush*, *khushi*); *dinghy* (< Hindi and Bengali *dingi*); *droshky* 'carriage' (< Russian *droshki*); *hickory* (earlier *pohickory*; < Algonquian *pawcohiccora*); *husky* 'dog' (< Newfoundland English *Huskemaw*, < the same root as *Eskimo*, see p. 256); *sherry* (earlier *sherris*, later taken to be a plural noun, as with *skate* < Dutch *schaats*; < Spanish place-name *Xeres*, now *Jerez*); *zany* (poss. via French < Italian *zani*, *zanni*).
    - *Whisky*/*whiskey* (< Irish Gaelic *uisce beatha(dh)*, Scottish Gaelic *uisge beatha*): by tradition, Scotch *whisky* and Irish *whiskey* are distinguished in spelling; similarly, the Canadian drink is generally written *whisky*, the American *whiskey*.

## z

z in English generally corresponds to z or [z] in the source or carrier languages, but may have other origins. See also under 'CZ', 'DZ', 'TZ'.

- In initial position:
  - Pronounced /z/: *zakat* 'Islamic tithe' (< Persian); *zany* (poss. via French < Italian *zani*, *zanni*); *zebra* (< Italian or Portuguese); *zen* (< Japanese); *ziggurat* 'Mesopotamian pyramid' (< Assyrian *ziqquratu*); *zinc*, *zither* (< German); *zombie* (< a West African language; e.g. Kikongo *zumbi* fetish, *nzambi* god); *zucchini* (< Italian).
    - *Zloty* 'Polish currency' (< Polish) has an unusual (for English) initial consonant cluster, but the sound–spelling correspondence is a predictable ZL = /zl/.
  - Pronounced /ts/: *zaddik* 'righteous person' (also *tsaddik*, *tzaddik*; < Hebrew *tsaddiq*); *zeitgeist* 'intellectual climate' (< German).
- In medial position, generally pronounced /z/: *azuki* 'bean' (also *aduki*, *adzuki*, *adsuki*; < Japanese); *bazaar* (< Persian *bazar*, prob. via Italian);

*banzai* 'Japanese cheer', *kamikaze*, *yakuza* 'criminal' (< Japanese); *bonanza*, *gazpacho* 'soup' (< Spanish); *borzoi* 'dog' (< Russian); *cadenza*, *influenza*, *stanza* (< Italian; all with /z/, but in *scherzo* z = /ts/); *chimpanzee* (via French < Kikongo *chimpenzi*); *Kwanzaa* 'African-American festival' (< Swahili); *marzipan* (< German); *mazuma* 'money' (< Yiddish *mezumen* < Hebrew); *mazurka* 'dance' (< Polish); *panzer* 'German tank', *schnauzer* 'breed of dog' (< German; in both cases z = /z/ as in core English or /ts/ as in German); *plaza* (< Spanish); *samizdat* 'clandestine literature' (< Russian); *vizier* 'government official' (< Turkish *vezir* < Arabic).
- In final position: *fez* (via French < Moroccan place-name); *kameez* 'tunic' (also *kamees*; Urdu *kamis* < Arabic); *kolkhoz* 'collective farm in USSR' (< Russian).
  - Phonologically final before a silent E: *booze* (< Dutch *busen*); *maize* (< former Spanish *mahiz*, now *maíz* < Taino *mahiz*); *schmooze* 'chat' (< Yiddish *shmues* < Hebrew).

### ZH

- In initial position, *zho* 'Tibetan ox' (also written *zo*, *dzo*; etc.; pronounced /zəʊ/ or /ʒəʊ/; < Tibetan *mdso*).
- In medial position, *muzhik* 'Russian peasant' (ZH = /ʒ/; < Russian).

### ZS

In medial position, *vizsla* 'breed of dog' (in which ZS = (/ʒ/; < Hungarian place-name).

### ZZ

In words of Italian derivation, ZZ is generally pronounced /ts/, sometimes alternatively /dz/; in non-Italian words, /z/.

- In medial position:
  - Pronounced /ts/, all from Italian: *intermezzo* (also /dz/), *mezzo* 'singer', *mozzarella* 'cheese', *palazzo* 'mansion', *paparazzi*, *piazza* (also /dz/), *pizza*, *pizzicato* 'musical instruction'.
  - Pronounced /z/: *jacuzzi/Jacuzzi* (< family name of inventor); *mizzen* 'sail' (< Italian *mezzana*); *muezzin* (< Arabic *mu'adhdhin*; the ZZ represents a regional pronunciation with /z/ rather than

classical Arabic /ð/); *schemozzle* 'muddle, rumpus' (poss. < Yiddish *shlimazl*); *schnozzle* 'nose' (prob. < Yiddish *shnoitsl*).

# Notes

1   This use of 'exotic' is not the same as that of Carney (1994), though many words with spellings belonging to Carney's 'Exotic' subsystem of English orthography will be covered in this chapter.
2   Languages referred to in this chapter and with which the reader may not be familiar are listed below:

Abenaki – a Native American language
Aleut – a language of the Aleutian Islands
Algonquian – a family of North American languages
Aramaic – a language closely related to Hebrew
Araucanian – a language of South America
Arawak – a group of languages spoken in Central and South America
Aymara – a language of South America
Balti – a language of Kashmir
Carib – a language of the Caribbean area
Chichewa – the national language of Zambia
Chinook Jargon – a Native American lingua franca
Choctaw – a Native American language
Cree – a Native American language
Dakota – a Native American language, a dialect of Sioux
Dharuk – an Australian Aboriginal language
Dhivehi – the language of the Maldives
Dzongkha – the national language of Bhutan
Evenki – a language spoken in Russia, Mongolia and China
Ewe – a language of West Africa
Fox – a Native American language
Ga – a language of West Africa
Gamilaraay – an Australian Aboriginal language
Guarani – a language of South America
Guugu Yimidhirr – an Australian Aboriginal language
Hopi – a Native American language
Igbo – a language of West Africa
Inuit – the language of the Eskimos of Greenland, northern Canada and Alaska.
Khoikhoi – a language of southern Africa
Kikongo – a language of West Africa
Kimbundu – a language of Angola

Lepcha – a language of Sikkim
Low German – a language of northern Germany related to Dutch
Luganda – the main language of Uganda
Malayalam – a language of southern India
Mandingo – a West African language
Marathi – a language spoken in western and central India
Massachusett – a Native American language
Mbuba – a language of Central Africa
Micmac – a Native American language
Nahuatl – the language of the Aztecs in Mexico
Narragansett – a Native American language
Nenets – a Siberian language
Nyungar – an Australian Aboriginal language
Ojibwa – a Native American language
Omaha – a Native American language
Pali – the Indian language of many early Buddhist scriptures
Quechua – a language of South America
Renape – a Native American language
Shawnee – a Native American language
Shona – a language of southern Africa
Tagalog – a language spoken in the Philippines
Taino – an extinct language of the Caribbean area
Tamil – a language of southern India and Sri Lanka
Telugu – a language of southern India
Tswana – a language of southern Africa
Tungus – a language of Siberia
Tupi – a language of South America
Turkic – a family of languages including Turkish and Tatar
Twi – a West African language
Wiradhuri – an Australian Aboriginal language
Wolof – a West African language
Yuwaaliyaay – an Australian Aboriginal language

3 For a description of the world's writing systems, see for example Coulmas (1989) and Sampson (1985).

4 The system of transliteration for Chinese developed by Sir Thomas Wade, first professor of Chinese at Cambridge University, and modified by his successor Herbert Giles. It has largely been replaced by the Pinyin romanization developed in the People's Republic of China in the 1950s.

# 9

# Reformers, Lexicographers and the Parting of the Ways

Early steps in spelling reform (in Orm's *Ormulum*; see p. 74) and spelling standardization (in the rise of Chancery usage; see p. 81) have already been discussed. The former had no influence on the development of English spelling, while Chancery usage was to a great extent adopted by the early printers, and thus were fixed – for better or for worse – many of the spellings that have come down to us today.

Moves towards standardization had not long progressed, however, before scholars began to comment critically on the inadequacies and illogicalities of English spelling and to propose various amendments and improvements. This final chapter in our history of English spelling will discuss the work of some of those who have concerned themselves with this aspect of the language, either as lexicographers or as spelling reformers (and some wearing both hats). Two men in particular have had an immense influence on current English spelling, one – Samuel Johnson – by his conservatism, the other – Noah Webster – by his innovativeness.

## Three Early Reformers

Amongst early would-be spelling reformers, three have already been mentioned in the Introduction: Sir Thomas Smith, John Hart and William Bullokar.[1] The first, Smith, was a scholar, statesman and diplomat. His

*The History of English Spelling*, First Edition. Christopher Upward and George Davidson.
© 2011 Christopher Upward and George Davidson. Published 2011 by Blackwell Publishing Ltd.

*De recta & emendata linguæ anglicæ scriptione, Dialogus* ('Dialogue on the correct and emended writing of the English language') was published in 1568, and in the book he proposes an English alphabet of 34 characters, along with a number of diacritics used, for example, to indicate and distinguish long vowels (e.g. *â* and *ä* for a 'long a'). With regard to consonants, he rejects the use of H in digraphs such as CH, SH and TH, recommending instead the use of <ð> or <∆> for /ð/ and <þ> or <Θ> for /θ/, and creates a new character for /ʃ/. Since Smith had studied law in Italy, it was perhaps his knowledge of Italian that led him to suggest that C be used to represent /tʃ/ (though he notes that it also had this use in Old English); S is always to be used for /s/, K for /k/ and Z for /z/. A new character is also proposed for the consonantal use of U/V to distinguish it from the vowel. Smith does not carry his proposed reforms to the point of one-sound-one-symbol, and seems at times to hesitate between the conventional spelling of a word and a phonetic one; he allows the continued use of Q and X, while noting that neither is required since KU is the same as QU and X is an abbreviation for KS. Among Smith's spellings are *bīt* 'bite', *huī* 'why', *sih* 'sigh', *tār* 'tear' (verb), *ðō/ðōu* 'though'.

A year later came John Hart's *An Orthographie conteyning the due order and reason, howe to write or paint thimage of mannes voice, most like to the life or nature*. Hart was a state official, the Chester Herald. We have already quoted (p. 2) from his condemnation of English spelling because of its 'confusion and disorder' and the fact that it is 'unfit and wrong shapen for the proportion of the voice'. Hart believes that a writing system should have the same number of symbols as there are sounds in the language, and he lists four ways in which spelling can be corrupt and unsatisfactory:

- 'diminution' – there are insufficient letters to represent all the sounds of the language;
- 'superfluity' – words may be spelt with more letters than there are sounds (i.e. there are silent letters that serve no purpose in representing sound, as is the case, Hart says, with the B in *doubt*, the O in *people*, the H in *authoritie* and the L in *souldiours* – note how the last two examples cast interesting light on the pronunciations of his time);
- 'usurpation' – the use of the wrong symbol to represent a sound, an error which arises because some letters have more than one 'power', as is the case of the G in *gentleness* and *together*;

- 'misplacing' – when letters are in the wrong order, an example being *fable*, which, says Hart, should be written *fabel* because we pronounce the E before the L.

As with Smith, Hart's remedy is to use both new characters and diacritics. He proposes new letters for /ʃ/, /θ/, /ð/ and the syllabic /l/, and the use of dots and accents to indicate vowel quality and length. He does away with the letters J, Q, W (for example, he writes HU for WH, as in *huen* 'when') and Y, and uses a special form of C for /tʃ/. He discusses the possibility of using a diacritic 'prick' or dot to distinguish pairs of voiced and voiceless consonants, but in the end opts to keep the conventional symbols. Other examples of Hart's proposed spellings are *ar* 'are', *az* 'as', *bei* 'by', *ius* 'use (noun)', *iuz*, 'use (verb)', *leik* 'like', *ov* 'of', *tu* 'to', *uant* 'want', *ui* 'we'.

William Bullokar, the third of our reformers, was a schoolmaster. His *Booke at large, for the amendment of orthographie for English speech* was published in 1580 (or possibly 1581). Bullokar notes that the reforms proposed by Smith and Hart have fallen on deaf ears, and suggests that this is because their proposals would have taken English spelling too far from what is known and familiar. For this reason he proposes to limit himself to just the 24 letters of the existing alphabet (that is, counting I/J and U/V as single letters), and to differentiate sounds by means of diacritics, though he also makes use of ligatures used at the time by printers, such as <æ> and a sign similar to ∞, as in *t∞* 'to', and of digraphs such as TH and WH. Bullokar indicates by means of a diacritic not only syllabic /l/, as Hart does, but also syllabic /m/, /n/ and /r/ as in *bottom, button* and *enter*. He is opposed to etymologically based spellings such as *debt* and *doubt*, and is also critical of the overuse of double consonants and final silent E's, preferring, for example, *fel* to *fell*, *flat* to *flatte* and *pin* to *pinne*. He deliberately distinguishes words that sound the same by means of different spellings. Among Bullokar's spellings are *ár* 'are', *az* 'as', *b∞k* 'book', *iz* 'is', *nót* 'note', *ón* 'one', *sillabl'* 'syllable'.

Another reformer worthy of mention is Alexander Gil, whose *Logonomia Anglica* was published in 1619, with a revised edition published in 1621. Like Bullokar, he was a schoolmaster. Milton was one of his pupils, and it is possible that Gil's spelling influenced that of Milton. The spelling system of the second edition uses fewer special characters than that of the first. Among Gil's spellings are *deljtful bourz* 'delightful bowers', *dïd* 'deed', *komon* 'common', *plai* 'play', *täk* 'take'.

# Right Writing of the English Tongue

Rather than being spelling reformers, some scholars – mostly, like Bullokar, school teachers – were more concerned with 'right writing' or 'true writing', that is, the correct spelling of words within the established conventional spelling framework of English, though some were not averse to some reforming as well. Richard Mulcaster was a scholar and school-master (he preceded Gil as the high master of St Paul's School) whose *First Part of the Elementarie* was published in 1582, a book 'which entreateth chefelie of the right writing of our English tung'. It has been described as the most important treatise on English spelling in the 16th century.[2] Like Bullokar, Mulcaster recognizes that proposed spelling reforms that are too radical and 'fly to innovations' will simply fail to gain acceptance, the problem being that the reformers 'cumber our tung with strange characts, & with nedelesse diphthongs'. He is therefore happy to follow current usage to a great extent, to use the 24 existing letters of the alphabet, and to accept that any one letter may represent more than one sound. His aim is to tidy up English spelling rather than radically overhaul it. Among his proposed spellings are: -IE at the end of a word 'if it sound gentlie' (as in *dictionarie, gentlie, manie, safetie, verie*) but Y when the vowel sounds 'sharp and loud' (as in *cry, defy, deny*); F instead of the Greek-derived PH (thus *filosofie, ortografie*); an avoidance of double consonants except across a syllable boundary (thus *duble* and *dăble* for *double* and *dabble*, but *budding, beginning, stripped*, though word-final LL is allowed, as in for example *generall, naturall, vowell, well*); K for Greek-derived CH (as in *monark, stomak*), the CH being 'mere foren'. Analogy and consistency play an important part in Mulcaster's thinking. If, for example, one writes *hear*, one should write *dear* and *fear*, but exceptions due to established usage must also be allowed: e.g. *here, there, where*. The key rule in writing is to adopt a single spelling for any given word and to keep to it. For this reason, the *Elementarie* includes a table of some 8,000 or so words with Mulcaster's recommended spellings. But recognizing the need for something more than a glossary of correct spellings, Mulcaster was also the first to express the hope that someone would produce a comprehensive dictionary of English:

> It were a thing verie praiseworthie in my opinion . . . if som one well learned and as laborious a man, wold gather all the words which we use in our English tung . . . out of all professions, as well learned as not, into one dictionarie, and besides the right writing . . . wold open to us therein, both their naturall force and proper use.

Such a dictionary was to come, though not immediately.

Edmund Coote was another teacher who was much concerned about 'right writing'. His *English Schoole-maister*, published in 1596, is a source book of information and advice for teachers; it includes a small glossary of English words with short definitions. Coote writes of teaching people the 'true orthographie' of words, though as he explains in his Preface, he means this to apply only to 'those words whose writing is determined: for there are many wherein the best English men in the land are not agreed'. As an example of such disagreement, Coote cites the word *malicious*, noting that some people write *malicious*, deriving it from *malice*, while others write *malitious*, deriving it from its Latin source *malitiosus*. (Coote opts for -c-.) Coote states that he is opposed to spelling reform as such 'because it lyeth not in us to reforme', advising his readers rather to 'observe the best, and follow that which wee have, than to labour for innovation, which we cannot effect'. It has been suggested that Coote probably contributed greatly to the spelling of English in its present form through the 54 editions of his book that were published up to 1737. His influence could doubtless also be traced through the dictionaries that were to follow the *English Schoole-maister* and which made much use of his material.

## The First Monolingual Dictionaries

The earliest English dictionaries were bilingual, especially Latin–English or French–English, but also Spanish–English, Italian–English and even Welsh–English. There were also short and simple English–English glossaries, such as the glossary of biblical words with English definitions which William Tyndale appended to his 1530 translation of the Pentateuch. But the first true monolingual English dictionary is Robert Cawdrey's *A Table Alphabeticall, conteyning and teaching the true writing and vnderstanding of hard usuall English wordes borrowed from the Hebrew, Greeke, Latine, or French, &c, with the Interpretation thereof by plaine English words, gathered for the benefit & helpe of Ladies, Gentlewomen, or any other unskilfull persons* (1604). Like Coote, Cawdrey was a schoolmaster, and as the long title of his dictionary tells us, he too was concerned with, among other things, the 'true writing' of words (although Cawdrey's notion of 'true writing' or correct spelling is clearly less strict than it would be today: he was content to have both 'wordes' and 'words' in the title of his dictionary even though this inconsistency was not forced on him by any need to justify the lines on the page). Cawdrey's *Table Alphabeticall* contains over 2,500 words, and consists to a great extent of material lifted from Coote and two other earlier sources, thus starting a stream of lexicographic plagiarism that continued through the next few dictionaries, and beyond. Cawdrey was a recorder, not a reformer, and there is little of note in his spelling; it follows the general patterns and conventions of 17th-century English. Cawdrey does not, for example, follow Mulcaster's suggested distinction between final -IE and final -Y (he has e.g. *accessorie, agonie, democracie, dignitie* as in Mulcaster but also *defie, deifie, fructifie, glorifie*; but there are examples of final -Y, such as *ly* = 'lie'; corresponding to Modern English adverbial and adjectival -LY, we find *abruptly, artificially, yearely*, etc., but also *craftilie, easilie*, etc.). Final -LL is standard (*buriall, fearefull, finall, gospell*), as is -ICKE for Modern English -IC (*hecticke, magicke, trafficke*, etc.). Modern English -NESS is represented by both -NES and -NESSE. One interesting spelling is *bisket* (= 'biscuit'), common in the 16th to 18th centuries and still found in Johnson's dictionary, though cross-referred by him to *biscuit*.

The dictionaries that followed Cawdrey's we will mention only briefly. John Bullokar's *An English Expositor* appeared in 1616, Henry Cockeram's *The English Dictionarie* in 1623, Thomas Blount's *Glossographia* in 1656, Edward Phillips's *The New World of English Words* – an interestingly modern-sounding title – in 1658, and John Kersey's *A New English Dictionary* in 1702. (Kersey's was the first dictionary to provide proper coverage of everyday words as well as 'hard' words.) And finally we have two dictionaries by Nathan Bailey: *An Universal Etymological English Dictionary*, published in 1721 and containing about 40,000 words, which ran through 30 editions between 1721 and 1802 and remained very popular even after the publication of Johnson's *Dictionary* in 1755; and the still larger *Dictionarium Britannicum* of 1730, used by Johnson as the working file for his own dictionary.

## Ascertainment of the English Language

In the second half of the 17th and the first half of the 18th centuries, a matter of great concern to many scholars and writers was the 'fixing' or 'ascertaining' of the English language, that is to say, the establishment and codification of the rules of correct usage so that the language would, hopefully, remain unchanged and unchanging thereafter, this ascertainment to be accompanied by a process of refinement by which perceived (or supposed) defects in the current language would be removed and any necessary improvements made. Among others, the poet and dramatist John Dryden (d. 1700) raised the matter several times; in 1712 the writer Jonathan Swift sent to the Earl of Oxford a *Proposal for Correcting, Improving, and Ascertaining the English Tongue*; and in 1756 the actor and lexicographer Thomas Sheridan, whom we have already quoted in the Introduction, similarly made a plea to the Earl of Chesterfield that he use his influence to stabilize the language.

One thing necessary for this process of ascertaining the language, it was generally agreed, was a reliable dictionary. Notwithstanding the works mentioned above, Dryden, writing in 1693, had noted the lack of 'a tolerable dictionary', and in 1707, the librarian and antiquarian Humphrey Wanley expressed the need for a new dictionary that would 'fix' the English language, just as had happened with French and Italian. Whether or not Bailey's dictionaries, written after this time, could have met this need adequately, several writers made plans for a new dictionary. The man who eventually brought the project to fruition, however, was Samuel Johnson.

# Samuel Johnson

With financial backing from a number of London booksellers, a contract for the new dictionary was signed in June 1746, and the following year Johnson produced his *Plan of a Dictionary of the English Language*, addressed to the Earl of Chesterfield. At this stage, Johnson too was a language 'fixer', though by the time he wrote the dictionary itself he recognized this to be an unattainable goal. The *Plan*, of course, discusses all aspects of the lexicographical task as Johnson saw it; here we will concern ourselves only with orthographical matters.

Johnson devotes four paragraphs of his *Plan* to the problems of spelling:[3]

> When all the words are selected and arranged, the first part of the work to be considered is the ORTHOGRAPHY, which was long vague and uncertain; which at last, when its fluctuation ceased, was in many cases settled but by accident, and in which . . . there is still great uncertainty among the best critics; nor is it easy to state a rule by which we may decide between custom and reason, or between the equiponderant authorities of writers alike eminent for judgment and accuracy.

The great orthographical contest has long subsisted between etymology and pronunciation. It has been demanded, on one hand, that men should write as they speak; but . . . it may be asked, with equal propriety, why men do not rather speak as they write. . . .

When a question of orthography is dubious, that practice has, in my opinion, a claim to preference, which preserves the greatest number of radical letters, or seems most to comply with the general custom of our language. But the chief rule which I propose to follow is, to make no innovation, without a reason sufficient to balance the inconvenience of change; and such reasons I do not expect often to find. All change is of itself an evil, which ought not to be hazarded but for evident advantage; . . .

The present usage of spelling, where the present usage can be distinguished, will therefore in this work, be generally followed, yet there will be often occasion to observe, that it is in itself inaccurate, and tolerated rather than chosen; particularly when, by the change of one letter or more, the meaning of a word is obscured, as in *farrier* for *ferrier*, as it was formerly written, from *ferrum*, or *fer*; in *gibberish* for *gebrish*, the jargon of *Geber*, and his chymical followers, understood by none but their own tribe. [This latter is in fact a false etymology.]

The key points to note from the above are:

- that current spellings have often been settled on 'by accident';
- that there is still uncertainty over some spellings among the best writers (though in fact, as Baugh and Cable observe,[4] English spelling in its modern form had been pretty well established about a century earlier, at least in writing intended to be made public[5]);
- that there may be a clash between 'custom' and 'reason', and between etymology and pronunciation, as the basis for spelling;
- that spellings which preserve the greatest number of radical letters (i.e. letters of the words from which the English words are derived) are in Johnson's view the most desirable; but
- that as a general rule Johnson intends to follow established usage regardless of other considerations.

This then was the statement of Johnson's opinions and intentions as he set out on his great work. What had he to say in the *Preface* to his *Dictionary* when the work was done? From the paragraphs Johnson devotes to questions of spelling, the following points may be noted:

In adjusting the ORTHOGRAPHY, which has been to this time unsettled and fortuitous, I found it necessary to distinguish those irregularities that are inherent in our tongue, and perhaps coeval with it, from others which the ignorance or negligence of later writers has produced. Every language has its anomalies, which, though inconvenient, . . . must be tolerated among the imperfections of human things . . . : but every language has likewise its improprieties and absurdities, which it is the duty of the lexicographer to correct or proscribe.

. . .

Some [words] still continue to be variously written, as authours differ in their care or skill: of these it was proper to enquire the true orthography, which I have always considered as depending on their derivation, and have therefore referred them to their original languages: thus I write *enchant, enchantment, enchanter*, after the *French* and *incantation* after the *Latin*; thus *entire* is chosen rather than *intire*, because it passed to us not from the *Latin integer*, but from the *French entier*.

. . .

Even in words of which the derivation is apparent, I have been often obliged to sacrifice uniformity to custom; thus I write, in compliance with a numberless majority, *convey* and *inveigh*, *deceit* and *receipt*, *fancy* and *phantom*. [And so must we to this day!] . . .

Some combinations of letters having the same power are used indifferently without any discoverable reason of choice, as in *choak, choke; soap, sope; fewel, fuel*, and many others; which I have sometimes inserted twice, that those who search for them under either form, may not search in vain.

In examining the orthography of any doubtful word, the mode of spelling by which it is inserted in the series of the dictionary, is to be considered as that to which I give, perhaps not often rashly, the preference. . . .

. . . I have endeavoured to proceed with a scholar's reverence for antiquity, and a grammarian's regard to the genius of our tongue. I have attempted few alterations, and among those few, perhaps the greater part is from the modern to the ancient practice; and I hope I may be allowed to recommend to those, whose thoughts have been, perhaps, employed too anxiously on verbal singularities, not to disturb, upon narrow views, or for minute propriety, the orthography of their fathers.

The above remarks need little further comment. We see from both the *Plan* and the *Preface* that Johnson's intention was not at all to be a spelling reformer and only occasionally to be a spelling corrector; for the most part, he accepted the already established usage, for better or for worse. Once more in the history of English spelling, an opportunity to make spelling less capricious and closer to the spoken form of the language was lost. And of course with the authority of Johnson's dictionary behind forms such as *doubt* and *receipt*, there was little hope of significant change thereafter, though some of his perhaps inadvertent inconsistencies (*pitfall* but *downfal*; *confessor* and *inheritor* but *possessour* and *oratour*; *exterior* but *interiour*) have been ironed out, and choices have been made between alternatives he allowed (*choke* and *choak*, etc. as mentioned above, and also *choir* and *quire*, *choose* and *chuse*, *click* and *klick*, *hearse* and *herse*, *scimitar* and *cimiter*, *screen* and *skreen*, *sponge* and *spunge*, *villainy* and *villany*) as well as for forms Johnson did not include (e.g. Modern English *reindeer*, Johnson *raindeer*,[6] both forms existing in English from the 16th century onwards). With regard to forms such as *critick, musick, politick*, etc., we have already noted (p. 49) Johnson's incorrect assumption regarding a 'Saxon κ' (but note Johnson himself writing 'critics' in his *Plan*; see above). Unfortunately, where Johnson rightly indicates a preference for a simpler form of a word over a more complex and etymologically unjustifiable one, such as *sithe* for *scythe* (< Old English *siðe*), English has not always followed his advice.

## Noah Webster and the Parting of the Ways

From Johnson's *Dictionary* of 1755, we now take a leap forward in time and westwards in direction to turn our attention to the work of the American lexicographer Noah Webster (1758–1843).

Already well known for his extremely popular *American Spelling Book* (1783),[7] the first part of his *Grammatical Institute of the English Language* which also included a grammar (1784) and a reader (1785), Webster produced two major dictionaries: *A Compendious Dictionary of the English Language* (1806), an abridged version of which was published the following year as *A Dictionary of the English Language; Compiled for the Use of Common Schools in the United States*; and the much larger *American Dictionary of the English Language* (1828). He also wrote a *Dictionary for Primary Schools* (1833).

Webster was at first as conservative as Johnson in his spellings. In his *Grammatical Institute*, for example, he rejected and ridiculed as 'absurdities' spellings such as *favor, honor* for *favour, honour* and *judgment* for *judgement*. And he had shown no interest in the proposals put forward by the American writer and scientist Benjamin Franklin, who had in 1768 brought out *A Scheme for a New Alphabet and a Reformed Mode of Spelling*. As Webster wrote in the *Grammatical Institute*, there was in his view little point in attempting 'a reformation [of spelling] without

302

advantage or probability of success'. But not many years later, in his *Dissertations on the English Language* (1789), he was of an entirely different opinion, agreeing now with Franklin that such an orthographical reformation was 'practicable and highly necessary', and advocating some quite radical changes to English spelling, among which were:

- the omission of superfluous or silent letters such as the A in *bread*, *head*, *realm*, the U of *built*, the final E of *give*;
- the replacement of some consonant and vowel graphemes by commoner and more predictable equivalents (e.g. *laf* for *laugh*, *tuf* for *tough*; the substitution of EE for the variously spelt /iː/ vowels in *mean*, *grieve*, *key*, *oblique*, etc.; K for CH in words such as *character* and *chorus* and for QUE in *oblique*, etc.)
  ○ hence, for example, *oblique* > *\*obleek*;
- the use of diacritical marks to distinguish different ways of pronouncing the same letter or letters, such as a stroke through TH to distinguish /ð/ from /θ/.

In Webster's opinion, such changes would render orthography 'sufficiently correct and regular'. They would also, he happily noted as an American patriot, serve to make American spelling quite different from British spelling. However, the reformed spellings he proposed met with such little favour that, when it came to publishing his dictionaries from 1806 onwards, he moderated his position and abandoned many of them, and of those he did advocate, fewer and fewer were to be found in each successive dictionary, with a steady retreat towards more traditional spellings. In his long section on orthography in the Preface to the *Compendious Dictionary*, Webster states his current position as follows:

> The correct principle respecting changes in orthography [is that] no great changes should ever be made at once, nor should any change be made which violates established principles, creates great inconvenience, or obliterates the radicals of the language. But gradual changes to accommodate the written to the spoken language, when they occasion none of these evils, and especially when they purify words from corruptions, improve the regular analogies of a language and illustrate etymology, are not only proper, but indispensable.

Corruptions in Webster's eyes are generally spellings which do not accurately or adequately reflect the spelling of the source word; thus he deplores, but still allows, spellings such as *leather*, *feather*, *weather*, the 'true orthography' being shown by Old English (Webster calls it Saxon) *lether, fether, wether*. Similarly, *hainous* is to be preferred to *heinous* on the grounds that it is derived from French *haine*, *heinous* being 'such a palpable error that no lexicographer can be justified in giving it his sanction'. *Tongue* was in Saxon written *tung, tonge* or *tunga*, but is now written 'most barbarously' as *tongue*. *Though* is a 'vitious [*sic*] orthography'. And so on.

The following are among the reforms introduced in the *Compendious Dictionary*:

- writing final -IC for earlier -ICK in *music, logic*, etc. (though inconsistently he still writes *frolick* and *traffick* and also *almanack, havock*);
- writing -ER in *theater, meter*, etc.;
- writing -OR in *favor, honor*, etc.;
- writing *defense, offense* for *defence, offence*;
- writing *check* for *cheque*, but still *masquerade* and *oblique* with QU (no *obleek* now!);
- dropping the final E from *determine, doctrine, examine*, etc.;
- dropping the B from *crumb*, but allowing both *thumb* and *thum*;
- allowing both *island* and *iland*; *leather, weather, wealth* and *lether, wether, welth*; *tho* (his preferred form) and *though*;
- writing *hainous* for *heinous*, *tung* for *tongue*, *wimmen* for *women*.

Where both -ISE and -IZE are possible, Webster generally prefers the latter. He still has a double letter in words such as *traveller* and *worshipper*, where American English would today have a single letter; the single-letter rule for *traveler, worshiper*, etc. was introduced in the *American Dictionary of the English Language* of 1828, in which the final -E was also restored in *determine, doctrine*, etc.

Of the above Websterian reforms, the first has entered British English, which also writes *music, public*, etc., as has to a great extent -IZE. The -ER, -OR spellings are distinguishing features of American English, as are *defense, check* and *traveling*, etc. Neither British nor American English has adopted forms such as *crum, hainous, tung* and *wimmen*, eventually abandoned either by Webster himself or by his later editors.

Spelling in Webster's popular spelling book, his main source of income throughout his life, remained much more conservative than that of his dictionaries. As Professor John Clark has remarked,[8] 'the joke on Webster was that he could not afford to publish his theories about reformed spelling except by using a mainly traditional spelling in his spelling books – which circulated so much more widely and had so much more influence (on spelling) than his other publications that only his tamest innovations ever became widely known or widely adopted', but nevertheless 'American spelling . . . is what it is almost entirely because of his theories'. In 1864, the US Government printing office adopted the Webster-inspired spellings that are so characteristic of present-day American English.

## English around the World

Having now traced the origins of the main spelling differences between British and American English, we will now consider briefly English spelling in some other parts of the world.

As Melchers and Shaw rightly remark,[9] spelling is not a major issue in the description of world Englishes. While regrettable – there is more to be said on spelling practices throughout the English-speaking world than many people might suspect – this state of affairs is perhaps not so surprising. Given that most of the English-speaking world is or was part of the British Empire, or more recently the Commonwealth – the notable exception being the United States, independent since 1776 – in these countries (Canada, Australia, New Zealand, South Africa, India, Pakistan, etc.) spelling generally or to a great extent follows the British standard, with, as we will see below, some input from American usage in some countries. While contributing much local material to the richness of English vocabulary, and thus contributing some interesting additions to the sound–spelling correspondences of English as outlined in Chapter 8, none of these countries has contributed anything to the general rules of English spelling as such. For this book, then, we will limit our comments to spelling practice in three countries, with particular mention of two of them.

Since Canada has historical political and cultural links to the United Kingdom while it is geographically attached to the United States, Canadian English is in a unique position. It is not surprising, therefore, that Canadian spelling is a mixture of both British and American spelling rules.[10] As Fee and McAlpine put it, most Canadians, whatever they think or say they do, use a mixture of British and American spellings. Canadians write *jail, tire* and *curb* in preference to *gaol, tyre* or *kerb*, but are unlikely to write *maneuver* or *check* (= 'cheque'). Most will follow British practice in *axe, catalogue, centre*, but American

305

practice in *analyze, peddler* and *plow*. (Americans have *tire centers*, the British buy tyres at *tyre centres*, but Canadians go to *tire centres*.) Final consonants are doubled before an added word-ending, as in *travelled, traveller*, as is standard in British English. Spelling practice varies from province to province, with Ontario tending most towards British spelling, followed by British Columbia and Newfoundland, while Alberta, Manitoba and Saskatchewan tend more towards American practice. Spelling is not even consistent within a given set of words: for example, *colour* is generally preferred to *color*, but *favorite* wins against *favourite*, and while *neighbour* is (or at least was in the recent past) preferred in all provinces except Alberta and Manitoba, *odor* is (or was) preferred in all but Ontario.[11]

Moving down to the southern hemisphere, we find a similar situation in Australia, but not in New Zealand, where British spelling conventions are the norm.[12] While Australian English spelling basically follows British tradition,[13] corpus-based studies have shown that usage varies considerably with regard, for example, to -OUR and -OR. (Note the name of the Australian Labor Party, as against the normal Australian -OUR spelling; the -OR spelling in the party name dates back to 1912.) With regard to pairs such as *cheque/check* and *tyre/tire*, British conventions are very much the norm, but -AM has almost completely supplanted -AMME in words such as *program/programme*.[14] We might also note the attempt by an Australian minister of health in the 1970s to introduce *helth* as an official Australian form for *health* (the change was short-lived, being reversed by his successor).

## The 'Simplified Spelling' Movement

With the later editions of the Webster dictionaries in America and the publication of the British-based *New English Dictionary on Historical Principles* (later the *Oxford English Dictionary*) from 1882 onwards, English spelling was to all intents and purposes finally and fully 'ascertained', albeit in two slightly differing standards, in the way that Dryden, Swift and so many others had hoped for two centuries earlier.

But the desire for reform was by no means dead, neither in the United Kingdom nor in the United States. Since, however, the work of the reform movements, like the efforts of the earlier reformers discussed above, has as yet had no significant, lasting effect on English orthography on either side of the Atlantic or elsewhere, we will confine ourselves here to no more than an outline of their history during the 20th century (there had already been similar movements in the late 19th) and some of the proposals put forward.[15]

## The Simplified Spelling Board

In March 1906, a Simplified Spelling Board was established in New York, backed by funding from the millionaire and philanthropist Andrew Carnegie. It hoped to appeal at all those who for educational or practical reasons wished to make English spelling easier to learn. Among its members were scholars and academics from universities such as Columbia, Harvard and Yale, dictionary editors and publishers, prominent statesmen, and the writer Mark Twain. Within a month, the Board had issued a list of 300 words with alternative spellings, one simpler or more regular than the other, asking people who supported them to sign a card undertaking to use the simpler, more regular forms as far as practicable. Among the words (with the recommended forms first) were *center/centre, honor/honour, judgment/judgement, ax/axe, catalog/catalogue, program/programme, fulfil/fulfill, tho/though, thru/through, plow/plough, surprize/surprise, rime/rhyme, sithe/scythe, archeology/archaeology, mold/mould.* (Slightly more than half of the recommended forms were already well established in American usage and American dictionaries.) Also recommended were past tense and past participle forms such as *fixt, kist* and *wisht* for standard *fixed, kissed* and *wished.*

Simplified spellings received backing from President Theodore Roosevelt, who ordered that they be used by the Government Printing Office. However, his order met with a great deal of resistance, and faced with negative reaction from both the public and the government (the House of Representatives passed a resolution stating that it would use the spellings found in most dictionaries and not the new simplified forms), the order was rescinded. With the death of Andrew Carnegie in 1919, the Board lost its main financial support and its activities declined, although it did in that same year publish a *Handbook of Simplified Spelling.*

There was some other support for simplified spellings. For a time in the mid-20th century, the Chicago *Tribune* adopted a number of simplified spellings, such as *agast, catalog, crum, harken, iland, lether,* but most of such simplifications were later abandoned. The dictionary publishers Funk & Wagnall included simplified spellings in their dictionaries until the 1940s. But little, if anything, was achieved beyond what Webster and his later editors had already accomplished. Nevertheless, the simplified spelling torch has not been completely extinguished: for example, the American Literacy Council, formerly the Phonemic Spelling Council, declares in its mission statement its continuing support for 'gradual unforced evolution of the written language toward more simple and consistent spellings' and states that 'spelling reform . . . continues to be part of the basic mission'.[16]

## The Simplified Spelling Society

Two years after the founding of the Simplified Spelling Board in the United States, the Simplified Spelling Society (now the English Spelling Society) was established in the United Kingdom. Like the American association, it has had throughout its history the support of some of the most eminent figures in language studies, literature, politics and society at large, among them the philologists and lexicographers Walter Skeat (the first chairman of the Society) and Sir James Murray, the phoneticians Daniel Jones, David Abercrombie, A. C. Gimson and John Wells, Archbishop William Temple, Dr Horace King (the Speaker of the House of Commons from 1965 to 1971), the writer H. G. Wells, the publisher and Member of Parliament Sir James Pitman, the founder of the Scout movement Sir Robert Baden-Powell, and the industrialist Sir George Hunter.

Having twice, in 1923 and 1933, failed to persuade the Board of Education to set up a committee to consider spelling reform – this in spite of immense support from scholars and academics, educational associations, writers, publishers, the church, and many others – the Society nearly achieved its aim through the actions of Dr Mont Follick MP (whose opinions of English spelling have been quoted in the Introduction), who in 1949 and again in 1953 introduced Private Member's Bills in support of spelling reform,[17] the former attempt being defeated by 87 to 84, the latter succeeding by 65 votes to 53. However, opposition to the proposal led to a compromise in which the government committed itself to no more than merely facilitating research into possible improvements in the teaching of reading by means of a system of simplified spelling. This led eventually to the development of the Initial Teaching Alphabet, but not to the development of any system of simplified spelling for general use.

Members and supporters of the Spelling Society, and others, have over the years put forward a number of proposed simplifications or reformations of traditional spelling, and continue to do so. It is impossible to mention and illustrate more than a few here:

- Anglic was developed by the Swedish scholar R. E. Zachrisson, and published in 1930. In this system, about 40 very frequent words keep their traditional spelling, while the rest are spelt phonetically using the most common of the traditional graphemes for each speech-sound. This means, Zachrisson claimed, that Anglic agrees with traditional orthography in more than half the number of words on any given page of text. The following is an example of Anglic:[18]

  > In its nue shape Anglic is 'Simplified Speling' braut up-to-date, wurkt out in evry deetale, puerified from evry dout and ambiguity.

- Out of Zachrisson's Anglic, the Simplified Spelling Society developed its New Spelling (or Nue Speling). The following is an example:[19]

  > We shood surtenly not kontinue to riet widh dhe prezent misleeding speling.

- In 1959, another Swedish linguist, Axel Wijk, brought out his system of Regularized English (or in his spelling 'Regularized Inglish'). The advantage of Regularized Inglish over New Spelling, Wijk claimed, was that, excluding certain changes in the use of final E and of the letter representing /z/ (where it is an S in traditional spelling), his system retained over 90 per cent of traditional spellings, whereas New Spelling altered the traditional spellings in about 90 per cent of English words. The following is an example of Regularized Inglish:[20]

  > At the first glaance a passage in eny reformd spelling looks 'queer' and 'ugly'. This objection iz aulwayz the first to be made; it iz perfectly natural; it iz the hardest to remoove.

- Finally, we may mention Cut Spelling, a spelling system developed by Christopher Upward and a working group of the (then) Simplified Spelling Society in the 1980s and 1990s which, by cutting out redundant letters, achieves a greatest possible regularization of spelling with the least disruption to traditional orthography. The following is an example of this system:[21]

  > We shud certnly not continu to rite with th presnt misleadng spelng.

## Some Benefits of Traditional Orthography

There remains one aspect of spelling reform to be discussed. As the philologist and lexicographer Henry Bradley, at one time editor of the

*Oxford English Dictionary*, once said,[22] 'many of the advocates of spelling reform are in the habit of asserting, as if it were an axiom admitting of no dispute, that the sole function of writing is to represent sounds'. Bradley's view is that 'this is one of those spurious truisms that are not intelligently believed by any one, but which continue to be repeated because nobody takes the trouble to consider what they really mean'.

Bradley is perhaps being a little harsh with those whose opinions he does not share: there are many who advocate or have advocated such a position who are/were by no means unintelligent. But he is not alone is his viewpoint. Sir William Craigie, who, like Bradley, was an editor of the *Oxford English Dictionary*, expresses his doubts about the 'commonly assumed . . . self-evident axiom that a phonetic spelling, or some near approach to this, must necessarily be the most suitable for any language, without regard to its character or history'.[23] And more recently Professor William Haas has stated that it may be 'advantageous for an orthography to deviate from a phonetically faithful representation of speech' and that 'various non-phonological factors need to be taken account of' in spelling.[24]

- One of the non-phonological factors that need to be considered is what we may call 'communicative clarity'. Written language is generally employed in situations where the communicator and the person(s) being communicated with are not present at the same place and/or time, and it is necessary, therefore, that there be as little scope for confusion and misunderstanding as possible. Homophones (= words that are the same in sound) present less possibility for confusion than do homographs (words that are the same in their written forms), and for this reason a spelling system that allows homographs is arguably to be preferred to one which does not. For example, while there is an immediately apprehensible difference between 'the rites of the Church' and 'the rights of the Church',[25] what one might intend by writing 'the riets of the Church' (assuming a simplified spelling *riet* for both *rite* and *right* in traditional orthography) is not clear at all. Similarly 'a mail carrier' and 'a male carrier' are clearly different, but 'a mael carrier' is ambiguous.[26] There are many examples of this type in English, although there are, of course, also potentially confusing homographs such as *read* (/riːd/, present tense) and *read* (/rɛd/, past tense) that would benefit in clarity from more phonetic spellings.

- Secondly, English is spoken in a large number of different accents with very different sound patterns. A spelling system that is designed to represent accurately the pronunciation of one accent will almost certainly fail to represent accurately pronunciation in at least some of the other accents. To take one example, *fir* and *fur* are pronounced /fɜː/ in a standard Southern British pronunciation but as /fɪr/ and /fʌr/ respectively in a Scots accent. No narrowly sound-based spelling system could accommodate this difference.

- Thirdly, a rigidly phonetic spelling system would lose many of the visual connections between related words, such as *photograph* and *photographer*, *injury* and *injurious*, *nature* and *natural*, etc. There is arguably something to be said in favour of a spelling system that makes words that are related in meaning graphically alike.

  ○ Similarly, it has been suggested that in a spelling system with complete consistency in sound–symbol correspondences, valuable features of symbol–meaning correspondence might be lost. For example, if the plural of *cat* is spelled with a final s but the plural of *dog* with a final z, a closer sound–symbol match may be achieved but at the cost of losing the visual relationship between s and the notion of 'plurality' that one has in current English spelling. How much of a problem this would actually be is not clear: many languages do have variable forms of plural marker.

- And fourthly, it has been suggested that in a world in which so much scientific and technical vocabulary is international, there are benefits to retaining spellings that are recognizably the same, or at least similar, in many languages, regardless of their pronunciation.

## A Final Word

Whether any reformation of traditional orthography will ever obtain general acceptance, one cannot say. To judge from the past, it seems clear that no radical overhaul of our spelling will do so, but it is nevertheless possible that some gentle and unthreatening amelioration may yet be achieved. There is of course the constant pressure from the language of advertising, with its deliberate misspellings in product names (*dreem*, *kleen*, *kool*, *kwik*, etc.),[27] though so far this has had little effect on English spelling (*lite* for *light* is now established as an acceptable spelling in certain contexts) and there seems to be no reason to think that it will have any greater effect in the future. Non-conventional spellings (e.g. *punx*, *anarkists*) can also be a symbol of rebellion or of group identity or solidarity,[28] but for that very reason may not spread much beyond the group. That the language of text-messaging will have any significant effect on everyday spelling is unlikely: there seems no reason to think that those who habitually key *u* and *gr8* when texting will cease to write *you* and *great* in other circumstances when these latter are the established forms printed in books, magazines and newspapers and taught in schools.

English spelling has developed, as we have seen, over some 13 centuries or more, incorporating many changes and additions along the way. It has now been fixed in something very close to its present form for more than 250 years, since the publication of Johnson's *Dictionary*. It may not be perfect, there may be room for some improvement here and there, but it has served, and continues to serve, its purpose very well. (It may be noted, for example, how the English of the 21st century exploits the grapheme distinction between F and PH for the sound /f/ – *phishing* is not the same as *fishing*.) Perhaps, as we come to the end of this study, we can agree with the words of Geoffrey Sampson already quoted in the Introduction that 'our orthography is possibly not the least valuable of the institutions our ancestors have bequeathed to us' but nonetheless also agree that, as the *Times Literary Supplement* stated not so very long ago,[29] 'there are very great advantages to be gained from reformed spelling' and that 'the case for change should be made regularly, forcefully, and audibly'.

# Notes

1   For a more detailed description of the work of Smith, Hart, Bullokar and other reformers than can be included here, see Vallins (1965), Dobson (1968).
2   Baugh and Cable (1993: 205).
3   The quotations from the *Plan* and the *Preface* to the Dictionary are taken from Crystal (2005).
4   Baugh and Cable (1993: 208). Brengelman (1980: 334) similarly states that 'during the middle half of the seventeenth century, English spelling evolved from near anarchy to almost complete predictability', commenting further that this process owed much more to the efforts of scholars and schoolmasters than to any interest that printers took in the matter. Mitton (1996: 17), on the other hand, suggests that it was the printers' spellings that were codified and taught to children, who would then expect the same

spelling conventions in whatever they read, an expectation printers would be careful to meet.

5   Sönmez (2000: 407) notes that private writings in the 17th century, such as letters and diaries, still show great variation in spelling. Similarly, Görlach (1991: 46) notes that spelling in private letters, diaries, etc. remains quite variable until the end of Early Modern English. And in J. Smith (1996: 76), mention is made of the differences between even Dr Johnson's published and private usage.

6   In keeping with his remarks about *farrier* and *ferrier* in his *Plan*, Johnson may have preferred the form *raindeer* on etymological grounds, deriving it as he does from the Saxon *hranar*.

7   The *American Spelling Book* sold in its millions. It is the most popular schoolbook ever published.

8   In Vallins (1965: 187–8, 186).

9   Melchers and Shaw (2003: 94).

10   Brinton and Fee (2001: 433), Fee and McAlpine (1997: 465).

11   Pratt (1993: 55), quoted in Brinton and Fee (2001: 433).

12   Melchers and Shaw (2003: 111).

13   Melchers and Shaw (2003: 104).

14   Collins and Blair (1989: 230). We should not forget, however, that British English has also been infiltrated by the *-am* spelling: one writes of *television programmes* but *computer programs*. The American spelling *disk* is similarly preferred to the British *disc* in the context of computers.

15   For a fuller discussion of the spelling reform movements, see for example Mencken (1963: 488–97), Scragg (1974: 106–17), Vallins (1965: 133–42).

16   Available online at www.americanliteracy.com/mission.html, accessed 17 March 2011.

17   For those who are not familiar with British parliamentary procedure, a Private Member's Bill is a bill presented to Parliament by an individual Member of Parliament rather than by the government.

18   From Zachrisson's 'Anglic and the Anglic Muuvment', *Simplified English Spelling*, published by the Simplified Spelling Society (1930). (Available online at www.englishspellingsociety.org/journals/pamflets/ses2.php, accessed 17 March 2011.)

19   From *Modernizing English Spelling: Principles & Practicalities*, published by the Simplified Spelling Society (2000) (available online at www. englishspellingsociety.org/aboutsss/leaflets/pandp.php, accessed 17 March 2011).

20   From Scragg (1974: 112).

21   Again from *Modernizing English Spelling: Principles & Practicalities*, published by the Simplified Spelling Society (see n. 19 above). See also Upward (1996).

22   'On the Relations between Spoken and Written Language, with special reference to English', read at the International Historical Congress in

1913; printed in the *Proceedings of the British Academy* vol. VI, and also reprinted by the Clarendon Press.

23  *Some Anomalies of English*, Society for Pure English Tract 59, 1942.

24  Haas (1970: 3–4).

25  The example is Bradley's, though the spelling 'riet' is ours.

26  The example is Craigie's, but the spelling 'mael' is ours.

27  Hughes (2000: 322) refers to the 'disturbing trend of aggressive illiteracy' and the 'destabilization of spelling', citing brand names such as *Eet-sum-mor*, *Ezkleen*, *Stafresh* and *tufpak*.

28  See Sebba (2007: especially 1–9, 26–57). The use of κ in place of other graphemes representing /k/, as in the *anarkists* example, is a common symbol of rebellion – and not just in English: in addition to the usually humorous use of *skool* for *school* and the counter-culture use of the spelling *Amerika*, we may note the similar use of κ in Spanish, e.g. in Spanish squatters' use of *okupación* 'occupation' for standard Spanish *ocupación* (Sebba 2007: 3). κ for c is also found in Italian graffiti (Sebba 2007: 48, footnote).

29  Editorial, *Times Literary Supplement*, 2 June 1972, quoted in Scragg (1974: 117).

# Glossary of Technical Terms

**accusative**   The noun or pronoun case typically indicating the object of a verb: e.g. *I saw him*.

**acute accent**   The sign ´ over a vowel, as in *é*.

**alphabetic principle**   The principle of unambiguous correspondence between the sounds of the spoken form of a language and symbols of the written form of the language, with pronunciation determining spelling.

**ash**   The Old English letter Æ.

**aspiration**   A puff of air following the release of a consonant, such as /p, t, k/ in *pin, tin, kin* in English, or before a vowel, as in Greek (see p. 214).

**aspirated**   Preceded or followed by aspiration.

**assimilation**   A process by which one sound becomes identical to or more like an adjacent sound, e.g. Latin AD- + *sentire* > Modern English *assent*.

**assimilated**   Having undergone assimilation.

**back vowel**   A vowel formed by the tongue making the narrowest opening towards the back of the mouth: e.g. [ɔ], [u].

**bilabial**   (A sound) formed by the action of the lips: e.g. [p], [m].

**carrier language**   The language by which a word is transmitted from one language to another.

**cedilla**   A small hook-like mark below a letter to indicate its pronunciation: e.g. French *façade* in which *ç* = [s] or Turkish *çakal* in which *ç* = [tʃ].

*The History of English Spelling*, First Edition. Christopher Upward and George Davidson.
© 2011 Christopher Upward and George Davidson. Published 2011 by Blackwell Publishing Ltd.

**circumflex (accent)**  The sign ˆ over a vowel, as in *ô*.

**cognate**  (Any of two or more words) having the same source word: French *mère* and Spanish *madre* are cognate (or cognates), both being derived from Latin *mater/matrem* 'mother'.

**combining form**  A word-forming element such as MICRO-, PHOTO-, RADIO-, -GRAPHY, -LOGY, which, like a prefix or a suffix, may be added to already existing words to form new words (e.g. *microwave, radioactive*), but which, unlike prefixes and suffixes, may combine with other combining forms to form words (*radiology, photography*).

**Cyrillic alphabet**  The alphabet used in writing Russian and some other languages of eastern Europe and the former USSR.

**dative**  The noun or pronoun case typically indicating the person or object receiving something: e.g. *I gave <u>him</u> the book.*

**derivative**  A word that is formed from another word, e.g. by the addition of some word-element (e.g. *walker* is a derivative of *walk*) or by some other process (e.g. the Latin verb *facere* 'to do, make' has Modern English derivatives such as *manufacture, perfect*).

**diacritic**  (A symbol or letter) used to indicate a particular pronunciation, such as the cedilla in *façade* or the U of *guest*.

**digraph**  Two letters used together to represent a single speech-sound: e.g. CH, TH, SH, OU, EE, OA.

**diphthong**  A vowel formed while the tongue moves from one point of articulation to another: e.g. /aʊ/ in *cow*, /eɪ/ in *hay*.

**doublet**  Two words deriving from the same ultimate source: e.g. *regal* and *royal*, both ultimately from Latin *regalis*, the former directly, the latter via French.

**eth**  The Old English letter ð.

**etymology**  The origin and development of a word or word-element, or the study or description of such histories.

**folk etymology**  The reforming of the shape of a word to make it resemble a more familiar word or words: e.g. Spanish *cucaracha* > English *cockroach*.

**fricative**  (A consonant) formed by air passing through a narrow opening between two parts of the mouth: e.g. [f], [z] or [ʃ].

**front vowel**  A vowel formed by the tongue making the narrowest opening towards the front of the mouth: e.g. [i], [ɛ].

**fronted**  With an articulation more towards the front of the mouth.

**futhark, futhorc**  The runic alphabet used for writing Old English before the introduction of the Roman alphabet.

**gemination** Double-length pronunciation, as in the DD in *midday* or the NN of *thinness*.

**geminated** With gemination.

**genitive** The case of a noun or pronoun which generally indicates possession.

**gerund** A verbal noun, such as *laughing* in *His laughing at her really irritated me*.

**gerundive** A Latin verb form expressing necessity: e.g. *agenda* 'things to be done'.

**grapheme** A letter or group of letters that represent a speech-sound: e.g. F or PH representing /f/, EE or EA representing /iː/.

**homograph** Any of two or more words that are the same in their written forms but different in pronunciation: e.g. *bow* of a ship and *bow* tie.

**homophone** Any of two or more words that sound the same but have different meanings: e.g. *scent/sent/cent*.

**infinitive** A verb form such as *to love* in English, *aimer* in French, *amare* in Latin.

**inflection** The changing of the form of a word to indicate its different grammatical relationships: e.g. *sing, sang, sung; talk, talked*. Also a grammatical element, such as -ED, used in such a process.

**inflected** Having an inflection.

**intervocalic** Between vowels.

**ligature** A character consisting of two, or sometimes more than two, letters joined together: e.g. Æ, Œ.

**macron** A bar over a vowel (as in *ā*), used for example to indicate that the vowel is long.

**metathesis** The transposing of two speech-sounds in a word, as in Old English *thurh, brid*, Modern English *through, bird*.

**minim** A short vertical stroke in a letter.

**mutation** A sound-change caused by adjacent or nearby sounds – e.g. *feet* < *\*foti*, the plural of *fot* 'foot' – or the result of such a change.

**mutate** to undergo mutation.

**nasalize** To pronounce a speech-sound with air passing through the nasal cavity, as in the vowels of French *vin blanc*.

**nasalization** The action of nasalizing a vowel.

**nominative** The noun or pronoun case typically indicating the subject of a verb: e.g. *The boy saw me*.

**palatal** (A speech-sound) made with the tongue touching or close to the hard palate: e.g. [j].

**palatalize**  To change the articulation of a consonant in the direction of the hard palate: e.g. [k] > [tʃ].

**palatalization**  The action of palatalizing a consonant.

**participle**  A verb form such as *going, writing,* the 'present participle', or *gone, written,* the 'past participle', or any equivalent form in another language.

**person**  Any of three forms of a verb or pronoun, referring to the speaker (*I, we*), the 'first person'; the person(s) or thing(s) spoken to (*you*), the 'second person'; and the person(s) or thing(s) spoken about (*he, she, it, they*), the 'third person'.

**phoneme**  Any of the contrasting speech-sounds of a language, such as /p/, /t/, /k/ in English, as in *pin, tin, kin.*

**prefix**  A lexical element added to the beginning of a word to form a different word: e.g. RE- in *rewrite.*

**quadruplet**  Four words derived from the same source word: e.g. *gentle, gentile, genteel* and *jaunty,* all ultimately < Latin *gentilis.*

**reflex**  A word, a word-element or a speech-sound that has developed from an earlier form; e.g. Modern English *stone* is a reflex of Old English *stan,* Modern English *-ence* is a reflex of Latin *-entia,* Modern English /ʃ/ as in *ship* is a reflex of Germanic /sk/.

**root**  The part of a word to which a word-ending is added; e.g. ANN- is the root to which the ending -US is added to form the Latin word *annus* 'year'. In a different sense, a root is the word from which a later form is derived; thus, Latin *annus* is the root underlying Modern English *annual.* See also **stem**.

**rough breathing**  Aspiration before a vowel in ancient Greek, or the symbol indicating this; also written above the letter rho.

**rounded**  Made with the lips rounded; [u] is a rounded vowel.

**rune, runic alphabet**  See **futhark**.

**schwa**  The vowel [ə], as in *about, father.*

**scriptorium**  The room in a medieval monastery where manuscripts were copied.

**semi-vowel**  A consonant such as /w/ and /j/.

**smooth breathing**  The absence of aspiration before a vowel in ancient Greek, or the symbol indicating this.

**source language**  The language from which a word ultimately derives; for example, *condor* entered English via Spanish, but the source language of the word is Quechua.

**stem**  The word or word-element to which a prefix or suffix is added: thus GOOD- is the stem of *goodness,* CLOS- the stem of *closure.* A stem may consist of a **root** plus some other word-element(s): thus the root of *occurrence* is Latin CURR-, and the stem is OCCURR-.

**suffix**   A lexical element added to the end of a word to form a different word: e.g. -NESS, -ITY in *goodness, chastity*.

**syllabic**   (Said of a consonant) forming a syllable without a vowel.

**thorn**   The Old English letter Þ.

**trigraph**   Three letters used together to represent a single speech-sound: e.g. EAU in *bureau*.

**triplet**   Three words derived from the same source words: e.g. *hospital, hostel, hotel*, all ultimately from Latin *hospitale/hospitalia*.

**unaspirated**   Without aspiration.

**unrounded**   Formed with the lips spread; [i] and [ɛ] are unrounded vowels.

**velar**   (A speech-sound) made with the tongue touching or close to the soft palate: e.g. [k], [g].

**voiced**   Said of a speech-sound made with vibration of the vocal cords: e.g. [b], [d], [g].

**voiceless**   Said of a speech-sound made without vibration of the vocal cords: e.g. [p], [t], [k].

**word-ending**   See **suffix**.

**wyn**   The Old English letter ƿ.

**yogh**   The Old English letter ȝ.

# Bibliography

Algeo, J. (ed.) (2001) *The Cambridge History of the English Language. Vol. 6: English in North America*. Cambridge: Cambridge University Press.

Baldick, C. (1990) *The Concise Oxford Dictionary of Literary Terms*. Oxford: Oxford University Press.

Barber, C. (1976) *Early Modern English*. London: André Deutsch.

Baugh, A. C. and Cable, T. (1993) *A History of the English Language*. 4th edn. London: Routledge.

Blake, N. F. (1996) *A History of the English Language*. London: Macmillan.

Boswell, J. (1934) *Life of Johnson* (ed. G. B. Hill; revised and enlarged by L. F. Powell), vol. 4. Oxford: Clarendon Press.

Brengelman, F. H. (1980) Orthoepists, printers, and the rationalization of English spelling. *Journal of English and Germanic Philology* 79: 332–54.

Brinton, L. J. and Fee, M. (2001) Canadian English. In: Algeo (2001: 422–40).

Brown, C. F. (1932) *English Lyrics of the XIIIth Century*. London: Clarendon Press.

Bullokar, W. (1580) *Bullokars booke at large, for the amendment of orthographie for English speech*. London: Henrie Denham.

Burnley, D. (1989) *The Language of Chaucer*. London: Macmillan.

Burrow, J. A. and Turville-Petre, T. (1996) *A Book of Middle English*. 2nd edn. Oxford: Blackwell. (3rd edn. 2005)

Campbell, A. (1969) *Old English Grammar*. Repr. with corrections. Oxford: Oxford University Press.

Carney, E. (1994) *A Survey of English Spelling*. London: Routledge.

Chomsky, N. and Halle, M. (1968) *The Sound Pattern of English*. New York: Harper & Row.

*The History of English Spelling*, First Edition. Christopher Upward and George Davidson.
© 2011 Christopher Upward and George Davidson. Published 2011 by Blackwell Publishing Ltd.

# Bibliography

Clarke, S. (ed.) (1993) *Focus on Canada*. Amsterdam: John Benjamins.

Collins, P. and Blair, D. (eds) (1989) *Australian English: The Language of a New Society*. St Lucia, Queensland: University of Queensland Press.

Coulmas, F. (1989) *The Writing Systems of the World*. Oxford: Blackwell.

Craigie, W. A. (1927) *English Spelling, Its Rules and Reasons*. New York: Crofts.

Crystal, D. (1987) *The Cambridge Encyclopedia of Language*. Cambridge: Cambridge University Press.

Crystal, D. (1988) *The English Language*. London: Penguin.

Crystal, D. (2005) *Johnson's Dictionary. An Anthology*. London: Penguin.

Dobson, E. J. (1968) *English Pronunciation 1500–1700*. 2 vols. 2nd edn. Oxford: Oxford University Press.

Elliott, R. W. V. (1989) *Runes*. 2nd edn. Manchester: Manchester University Press.

Fee, M. and McAlpine, J. (1997) *Guide to Canadian English Usage*. Toronto, New York and Oxford: Oxford University Press.

Fennell, B. A. (2001) *A History of English: A Sociolinguistic Approach*. Oxford: Blackwell.

Fisher, J. H. (1996) *The Emergence of Standard English*. Lexington: University Press of Kentucky.

Fisher, J. H., Richardson, M. and Fisher, J. L. (1984) *An Anthology of Chancery English*. Knoxville: University of Tennessee Press.

Fisiak, J. (1968) *A Short Grammar of Middle English. Part 1: Graphemics, Phonemics and Morphemics*. Warsaw: Pañstwowe Wydawnictwo Naukowe.

Follick, M. (1965) *The Case for Spelling Reform*. London: Pitman.

Gimson, A. C. (1962) *An Introduction to the Pronunciation of English*. London: Edward Arnold.

Görlach, M. (1991) *Introduction to Early Modern English*. Cambridge: Cambridge University Press.

Haas, W. (1970) *Phono-Graphic Translation*. Manchester: Manchester University Press.

Hanna, P. R., Hodges R. E. and Hanna, J. S. (1971) *Spelling: Structure and Strategies*. Boston: Houghton Mifflin.

Hart, J. (1569) *An Orthographie: conteyning the due order and reason, howe to write or paint thimage of mannes voice, most like to the life or nature*. London: William Seres.

Hogg, R. M. (ed.) (1992a) *The Cambridge History of the English Language. Vol. 1: The Beginning to 1066*. Cambridge: Cambridge University Press.

Hogg, R. M. (1992b) Phonology and Morphology. In: Hogg (1992a: 67–167).

Hughes, G. (2000) *A History of English Words*. Oxford: Blackwell.

Jackson, K. (1953) *Language and History in Early Britain*. Edinburgh: Edinburgh University Press.

Jespersen, O. (1905) *Growth and Structure of the English Language*. 1st edn. Leipzig: B. G. Teubner. (9th edn, 1956. Oxford: Blackwell.)

Jespersen, O. (1933) *Essentials of English Grammar*. London: George Allen & Unwin.

Jespersen, O. (1949) *A Modern English Grammar on Historical Principles. Part 1: Sounds and Spellings*. London: George Allen & Unwin.

Kastovsky, D. and Mettinger, A. (eds) (2000) *The History of English in a Social Context*. Berlin and New York: Mouton.

Landau, S. (1989) *Dictionaries: The Art and Craft of Lexicography*. Cambridge: Cambridge University Press.

Lass, R. (ed.) (1969) *Approaches to English Historical Linguistics*. New York: Holt, Rinehart & Winston.

Lass, R. (1987) *The Shape of English: Structure and History*. London: Dent.

Melchers, G. and Shaw, P. (2003) *World Englishes: An Introduction*. London: Arnold.

Mencken, H. L. (1963) *The American Language*. Abridged, with annotations and new material, by Raven I. McDavid. New York: Alfred A. Knopf.

Mitton, R. (1996) *English Spelling and the Computer*. London and New York: Longman.

Murray, J. A. H., Bradley, H., Craigie, W. A. and Onions, C. T. (eds) (1884–1928) *A New English Dictionary on Historical Principles* (later *The Oxford English Dictionary*). Oxford: Clarendon Press.

Nolst Trenité, G. *The Chaos*. Quoted in Upward (1994).

Page, R. I. (1987) *Runes*. London: British Museum Publications.

Pearsall, J. (ed.) (1998) *The New Oxford Dictionary of English*. Reissued with corrections (2001). Oxford: Oxford University Press.

Pei, M. A. (1953) *The Story of English*. London: George Allen & Unwin.

Pope, M. K. (1952) *From Latin to Modern French, with Especial Consideration of Anglo-Norman*. 2nd edn. Manchester: Manchester University Press.

Pratt, T. K. (1993) The hobgoblin of Canadian English spelling. In: Clarke (1993: 45–64).

Pyles, T. and Algeo, J. (1982) *The Origins and Development of the English Language*. 3rd edn. New York: Harcourt Brace Jovanovich.

Richardson, M. (1980) Henry V, the English Chancery and Chancery English. *Speculum* 55: 726–50.

Robertson, S. (1936) *The Development of Modern English*. London: Harrap.

Sampson, G. (1985) *Writing Systems*. London: Hutchinson.

Samuels, M. L. (1963) Some applications of Middle English dialectology. *English Studies* 44: 81–94. Repr. in Lass (1969: 404–18).

Schwarz, C., Davidson, G., Seaton, A. and Tebbit, V. (eds) (1988) *Chambers English Dictionary*. Cambridge, Edinburgh, etc.: Chambers Cambridge.

Scragg, D. G. (1974) *A History of English Spelling*. Manchester: Manchester University Press.

Sebba, M. (2007) *Spelling and Society*. Cambridge: Cambridge University Press.

Serjeantson, M. S. (1935) *A History of Foreign Words in English*. Repr. (1961). London: Routledge & Kegan Paul.

Sheridan, T. (1780) *A General Dictionary of the English Language*. London: Dodsley, Dilly & Wilkie.

Simpson, J. and Weiner, E. (eds) (2000, with subsequent updates) *The Oxford English Dictionary Online*. Oxford: Oxford University Press.

Smith, J. (1996) *An Historical Study of English: Function, Form and Change*. London: Routledge.

Smith, T. (1568) *De recta & emendata linguae Anglicae scriptione, Dialogus*. Paris. Repr. (1968) Menston: Scolar Press.

Sönmez, M. J.-M. (2000) Perceived and real differences between men's and women's spellings of the early to mid-seventeenth century. In: Kastovsky and Mettinger (2000: 405–39).

Strang, B. M. H. (1970) *A History of English*. London: Methuen.

Toon, T. E. (1992) Old English dialects. In: Hogg (1992a: 405–91).

Upward, C. (1994) The classic concordance of cacographic chaos. *Journal of the Simplified Spelling Society* 2: 27–30. Retrieved on 28 February 2011 from http://www.spellingsociety.org/journals/j17/caos.php

Upward, C. (1996) *Cut Spelling: A Handbook to the Simplification of Written English by Omission of Redundant Letters*. 2nd edn. Birmingham: Simplified Spelling Society.

Vachek, J. (1973) *Written Language: General Problems and Problems of English*. The Hague: Mouton.

Vallins, G. H. (1965) *Spelling*. Rev. D. G. Scragg. London: André Deutsch.

Wakelin, M. F. (1988) *The Archaeology of English*. London: Batsford.

Wandruszka, M. (1990) *Die europäische Sprachengemeinschaft*. Tübingen: Francke Verlag.

Wells, J. C. (1990) *Longman Pronunciation Dictionary*. Harlow: Longman.

Whitelock, D. (1967) *Sweet's Anglo-Saxon Reader in Prose and Verse. Revised throughout by Dorothy Whitelock*. Oxford: Clarendon Press.

Williams, J. M. (1975) *Origins of the English Language: A Social and Linguistic History*. New York: Free Press.

Wingate, P. (1988) *The Penguin Medical Encyclopaedia*. 3rd edn. Harmondsworth: Penguin.

Wright, J. and Wright, E. M. (1924) *An Elementary Historical New English Grammar*. London: Oxford University Press.

Wyld, H. C. (1936) *A History of Modern Colloquial English*. Oxford: Blackwell.

# Language and Dialect Index

# Word and Word-Element Index

- Since Old English, etc. words are generally not glossed if they are identical or very similar in form to Modern English words form, the index below includes Modern English words that are not actually found in the text on the pages specified. For example, although corn is listed below as appearing on page 37, it is only the Old English word corn that is specifically mentioned on that page, the Modern English word being implied rather than stated.
- Words may appear below in their American English as well as their British English spellings even if the American English forms are not specifically found in the text on the pages referred to.

-IAL 97
iamb 205
-IAN 88
-IBLE 127–8, 136
-IC 95, 128, 298, 304
ice 55, 180
-ICE 128
iceberg 250
ichthyosaurus 203
icicle 44
icon 216, 221
iconoclastic 205
-iction 127
-ID 128
idea 195, 216
ideology 208
-IDGE 88
idiom 209, 216
idiot 216
idle 108
idol 208, 216, 221
idolatry 221
idyl(l) 208, 221
idyllic 208
IE 41, 105, 125, 176–8, 254
-IE 125
I–E 41, 48, 63, 123–4, 177
-IER 128
if 44
-IFY 127
IGH 41, 82–3; see also GH
igloo 250, 253, 267, 284
ignore 117, 143, 150
iguana 235, 252–3
IH 254
ikebana 253, 261
-IL 128
ilang-ilang see ylang-ylang
ill 28
illegal 136
illicit 130, 136
illuminate 136
illustrate 136
IM- 127
image 127
imagery 111
imagine 117, 129

imam 253, 260
imbibe 107, 138
imbroglio 251
immediate 101, 103
immense 112, 138–9
immigration 138
imminent 140
immune 107
impala 253, 259
impeach 104
impeccable 96
implicit 130
imply 127
important 158
impotent 107
impresario 253, 283
impressionism, -ist 130
impressive 153
impromptu 162
improve 107
impulse 138
in situ 162, 283
IN- 107, 127
-IN 128–9
inaugurate 91
incantation 301
inch 32n
include 107
incognito 252–3
incommunicado 260
increase 95, 108
-INCTION 127
index 167
indicate 95
indict 95, 124, 191
indigo 250, 253
indulge 118
industry 125, 152
-INE 129, 237
inertial 97
infancy 126
infant 116
inferior 116
inferno 253
infinite 130
infirmary 126
inflammation 138

inflection/-xion 167–8
inflict 127
influenza 253, 261, 282, 290
-ING 136
inhalation 121
inheritor 302
inhuman 121
initial 97
injure 134
injurious 311
injury 126, 311
innate 140
inner 25
innocent 140
innovation 189
inquire 6
inscribe 155
insist 155, 167, 189
inspire 123, 155
instil(l) 128
instinct 155
insulin 129
insure 108
intaglio 251
INTEL- 127
intellect 127, 136, 151
intelligent 127, 136, 151
intelligentsia 250, 253, 259, 281
intensity 158
INTER- 127, 151
interact 127
intercede 103
intercept 127
intercourse 127
interdependent 127
interest 108, 127
interfere 127
interim 138
interior 144, 302
intermezzo 290
intermittent 158
interpret 127
interrogate 127, 151
interrupt 151
intervene 164
intimacy 125
intrigue 113, 132

354

utopia, Utopia 217, 222
utter 60
UU 285

v 42–3, 164–5, 176, 285–6
vague 113, 120, 163
vain 182
valet 111
valium 164
valley 106, 136
value 113, 137, 163
vamoose 247, 268, 276, 285
vampire 270, 285
vane 43
vanilla 259, 285
varmint 103, 160
varnish 103
varsity 103
vary 126
vast 164
vat 43
vaunt 92
veal 68
veer 132
vehement 121, 164
vehicle 121
veil 105
vein 105, 169, 182
veld 244, 285
veldskoen 265
vendetta 235, 281, 285
veneer 132, 285
veranda(h) 237, 285
verboten 285
verge 118
vermicelli 241
vermin 103, 129, 160
verse 1, 43, 153
very 151, 295
vestige 118
vex 167
viable 164
vial 43
vibrant 139
vicar 127
vice (in place of) 114
vicious 185

victory 126, 144, 189
victuals 95, 191
vicuña/vicuna 262
vie 127
view 60, 161, 166
vigilante 285
village 88, 137
villain 90
villainy 302
villein 90
violin 129, 258
virgin 129
virtue 62, 166
viscacha 285
viscount 124
visible 127
vision 131, 152, 185
visit 158
vitamin 129
vivid 164
vixen 43
vizier
vizsla 290
vodka 235, 244, 256, 264, 285
vogue 120
voice 98, 112, 144
void 101
volcano 285
vole 247, 264, 285
volk 285
volley 106, 142
volume 138, 140, 164
voodoo 267
vote 112
vow 146, 188
vowel 109, 146, 188, 295
voyage 145, 169
voyeur 145
vrou 285
vulgar 117
vulnerable 139, 164

w 32n, 60–2, 165–6, 176,
  189–90, 286–7
wadi 286
waffle 249
wag 179

wage 166
wag(g)on 50, 250, 261, 286
waif 116
wain 50
waistcoat 193
waiter 110
wake 38
walk 49, 185–6
wall 32n
wallah 286
wallaroo 286
walrus 276, 283
waltz 235, 282, 286
wampum 270
wand 179
wanderlust 287
want 2, 28, 179, 295
wapiti 270
war 60, 179
ward 119, 166
warder 70
warm 41
warranty 70, 119
warrior 144
wasabi 286
wash 55, 179
wassail 28
waste 86
watch 38, 159
water 35
wax 62, 179
way 40, 46
we 40, 295
weak 30
wealth 304
wealthy 58
weapon 61
weary 40
weasel 54
weather 303–4
weave 40
wedge 46
Wednesday 193
Wehrmacht 287
weigh 46
Weimaraner 248, 287
well 295

# General Index